Spiritual Homelands

Perspectives on Jewish Texts and Contexts

Edited by
Vivian Liska

Editorial Board
Robert Alter, Steven E. Aschheim, Richard I. Cohen, Mark H. Gelber,
Moshe Halbertal, Christine Hayes, Moshe Idel, Samuel Moyn,
Ada Rapoport-Albert, Alvin Rosenfeld, David Ruderman, Bernd Witte

Volume 12

Spiritual Homelands

The Cultural Experience of Exile, Place
and Displacement among Jews and Others

Edited by
Asher D. Biemann, Richard I. Cohen
and Sarah E. Wobick-Segev

DE GRUYTER

Printed with the generous support of the Jewish Studies Program at the University of Virginia and Daat Hamakom.

Supported by the I-CORE Program of the Planning and Budgeting Committee and the Israel Science Foundation (Grant No. 1798/12).

ISBN 978-3-11-077746-8
e-ISBN (PDF) 978-3-11-063756-4
e-ISBN (EPUB) 978-3-11-063761-8
ISSN 2199-6962

Library of Congress Control Number: 2019946010

Bibliographic information published by the Deutsche Nationalbibliothek
The Deutsche Nationalbibliothek lists this publication in the Deutsche Nationalbibliografie; detailed bibliographic data are available on the Internet at http://dnb.dnb.de.

© 2021 Walter de Gruyter GmbH, Berlin/Boston
This volume is text- and page-identical with the hardback published in 2019.
Cover image: akg-images
Felix Nussbaum: Der wandernde Jude (Wanderer im Gebirge)
Typesetting: Integra Software Services Pvt. Ltd.
Printing and binding: CPI books GmbH, Leck

www.degruyter.com

Contents

Asher D. Biemann, Richard I. Cohen, and Sarah E. Wobick-Segev
Introduction —— 1

Part 1: Exile and Erasures

Pierre Birnbaum
The End of Exile? The Metz Contest of 1787 Revisited —— 11

Nina Fischer
Remembering/Imagining Palestine from Afar: The (Lost) Homeland in Contemporary Palestinian Diaspora Literature —— 31

Part 2: Writing the Homeland

Regina Range
Worlds, Words, and Womanhood: Gina Kaus and the Formation of a Spiritual Homeland —— 59

Diego Rotman
Performing Homeland in Post-Vernacular Times: Dzigan and Shumacher's Yiddish Theater after the Holocaust —— 81

Part 3: Language in Exile

Stefani Hoffman
The World as Exile and the Word as Homeland in the Writing of Boris Khazanov —— 101

Judith K. Lang Hilgartner
Uncovering Accent and Belonging in Juan Gelman's *Dibaxu* —— 129

Part 4: Multiple Exiles, Contingent Homelands

Jeffrey A. Grossman
France as *Wahlheimat* for Two German Jews: Heinrich Heine and Walter Benjamin —— 153

H. Esra Almas
The Girl from the Golden Horn: Kurban Said / Lev Nussinbaum's Vision of Home and Exile in Interbellum Berlin —— 183

Anna M. Parkinson
"In der Fremde zu hause": Contingent Cosmopolitanism and Elective Exile in the Writing of Hans Keilson —— 205

Part 5: Of Other Spaces: Travel and Trauma

Agnes C. Mueller
Israel as a Place of Trauma and Desire in Contemporary German Jewish Literature —— 233

Doerte Bischoff
Paper Existences: Passports and Literary Imagination —— 253

Judith Müller
Neither *Heimat* nor Exile: The Perception of Paris as a Historical Blind Spot in Three Israeli Novels —— 277

Notes on Contributors —— 299

Index —— 303

Asher D. Biemann, Richard I. Cohen, and Sarah E. Wobick-Segev
Introduction

This volume of essays began by happenstance. An interdisciplinary center of excellence in Israel, Daat Hamakom, Center for the Study of Cultures of Place in Jewish Modernity, supported by the Israel Science Foundation, began its activities in 2012 with the goal to further academic cooperation and intellectual pursuit with colleagues and centers in Israel and abroad. By chance, as things often happen in the academic world, colleagues at the University of Virginia, and in particular Professor Asher Biemann, were in the throes of thinking of expanding their scholarly interests and horizons in issues of Homeland, Exile, Imagined Homelands and the like, and were involved in discussions on creating a conference on these themes. Our interests coincided and thus we embarked on a joint venture that began with an international conference in Charlottesville, Virginia in 2015 and a sequel workshop with some of the original participants in Yad Hashmona, Israel in 2017. Fortunately, Dr. Sarah Wobick-Segev, a historian of modern Jewish history, who joined us on the eve of the workshop in Israel and has been a wonderful collaborator from that point on, has taken on many responsibilities for the editorial process, not the least of which was her active participation in the composition of this introduction.

Colleagues from both centers and participants have been acutely aware that these themes relating to place touch dramatically on contemporary society in which hundreds of thousands of refugees are leaving their homes for a host of reasons and seek a new homeland, often at high risk to their lives. Interestingly, the papers collected here make no allusions to the plight of these people, but their analyses of literary and historical phenomena offer insight to the burden of our times. This volume brings together mutual contemplations of both venues.

"Place" and the multiple expressions Jews developed for a particular place was an overriding theme of Daat Hamakom. The term *makom*, in Hebrew מקום, carries innumerable meanings and associations – geographic, theological (for example, God is referred to as *Makom*), philosophical, and existential. Indeed, the presence of "place" has permeated Jewish life and consciousness from time immemorial but has taken dramatic turns in modern times. Place in this context is a feature of modern cultural adaptation that relates to the cultural dilemmas of loss, nostalgia, utopia, travel, longing, but also in terms of boundaries, languages, and space, and the cultural dilemmas associated with being "misplaced" and "displaced" as well as "re-placed."

The geography of culture can be viewed as a means of "mapping" where and how certain modes of creativity and their traditions became rooted, or – in many cases – when and how they became uprooted and were then transported to new contexts and transformed. The turn to spatial and geographic concerns in the study of the humanities can be fruitfully and imaginatively applied to the Jewish case and that, in turn, can enrich scholarly discourse from this particular angle of vision. The idea of "place" anchors this volume in a field of research related to the overall question: how do *realia* of particular places influence behavior, consciousness, beliefs, and creativity?

Spiritual Homelands poses these questions anew from a variety of disciplinary approaches, including history, literary criticism, ethnography, and cultural studies. It is an exploration into a world of boundary crossings and of desired places and alternate identities, into a world of adopted kin and invented allegiances. What makes this theme relevant is that the election of a homeland is no mere fantasy and projection of the mind, but a transformative and mutually constitutive process. Scholars such as Arjun Appadurai and Homi Bhabha have recently created theoretical frameworks for communities of sentiment and narrative identities co-existing with larger transnational realities. Others, such as Barbara Kirshenblatt-Gimblett, have reconsidered the fixity of locations as "accidents of proximity" and the old dichotomies of here and there, home and exile, as "spaces of dispersal."[1] The intention of the present volume is to discuss the role of *choosing alternate places* and of identifying with cultures not necessarily one's own, a process, which can neither be subsumed under "rootless" cosmopolitanism nor merely be labeled romantic exoticism. Nor, for that matter, does the language of "assimilation" or, in more recent scholarship, "co-constitution" suffice to describe the agency of choosing and the awareness of self-fashioning. It is not the imitative impulse that defines this volume's theme, not the erosion of selfhood, but the creative imagination of an expanded self beyond the facts of natural kinship and given place. Spiritual homelands, however naïve and imaginary they may be, are works of self-formation and "self-othering" that question existing geographies and cultural-political orders. They are places of elective affinity and imagined familiarity. But this does not render them less real, or "authentic." Choosing a homeland is an act of election that simultaneously implies a process of un-election and conscious dissociation. If the modern condition, as Erich Auerbach wrote from his own place of exile, involved "the task of making oneself at home in existence without fixed points of support," then the election of place is both an act of self-orientation and one of defiant rootedness in a "boundless and incomprehensible" world.[2] Spiritual homelands are fixed

---

[1] Arjun Appadurai, *Modernity at Large: Cultural Dimensions of Globalization* (Minneapolis and London: University of Minnesota Press, 1996); Barbara Kirshenblatt-Gimblett, "Spaces of Dispersal," *Cultural Anthropology* 9, no. 3 (August 1994): 339–44.

[2] Erich Auerbach, *Mimesis: The Representation of Reality in Western Literature*, trans. Willard R. Trask (Princeton, NJ: Princeton University Press, 1968), 311.

points in a fluctuating, accidental geography. But their elective topography is also an acknowledgment of the transience of human space and the uncertainty of belonging. Spiritual homelands at once seek places and betray a sense of placelessness. They are, paradoxically, homecomings into an elsewhere. And as such, they frequently function as forms of cultural critique and statements of dissent and protestation, though they can also become sites of disguise and hiding.

Not all election of place, of course, is one of free agency and conscious choice. More often than not, spiritual homelands emerge from conditions imposed by power and force. They belong to complex stories of migration and exile, which, in one form or another, have always been part of human history – despite claims to the contrary made by waves of nativist movements throughout the modern era.[3]

Though the various terms to explain the loss of home change from language to language and over time, there appears to be a fundamental commonality to the visceral nature of this experience.[4] Moreover, most if not all cases of expulsion and exile during the early modern and modern eras have been essentially, as Joseph Carens suggests, "by-products" of the way we organize the world politically.[5] The last century's massive political readjustments and human displacements exemplify this. As Peter Gatrell has averred, "the collapse of multinational empires, the emergence of the modern state with a bounded citizenship, the spread of totalizing ideologies that hounded internal enemies, and the internationalization of responses to refugee crises" resulted in unprecedented waves of exile.[6]

By the early twentieth century, as old homelands disintegrated and were replaced with new states, many people lost their footing, along with their previous political affiliation. Looking for mooring, some tried to find solace in new conceptualizations of cosmopolitanism, which they saw as the antithesis of the rabid nationalism that surrounded them.[7] The famous Austrian-Jewish author Stefan Zweig, for example, would write a number of biographies on historical figures whom he understood as serving as guiding lights in dark times. Zweig's work on Erasmus pitted the humanist against Luther and was, as such, a parable on the dangers of nationalism and fanaticism. Erasmus, in Zweig's reading, was

---

[3] For the early modern era, consider the cases of the Jews and Muslims expelled from Spain in 1492, as well as the French Huguenots in 1685. Peter Gatrell, *The Making of the Modern Refugee* (Oxford: Oxford University Press, 2013), 2.
[4] Peter Burke, *Exiles and Expatriates in the History of Knowledge, 1500–2000* (Waltham, MA: Brandeis University Press, 2017), 2–4.
[5] Joseph Carens, *The Ethics of Immigration* (Oxford: Oxford University Press, 2013), 208.
[6] Gatrell, *Making of the Modern Refugee*, 2.
[7] Michael Miller and Scott Ury, "Cosmopolitanism: The End of Jewishness?" *European Review of History – Revue européenne d'histoire* 17, no. 3 (June 2010): 337.

not only "the first conscious European, [but also] the first to fight on behalf of peace."[8] Other thinkers of Zweig's time, including Paul Kristeller, Ernst Cassirer, Hans Baron, and Ernst Kantorowicz,[9] sought in Renaissance humanists role models for a humane and enlightened engagement with the Other. The Renaissance became their own virtual "dreamland."[10]

The refugee crises of the twentieth century in general and the Holocaust in particular have become paradigmatic case studies for philosophers and political ethicists. Carens has argued that the Holocaust is the watershed moment that proves the state's responsibility to welcome those in critical need.[11] To be sure, this perspective also has roots in Kantian cosmopolitanism. The latter is not the facile and oft derided belief that each person can and should see herself as a citizen of the world, supposedly at home everywhere, but according to critics, truly at home nowhere. Rather, Kant contended that states had the moral duty to provide hospitality to the stranger. Kant's notion of openness arose from his belief that as humans we all share the earth. However, by this he did not mean to suggest that humans could or were supposed to shed their need for a concrete home or homeland, rather that everyone has the right to (at least temporarily) security and shelter.[12]

More recently Jacques Derrida has returned to Kant's concept of cosmopolitanism and advocated with others for "cities of refuge."[13] Yet much of this Kantian-inflected discussion of the ethics of cosmopolitanism is top-down,

---

[8] Stefan Zweig, *Erasmus of Rotterdam*, trans. Eden and Cedar Paul (New York: Viking Press, 1934), 4. Sadly, Erasmus's noble humanism did not prevent his own moments of antisemitism. See, for instance: James D. Tracy, *Erasmus of the Low Countries* (Berkeley and Los Angeles: University of California Press, 1996).
[9] Kay Schiller, *Gelehrte Gegenwelten: Über humanistische Leitbilder im 20. Jahrhundert* (Frankfurt am Main: S. Fischer Verlag, 2000).
[10] See most recently, Emily Levine, *Dreamland of Humanists: Warburg, Cassirer, Panofsky, and the Warburg School* (Chicago and London: University of Chicago Press, 2013).
[11] Carens, *The Ethics of Immigration*, 194 and 195.
[12] Kant's reflections on "perpetual peace" had a significant impact on Weimar Jewish intellectuals, especially Hermann Cohen, whose 1919 *Religion of Reason* included a theo-politics akin to Kant's republicanism, and Cohen's own student Cassirer, whose 1928 decennial speech on the Weimar Constitution fused Cohen's prophetic and Kant's cosmopolitan visions. See Immanuel Kant, *Zum Ewigen Frieden: Ein philosophischer Entwurf*; idem, *Werke in Sechs Bänden*, vol. 6, ed. Wilhelm Weischedel (Darmstadt: Wissenschaftliche Buchgesellschaft, 1964), 195–254; Hermann Cohen, *Religion der Vernunft aus den Quellen des Judentums* (Frankfurt am Main: J. Kauffmann, 1929); Ernst Cassirer, *Die Idee der Republikanischen Verfassung. Rede zur Verfassungsfeier am 11. August 1928* (Hamburg: de Gruyter, 1929).
[13] Jacques Derrida, *On Cosmopolitanism and Forgiveness* (London and New York: Routledge, 2001), 3–5.

focused on the responsibilities of the state (or city) toward those who seek its hospitality. What of the exiles themselves? For as much as cosmopolitanism seemed to offer a way out for some in the face of exile or nationalism or religious particularism, the need for belonging and a concrete place to call home has remained pressing, even for the most committed humanists and cosmopolitans.

Additionally, there is an important distinction between a guest's right to hospitality and shelter in times of need and the right to a *home* beyond the place of one's birth. Does such a right even exist? And assuming that the exile is allowed in, will she ever feel truly at home? Here the answers remain more complicated. And here is where our volume seeks to make important interventions.

The challenges of exile are well known. Edward Said's assessment of exile, for instance, is absolute in its pessimism. For him, exile is a "condition of terminal loss," and "the achievements of exile are permanently undermined by the loss of something left behind forever."[14] Siegfried Kracauer, less absolute but not particularly more optimistic, has suggested that the exile "will never fully belong to the community to which he now in a way belongs" but instead lives, "[i]n the near-vacuum of extra-territoriality, the very no-man's-land … The exile's true mode of existence is that of a stranger."[15] Certainly, many of his fellow German-Jewish refugees lost hope and never found comfort in the lands in which they would find temporary shelter. It was far from easy to build a new future in foreign lands. Finding secure, long-term employment was notoriously complicated for many. Working and communicating in new languages and in new cultures was often frustrating and left individuals feeling alienated. Loneliness and a sense of loss overwhelmed others. Indeed, the despair and psychological toil provoked a number of exiles of Kracauer's generation to take their own lives – including Stefan Zweig, Walter Benjamin, and Ernst Toller, though each of them experienced flight and exile in ways that cannot be necessarily compared. Others like Joseph Roth would self-destruct, dying from complications of alcoholism.[16]

For those in exile, the most profound challenge has been to create a home without, at least initially, the support networks and emotional rootedness we assume, at least idealistically, come with the very word *home*. Yet there were some who were (more) successful, and the experience of remaking a home in a chosen homeland could be socially and culturally productive acts. Even Kracauer was willing to admit that there were advantages to exile. Namely, that the experience

---

14 Edward Said, "Reflections on Exile," in *Reflections on Exile and Other Essays* (Cambridge, MA: Harvard University Press, 2000), 173.
15 Siegfried Kracauer cited in Gertrud Koch, *Siegfried Kracauer: An Introduction* (Princeton, NJ: Princeton University Press, 2000), 114–15. Burke, *Exiles and Expatriates*, 22–23, 27.
16 Burke, *Exiles and Expatriates*, 5–7.

promoted a sharp sense of cultural criticism.[17] Historian Peter Burke's recent book on the intellectual contributions of exiles and expatriates offers countless examples of how this condition of distance and displacement has fostered deep scholarly insights.[18] The sheer length of the list of exile/scholars compels the reader to consider where modern scholarship would be today were it not for these trying but ultimately productive experiences.

Yet, the process of building a home in a new land – not just the distance from one homeland to a new one – is not merely a catalyst for critical thought, it constitutes new identities. Martin Heidegger has argued in his post-war essay on building and dwelling that "we attain to dwelling, so it seems, only by means of building."[19] Yet to build is not merely a physical task; it is intrinsically connected, Heidegger continues, by acts of cultivating, caring for, protecting, and ultimately of being at peace.[20] To be at home is thus to care and be cared for – deeply charged emotional acts of mutual concern and protection. Home is thus not only a place – "the home is also a site of cultural meaning, social relations and emotional attachments. Home is a key space in which our identities are (re)produced."[21] The emotional need for a home (and a homeland) is linked directly to a sense of belonging, which is in turn created through our affective attachments.[22] Similarly, Michel Foucault has asserted that space can be described through a network of relations; and in fact the importance of relations, of relatedness is key to the meaning of place and to home, in particular.[23] Home is an obvious embodiment of the emotional connections we attribute to it. These connections can, of course, also be negative ones. As gendered critiques of the home remind

---

[17] Siegfried Kracauer, *History: The Last Things Before the Last* (Princeton, NJ: Markus Wiener, 1994), 83–84.
[18] For a comprehensive study on exile and exiles see Eckart Goebel and Sigrid Weigel, eds., *"Escape to Life." German Intellectuals in New York: A Compendium on Exile after 1933* (Berlin et al.: De Gruyter, 2012).
[19] Martin Heidegger, "Building, Dwelling, Thinking," in Martin Heidegger, *Poetry, Language, Thought*, trans. Albert Hofstadter (New York: Harper Perennial Modern Classics, 2001), 145.
[20] Ibid., 147–49.
[21] Carla Barrett, "Lesbians at Home: Gender and Housework in Lesbian Coupled Households," in *Lesbian Geographies: Gender, Place and Power*, ed. Kath Browne and Eduarda Ferreira (London and New York: Routledge, 2016), 56.
[22] Peter van der Graaf, "Feeling at Home and Habitus: How Spaces Matter for Emotions," in *Die Ambivalenz der Gefühle*, ed. J. Kleres and Y. Albrecht (Wiesbaden: Springer, 2015), 25: "Moreover, place attachment theory argues that these social interactions serve a distinct purpose: place affiliations are used to symbolize or situate identity, also known as place identity. Like other forms of identity, place identity answers the question 'Who am I?' by countering 'Where am I?' or 'Where do I belong?'"
[23] Michel Foucault, "Of Other Spaces," trans. Jay Miskowiec, *Diacritics* 16, no. 1 (1986): 23 and 24.

us, the home is formative just as much, if not more, for the conflicts that take place within its walls, with ethnic, gender and class differences enacted against dominant norms.[24] The conflicts that emerge at home do not, nonetheless, take away from the need for a space of familiarity and comfort, even if tensions and conflict – both domestic and national – lead the individual to leave and build a new home, and homeland, in another space. Spiritual homelands are homes built elsewhere, homes built with multiple and often contradictory affiliations and affinities. Homecoming itself is a paradoxical term, for the homecomer, as Alfred Schutz wrote in 1944, "is not the same man who left. He is neither the same to himself nor for those who await his return."[25] The homecomer has always already tasted the "magic fruit of strangeness," and every return, in this respect, is a strangely intimate encounter of unfamiliar faces. Homecoming renders every homeland an unfamiliar place; to the homecomer, every home is an imaginary one, a spiritual homeland yet to be built and truly inhabited.

The stories in our volume are stories of building, of creating homelands in strange places, of choosing belonging; they are stories of election and defiance; and most of all, stories of self-fashioning. The majority of our voices focus on Jewish biographies. But this should not obscure the fact that exile, migration, and the search for homelands are universal human experiences, demanding our urgent attention and engagement. Rather, the modern Jewish experience has become symbolic of a plight shared by many groups displaced and labeled as "other," and it can offer us a common thread that will allow the reader a perspective, a historical point of reference, whose contemporary significance is painfully apparent.

Indeed, generations of Jews in the modern period struggled and yearned for a place that would offer them a home. Many developed a profound attachment to their native or acquired land in the diaspora or in the Land of Israel (*Eretz Israel*). They acquired the language of the country, the habits of its people, the tunes and rhythms of its culture, yet often maintained elements of their own tradition, albeit with nuances and influences of the native spirit. Manifesting their inner desire to belong and feel part of that culture/place, their diverse forms of creativity emphasized the multiple layers of their existence. Music, theater, poetry, synagogues,

---

24 For instance, queer gender identities resist and subvert the dominant heterosexual reproductive role of the nuclear family. See Risa Whitson, "Spaces of Culture and Identity Production: Home, Consumption, and the Media," in *Feminist Spaces: Gender and Geography in a Global Context*, ed. Ann M. Oberhauser, et al. (New York: Routledge, 2018), 47–75; Allison Weir, *Identities and Freedom: Feminist Theory Between Power and Connection* (Oxford: Oxford University Press, 2013), 49.
25 Alfred Schutz, "The Homecomer," in Alfred Schutz, *Collected Papers*, vol. 2: *Studies in Social Theory*, ed. Arvid Brodersen (The Hague: Martinus Nijhoff, 1964), 116.

liturgy, and language drew from many sources, but the dialogue with the geography, the place in which they lived took a privileged role. Languages and traditions became intertwined and confused. The ways in which Jews in Istanbul and Paris, Jerusalem and Berlin, bridged these worlds, left a mark on their form of belonging and attachment to that particular place, can be seen in the diverse essays in this volume. Yet, at times, either as a result of voluntary action or forced displacement, Jews sought new homes, surroundings, and traditions. Dis-placed but not totally acculturated to the novel situation, the power and attraction of the former place, its sensitivities and formal structures loomed large. Thus the Jews from Italy, for example, found a new home in different countries but often continued to pray in the rite of Italian Jewry, or of a specific community in Italy, nostalgically and/or consciously, remaining in contact with the former place. The sounds of the past place continued to reverberate in the new one. Exploring the ways in which Jews shaped the culture they cultivated in one place and how they translated it into another requires the attention to many voices and sights.

The diverse group of scholars in this volume have in their research sought out the ways in which individuals created, remembered, dreamt of a place, physical or imaginary, revealing some of the major intricacies of Jewish life in modern times. The sense of being of a place, and being out of place, has been part of the Jewish experience in the diaspora and *Eretz Israel*; how this was translated into the minds and imaginations of authors and thinkers, is at the center of our attention. Viewing this concern within a comparative context (by concentrating on a range of authors who developed forms of attachment and belonging to different places) and theoretical underpinnings of cultural studies, the volume enables us to further understand some basic notions of identity, traditions, and forms of attachment and belonging in the modern era. The lessons of the past remind us of the very palpable need for homes and homelands for all.

****

The editors are indebted to Dr. Sharon Assaf for her meticulous copy editing of the essays. Her dedicated attention to issues small and large has added considerably to the quality of the manuscript. Professor Vivian Liska graciously agreed to review the text and her favorable attitude to adding it to her series is deeply appreciated. Katja Lehming, the content editor, and Lukas Lehmann, the production editor of De Gruyter Press, have been wonderful and congenial partners in the production of the manuscript, for which we are most grateful.

Asher D. Biemann, Richard I. Cohen, Sarah E. Wobick-Segev
May 2019

Part 1: **Exile and Erasures**

Pierre Birnbaum
The End of Exile? The Metz Contest of 1787 Revisited

Jews have long been scattered throughout the world. One might ask: over these many millennia of dispersion, have they experienced a specific sense of being in exile? Moreover, have they been perceived as foreigners dreaming to return to the Land of Israel? Engagement with these questions requires neither the logic of the history of ideas nor a kind of lachrymose vision of history leading to, for instance, Yitzhak Baer's wholly negative assessment that "all that we accomplished in a foreign country was a treason of our own spirit."[1] And Baer is far from alone. Nowadays, too, *galut* has been construed as purely "pathological."[2]

What is called for in this context is an alternative approach; namely, that of comparative historical sociology. Such a perspective will allow us to gain a good idea of the meaning of *galut* for Jews living in different countries. At this point we might invoke Albert Hirschman,[3] who noted that Jews, like their peers in different faith communities, always had multiple paths available to them. They could, for instance, experience allegiance to the prince or the state, without any feeling of being in exile; they could advocate on their own behalf; and finally, they could be cognizant of a certain foreignness, of being alien to their society. This latter stance was embodied in the Wandering Jew and the messianic Jew and, later on, the immigrant Jew dreaming of Ellis Island and the Zionist Jew dreaming of Zion. Rather than praying for the well-being of the state, instead of fighting for their rights, exile for this group meant following an exit strategy. Yet each of these methods was implemented within different kinds of states, state/church relations, public spaces, and economic conceptions. For Jews as well as for others, various paths of emancipation led to diverse interpretations of being in exile.[4]

---

[1] Yitzhak Baer, *Galout, l'imaginaire de l'exil dans le judaïsme* (Paris: Calmann-Lévy, 2000), 211. This sentence can be found in the epilogue to the American edition published in 1947 and translated in the French edition.
[2] A.B. Yehoshua, *Pour une normalité juive* (Paris: Liane Levi, 1992).
[3] Albert Hirschman, *Exit, Voice and Loyalty* (Cambridge, MA: Harvard University Press, 1970).
[4] Frances Malino and David Sorkin, eds., *From East and West: Jews in a Changing Europe, 1750–1870* (Oxford: Blackwell, 1990). Jonathan Frankel and Steven Zipperstein, eds., *Assimilation and Community: The Jews in Nineteenth-Century Europe* (Cambridge: Cambridge University Press, 1992). Pierre Birnbaum and Ira Katznelson, eds., *Paths of Emancipation: Jews, State and Citizenship* (Princeton, NJ: Princeton University Press, 1995). Lois Dubin, *The Port Jews of Habsburg Trieste: Absolutist Politics and Enlightenment Culture* (Stanford: Stanford University Press, 1999). See

In this article, I wish to take a close look at some mostly unknown documents from the famous Metz essay contest of 1787. This contest marked a pivotal moment between the failure of the Jew Bill in England, the Edicts of Tolerance issued by Emperor Joseph II, the publication of Christian Wilhem Dohm's seminal work, *On The Civic Improvement of the Jew*, the successful limited entrance of French Protestants within the public realm, and the final emancipation of French Jews in September 1791. To what extent did emancipation by virtue of strong state action imply being simply a citizen among others and the end of the idea of exile? Did Jeremiah's letter to the Jews expelled to Babylon lose its coherence in such context, in which the advantages of citizenship blunted so fully the pain of exile? Taking a different tack, did emancipation gained in a weak state but a strong liberal and pluralistic society based on commerce and exchange permit the persistence of a Jewish collective identity, and with it the memory of being in exile? Put another way, we might ask: in the eighteenth century, was the remembrance of the Land of Israel, the impression of being in exile, different, say, in England, Holland or the Italian ports on the one hand, and in France or Prussia, on the other?[5]

From Venice and Livorno to the Netherlands and England, we can discern a pattern: within the framework of a weak state, a strong pluralistic civil society based on commerce and foreign trade was able to grow. In this context, Jewish thinkers such as Simone Luzzatto and Menasseh ben Israel, but also non-Jewish ones like John Toland, argued that the end of exile could be constructed upon profit and fidelity. In his *Petition to Cromwell* for readmittance of the Jews to England, Menasseh ben Israel thus described what the English can expect from the Jews: "Profit, they may receive from them, Fidelity, they hold toward their Princes, and the Nobleness and purity of their blood."[6] In Toland's view, entry

---

also David Sorkin, "Port Jews and the Three Regions of Emancipation," *Jewish Culture and History* 4, no. 2 (2001): 31–46, and Evelyne Oliel-Grausz, "Networks and Communication in the Sephardi Diaspora: An Added Dimension to the Concept of Port Jews and Port Jewries," *Jewish Culture and History* 7, nos. 1–2 (2004): 61–76. Francesca Bregoli, *Mediterranean Enlightenment. Livornese Jews. Tuscan Culture and Eighteenth-Century Europe* (Stanford: Stanford University Press, 2014).

5 Isaac Barzilay may be the sole scholar who has considered this sort of opposition among various eighteenth-century thinkers. For him, "On the continent, the attitude toward Jewish national aspirations was different. Even before the Revolution, the concept of the national state was gaining acceptance." Hence, the political integration pattern implied the weakening of the sense of being in exile. Isaac Barzilay, "The Jew in the Literature of the Enlightenment," *Jewish Social Studies* 18 (1956): 259.

6 Quoted by Yosef Kaplan, "Political Concepts in the World of the Portuguese Jews of Amsterdam during the Seventeenth Century: The Problem of Exclusion and the Boundaries of Self-Identity," in *Menasseh ben Israel and His World*, ed. Yosef Kaplan, Henry Méchoulan, and Richard Popkin (Leiden: Brill, 1989), 50.

would not be temporary: "for where the Jews are once kindly received, they make a firm resolution never to depart from there, feeling that they have no place of their own."[7] Benjamin Ravid has noted that the terms "profit" and "fidelity" used by Menasseh ben Israel and Toland can be traced directly to Simone Luzzatto.[8] In this vein, Isaac Barzilay has pointed out that Toland "repeats all the arguments of Luzzatto, describing the Jews as 'obedient, peaceable and advantageous as any.'"[9] For Barzilay, Toland's work is "an elaboration of the views of Luzzatto and their application to the English case."[10] Thus concludes Luzatto: "The Jews are fearful, obedient, submissive, always ready to bendt their heads before the rulers ... and to comply promptly with all demands of taxes and payments made on them ... having no country of their own to which they may desire to transfer their wealth ... they are resolved never to leave those places where they are treated in amity."[11] And Toland writes: "[Jews] having no country of their own, in which they might retire, after having got estate here ... the Jews being better used with us, than any where else in the world, are sure to be ours for ever."[12]

Oddly, in 1718, Toland published a short essay titled, "Two Problems Concerning the Jewish Nation and Religion," in which he offered the contradictory logic that despite their dispersion, Jews "have nevertheless preserved themselves as a distinct people with their ancient rites"; he asked himself whether it is in the "interest and duty of Christians to assist them in regaining their country."[13] Perhaps the strong messianism of those years can account for this conflicting view, but as Barzilay, citing this line, notes: "those who were ardent believers in the future restauration of the Jews also pleaded for their admission into England

---

7 *Menasseh ben Israel's Mission to Oliver Cromwell*, ed. Lucien Wolf (London: Macmillan, 1901), 84.
8 Benjamin Ravid, "How Profitable the Nation of the Jews Are: The Humble Addresses of Menasseh ben Israel and the Discorso of Simone Luzzatto," in *Mystics, Philosophers and Politicians. Essays in Jewish Intellectual History in Honor of Alexander Altmann*, ed. Jehuda Reinharz and Daniel Swetschinski (Durham, NC: Duke University Press, 1982), 159–80.
9 Isaac Barzilay, "John Toland's Borrowings from Simone Luzzatto's Discourse on the Jews of Venice (1638), the Major Source of Toland's Writing on the Naturalization of the Jews in Great Britain and Ireland (1714)," *Jewish Social Studies*, no. 2 (1969): 79.
10 Ibid., 81.
11 Ibid., 79.
12 John Toland, *Reasons for Naturalizing the Jews in Great Britain and Ireland, on the same foot with all other Nations. Containing also a Defence of the Jews against all Vulgar Prejudices in all Countries* (London, 1714) 54, 56.
13 Sylvia Berti, "At the Roots of Unbelief," *Journal of the History of Ideas* 56, no. 4 (1995): 569. She found this kind of proto-Zionism surprising, but does not discuss the relation between this view and the demand for naturalization. On Toland and the Jews, see Paolo Bernardini and Diego Lucci, *The Jews, Instructions for Use* (Boston: Academic Studies Press, 2012).

as naturalized citizens. Jewish national aspirations did not appear to these Gentiles, like Toland, to conflict with their partial emancipation."[14]

Jonathan Karp has rightly noted that Toland diverged from Luzzatto in the former's insistence that Jews ought to own land and even become soldiers.[15] Nonetheless, the "politics of Jewish commerce" still frame Toland's thinking. From Luzzatto to Menasseh ben Israel to Toland, we thus identify a common process: leveraging commerce and utility, Jews would refrain from requesting political rights and steer clear of politics. They ought to then integrate within their specific societies, be naturalized, settle down, hold fast to their religious values and forget the feeling of being in exile.

One can say that the general atmosphere of philosemitism,[16] the influence of the Hebraist republic[17] in England, the so-called "Second Israel," led to the slow integration of the Jews, loyal to their country but also to their Jewish values and rituals. This process of inclusion spelled the end of the Jews as a nation for Luzzatto: "Like a river winding its way through vast stretches of land, whose waters receive the coloration of the various soils through which they pass, the Jews also receive various customs from the peoples in the midst of whom they live. Consequently, the mores of the Jew of Venice differ from those of the Jew of Constantinople, Damascus or Cairo, as they in turn differ among the German and Polish Jews."[18] And for Toland: "Since their dispersion, they have no common or peculiar inclination distinguishing them from others; but visibly partake of the nature of those nations among which they live and where they were bred. The ordinary sentiments and manners of the Portuguese or Italian Jews differ from those of the Polish Jews as much as Poles do from Germans and so do those of Ispahan or Constantinople from such as born at London or Amsterdam."[19]

England, for its part, is a pluralistic and deeply religious society. For English Jews, the end of the feeling of being in exile never implied the jettisoning of Jewish identity, keeping a kosher kitchen and even of staying within several *eruvim* (boundaries of the Sabbath and festival days).[20] In their prayers to the

---

14 Barzilay, "The Jew in the Literature of the Enlightenment," 259.
15 Jonathan Karp, *The Politics of Jewish Commerce in Europe, 1638–1848* (Cambridge: Cambridge University Press, 2008), 26.
16 David Katz, *Philo-Semitism and the Readmission of the Jews to England, 1603–1655* (Oxford: Clarendon Press, 1982), chap 6.
17 Eric Nelson, *The Hebrew Republic* (Cambridge, MA: Harvard University Press, 2011).
18 Quoted in Isaac Barzilay, "The Jew in the Literature of the Enlightenment," 259.
19 Toland, *Reasons*, 60.
20 Eugene Black, *The Social Politics of Anglo-Jewry, 1880–1920* (New York: Blackwell, 1988). See also, Steven Singer, "Jewish Religious Observance in Early Victorian London, 1840–1860," *Jewish Journal of Sociology* 28, no. 2 (1986): 117–37.

monarchy, English Jews openly referred to themselves as the "People of Israel" that has settled permanently in England.[21] Along these lines, an Orthodox leader of the Jewish community in England declared:

> We ourselves ... must be thankful for the English government and it is our sacred duty to pray for long life to our Queen and all the royal family and I cannot understand how real Judaim should be against anglicism, the contrary, the Jew who prays everyday and keeps the dietary laws, that Jews know the tradition, "Thou shall pray for the welfare of the Kingdom." And we are certain that the government does not require us to throw out our religion on the other side of the sea.[22]

This declaration tells us a great deal about the logic of English Jewry, one that is entirely foreign to the French tradition. In societies with weak states, such as England, mercantilism was a central value and Jews became a legitimate part of the host nation. Along the way, Judaism was transformed into a religion and Jews lost the notion of nationhood. No longer perceiving themselves to be in exile, they nonetheless shared a common identity; they still recalled *Eretz Israel* (the Land of Israel), and the idea of Zionism would, later on, find much support among them. As Todd Endelman notes, "In the English debate, those who favored emancipation did not make their support conditional ... Whether they continued to pray for their return to Jerusalem and the restoration of the Davidic monarchy and Temple cult or to socialize and marry exclusively among themselves was of little interest."[23]

Conversely, in societies with strong states, the political element predominated, commerce was sidelined, and Jewish culture was to be kept out of the public space. This produced a very different kind of "end of exile" feeling than the English one. In the context of Continental enlightened despotism, far from the Netherlands and England, it was the emperor of a bureaucratic state who issued edicts in favor of the Jews, a Prussian civil servant who wrote his major work on the civic status of Jews, and from Malesherbes to Louis XVI himself, the French state that stood resolutely at the heart of such a shift.

In this vein, Robert Liberles shows that, in Prussia for instance, "Dohm totally ignored the existing economic apologetics on behalf of the Jews as merchants that had appeared over the course of the previous 140 years, beginning with Simone Luzzatto in Venice and followed in England by Menasseh ben Israel,

---

[21] Pierre Birnbaum, *Prier pour l'État. Les Juifs, l'alliance royale et la démocratie* (Paris: Calmann-Lévy, 2005), 28–30.
[22] Quoted in David Feldman, *Englishmen and Jews. Social Relations and Political Culture, 1840–1914* (New Haven: Yale University Press, 1994): 336.
[23] Todd Endelman, *The Jews of Britain, 1656 to 2000* (Berkeley: University of California Press, 2002), 109.

John Toland and the supporters of the Jews during the Jew Bill controversy ... he transformed the question into a political one by proposing citizenship."[24]

For Karp, this break with Luzzatto and Toland was hence a "radical" one.[25] The end of exile had come to be mainly imposed by a political integration within the public sphere. Dohm, as a state civil servant, pleaded in favor of this path of emancipation within the strong Prussian state:

> Could we possibly persuade ourselves that so many honest and industrious people will not be useful to the State, simply because they come from Asia and are distinguished by their beards and circumcision, and by having a particular way of worshiping the Supreme Being ... In every country where there are Jews, they are more acclimated and integrated than foreigners could be, even after an extended amount of time. They know of no other homeland than the one they will gain and have no longing for a distant native land. They are not wild and uncivilized Bohemians, neither are they ignorant, unmannered fugitives.[26]

In another lesser known letter, Dohm added that Jews pray for their redemption but work quietly as though they will stay forever.[27] For Dohm, then, Jews ought to become citizens and integrate within the state as equals to Christians, demonstrating their utility while keeping their customs. In this way, they will be "incorporated and dream no longer of a distant native land," effectively causing the end of the idea of exile and of any messianic redemption. Johann David Michaelis, for his part, disagreed. For him, their "oriental" character meant Jews will remain forever foreigners; they will never "blend in" with other Europeans and must return to the historic Land of Israel: "The Jews will always view the state as a temporary dwelling, which, if they are lucky, they will be able to leave so as to return to Palestine ... A people that has such hopes will never become completely native. They will, at least, always lack the proper patriotic love for the paternal fields."[28]

Let us now consider the contemporary French case. We are dealing here with a strong centralized state within a nearly unified Catholic society. Commerce plays

---

24 Robert Liberles, "From Toleration to Verbesserung: German and English Debates on the Jews in the Eighteenth-Century," *Central European History* 22, no. 1 (1989): 24–30.
25 Karp, *The Politics of Jewish Commerce in Europe*, 96.
26 English translation from Christian Wilhem Dohm, *De la réforme politique des Juifs* (Paris: Stock, 1984), 38, 65.
27 "Les Juifs prient pour le retour dans leur terre comme les Chrétiens pour une rédemption prochaine; les deux vaquent à leurs affaires comme s'ils devaient rester ici éternellement" (The Jews pray for the return to their land as do the Christians for the forthcoming redemption; both go about their business as if they were here to stay). Quoted in Dominique Bourel, "Préface," in Dohm, *De la reforme politique des Juifs*, 18.
28 Quoted in Jonathan Hess, *Germans, Jews and the Claim of Modernity* (New Haven: Yale University Press, 2002), 68.

a decidedly lesser role in such a state-run society. Only at the Atlantic periphery, from Bordeaux to Nantes and Bayonne, Jews of Sephardic origin, like their brethren in England and Holland, followed the economic pattern of assimilation through international trade. But in this strongly centralized society, as against the English pattern, Jews were obliged to adopt the local customs. They were expected to cut off their beards, follow an exogamic strategy, and in general behave like their bourgeois neighbors. The idea of being a nation in exile went by the wayside.[29]

Yet Jews in Lorraine and Alsace, like those in Prussia and the Austro-Hungarian Empire, were still ensconced within an agricultural economy, a physiocratic economy organized by the state. Hence, it is no surprise that when the Metz contest opened with the question "Are there means to render the Jews more useful and happier in France?" the notion of utility was seen mainly from the perspective of the state. The contest was organized by Pierre Louis Roederer, a civil servant later appointed to the state council, that is, the Conseil d'Etat, and soon to become Napoleon's minister. Like Dohm in Prussia, several members of the jury and some contributing authors also had ties with the state.

It was opened in 1785 and the prizes were allocated in 1788, just several months before the French Revolution. During the same period, in 1787, the Protestants at last were recognized almost as equal citizens while the Jews remained excluded from this important reform. Nevertheless, King Louis XVI asked Malesherbes whether it was also possible to improve the Jews' status. The question of the emancipation of the black slaves from the Islands was also discussed. The Metz contest attracted much attention and for that reason was seen by Heinrich Graetz and other Jewish historians as a turning point in modern Jewish history.

The first round of the Metz contest, organized by the Metz Academy saw nine essay entries; the jury selected two for the second round, two other entries were added, and three were awarded a prize. Of the prize-winning essays, two were published in the twentieth century (those of the Abbé Grégoire and Zalkind Hourwitz), while the third (by Claude-Antoine Thiery) was published almost only confidentially. Several entries were thought to have disappeared.[30] Grégoire's first Metz entry was discovered recently by Alyssa Sepinwald, and

---

[29] Frances Malino, *The Sephardic Jews of Bordeaux* (Tuscaloosa: University of Alabama Press, 1978).

[30] For a general overview, Abraham Cahen, "L'émancipation des Juifs devant la Société Royale des sciences et des arts de Metz en 1787 et M Roederer," *Revue des Etudes Juives* 1 (1880): 83–104. David Feuerwerker, *L'émancipation des Juifs en France, de l'Ancien Régime à la fin du Second Empire* (Paris: A. Michel, 1976), and H. Tribout de Morembert, "Est-il des moyens de rendre les Juifs plus utiles et plus heureux?" Tiré à part des *Mémoires de l'Académie Nationale de Metz*, T.1. (Lorrain, 1974). Bibliothèque de Metz, LOBR in 8° 238.

I myself found another manuscript written by Haillecourt.[31] For some devout Catholic contestants, such as Michaelis in Prussia, Jews as orientals must simply return to Palestine, where they belong. For others, they should convert to Catholicism and join the Catholic nation. Still others argued that they ought to become universal citizens, relinquishing their rituals and any consciousness of being a nation in exile. The common ground among these opinions was that belonging to French society and feeling a kinship with Palestine were deeply incompatible impulses.

We will now consider this question of exile in light of some of these documents. Dom Chais was a Catholic priest, among those most hostile to the Jews. His first-round entry comes out clearly against any integration. Like Michaelis in Prussia, he believed that Jews indeed would be more useful and happier in their ancestral land.

> All the nations on Earth have a home, a homeland, a country or a province, as small as it may be. Each citizen is free to travel, journey, and trade, no doubt; but in the end, each comes home; one would not say of the Dutch that they are scattered to the four corners of the earth, but that they range far and wide, running to wherever commerce takes them. But the Jew is strewn, scattered, flung as if by chance, and carried off like dust to all parts of the world, where he is domiciled, but not at home. When one asks a Portuguese Jew, why are you here? He answers, I was born here, my father died here, and here I will live out my life: Portugal is therefore your homeland, is it not: Not at all, it is a strange land, I have no homeland other than Judea, where our Temple stood.
>
> If one were to ask the same question of a Chinese Jew or an American, he would answer similarly; they are all born with the love of a homeland that they do not possess, have never seen, and will never see; nevertheless, they sigh as they wait to see it once more, or to possess it. For the last 1,800 years, only death has put an end to their longing; without changing this illusory love for a land, with which they are all generally born, a whit; a land that they were promised; that they were given to possess; and of which they were dispossessed and have been chasing after for so many centuries. This prodigious lapse of time, that devours everything, and causes all to be forgotten, has no hold against this uniformly Jewish characteristic.[32]

---

31 It is also worth noting, between the two rounds, the publication of a pamphlet by Berr Bing, a renowned Jewish figure from Metz hostile to the idea of *galut* who, following Jeremiah's letter, wrote on this question that "The Eternal instructed Jeremiah to tell the captive nation in Babylon in His name that 'the well-being of the city to which I have brought you shall be dear to you; pray to your Lord for it.'" *Lettre du S.I.B.B, Juif de Metz*. Metz. 1787. Bnf Ld 184 67 A, 11. One can read for the first time all the manuscripts including the first unpublished manuscript of Grégoire in *"Est-il des moyens de rendre les Juifs plus utiles et plus heureux?" Le Concours de l'Académie de Metz, 1785*, ed. Pierre Birnbaum (Paris: Le Seuil, 2017).

32 Ms 1349. Bibliothèque de Metz (first manuscript). These paragraphs do not appear in the second manuscript.

Thus, for Dom Chais, any Jew living in Holland, Portugal, China, or America would recognize that he lives in a foreign nation. His only real nation is Judea, where his Temple had been. Two years later, in the midst of the Revolution, the greatest opponent of Jewish emancipation, the Bishop of Nancy, Mgr La Far, espoused a very nearly identical position:

> This nation, torn from the land of its fathers, dispersed throughout the earth ... has been crisscrossing through the generations of other nations for seventeen centuries without allying itself or integrating itself with them ... It carries with it, without alteration, its religion, its laws, its mores and its prejudices. In the bosom of the states that have taken in the errant members of this scattered nation, one sees it always particular and distinct ... In whichever kingdom in which it resides, it is and will always be the Jewish People ... France cannot admit a tribe whose eyes turn incessantly toward the shared homeland that is destined to reunite its scattered people one day, [a tribe] which therefore cannot swear an allegiance of any substance to the country that hosts it.[33]

In La Fars' opinion, the Jews were a tribe seeking to reunite its scattered members as a common nation that has no link at all with French soil. Thus, for Dom Chais as for La Far, Jews should renounce the idea of exile and return to the Land of Israel, leaving the nations where they will forever be foreigners.

In sharp contrast to this interest in a Jewish return to *Eretz Israel*, Grégoire wished to convert the Jews and bring them within the French Catholic nation, thereby breaking any other national tie. Using almost identical language in the first and second round of essays, he laments that,

> Even commerce, which tends to erase the national character of nations, to integrate them, or to leave them only with nuances [of difference] has left the [national character] of the Hebrew nation almost intact. It has barely been modified by the difference in climate, because the uniformity of its living habits combats and weakens this influence. So too, far from diminishing its native traits, the difference of the centuries and countries has only reinforced its character. One [attempts to] obstruct its genius in vain; no one has been able to change it and perhaps the Jews of Ethiopia resemble the Jews of England more than the inhabitants of Picardy do those of Provence.
>
> This is why, as was observed in London, the Jew is not English; he is not Dutch in The Hague, nor is he French in Metz. It is always a nation apart, a State within a State, and how

---

33 "Opinion de M L'Evêque de Nancy, Député de Lorraine sur l'admissibilité des Juifs à la plénitude de l'état civil et des droits de citoyens actifs," in *La Révolution française et l'émancipation des Juifs*, 7: 2. The Prince of Colmar, another enemy of the Jewish emancipation in the same discussion, said that Jews, as "*cosmopolites*" preserve "their religion, their habits, the superstitious hope that causes them to wait continually for their Messiah and glory ... leaving them strangers, essentially, in the country in which they live." "Opinion de M le Prince de Broglie, député de Colmar sur l'admission des Juifs à l'état civil," in *La Révolution française et l'émancipation des Juifs*, 7: 4.

absurd to reproach it of almost never having had a homeland when nowhere, or nearly so, has its right to a homeland been conceded.[34]

In his first and second essays, Grégoire objects to the idea, articulated by Michaelis, that all Jews are simply waiting to return to Palestine. In his view, once they will become a member of the nation, bound to the laws of the state, they will lose their consciousness of being a member of a group and embrace their actual nation:

> Mr. Michaelis claims that they will always see Palestine as their place of rest and will never connect to other countries, seeing them as nothing but crossing points. Whom shall we believe – him or Boulanger? This one assures us that the fanaticism of the Jews is cooling off and that eventually it may be completely extinguished. We can only assess this claim by dint of future experience; but different traits about which we have read and which we will read in this work favor the latter view. The Jew hopes to return to Palestine, but at the same time, he hopes to conquer the universe, thus securing his possessions in other countries. In any case, in his view, this return is to take place at an indeterminate time, and as he has as much sense as we do, his hopes are not a reason to abandon his current pleasures, as long as he can have them.
>
> Though misfortune weighs upon him and he tremblingly eats bread that is wet with his tears; and sighs for the coming of the messiah; his coming seems less desirable when the humanity of the nations allows him to breathe easily under paternal roofs inhabited by tranquility and happiness which have all the charm of novelty for him. Once he has become a member of the nation, committed to the law, to the State, by the ties of pleasure, security, liberty, ease, we will see his group allegiance diminished. He will cherish his mother, that is to say his homeland, whose wellbeing will be one and the same as his, and he will not take his wealth elsewhere. Tolerance and his lands will secure him to the country in which he will have acquired them. Toland insists strongly on this last reason in his work on the naturalization of the Jews in England.[35]

Yet in the second essay, the winning text, we find a further passage that counters this view:

> Their gaze is ever turned toward their ancient metropolis; and if liberty were to now stretch out its arms to the frontiers of Palestine, they would fly there from the four corners of the globe with their books, their rites, and their law. Seventeen centuries have not been able to remove their hope of a liberator, and when Sabbatei Zevi announced himself as such, the Jews of Metz, Italy, Germany were already ready to sell everything in order to join him …

---

[34] L'Abbé Grégoire. First unpublished manuscript. Ms1349. Bibliothèque de Metz. These sentences can be found in *Essai sur la régénération physique, morale et politique des Juifs* (Paris: Flammarion, 1988), scattered through chapters 5 and 16.

[35] Ibid. In the second published manuscript, he used a less interrogative formula when wondering about Michaelis's opinion; Toland's name disappears from the text, reappearing only in a note. On Grégoire see Alyssa Goldstein-Sepinwall, *The Abbé Grégoire and the French Revolution* (Berkeley: University of California Press, 2005).

> Why then are the Hebrews ... currently attached not only to Mosaic law but also to delusional fantasies in which they display blind credulity?[36]

Grégoire expected, in accordance with strong-state logic, that the state would act vigorously to destroy this residual collective identity even commercial activity had not managed to obliterate. In the second essay, he used much harsher language to describe such state action. Here, he made numerous hostile remarks, such as his oft-quoted line concerning Yiddish ("ce jargon tudesco-hébraico-rabbinique" [the German-Hebraic rabbinical language]) and negative views on the Talmud (for example "rêveries talmudiques" [Talmudic dreams]). In this second text, Jews even appear to be responsible for ritual murder.

Thus the title of Grégoire's text specifically signals rebirth and effacement of previous identity. In this essay, Grégoire calls repeatedly for a regeneration of French Jews through state action. Moreover, he describes, using brutal terms, the way the state is to deal with the Jews (for example, "lions les," and "emparons nous" [bind them, seize them]), so that any idea of being a collective body related to a nation located in Palestine will be eradicated. For Grégoire, the logic of the strong state is sure to obviate any kind of external remembrance. Precisely through political means the Jews will no longer experience exile. The very idea of a Jewish nation, of a wished-for collective body, will disappear in this strong state, where Jews will be spread throughout the country and encouraged to forget their values, and once bound to the state and its laws, will embrace the "*patrie*," homeland, and dream no more of Palestine. In the French context, commerce failed to make the Jews forget Jerusalem, but where trade failed, the state may succeed by reshaping the values, education, and customs of the Jews, with an eye toward their conversion.

The majority of essays submitted to the Metz contest dealt in one way or another with the question of exile. Differently from Dom Chais, with his willingness to return the Jews to Palestine, or Grégoire's ridicule of Palestinian credulity and suggestion that the state strong-arm the Jews into joining the Catholic nation, a third category of author was convinced that Jews, by retaining some of their values but dropping the dream of Palestine, are already prepared to enter French society. As a civil servant of a small town in the north of France, Valioud, for instance, who competed only in the contest's first round and was quite favorable to the emancipation of the Jews, saw the Jewish conquest of Palestine as a "chimera." He held that the Jews will find "true happiness" in their actual societies, when they are no longer humiliated. Valioud also voiced a premonition that

---

[36] Grégoire, *Essai*, 62. In the first manuscript, we find in note 29: "We can count more than twenty false messiahs, until Sabbathai-Zevi who appeared in the last century."

should such a reality – the Jewish conquest of Palestine – ever materialize, one would see both Christian and Muslim armies joined against the Jews.

> Having failed to attain the happiness to which they could aspire on Earth, could the Jews still flatter themselves that they will one day find a conquerer, a co-religionist, who will gather them, and bring iron and devastation to their ancient land of Judea with the ferocity of a Tartar chief, and rout all the nations who live there, and become its formidable possesser, causing their crown to be respected, and rebuilding a temple to the Living God, and renewing the sacrifices? There is no nation today that does not feel the ridiculousness of this delusion, and that does not conceive in advance the impossibility of even a shadow of success. If this were to happen we would see the idea of deicide in all its horror, with millions of arms, the two religions that have divided the earth would join forces in order to mete out explosive punishment. We would witness [hitherto] inconceivable agreement in matters of religion, supported by well understood policy, Ottoman flags together with those of the Cross, emerging from the four corners of the earth, and marching against the new standards of the God of the armed, they would not fear to attack them, as if they were marked by their own confession by their hands, stained by the greatest of crimes, venging themselves for a second time for the attack on the person of the Son, reaching them even in the new tabernacles of the Father, and perhaps extinguishing a name that has become more odious than ever, in the blood of the last of the unfortunates who will have brought victory. Thanks to the events that the centuries and Providence have allowed to unfold, these horrors will never be seen. Educated Jews in possession of their writings are very far from these ideas. They have entirely lost the thread of their calculations. They no longer know anything of the epochs in which they were arranged. The times which were meant to have brought deliverance have passed, and deliverance never came. Now, reduced to a vague and loose hope to which they see no end or certainty, and in which they cannot even discern anything solid, they would sooner take a real and unique state of happiness, one which will redeem the humiliation that they experience; and if they do not honor the prince who will remove their humiliation with the name of Savior, at least they will name him Benefactor and Envoy of the Heavens, sent for their felicity.[37]

Valioud held that Jews could find within the French nation their "lost" Promised Land; they would no longer need to await any messiah. Respectful of Jewish values and rituals, Valioud contended that Jews might achieve happiness in France without any regeneration.

Thiery, the second winner of the Metz contest, also set forth this question in his second essay but, unlike Grégoire, did not advocate for the state's use of force:

> They are accused, I know, of seeing themselves as passengers among the other Nations; we claim that they wait ceaselessly for the day of the arrival of a Messiah who will reunite them and avenge them at last; we conclude that therefore we could never turn them into Citizens, that they can never behave like Citizens or feel like them ... It seems to me that experience destroys these allegations, they create establishments everywhere, everywhere they bind

---

37 Valioud, Ms 1349. First and only manuscript. Bibliothèque de Metz.

themselves by ties that are most difficult to sever, everywhere they are loyal and submissive subjects; ... In this Messiah, they wait for an avenger and a support ... Well then, let us be that ourselves, let us secure them through benevolent acts, let us offer them some of the enjoyment that it pleases us to offer other Foreigners, and soon we will see them ... their Promised Land will be the one in which they finally find peace and tranquility.[38]

Thiery's winning text affirmed – recalling to a certain extent Grégoire – that French Jews had already found their "Promised Land" in France, and supported his contention by adducing the examples of England, Italy, and Holland where Jews were peacefully integrated. These examples fill four full pages of his second essay but took up barely three lines in his first. Moreover, and crucially, Thiery's second essay contains nearly ten pages on the successful integration of Nancy's Jews compared to those of Metz (the first essay has a single line on Nancy, in a footnote). Thus, in the winning text, Nancy's Jews have become the prototype of a social integration that can be compared to that of the English or the Dutch, namely, through modernization, commerce, and enlightenment:

> With no external distinguishing marks, the Nation does not find it repugnant to approach them, it is not surprised to find them sometimes dignified in their appearance, there is finesse in their furnishings and their apparel ... Where can this difference that places the Jews from Metz two centuries away from the Jews of the neighboring City come from, if not these external marks that the former are obliged to wear all the time ... Furthermore, among these external marks, we find some that are imposed by *us* and I do not think that we should encounter great difficulty in abolishing them; others, such as the beard for men, the veils which cover the hair of the married women, represent less rigorous rules. And already, the first of them allow themselves to be entirely clean-shaven whereas the others [the women] ... have been able to catch our eyes and recall, at least to our imagination, an ornament that they would regret keeping hidden from us.[39]

The Jews of Nancy were entering the various professions; as a result, they did not wear any particular sign on their clothes or heads, they were clean-shaven, and women did not cover their hair. A peaceful and non-violent assimilation brought the Jews within French society: they can keep their values in their private sphere, they don't have to convert, and in France they shall find their Promised Land. Implicitly, Thiery takes exception to Diderot's lauding "*les rasés*" but condemning "*les barbus*," who were perceived as dangerously dreaming of rebuilding the Temple in Jerusalem:

---

[38] Thiery, *Dissertation sur cette question: "Est-il des moyens de rendre les Juifs plus heureux et plus utiles en France?"* (Paris: EDHIS, 1968), 2: 52.
[39] Ibid., 63–72.

> The Jews are nowhere so close to the condition of other citizens. They have their neighborhood; there are clean-shaven ones, there are bearded ones ... The clean-shaven Jews are rich and pass for honest men; one must be on one's guard with the bearded ones, who are not as infinitely scrupulous ... We recognize as holy ground only the temple in Jerusalem, which no longer exists, says one rabbi, and we will have no real synagogue until it will be rebuilt, which will happen sooner or later; you can be certain that the messiah will come if we give him enough time to do so.[40]

In his prize-winning essay, Thiery, like Valioud, advocates in favor of a peaceful assimilation that holds Jewish culture in tact: neither the Talmud nor the Yiddish language is derided, and if up to him, Jews could work on Sunday rather than Saturday, when they pray and rest. Therefore France shall be the new Promised Land.

Thiery's vision does not fit with Ronald Schechter or David Nirenberg's recent analysis of the French Enlightenment's interest in the Jews, who in their view, "provided the perfect proving ground for the powers of Enlightenment. Perfect because Enlightenment won either way. If even the Jews could be 'regenerated,' then there were no limits to the emancipatory powers of Enlightenment anthropology. But if they could not, it simply means that reason has reached the boundaries of its authority and that Jews lay on the other side."[41] For Valioud, Thiery, Mirabeau and Dohm,[42] the French Enlightenment should have allowed the Jews to enter civil society without any conversion but also without any radical regeneration of their souls and bodies. They advocated for compromises ("*accomodement*") that would allow Jews to feel at home in their new Promised Land.

This was exactly the vision of Zalkind Hourwitz, the third winner, and only Jewish contestant, of the Metz contest. He advocated to "[g]rant them the rights of citizenship and you will see that they are French just like all others subjects of the kingdom. It is true that they do not believe they will remain permanently in the country they inhabit and that they await the arrival of a messiah who will re-establish them in Palestine but they await death with even more certitude and this does not prevent them or for that matter anyone from sowing and planting wherever permitted."[43]

---

40 Denis Diderot, *Voyage de Hollande*, in *Œuvres Complètes* (Paris, 1819), 96–98. On this distinction, Dominique Bourel, "Les rasés et les barbus. Diderot et le judaïsme," *Revue philosophique de la France et de l'étranger* 174, no. 3 (1984): 275–85.
41 David Nirenberg, *Antijudaism. The Western Tradition* (New York: Norton, 2013), 350–51. Ronald Schechter. *Obstinate Hebrews. Representations of Jews in France, 1715–1815* (Berkeley: University of California, 2003).
42 See above n. 27.
43 "[O]n ne déménage pas si facilement d'un pays comme d'une maison." Zalkind Hourwitz, *Apologie des Juifs en réponse à la question, Est-il des moyens de rendre les Juifs plus heureux et plus utiles en France* (Paris: EDHIS, 1968), 4: 77. This sentence is absent from the first manuscript. On Hourwitz, Frances Malino, *A Jew in the French Revolution. The Life of Zalkind Hourwitz* (London:

Following Jeremiah's letter to the Jews of Babylon, then, Jews will dwell in their countries, work, build, and lead an ordinary life there and as Thiery and Valioud argue, they will no longer dream of Palestine. In his second round essay, Hourwitz also compared between Jews from Nancy (or from Bordeaux) and Metz. In this winning text he notes that "one does not move as easily from a country as from a house."[44]

With the French Revolution, these interpretations of the Jewish destiny within the French nation could be applied. Deriving from the universalist Enlightenment, the Revolution forced society to homogenize, challenged all forms of particularism, and combatted the remnants of social and cultural pluralism by imposing a public sphere that was unfavorable to religion. It wanted particularistic groups to assimilate, whether Britons, Occitans, or Jews. According to the words of Clermont Tonnerre, "We must refuse everything to the Jews as a Nation, in the sense of a corporate body, and accord everything to the Jews as individuals." Jews disappeared as a nation only to be reborn as individuals sharing specific values. For most of them, France had became their home and they celebrated it in their prayers:

> O Israel! For too long you have been persecuted by cruel intolerance ... Awaken to the ring of Liberty, the days of your happiness have arrived ... Let out a stream of thanksgiving, O my brothers; the sacred land on which we live has become our Homeland; the laws of the French Republic are also our laws; a holy alliance has placed us in the great family of free men.[45]

And after the revolution, they celebrated Napoléon Bonaparte in the same way:

> But what do I see? O Zion, in solace you are reborn!
> Rise up, you are no longer captive and desolate!
> Come teach it to the land, to the empire of the seas
> That Napoleon is the greatest of heroes.[46]

Blackwell, 1996). Malino translated this paragraph: "When we accord them the rights of citizenship, we will see that they are as French as other subjects of the Kingdom. It is true that they do not believe that they will always stay in the country in which they currently live, and that they await the arrival of the Messiah who will re-establish them in Palestine; but they await death with even more certitude, this does not prevent them, just like other men, from building, sowing and planting anywhere we allow them to do so" (49). Mirabeau penned nearly the same line: "Waiting for the messiah will no more prevent the Jews from becoming good citizens than it hinders the Christians, who have been waiting for the return of Christ since Justin, Irénée, Tertilien, Suplice and others." *Sur Moses Mendelssohn: sur la réforme politique des Juifs* (Paris: EDHIS, 1968), 1: 123.
44 Hourwitz, *Apologie des Juifs*, 82. This does not appear in the first essay.
45 Pierre Birnbaum, *Prier pour l'État*, 49. See also, Ronald Schechter, *Obstinate Hebrews* (Berkeley: University of California Press, 2003).
46 Birnbaum, *Prier pour l'État*, 58.

France was the new Land of Israel and the Seine, the new Jordan. Far from Dom Chais's wish to send the Jews to Palestine or Grégoire's conception of complete regeneration, Jews were to be transformed into Frenchmen without any preconditions. Within the new universalist public space, they would have free access to state positions – but no sense of being in exile or of a collective Jewish identity. The key was the notion of commonality: Jews would eat what other citizens ate and at the same table, pray for the health of the king or the state, and surrender their sense of belonging to the People of Israel.[47] Even if, in reality, numerous bonds of solidarity remained,[48] French Jews were to restrict their Judaism to the private sphere. For Joseph Reinach, hero of the Dreyfus affair, symbol of the state Jew who loves the Republic and an important political actor of the Third Republic:

> If one understands Zionism to be the establishment of a Jewish State in Palestine, I say distinctly, resolutely, no ... the very idea that a State could be based on a religion contradicts all the principles of the modern world ... There has not been a Jewish nation for twenty five centuries ... Since the Revolution declared the equality of all religion through Mirabeau and Abbot Gregory, it is no longer permissible to speak of French Jews. There is, therefore, no Jewish race nor Jewish nation, as there is only a Jewish religion, Zionism is certainly a foolishness, a historical, archeological, ethnic triple error.[49]

Throughout the nineteenth century, Zionism would be more or less an alien notion to French Jews.[50] Even the Dreyfus affair did not shake their allegiance to the strong state. Confronted with a strong antisemitic movement, they remained loyal to the strong state still protecting their lives and livelihoods. They seldom converted like in Prussia or Austria and were eager to be seen as French citizens sharing just their Jewish religion organized under the umbrella of their strong state since Napoléon Bonaparte's Sanhedrin. Jewishness therefore became a legitimate religion within a strongly secularized public space. It lost its national dimension in accordance with the logic of the integration process of the French homogenized nation shaped by the French Revolution's emancipatory values. This explained the weakness of French Zionism seen by native French Jews as a shocking rupture of the Franco-Jewish wedding. André Spire, one of the very few state Jews aligned with the Zionist movement, contrasting the French, English, and the American case, noted:

---

47 Pierre Birnbaum, *La République et le cochon* (Paris: Le Seuil, 2013), 263.
48 Lisa Moses Leff, *Sacred Bonds of Solidarity* (Stanford: Stanford University Press, 2006).
49 Quoted in Pierre Birnbaum, *Les deux maisons. Essai sur la citoyenneté des Juifs en France et aux Etats Unis* (Paris: Gallimard, 2012), 263.
50 Michel Abitbol, *Les Deux Terres promises. Les Juifs de France et le sionisme* (Paris: Olivier Orban, 1989).

Our Jewish elite calls itself French, believes itself to be French, and it has really proven that it is so by giving France the best of its blood: that of its sons. But in fighting Zionism, it does not perceive at all that its egoism and incomprehension cause it to fail its most manifest French duty.

Whether it is informed, then, by the great Zionist agitation that has been developing for the last three years as much in England as in America, or ... Jews and non-Jews, bourgeois and laborer, call for, in [addition to] individual liberties, the Congress of Peace to grant the Jews national lands and national rights, and that all ease be granted the Jews toward the colonization of Palestine.[51]

Zionism exerted much appeal to Jews living in societies with pluralistic, weak states. They built powerful Zionist organizations led by renowned figures such as Louis Brandeis. For Brandeis, Zionism and Americanism were one and the same notion: "I understood slowly that to become a good American, we must become good Jews and to be good Jews, we must become Zionists."[52] By way of contrast, in France, the strong-state emancipation of the Jews and extirpation of the idea of exile had profound consequences: a resolute resistance to any Zionist vision.

Bibliography

Abitbol, Michel. *Les Deux Terres promises. Les Juifs de France et le sionisme*. Paris: Olivier Orban, 1989.
Baer, Yitzak. *Galout, l'imaginaire de l'exil dans le judaïsme*. Paris: Calmann-Lévy, 2000.
Barzilay, Isaac. "John Toland's Borrowings from Simone Luzzatto's Discourse on the Jews of Venice (1638), the Major Source of Toland's Writing on the Naturalization of the Jews in Great Britain and Ireland (1714)." *Jewish Social Studies* 31, no. 2 (1969): 75–81.
Barzilay, Isaac. "The Jew in the Literature of the Enlightenment." *Jewish Social Studies* 18, no. 4 (1956): 243–261.
Birnbaum, Pierre, ed. *"Est-il des moyens de rendre les Juifs plus utiles et plus heureux?" Le Concours de l'Académie de Metz, 1785*. Paris: Le Seuil, 2017.
Birnbaum, Pierre. *La République et le cochon*. Paris: Le Seuil, 2013.
Birnbaum, Pierre. *Les deux maisons. Essai sur la citoyenneté des Juifs en France et aux Etats Unis*. Paris: Gallimard, 2012.
Birnbaum, Pierre. *Prier pour l'État. Les Juifs, l'alliance royale et la démocratie*. Paris: Calmann-Lévy, 2005.
Birnbaum, Pierre and Ira Katznelson, eds. *Paths of Emancipation: Jews, State and Citizenship*. Princeton, NJ: Princeton University Press, 1995.
Black, Eugene. *The Social Politics of Anglo-Jewry, 1880–1920*, New York: Blackwell, 1988.
Bourel, Dominique. "Les rasés et les barbus. Diderot et le judaïsme." *Revue philosophique de la France et de l'étranger* 174, no. 3 (1984): 275–285.

---

51 André Spire, *Souvenirs à Bâtons rompus* (Paris: A. Michel, 1962), 98.
52 Louis Brandeis, *Brandeis on Zionism*, reprint (Washington, DC: Zionist Organization of America, 1999), 50.

Brandeis, Louis D. *Brandeis on Zionism*. Reprint, Washington, DC: Zionist Organization of America, 1999.
Bregoli, Francesca. *Mediterranean Enlightenment. Livornese Jews. Tuscan Culture and Eighteenth-Century Europe*. Stanford: Stanford University Press, 2014.
Cahen, Abraham. "L'émancipation des Juifs devant la Société Royale des sciences et des arts de Metz en 1787 et M Roederer." *Revue des Etudes Juives* 1 (1880): 83–96.
Dohm, Christian Wilhem. *De la réforme politique des Juifs*. Paris: Stock, 1984.
Dubin, Lois. *The Port Jews of Habsburg Trieste: Absolutist Politics and Enlightenment Culture*. Stanford: Stanford University Press, 1999.
Endelman, Todd. *The Jews of Britain, 1656 to 2000*. Berkeley: University of California Press, 2002.
Feldman, David. *Englishmen and Jews. Social Relations and Political Culture, 1840–1914*. New Haven: Yale University Press, 1994.
Feuerwerker, David. *L'émancipation des Juifs en France, de l'Ancien Régime à la fin du Second Empire*. Paris: A. Michel, 1976.
Frankel, Jonathan and Steven Zipperstein, eds. *Assimilation and Community: The Jews in Nineteenth-Century Europe*. Cambridge: Cambridge University Press, 1992.
Goldstein-Sepinwall, Alyssa. *The Abbé Grégoire and the French Revolution*. Berkeley: University of California Press, 2005.
Hess, Jonathan. *Germans, Jews and the Claim of Modernity*. New Haven: Yale University Press, 2002.
Hirschman, Albert. *Exit, Voice and Loyalty*. Cambridge, MA: Harvard University Press, 1970.
Kaplan, Yosef. "Political Concepts in the World of the Portuguese Jews of Amsterdam during the Seventeenth Century: The Problem of Exclusion and the Boundaries of Self-Identity." In *Menasseh ben Israel and His World*. Edited by Yosef Kaplan, Henry Méchoulan, and Richard Popkin, 45–62. Leiden: Brill, 1989.
Karp, Jonathan. *The Politics of Jewish Commerce in Europe, 1638–1848*. Cambridge: Cambridge University Press, 2008.
Katz, David. *Philo-Semitism and the Readmission of the Jews to England, 1603–1655*. Oxford: Clarendon Press, 1982.
La Révolution française et l'émancipation des Juifs. Paris: EDHIS, 1968.
Liberles, Robert. "From Toleration to Verbesserung: German and English Debates on the Jews in the Eighteenth-Century." *Central European History* 22, no. 1 (1989): 3–32.
Malino, Frances. *A Jew in the French Revolution. The Life of Zalkind Hourwitz*. London: Blackwell, 1996.
Malino, Frances. *The Sephardic Jews of Bordeaux*. Tuscaloosa: University of Alabama Press, 1978.
Malino, Frances and David Sorkin, eds. *From East and West: Jews in a Changing Europe, 1750–1870*. Oxford: Blackwell, 1990.
Moses Leff, Lisa. *Sacred Bonds of Solidarity*. Stanford: Stanford University Press, 2006.
Nelson, Eric. *The Hebrew Republic*. Cambridge, MA: Harvard University Press, 2011.
Nirenberg, David. *Antijudaism. The Western Tradition*. New York: Norton, 2013.
Ravid, Benjamin. "How Profitable the Nation of the Jews Are: The Humble Addresses of Menasseh ben Israel and the Discorso of Simone Luzzatto." In *Mystics, Philosophers and Politicians. Essays in Jewish Intellectual History in Honor of Alexander Altmann*. Edited by Jehuda Reinharz and Daniel Swetschinski, 159–180. Durham, NC: Duke University Press, 1982.
Schechter, Ronald. *Obstinate Hebrews. Representations of Jews in France, 1715–1815*. Berkeley: University of California, 2003.

Sorkin, David. "Port Jews and the Three Regions of Emancipation." *Jewish Culture and History* 4, no. 2 (2001): 31–46.
Spire, André. *Souvenirs à Bâtons rompus*. Paris: A. Michel, 1962.
Toland, John. *Reasons for Naturalizing the Jews in Great Britain and Ireland, on the same foot with all other Nations. Containing also a Defence of the Jews against all Vulgar Prejudices in all Countries*. London, 1714.
Yehoshua, A. B. *Pour une normalité juive*. Paris: Liane Levi, 1992.

Nina Fischer
Remembering/Imagining Palestine from Afar: The (Lost) Homeland in Contemporary Palestinian Diaspora Literature

For thousands of years Jews have longed, prayed, and waited for the return to Zion, and culture – literature in particular – has had a significant role in upholding collective memory and identity as related to place.[1] Through the political movement of Zionism and Israel's establishment in 1948, leaving the diaspora for a once spiritual homeland became a lived reality for many Jews. But the Israelis' fight for their state led to the displacement of fifty percent of Mandate Palestine's Arab inhabitants. The *Nakba* – the destruction of historical Palestine and the displacement of a large percent of the Arab inhabitants – thus functions inversely to the Jewish experience. Now, Palestinians, whether Christian or Muslim, long for and write about their homeland, which has similar geographical outlines as the land Jews have held dear for so long. Focusing on the English-language literature of diaspora Palestinians, I will use Sidra Ezrahi's thinking about the role of Zion in Jewish literature and cultural identity as a springboard to explicate the role of the homeland in Palestinian collective memory, identity, and political aspirations. Contemplating the hold this land has on both peoples might aid in understanding the intricacies of the ongoing conflict over it.

Today, only about half of the world's twelve million Palestinians live in Israel, East Jerusalem, the West Bank, and Gaza, that is, in areas of historical Palestine. Due to the disputed narratives of Israel and Palestine's history and present, the unresolved political conflict – including the occupation, the status of Jerusalem, the Israeli settlements, and the location of any future borders, as well as the

---

Note: This chapter is published in the framework of the Hessian Ministry for Science and Art, funded by the LOEWE research hub "Religious Positioning: Modalities and Constellations in Jewish, Christian and Muslim Contexts" at the Goethe University Frankfurt / Justus-Liebig-Universität Gießen. I want to thank especially the editors and other authors of this book for their comments on my chapter. Others who offered important input and to whom I owe thanks include: Dareen Ammouri, Louise Bethlehem, Daniel Feldman, Osama Iliwat, Natasha Rowland, and Hannah Wirth-Nesher.

A related German-language piece using similar material has been published as "Literatur als kultureller Widerstand. Palästinabilder aus der Diaspora." *WestEnd: Neue Zeitschrift für Sozialforschung* 16, no. 1 (2019): 33–53.

[1] Sidra DeKoven Ezrahi, "'To What Shall I Compare You?': Jerusalem as Ground Zero of the Hebrew Imagination," *PMLA* 122, no. 1 (2007): 220–34.

https://doi.org/10.1515/9783110637564-003

ongoing refugee status of some five million Palestinians – the issue of homeland is both urgent and multilayered for all Palestinians, no matter where they live. Political scientists, peace and conflict scholars, and historians have long debated the past, present, and future of Palestine, but today, literary scholars are also called upon to participate. In recent years, a wave of Palestinian literature has appeared that grapples with understandings of home and exile. In the collection *Seeking Palestine: New Palestinian Writing on Exile and Home*, editor Penny Johnson states: "Palestine evokes a particular obligation of belonging in its far-flung 'inhabitants' for whom insistent memory becomes a mode of habitation."[2] Writing at the intersection of memory, imagination, and fraught political issues, the authors contemplate what belonging to Palestine means for its children in the diaspora, providing a striking example of this new Palestinian writing.

Exploring similar questions of belonging, memory, and politics related specifically to Palestine as homeland – lived, lost, and still embattled – I read contemporary English-language literature written by authors displaced in 1947/8 and those born in exile. While an "insistent memory" of Palestine is at the center of the entire corpus, I argue that there are distinct generational approaches to considerations of the homeland. The first generation writes texts of lived experience populated with memories of accurately described places, full of people, sounds, smells, and tastes representing "home." The next generations, in contrast, produce more diffuse and yet diverse images of Palestine, often in fictional form, created from the imagination, transgenerationally transmitted narratives of a former life, media reports, and sometimes, visits. For the diaspora-born authors, the homeland is much more metaphorical rather than a lived reality as it is for authors born in Palestine, both those who fled and those who remained. But even though the homeland is more abstract, it is nonetheless a central site of Palestinian identity and at the heart of the next generations' writing.

Sociologist Keith Jacobs maintains that all migrant literature is "a response to and contemplation on the meaning of home,"[3] but I want to suggest that the prominence of the homeland, which moves from a Palestine remembered to a Palestine imagined, is more than a characteristic literary feature of Palestinian diaspora writing. Given the unresolved conflict, in this case, expressive culture has a political function, too. After the devastating losses of the second Intifada, which showed that violence brought no improvement and instead left the peace

---

[2] Penny Johnson, "Introduction: Neither Homeland nor Exile are Words," in *Seeking Palestine: New Palestinian Writing on Exile and Home*, ed. Penny Johnson and Raja Shehadeh (Northampton, MA: Olive Branch Press, 2013), xi.

[3] Keith Jacobs, *Experience and Representation: Contemporary Perspectives on Migration in Australia* (Farnham and Burlington: Ashgate, 2011), 102.

process in tatters, these authors turned to culture as a new way to challenge the status quo, by promoting a Palestinian narrative of the past and present of the land that is often unknown in the West. My corpus represents a collective attempt to write Palestine and the Palestinian narrative of the homeland – past and present – into global consciousness, just like American-Jewish author Leon Uris's *Exodus*[4] did for the Israeli narrative. Literature offers thus more than just an aesthetic longing or memory work within the Palestinian community; it is a cultural tool to reach out to the broader public. The language choice shows that these texts are not intended for an internal Arab audience, as much as it indicates that we are dealing with a diaspora literature where the next generation speaks English natively, and tells a specifically Palestinian story often unknown to non-Palestinians in recognizable formats. There are many Palestinian diaspora communities around the world and I chose language as the basis for my selection because of its direct address to the West, both linguistically and culturally.

Placing this article within the theoretical frameworks of migration and memory studies, I will contemplate how the *Nakba* impacts the workings of memory in relation to the homeland, also for the generations born in the diaspora. While I do not compare the *Nakba* and the Holocaust as historical events, I understand them as traumatic chasms for each community that shape collective memory and identity. I will therefore also use memory studies theory developed in relation to the Holocaust to explore the mnemonic aftermath of dispossession and losses for Palestinians.

1 Theoretical Considerations: Palestinian Nationhood, Land, Loss, and Literature

Palestinian identities are bound to the land. The tribal system of clans is held together by the paternal line and land ownership. Palestinian expressions reflect the significance of the land, for instance: If you ask where a person lives, you literally ask where their lands are: وين اراضيك ؟ "*Wein aradak*?" The land is also inscribed in customs: Palestinian songs are primarily about it and traditional embroidery designs show what town or area a woman is from, much like last names often indicate a family's place of origin.

Today, most Palestinians do not live on their land anymore, but the homeland nonetheless binds the nation together. Rashid Khalidi's groundbreaking study

---

4 Leon Uris, *Exodus* (New York: Bantam, 1958).

on Palestinian identity shows that the land has been the basis of the national movement and self-understanding long before the *Nakba* and the ensuing division of society.[5] The homeland, constructed between memory and politics, is central to what Middle East scholar Rosemary Sayigh calls "the shared sense of 'Palestinianness'"[6] among a fractured community: those living in the West Bank and Gaza, East Jerusalemites, those with Israeli citizenship (many internally displaced from their ancestral villages and towns), and those in the diaspora. National identities affirm the belonging to a community and place: it is no surprise that *wattaniyeh* – nationalism or patriotism – is derived from *al-watan*, the homeland.

In the terminology of memory studies, sites of memory, that is, elements of the past in which "memory crystallizes and secretes itself"[7] give meaning in the present as they create focal points of collective identity especially in nation-building processes. Palestine – as a location—is a site of memory in its most literal sense. Sociologist Maurice Halbwachs argued that places keep groups connected; a community's existence in one place represents its continuity across generations as is evident in Palestinian self-understanding. However, if historical events such as the *Nakba* shatter the permanence of "generational sites," the group's relationship to place and the collective memory of it change drastically.[8] Historian Peter Read calls such locations "lost places" and describes them as sites of communal life that have been destroyed literally and metaphorically, but loom large in the memory of those who lost them.[9] Given the unresolved questions surrounding what "Palestine" means today and will look like in the future, however, both concepts need to be reconsidered for this specific case of a homeland that has varying shapes depending on peace negotiations and the political stance of the beholder. Literary texts engaging with the homeland from different generational perspectives offer new and previously often under-valued material for such considerations.

Much of Palestinian collective memory of the homeland is built around the experience of losses – during the *Nakba*, the Six-Day War, and land dispossessions continuing to this day. The need to remember Palestinian lives *in situ* is exacerbated by Zionist narratives that shed doubt on their existence in this con-

---

[5] Rashid Khalidi, *Palestinian Identity: The Construction of Modern National Consciousness* (New York: Columbia University Press, 1997).
[6] Rosemary Sayigh, "Palestinian Refugee Identity/ies: Generation, Region, Class," in *Palestinian Refugees: Different Generations, but One Identity*, ed. Ibrahim Abu-Lughod (Birzeit: Birzeit University Press, 2012), 13.
[7] Pierre Nora, "Between Memory and History: Les Lieux de Mémoire," *Representations* 26 (1989): 7.
[8] Maurice Halbwachs, *On Collective Memory*, trans. Lewis A. Coser (Chicago: University of Chicago Press, 1992), 186.
[9] Peter Read, *Returning to Nothing: The Meaning of Lost Places* (Cambridge: Cambridge University Press, 1996).

tested land.[10] The history and continuation of territorial losses and the challenge to narratives qualify as threats to belonging, providing more reasons for the prominent role of the homeland in Palestinian lives, memories, and narratives. Nira Yuval-Davis, a sociologist, maintains that belonging "becomes articulated and politicized when it is threatened in some way."[11] Memory establishes belonging and voicing it is a form of cultural resistance. Ahmad Sa'di and Lila Abu-Lughod, editors of the preeminent study of *Nakba* memory, even argue, "Making memories public affirms identity, tames trauma, and asserts Palestinian moral and political claims to justice, redress, and the right to return."[12] Literature is a powerful way of making memories public, since, after all, it tells stories and allows readers to identify, making this one juncture where literature becomes engaged in the political conflict. Selma Dabbagh, a British-Palestinian author, for instance, believes "in the power of literature to transport both writers and readers into the skins of other people."[13] Many call for telling Palestinian stories; to illustrate, Hanan Ashrawi, a senior Palestinian Authority politician with a PhD in literature, after reading an essay by American-Palestinian Susan Abulhawa, asked her to write more about Palestine, because, "We need such a narrative."[14] Abulhawa's novel *Mornings in Jenin*,[15] a bestseller translated into twenty-six languages, indeed brought the Palestinian experience to a global audience. She tasks Palestinian authors with countering "Israel's narrative that has dominated literature until recently."[16]

---

10 This is codified in the trope "A land without people for a people without a land," which, in the words of Edward Said, is an example of Israeli hopes to "cancel and transcend an actual reality – a group of resident Arabs – by means of a future wish – that the land be empty for development by a more deserving power" (Edward Said, *The Question of Palestine* [New York: Times Books, 1979], 9). The sentence, most famously used by Israel Zangwill and Golda Meir, has received much critical attention. Historian Anita Shapira, for example, explores its role in Zionist discourses (Anita Shapira, *Land and Power: The Zionist Resort to Force, 1881–1948* [Oxford: Oxford University Press, 1992], 41ff). Said and Khalidi (*Palestinian*, 101), have studied the implications for Palestinians.
11 Nira Yuval-Davis, "Belonging and the Politics of Belonging," *Patterns of Prejudice* 40, no. 3 (2006): 197.
12 Ahmad H. Sa'di and Lila Abu-Lughod, eds., *Nakba: Palestine, 1948, and the Claims of Memory* (New York: Columbia University Press, 2007), 3.
13 David B. Green, "A Conversation with British-Palestinan Writer Selma Dabbagh," *Haaretz*, October 1, 2012. http://www.haaretz.com/jewish/books/a-conversation-with-british-palestinian-writer-selma-dabbagh-1.467660 accessed June 6, 2016.
14 Olivia Snajie, "The Many Lives and Languages of a Palestinian Novel," *Publishing Perspectives*, March 21, 2012. http://publishingperspectives.com/2012/03/the-many-lives-and-languages-of-a-palestinian-novel/.
15 Susan Abulhawa, *Mornings in Jenin* (New York: Bloomsbury, 2010.).
16 Snajie, "Many Lives."

Much recent Palestinian literature reflects the impetus of working for a common goal in interesting relational forms that introduce more than just individual life stories. The Palestine memories brought together in this chapter participate in building a place of individual and collective experience and belonging, too. Especially in life writing, the texts themselves are relational in that they tell the story of the writer along with the story of her family and community, bringing the Palestinian cause – as a whole – to the fore. The sheer number of anthologies speaks to a concerted collective effort to make Palestinian voices heard.[17] Even academic studies of contemporary Palestinian identities, in which interviewees tell their stories,[18] contain "the fragments of a collective national journey."[19]

Most of these collections are arranged along the experiences of generations and their incisive political events such as 1948, 1967 (the *Naksa*, the "setback"), and the Intifadas.[20] As the literary texts show, diaspora Palestinians were shaped by the experiences of migration, too. Human rights scholar Victoria Mason maintains that for the Palestinian case, researchers need to consider what exilic generation a person belongs to because the question of displacement is not resolved politically and thus continues for many.[21] Or, as American-Palestinian Randa Jarrar writes in her novel *The Map of Home* that depicts a refugee family's continued search for a place of long-term belonging: "Baba said that moving was part of being Palestinian."[22]

But it is not only one's generation that influences outlook and texts; contexts are also significant. The meaning of the homeland or opinions on the right of return differ depending on the situation people live in, whether under Israeli occupation, in a destitute refugee camp in war-torn Syria, or as German citizens,

---

[17] Cf. Jo Glanville, ed., *Qissat: Short Stories by Palestinian Women* (London: Saqi, 2006); Johnson and Shehadeh, *Seeking Palestine*; Ismail Khalidi and Naomi Wallace, eds., *Inside/Outside: Six Plays from Palestine and the Diaspora* (New York: Theatre Communications Group, 2015); Yasir Suleiman, ed., *Being Palestinian: Personal Reflections on Palestinian Identity in the Diaspora* (Edinburgh: Edinburgh University Press, 2016).
[18] Cf. Diana Allan, *Refugees of the Revolution: Experiences in Palestinian Exile* (Stanford: Stanford University Press, 2014); Fiorella Larissa Erni, *Tired of Being a Refugee: Social Identification among Young Palestinian Refugees in Lebanon* (Geneva: Graduate Institute Publications, 2014); Dina Matar, *What It Means to Be Palestinian: Stories of Palestinian Peoplehood* (London: I.B. Tauris, 2010); Arthur Neslen, *In Your Eyes a Sandstorm: Ways of Being Palestinian* (Berkeley: University of California Press, 2011).
[19] Neslen, *Sandstorm*, 4.
[20] Julie Peteet, *Landscape of Hope and Despair: Palestinian Refugee Camps* (Philadelphia: University of Pennsylvania Press, 2005), 98.
[21] Victoria Mason, "Children of the 'Idea of Palestine': Negotiating Identity, Belonging and Home in the Palestinian Diaspora," *Journal of Intercultural Studies* 28, no. 3 (2007): 271–85.
[22] Randa Jarrar, *A Map of Home* (New York: Penguin, 2008), 9.

to name but some possibilities. In a sociological study of Canadian-Palestinian diaspora identities, Ismat Zaidan finds that even though none of her interviewees consider Palestine a future place to live,[23] "Homeland remains the key element in understanding notions of identity and home."[24] The geographer's subjects are comparable to the authors' in my corpus and her finding about the centrality of the homeland is also mirrored in the literature of the English-speaking diaspora.

2 "What Am I Without Palestine? And What Is Palestine Without Me?" The Homeland of the *Nakba* Generation

Authors from the *Nakba* generation explore questions of an inhabited homeland, displacement, and exile, throughout driven by a sense of loss.[25] Sociologist Zarefa Ali writes, "Displaced Palestinians give the impression that in Palestine they lived in paradise, and as the Zionist forces occupied the lands, destroyed their homes, and forcefully displaced them, they were turned into refugees whose problem is left without solution until today. This has become the central theme of narration of Palestine as 'the lost paradise.'"[26] Most commonly, these voices longing for a lost home are recorded in oral testimonies, a significant source in the scholarship of Palestinian history and culture.[27] English-language literature by authors who

---

[23] Ismat Zaidan, *Palestinian Diaspora in Transnational Worlds: Intergenerational Differences in Negotiating Identity, Belonging and Home* (Birzeit: Birzeit University Press, 2012), 87.
[24] Zaidan, *Palestinian Diaspora*, 92.
[25] The quotation in the section heading is from Jean Said Makdisi, "Becoming Palestinian," in *Seeking Palestine: New Palestinian Writing on Exile and Home*, ed. Penny Johnson and Raja Shehadeh (Northhampton, MA: Olive Branch Press, 2013), 177. The authors' retelling of 1948 and other events of Palestinian history also works along relational lines. Communications scholar Lena Jayyusi has argued about *Nakba* memories that "Each new tale is an echo within the echo, focusing and conjuring the collective predicament through the individual, and ramifying the significances and symbolic meaning of the individual experience through the collective." Lena Jayyusi, "Iterability, Cumulativity and Presence: The Relational Figures of Palestinian Memory," in *Nakba: Palestine, 1948, and the Claims of Memory*, ed. Ahmad H. Sa'di and Lila Abu-Lughod (New York: Columbia University Press, 2007), 110.
[26] Zarefa Ali, *A Narration Without an End: Palestine and the Continuing Nakba* (Birzeit: Birzeit University Press, 2013), 5.
[27] Laleh Khalili, *Heroes and Martyrs of Palestine* (Cambridge: Cambridge University Press, 2006), 66–7.

fled Palestine is much less common than oral history. The corpus is also small compared to the following generations.

Historian Annette Wieviorka has shown how, in the wake of the Holocaust, the witness became an increasingly important social figure. Within the contemporary cultural regime of memory, witnesses who lived through and now testify to horrific events shape our understanding of the past. By choosing life writing in its most testimonial form, the generation of the *Nakba* also establishes itself as witnesses who are documenting a lost life in Palestine. The witnessing stance gives historical gravitas and is, by definition, an embodied one, as the witness's body attests "to the past and to the continuing presence of the past."[28] By including tastes, smells, and sights, the body and its sensual memories are brought into the text and place the authors and, by extension, also the readers, in the homeland. Linking this with the experience of displacement, the readers encounter Palestine first as lived-in, then lost and longed for.

Frequently, texts are penned by former Jerusalemites, a Palestinian urban community that was particularly well-educated. They write about the city that figures in the cultural memory of all Abrahamic religions and therefore translates also for non-Palestinians, meaning that a Western audience might identify with the texts and their political impetus. But the Jerusalem we encounter is not that of Scripture; instead, the central motif is home. Such life writing portrays pre-1948 Palestine as a place of family, community, tradition, and everyday life. These images are interwoven with memories of the *Nakba*, life in exile in the wound of displacement that never healed, and discussions of the ongoing conflict. These elements go beyond the task of life writing; they are part of the political charge of Palestinian literature: writing the pre-*Nakba* experience means writing against a Zionist narrative that challenges Palestinian history on the land. Writing the *Nakba* experience personifies their losses, and writing the post-*Nakba* experience means bringing an unresolved situation to the reader's awareness.

One of the first well-known diasporic English-language texts relating the *Nakba* experience is Ghada Karmi's *In Search of Fatima: A Palestinian Story*. The titular Fatima worked for the Karmi family and was a mother figure to Ghada. The Karmis lived in Qatamon in West Jerusalem, along with other Muslim, Christian, and some Jewish families. The memoir is not only a transnational history of the family; it also includes a history of Arab Jerusalem, including a description of Qatamon as a secular, mixed neighborhood where the relations between the religious and ethnic groups were harmonious. Indeed, after the *Irgun*, a Zionist paramilitary group,

---

[28] Annette Wieviorka, *The Era of the Witness*, trans. Jared Stark (Ithaca, London: Cornell University Press, 2006), 88.

attacked the King David Hotel and killed ninety-one people in 1946 during the battle for independence from the British Mandate,[29] Karmi reports that German-Jewish refugee neighbors condemned the attack, believing that the Jewish underground's actions "will destroy everything we have worked so hard to create here."[30]

When the violence between Jews, Arabs, and the British forces that preceded the end of the British Mandate in the years 1947–8 took over Jerusalem, it left a lasting impression; even the eight-year-old sensed how "events succeeded each other with a relentless momentum, heading for some cataclysm. And we were being pushed uncontrollably by this momentum, powerless to stop it."[31] The Deir Yassin massacre of April 1948 caused widespread fear among Arabs in Palestine.[32] It also precipitated the Karmi family's flight. When leaving Jerusalem, the girl turns around in the backseat of the car for a last glimpse of Fatima and their family dog, a moment that stays with her forever. The image signifies the lost homeland – Karmi never sees either one again: "Like a body prematurely buried, unmourned, without coffin or ceremony, our hasty, untidy exit from Jerusalem was no way to have said goodbye to our home, our country and all that we knew and loved."[33] The Palestinians might not have had a state, but nonetheless, calling Palestine "her country" encapsulates the author's sense of localized belonging.

Growing up in the United Kingdom, Karmi suppresses her memories, partially because she wanted to assimilate and partially because she observed how debilitating her parents' losses during the *Nakba* and their longing for the lost homeland were for their later lives. But childhood memories erupt when she sees footage of a victorious Israel in 1967, against the backdrop of Jerusalem's most iconic site: "The vast tiled courtyard in front of the Dome of the Rock used to make a perfect playground for hopscotch, and the historic arches, pillars and holy sanctuaries were ideal for games of hide-and-seek."[34] For her, the Dome of the Rock and the Al Aqsa mosque are childhood memories, placing her in Jerusalem-as-home.

---

[29] On June 22, 1946, the *Irgun* bombed the building, which at the time housed the British Mandate Authority's central offices, including its governmental and military headquarters for the area. The ninety-one victims were not only British, indeed, the largest number were Arab, as well as some Palestinian Jews and others. Another forty-six people were injured.

[30] Ghada Karmi, *In Search of Fatima: A Palestinian Story* (London: Verso, 2002), 71.

[31] Karmi, *In Search*, 113.

[32] On April 9, 1948, fighters of two Zionist militia groups, *Irgun* and *Lehi*, attacked the Jerusalem village of Deir Yassin and killed over one hundred Palestinian villagers, though the number is still contested. Afterwards, the forces took some survivors and paraded them through the streets of Jerusalem. Both acts were condemned by the *Haganah*, the Jewish leadership's paramilitary force but nonetheless caused terror among Palestinian Arabs.

[33] Karmi, *In Search*, 123.

[34] Ibid., 370.

Returning for the first time in 1998, thirty years after this awakening and fifty years after her departure, Karmi encounters a city she does not know. She only finds her Jerusalem when she hears the Al Aqsa muezzin's call to prayer: "Mesmerised, I went to the balcony windows and threw them open, the better to hear it. On it came, over the Wailing Wall, over the huddle of poor Arab housing, over Israel's brash buildings, its luxury hotels, its noisy traffic. The unmistakable sound of another people and another presence, definable, enduring, continuous. Still there, not gone, not dead."[35] In sounds, she finds parts of her childhood home in a place that is now layered with other realities, a moment that has meaning far beyond a sensual recovery of memory.

In 2015, Karmi published a follow-up memoir in which she relates her experiences from 2005, the year she spent in Ramallah volunteering for the Palestinian Authority (PA). *Return: A Palestinian Memoir* complicates Karmi's previously clear notions of Palestine, as she encounters a developing country run by bureaucrats and often contentious internal politics while under military occupation. She identifies changes at odds with the displaced person's understanding of the homeland: first, Palestine has become the West Bank and Gaza; second, what she believed was an absolute stance concerning the refugees' right of return has been shattered even among Palestinians living under PA control; and finally, the realization that her memories have little to do with the contemporary reality. She has "travelled to the land of my birth with a sense of return, but it was a return to the past, to the Palestine of distant memory, not to the place that it is now."[36] Life has moved on and the hopes and dreams of those living in the area of historical Palestine are not those of diaspora Palestinians. This makes *Return* a story of disappointment, of a failed recovery of space and memory.

While Karmi repeatedly writes about Jerusalem itself, the sense of being out of place, that is, in exile, is at the heart of much of Edward Said's writing. He describes his Jerusalemite childhood and flight from Palestine in his poignantly entitled *Out of Place*. Providing the foundation for his life-long intellectual (and presumably personal) struggle with the question of exile, his memoir is more focused on being "in place" than on the period after the family's flight when he was twelve in December 1947. And yet, starting out, Said declares his intention: to record "an essentially lost or forgotten world" because "many of the places and people that I recall here no longer exist, though I found myself frequently amazed at how much I carried of them inside me in often minute, even startlingly concrete, detail."[37] These memories are driven by his sense of displacement: "it is geog-

---

35 Ibid., 451.
36 Ghada Karmi, *Return: A Palestinian Memoir* (London: Verso, 2015), 313.
37 Edward Said, *Out of Place* (New York: Knopf, 1999), ix.

raphy – especially in the displaced form of departures, arrivals, farewells, exile, nostalgia, homesickness, belonging, and travel itself – that is at the core of my memories of those early years."[38] To illuminate the experience of displacement, Said retains and discusses specific memories of placement in Palestine, whether it is the family's book business in Jerusalem, a summer spent in Ramallah, or even more naturalized memories of belonging. To illustrate, in his school, St. George's, which most of his male relatives had attended, he "felt totally at home; for the first and last time in my school life I was among boys who were like me."[39] Belonging here means similarity – the opposite of being the Other and of being in exile.

The Saids lived in Talbiyeh, a West Jerusalem area that after 1948 became Israel. Like Qatamon, it was a majority Arab neighborhood, a fact today often ignored. For Said, this means an erasure even of his memories. He finds it challenging "to accept the fact that the very quarters of the city in which I was born, lived, and felt at home were taken over by Polish, German, and American immigrants who conquered the city and have made it the unique symbol of their sovereignty, with no place for Palestinian life, which seems to have been confined to the eastern city, which I hardly knew. West Jerusalem has now become entirely Jewish, its former inhabitants expelled for all time by mid-1948."[40] This erasure of a pre-*Nakba* Arab presence in West Jerusalem is akin to what has happened to the destroyed Palestinian villages in what is now Israel. Not only were their inhabitants displaced from the land and from mainstream Israeli memory, in *Sacred Landscape: The Buried History of the Holy Land since 1948*, historian Meron Benvenisti shows how Israel renamed formerly Arab locations to create a Jewish narrative of the land.[41] Yet, while Qatamon and Talbiyeh officially became Gonen and Komemiyut, these names never took hold in everyday use. Today, the memory of its former residents is primarily found in the Arab architecture and in texts like Said's, since even the Arabic names have been converted into Hebrew.

Said's younger sister, Jean Makdisi Said, also describes Talbiyeh in her memoir. Born in 1940, she only has a girl's memories of Jerusalem, but her childhood recollections feature centrally in *Teta, Mother, and Me: Three Generations of Arab Women* as a structural device to tie the transnational family history to Palestine, while also drawing a vivid image of the city as home. Having only lived in Palestine as a child, Makdisi is helped by external mnemonic aids like photographs to recall her homeland. One memory, however, is different and tangible:

---

38 Ibid., xiv.
39 Ibid., 106.
40 Ibid., 109.
41 Meron Benvenisti, *Sacred Landscape: The Buried History of the Holy Land since 1948*, trans. Maxine Kaufman-Lacusta (Berkeley: University of California Press, 2000).

"Jerusalem often comes back to me in a series of scents. I smell Jerusalem in the jasmine and the orange blossom, the smell of a lemon being squeezed, the smell of cinnamon sticks in syrup, the bay leaf and olive oil of the soap from Nablus they used to wash us with."[42] Memories triggered by smells and tastes tend to be strong, characterized by an immediacy seldom achieved in less embodied forms of memory.[43] While establishing herself as an embodied witness of a Palestinian Jerusalemite community, Makdisi simultaneously reminds her readers that she is also an exile, as smells bring back her lost home in other places.

Losing Jerusalem is much more than the loss of a home; it is also the loss of the Palestinian homeland that defines personal and collective memories and identity. These losses also underlie Makdisi's essay "Becoming Palestinian." She writes: "My native Jerusalem, of which I only have some childhood memories, continues to be the ideal model of home, my *heimat*, where the past, present and future meet in my mind."[44] Despite and perhaps because of the experience of exile, Jerusalem is the "ideal" home; it is her *Heimat*. The place anchors her memory of idealness, offering a sense of unquestioned belonging before displacement.

The memory of lost wholeness and the unresolved conflict make Makdisi's writing political: "To be from Jerusalem, and to have lost it, is to be attached to the struggle for Palestine and therefore to the heart of Arab history."[45] Voicing memories allows establishing the lost home as real and reifies it against a double loss – in reality and in memory:

> Holding on to the past clutching at it as it flies away and would otherwise fade into oblivion, embodying it and rendering it concrete in individual memories, memories of places and faces, clothes, foods and rituals. This is not a futile and damaging personal fixation; it is a politically charged community action which feeds the urge for redeeming justice ... Remembering restores my mother's rightful place in her native Galilee where her father, the pastor, taught her to identify and love the fields where Christ walked.[46]

Here, Makdisi highlights the significance of nationality and ethnicity over religion – their Palestinian identity unites all the authors, no matter whether they are Muslim or Christian. Simultaneously, she also brings in Palestinian places beyond Jerusalem.

---

[42] Jean Said Makdisi, *Teta, Mother, and Me: Three Generations of Arab Women* (New York, London: W.W. Norton & Co. 2005), 27.
[43] Andreas Hartmann, "Geschmack in der Kulturwissenschaft," in *Gedächtnis und Erinnerung: Ein interdisziplinäres Lexikon*, ed. Nicolas Pethes and Jens Ruchatz (Hamburg: Rowohlt, 2001), 231.
[44] Makdisi, "Palestinian," 160.
[45] Makdisi, *Teta*, 28.
[46] Makdisi, "Palestinian," 166.

Recently, more *Nakba* generation memoirs have been published that bring to life other locations in historical Palestine, among them the writings of historian Hisham Sharabi, an American Palestinian who remembers Jaffa in *Embers and Ashes: Memoirs of an Arab Intellectual*[47] and Salman Abu Sitta who published the only English-language memoir about pre-*Nakba* Palestinian life in the Beersheba district.[48]

Taking a new perspective and adding one significant contemporary Palestinian location – the refugee camp – poet and environmental scholar Sharif S. Elmusa contemplates his life, which was shaped by both 1948 and 1967, in "Portable Absence: My Camp Re-membered." Elmusa has no personal memories of pre-*Nakba* Palestine, even though he was born in the ancestral village near Jaffa. He was a few months old when his family fled Al-Abbasiya, and found refuge in the Al-Nuwayma camp close to Jericho: "still in historic Palestine and yet across a new border from my parents' home on the coast."[49] Studying in Cairo in 1967, Elmusa also lost this second home, the liminal space of the refugee camp, now a conscious experience repeating his parents' fate. Since he was absent during the war, "Israel denied me, as it did hundreds of thousands of other Palestinians, the right to go back not only to the territory that became Israel in 1948, it barred us in a similar fashion from the West Bank and my camp, Al-Nuwayma. I became, as a consequence, a 'displaced person,' in the UN's legal lexicon, a refugee from a refugee camp."[50]

In 1971, Elmusa moved to the United States to continue studying and this voluntary migration after two forced displacements causes him to further contemplate the meaning of home and "the quandaries of exile and unrequited homesickness."[51] He states that an exile, unlike the expat who will go home, or the immigrant who wants to belong to a new place, "lingers in a state of suspense, floats, lighter than the social liquid, does not fuse."[52] The meaning of "homeland" is particularly significant to the man who grew up in a refugee camp, which "was by definition not a home – it was a temporary transit station, even if my childhood there, despite the lack of modern technological comforts, was largely a happy one, filled with play and warmth of family and friends, and was

---

47 Hisham Sharabi, *Embers and Ashes: Memoirs of an Arab Intellectual*, trans. Issa J. Boullata (Northampton, MA: Olive Branch Press, 2008).
48 Salman Abu Sitta, *Mapping My Return: A Palestinian Memoir* (Cairo: The American University in Cairo Press, 2016).
49 Sharif S. Elmusa, "Portable Absence: My Camp Re-membered," in Johnson and Shehadeh, *Seeking Palestine: New Palestinian Writing on Exile and Home*, 23.
50 Ibid., 30.
51 Ibid., 23.
52 Ibid., 26.

a 'looking-forward.' No one had any desire to stay in the camp or acknowledged it as his or her home."[53] For Elmusa, life in a refugee camp is the "quintessential Palestinian experience, both actual and symbolic" and adds further urgency to the unresolved questions surrounding Palestinian homeland and refugees.[54]

After Elmusa became an American citizen, he managed to visit the area of the ancestral village and the refugee camp, both of which were razed to the ground. His family places were thus all lost to the visitor: the village because it was never truly his and was then destroyed; the camp because it was only ever a liminal space rather than a home, and happy childhood memories could not and cannot change this sense of eternal homelessness. He stays "in a frame of mind akin to the blues – feeling homesick when you don't have a home."[55] Home is a complicated notion, most of all because in the refugee camp: "Home was Palestine, the opposite of the camp, and the future was going to be the reverse of the here-and-now."[56]

Elmusa interweaves his contemplations with poetry, adding layers of sensuous memories. The first poem, for instance, which opens the essay, describes the hills of Palestine, with "red poppies swaying in the breeze" of winter.[57] The poems show that the landscape, that is, nature itself, is a kind of home for the author born into the loss of a definable location. In this, his experience differs greatly from that of the authors above who have lived memories of a homeland and can place themselves in a Palestine in which they belong unquestionably.

3 "What Is It that Ties Us All Back to Palestine?" The Homeland of the Exilic Generations

In the case of diaspora-born authors, the similarities of the witnessing texts dissolve even more as they already do with Elmusa; we encounter diverse conceptions of the homeland.[58] Nonetheless, Palestine and its past and present, both as a country and as a site of memory, feature centrally with significant points of interest being Jerusalem and the refugee camps. This corpus, which is larger than that of the *Nakba* generation, also employs a wider choice of genres than the

---

53 Ibid., 27.
54 Ibid., 23–24.
55 Ibid., 41.
56 Ibid., 27.
57 Ibid., 22.
58 The quotation in the section heading is from Mischa Hiller, "Onions and Diamonds," in Johnson and Shehadeh, *Seeking Palestine: New Palestinian Writing on Exile and Home*, 179.

authors who document the loss of the land in life writing. Fitting with the need to imagine historical Palestine, the novel, which Edward Said drawing from Georg Lukács, calls "*the* form of 'transcendental homelessness',"[59] becomes a frequent generic choice.

Growing up in the diaspora influences the writers and their texts in multiple ways. Not only is their English native, but questions of hyphenated identities, the connection to Palestine as the homeland, and what it means to be Arab in the West also loom large. Moreover, the advantage of having a Western passport figures prominently: some authors – unlike Palestinians living in Arab countries – could visit Israel, Jerusalem, the West Bank, and Gaza.

Given that these authors were born in the wake of a catastrophe that cut off connections to families, land, and tradition, their literary texts perform "memory work." Elsewhere, I introduced the concept of memory work as "an individual's conscious, voluntary, and methodical interrogation of the past within collective frameworks, predominantly the familial one" for children of Holocaust survivors' engagement with both their parents' survival and the lost European Jewish origins.[60] The significance of the past also underlies the texts of most authors who, in the words of historian Beshara Doumani, himself a son of *Nakba* refugees, were "born after Palestine."[61]

The daughter of 1967 refugees, Susan Abulhawa was born in Kuwait, spent part of her childhood in Jerusalem's Dar Al-Tifl Al-Arabi orphanage and came to America as a teenager. She knows her place of origins and in her novel *Mornings in Jenin* the representations of Jerusalem and the West Bank are vivid, but historical Palestine is only accessible through memory work and the imagination. Her sweeping family saga tellingly begins in a bucolic pre-*Nakba* Palestine and we encounter the olive tree, the steadfast villager, bread baking in a *taboon*, and the gold anklets of the young Bedouin. This assembly presents recognizable images recreated from Palestinian sites of memory and transgenerationally transmitted narratives not drawn from lived experience.

The protagonist Amal was born in the Jenin refugee camp after her parents escaped their village during the Nakba, and she dies in Jenin during the 2002 IDF incursion while visiting the homeland with her American-born daughter. Abulhawa's description of the refugee camp, the setting of world-changing history and

---

[59] Edward Said, "Reflections on Exile," in *Altogether Elsewhere: Writers on Exile*, ed. Marc Robinson (Boston: Faber & Faber, 1994), 144.
[60] Nina Fischer, *Memory Work: The Second Generation* (Houndsmills: Palgrave Macmillan, 2015), 2.
[61] Doumani, Beshara. "A Song From Haifa," in *Seeking Palestine: New Palestinian Writing on Exile and Home*, ed. Penny Johnson and Raja Shehadeh (Northampton, MA: Olive Branch Press, 2013), 18.

everyday events, is evocative of Elmusa's childhood teachings that a camp is not a home, the "United Nations refugee camp stretched below me in one square kilometer, so many souls packed in for the long and stubborn wait to return to their Palestine."[62]

More than any other place, Jerusalem speaks to Amal who, like the author, lived in Dar Al-Tifl orphanage before her migration: "I am the daughter of this land, and Jerusalem reassures me of this inalienable title, far more than yellowed property deeds, the Ottoman land registries, the iron key to our stolen homes, or UN resolutions and decrees of superpowers could ever do."[63] Even though neither Abulhawa nor her protagonist lives there, Jerusalem is the central site of Palestinian belonging and not a lost place, not least because of its contested status. The city itself is family to which she has a natural connection, a sense of belonging the refugee camp can never provide.

In other texts, this unbreakable link is more tenuous. In Susan Muaddi Darraj's *The Inheritance of Exile: Stories from South Philly*, the different generational experiences are presented in a range of female Palestinian-American characters – four mothers and their daughters – who together provide a tapestry of the Palestinian experience in America. The mothers' memories revolve around life in Palestine during the *Nakba* as well as under Jordanian and Israeli rule, but for the daughters, the homeland is created out of family and cultural memory enhanced by imagination.

Siham's vivid Jerusalem memories bring in a strong lived presence of the homeland. Even visually the city is part of her family's American life; on her wedding picture the "Dome of the Rock, with its golden cupola, was visible in the background."[64] The golden dome is a central icon of Palestinian identity and a visual symbol of the Arab past and present in Jerusalem.[65] This preeminent site of memory of the Palestinian people draws the community together like an ekphrastic description of the Western Wall in a Jewish diaspora text.

Like in Abulhawa's *Mornings in Jenin*, the other contemporary Palestinian space is the refugee camp where Huda, like Siham belonging to the maternal generation, grew up. Upon his first visit, her American-Palestinian husband was

---

[62] Abulhawa, *Mornings*, 162.
[63] Ibid., 140.
[64] Susan Muaddi Darraj, *The Inheritance of Exile: Stories from South Philly* (Notre Dame: University of Notre Dame Press, 2007), 29.
[65] Nina Fischer, "Seeing and Unseeing the Dome of the Rock: Conflict, Memory, and Belonging in Jerusalem," in *Spatialising Peace and Conflict: Mapping the Production of Place, Sites and Scales of Violence*, ed. Annika Björkdahl and Susanne Buckley-Zistel (Houndsmills: Palgrave Macmillan, 2016).

shocked: "his hands shook when he saw the children playing in the open sewers, and the holes, like gaping mouths filled with jagged teeth, that opened the surfaces of many of the homes. 'You lived like *that*?' he seethed for days afterwards."[66] For daughter Hanan, the camp is an open wound she had never seen but always envisioned: "After all, I'd spent all my life hearing about them for myself: cement shacks with hastily thatched roofs, children running barefoot on dirt paths, sidestepping donkey dung as they scampered about, old men sitting on wooden crates playing *tarneeb* with a badly worn deck of cards. The women in the camp wore clean but threadbare clothes, and flashed smiles that displayed missing teeth."[67] But Huda was born in Haifa and the book concludes with her memories of the family's hasty exodus and its traumatic aftermath. A recognizable motif of her work is that the camp "had never been our home – Haifa would always be our real home."[68]

The young protagonists to whom the title refers, those born with an "inheritance of exile," are tied to the homeland differently. Only one, Aliyah,[69] could ever visit:

> Mama and Baba always spoke to me about "back home," and that was why I had finally gone that summer. Mama's parents had brought her to the States during one of the wars, but died before they could return. Sidi, Baba's father, had never left. His land and farm outside Jerusalem had been seized to build settlements, so he moved his family to Ramallah. So I wasn't going to the home Baba had been born in. I never could return because it had been replaced by a walled-in city to which my dark skin and last name denied me access.[70]

Aliyah's visit is a complex experience not only because she encounters Palestinian life under occupation. The trip also encapsulates her sense of being a diaspora Palestinian who struggles in both her "homes" – in America she is a stranger because of her ethnicity, and in Ramallah she is a stranger because of her Americanness and accent. But one location changes this – the Dome of the Rock: "*The room was enormous, and beautiful arabesques adorned the walls and interior Dome, whose golden exterior I had seen crowning pictures of Jerusalem. Now I was here, finally inside the picture.*"[71] This scene, included in documentary form, in other words, presented as drawn from her travel diary, shows the significance of the Dome of the Rock as the national symbol of all Palestinians as the

---

66 Muaddi, *Exile*, 101.
67 Ibid., 136.
68 Ibid., 192.
69 For readers who are knowledgeable about Israel and Judaism, the name Aliyah, which in Hebrew is the term describing immigration to Israel, might seem surprising in an Arab context, however, it is a common feminine given name, meaning "exalted" or "praised."
70 Muaddi, *Exile*, 70.
71 Ibid., 72. Emphasis in the original.

next sentence starts with *"My finger rubbed the golden cross around my neck."*[72] For the Christian Palestinian-American, being here means that she is finally not only "inside the picture," but also "the first time I felt comfortable in Palestine."[73] Once again, we encounter the national positioning of these homeland texts, where even the famous Islamic building has reduced religious meaning.

During her trip, she meets a young, local man. When their engagement fails, her American-Palestinian friends explain it as an outcome of their cultural difference. Aliyah, who felt a sense of belonging in Ramallah, does not want to accept that she is primarily American: "But I want to be *more* than that," I insisted. "That summer, I fit in. I really liked it there."[74] For this young woman, both places are part of her and she belongs to both: giving up on Palestine is not an option, even if it is challenging.

The motif of the "return journey" to a former generational site, which already emerged in the writings of Elmusa and Abulhawa, can be found in much of contemporary Palestinian writing. Such transnational memory work voyages are common today, including Jewish returns to Eastern Europe, and have attracted scholarly interest. For example, Marianne Hirsch and Nancy K. Miller's edited volume *Rites of Return: Diaspora Poetics and the Politics of Memory*[75] explores the dynamics of return journeys taking place in the wake of violence, including the Holocaust, the *Nakba*, and American slavery.

Najla Said's *Looking for Palestine: Growing up Confused in an Arab-American Family* describes her life as Edward Said's daughter, including a family trip to Israel and Palestine in 1992. Studying in a New York high school with a primarily Jewish student body, Najla writes that by the time of graduation "most of them had been to my 'homeland' (which to them was Israel), but I still had not,"[76] with the quotation marks indicating the complexities ingrained in the concept of the Palestinian homeland within contemporary political realities. The trip is complicated: already before landing, Najla expects that they will "end up in jail for trespassing on Israel."[77] Najla's impression of the land that has always been a presence in her family life is shaped by conflict and occupation: "everywhere that there was a small Arab town it seemed to be surrounded by concrete slabs of

---

[72] Ibid. Emphasis in the original
[73] Ibid.
[74] Ibid., 74.
[75] Marianne Hirsch and Nancy K. Miller, eds. *Rites of Return: Diaspora Poetics and the Politics of Memory* (New York: Columbia University Press, 2011).
[76] Najla Said, *Looking for Palestine: Growing up Confused in an Arab-American Family* (New York: Penguin, 2013), 156.
[77] Said, *Looking*, 159.

unmovable earth. These, I learned, were "settlements."[78] Moreover, "We visited the Arab towns of Bethlehem, Nablus, Nazareth. There were Israeli soldiers everywhere we went, on the side of every street, outside every tourist site."[79]

In Jerusalem, they visit the former family home in Talbiyeh, which Edward Said had described as a "two-story stone villa with lots of rooms and a handsome garden in which my two youngest cousins, my sisters, and I would play."[80] His daughter – lacking such personal memories – instead watches her father who "circled the house feverishly with my camera, shooting picture after picture of the façade."[81] Opposite this lost place, her own memory work is minimal; she listens to and later documents his memories. Unlike Muaddi's protagonist Aliyah, at the end of her trip, Najla concludes that in the current situation, neither Israel nor the Occupied Palestinian Territories are a place she can imagine herself living in, despite Palestine's significance as the family's homeland.

Lila Abu-Lughod, a Palestinian-American anthropologist, also accompanied her father, historian Ibrahim Abu-Lughod, to Jaffa from which he fled when he was nineteen. Her life writing essay "Return to Half-Ruins: Memory, Postmemory and Living History in Palestine"[82] contemplates what "return" can mean for Palestinians. Abu-Lughod starts by discussing the charged term ʿawda, return, which has been impossible despite UN Resolution 194. Abu-Lughod also introduces her father's initial return in 1991, followed by his return to live on Palestinian land in Ramallah with the help of his American passport and tourist visas. This passport also allowed repeated returns with visitors, including his daughter, to retrace the ghostly presence of Palestine under the Israeli topography as "his memories now became the guide to a living history and real place."[83] But "Half-Ruins" also contains his ultimate return, his burial in Jaffa, the closest thing to an ʿawda.

For the daughter, visiting Jaffa, "the heart of my father's Palestine" meant observing him "claiming and reclaiming the city in which he had been born, the sea in which he had swum as a boy, and the home he had been forced to flee in

---

78 Ibid., 160.
79 Ibid., 165.
80 Ibid., 21
81 Ibid., 164.
82 Lila Abu-Lughod, "Return to Half-Ruins: Memory, Postmemory, and Living History in Palestine," in *Nakba: Palestine, 1948, and the Claims of Memory*, ed. Ahmad H. Sa'di and Lila Abu-Lughod (New York: Columbia University Press, 2007). The chapter is reprinted in Hirsch and Miller's collection on return journeys, serving as the Palestinian example for the cultural phenomenon. Cf. Lila Abu-Lughod, "Return to Half-Ruins: Fathers and Daughters, Memory and History in Palestine," in *Rites of Return: Diaspora Poetics and the Politics of Memory*, ed. Marianne Hirsch and Nancy K. Miller (New York: Columbia University Press, 2011).
83 Ibid., 82.

1948."[84] Referring to Marianne Hirsch's concept of postmemory, which combines generational distance with a paradoxically close relationship to the parental past,[85] Abu-Lughod redefines the term for Palestinians: "What I, as the daughter of someone who lived through the *Nakba* learned from my father's return to Palestine, was that, for Palestinians, both memory and Postmemory have a special valence because the past has not yet passed."[86] The continuing pasts, whether in the ghostly presence of her father's erased Jaffa or in the occupation, structure her visit. The father tells the story of a city that is mostly gone, but for his daughter, seeing the evidence is difficult even when "he would point out the arched windows of old Arab houses that had somehow escaped destruction. Half-ruins he built in his imagination, while I strained to make them out amidst the ugly concrete."[87]

While Abu-Lughod literally strains to see her father's Palestine in contemporary Jaffa, other authors acknowledge the difficulty of engaging with a lost place by presenting a physical absence of land- and cityscapes. Selma Dabbagh barely depicts the landscapes, as if authors born far from historical Palestine – in time and space – are too, cut off from the land to which they are nonetheless linked. Dabbagh has visited Israel, the West Bank, and Gaza but both her short story "Me (the Bitch) and Bustanji"[88] set in the Kuwaiti-Palestinian community and her novel *Out of It*,[89] though depicting Gaza, remain obscure when it comes to place descriptions of Palestine. In her Gaza-set novel, we learn only about the same human and urban scars of the second Intifada readers might recognize from news reports. Dabbagh's city is primarily a place of human connections, family, and different ways in which Palestinians are engaged in their national struggle. She aimed to "present a state of war, a state of being, a state of pressure, of siege."[90] London, the novel's other setting and Dabbagh's hometown, however, is recognizable in its cityscape.

Similarly, British-Palestinian Mischa Hiller sets *Sabra Zoo*[91] in the Sabra refugee camp in Beirut against the backdrop of the Lebanese civil war and the 1982 massacre in the camp; Palestine only functions as a present absence and refugees' place of longing. In *Shake Off*[92] the protagonist, a London-based

---

[84] Ibid.
[85] Marianne Hirsch, *Family Frames: Photography, Narrative, and Postmemory* (Cambridge: Harvard University Press, 1997), 22.
[86] Abu-Lughod, "Return," 79.
[87] Ibid., 83.
[88] Selma Dabbagh, "Me (the Bitch) and Bustanji," in *Qissat: Short Stories by Palestinian Women*, ed. Jo Glanville (London: Saqi, 2006).
[89] Selma Dabbagh, *Out of It* (London: Bloomsbury, 2011).
[90] Green, "A Conversation with British-Palestinan Writer Selma Dabbagh."
[91] Mischa Hiller, *Sabra Zoo* (London: Telegram Books, 2010).
[92] Mischa Hiller, *Shake Off* (London: Mulholland Books, 2011).

PLO operative, is also born and raised in the camp. Unsurprisingly, Palestine's national struggle is the heart of the narrative and the center of the protagonist's identity, but no landscapes are imagined. That his handler ultimately turns out to be a Mossad double agent adds depth and complexity to the novel: Palestine and Israel are interconnected entities.

Hiller's essay "Onions and Diamonds" explicates his stance on the land today: historical Palestine is gone and the current political situation dismantles its remnants. The fact that Hiller did not personally lose his homeland also means that it is not his to return to; after all, that would make him no different from Jewish immigrants to Israel who reclaim a land that they have only a spiritual, and not personal-biographical, connection to and where other people live. The Palestinian option now is a state in the West Bank and Gaza: "We can only move forwards, not backwards. We are already re-imagining a Palestine that reflects who we are now and who we hope to become."[93] But since this state has yet to be built, Hiller and his people's identity are still that of a displaced community, but "when that [state founding] happens, I reserve the right to graduate from being dispossessed to becoming an exile."[94] Today, the Palestinian diaspora is one that results from involuntary displacement, but with a politically confirmed homeland, Hiller would live in the diaspora, or exile, as he defines it, by choice. While he does not necessarily imagine living as a self-imposed exile from a future country in which he might not want to live, he still leaves his options open and acknowledges his complex identity and legacy.

My final example, which offers another take on the Palestinian homeland, is by British-Palestinian Samir el-Youssef. Unlike the other authors and most Palestinians, el-Youssef refutes a Palestinian right of return, his novel is even entitled *The Illusion of Return*. Opening the book, the narrator, like the author originally from a refugee camp in Lebanon and now living in London, wants to demonstrate in his doctoral thesis that the refugees have left behind the dream of return because they have entered middle-class Lebanese society. He says: "we ought to be realistic and forget about an actual return;"[95] for this, other Palestinians attack him. The novel only contains memories of the refugee camp and while many are negative, Lebanon is the narrator's place of origin and roots, whereas historical Palestine is Israel. This understanding of place mirrors the opinion of the author who said in an interview: "The idea that every single person whose parents came from Palestine should have an automatic right of return is ridicu-

---

93 Hiller, "Onions," 185.
94 Ibid., 185.
95 Samir El-Youssef, *The Illusion of Return* (London: Halban, 2007), 13.

lous ... I don't believe in the right of return, ... and don't want to return, but I do want an acknowledgment from the Israelis that I don't come from nowhere."[96] El-Youssef thus engages with the refugee camp as a significant Palestinian space, but also offers a take on the homeland that shows the range of stances across the exilic generations.

4 Conclusion

Historian Simon Schama contends that, "landscape is the work of the mind. Its scenery is built up as much from strata of memory as from layers of rock,"[97] highlighting that neither landscapes nor memory exist as a stable reality; they are always created and recreated. In the context of Palestinian memory and imagination of the homeland, this means that we encounter many "Palestines," which sometimes have little to do with the contemporary landscape. Migration scholarship has started exploring how migrants are "simultaneously embedded in the multiple sites and layers of the transnational social fields in which they live."[98] In the Palestinian case of forced displacement and ongoing conflict, such multiplicity stays virulent: the status of the lost home is still embattled. Thus, the portrayals between experience, memory, and the imagination, by authors who are far removed in time and space from historical Palestine and often also from today's Israel and Palestinian Territories, add another layer to the landscape long imagined by believers of Abrahamic faiths and today given intense media attention.

My corpus shows a generational development from a Palestine remembered to one imagined, from a place that connotes "home" to a lost place, defined by transgenerationally transmitted narratives and knowledge of loaded sites such as Jerusalem or the refugee camps. In "Memory, Invention, and Place," Edward Said shows how Zionism has realized a narrative of return, whereas by 2000, when he was writing, Palestinians, while observing this Jewish return, had yet to publicly uphold a narrative in which they belong to this land.[99] The proliferation of literary voices telling a story of the Palestinian homeland attests to a "powerful re-emergence of Palestine as a cultural force" and a collective effort to establish

---

[96] Mathew J. Reisz, "Samir el-Youssef: At Home with the Heretic," *The Independent*, January 18, 2007 http://www.independent.co.uk/arts-entertainment/books/features/samir-el-youssef-at-home-with-the-heretic-432650.html.
[97] Simon Schama, *Landscape and Memory* (New York: HarperCollins, 1995), 6–7.
[98] Peggy Levitt and B. Nadya Jaworsky, "Transnational Migration Studies: Past Developments and Future Trends," *The Annual Review of Sociology* 33 (2007): 130.
[99] Edward Said, "Invention, Memory, and Place," *Critical Inquiry* 26, no. 2 (2000): 184.

this narrative.[100] But more than that, the Palestinian homeland, even if often spiritual and barely a physical location, is also an open wound and central to the national identity that spans the fragmented community.

Both Jews and Palestinians have experienced exile, and the loss of the people-land bond is central to their collective identities and cultural memories.[101] As indicated in the introduction, Sidra Ezrahi has pointed to the importance of literature in upholding the meaning of Zion for Jews in the diaspora for thousands of years. The recent wave of publications in which Palestine features so prominently shows that diaspora Palestinians will not give up on their homeland. Instead, within the unresolved conflict, memories become a claim to existence in place: "*al-Quds al-Sharif*, noble Jerusalem, is not to me merely a mythical location, a historical metaphor, but a real place, where my father was born and grew up, where my brother Edward and I were born."[102]

The next generations might not have these personal memories, and yet Palestine, no matter how diffuse as an actual space, is still a generational site, even if lost; it calls on connection, structures identities, and provides the material for writing. Or, in the words of Palestinian-Canadian Danah Abdulla: "After all, I was told that if I let go of Palestine it would no longer exist."[103] Indeed, the absence of Palestine as a landscape in the next generation's texts, or as a livable place in cases such as Najla Said, speaks loudly, as it brings this homeland to a Western audience. Additionally, the notion of the "homeland," so prominent in Palestinian diaspora texts, evokes a universal human experience the meaning of which is understandable to us all, or to use the words of philosopher Simone Weil: "to be rooted is perhaps the most important and least recognized need of the soul."[104] Here, the political charge of this corpus once again becomes prominent: the texts can speak to readers, not only because they engage with the "Holy Land," but also with eternal question of home, belonging, and rootedness.

---

100 Samar H. Al-Jahdali, "Venturing into a Vanishing Space: The Chronotope in Representing Palestinian Postcoloniality," *Journal of Postcolonial Writing* 50, no. 5 (2014): 226.
101 Cf. Carol Bardenstein, "Trees, Forests, and the Shaping of Palestinian and Israeli Collective Memory," in *Acts of Memory: Cultural Recall in the Present*, ed. Mieke Bal, Jonathan Crewe, and Leo Spitzer (Hanover: University Press of New England, 1999).
102 Makdisi, "Palestinian," 162.
103 Danah Abdulla, "Only Icons," in *Being Palestinian: Personal Reflections on Palestinian Identity in the Diaspora*, ed. Yasir Suleiman (Edinburgh: Edinburgh University Press, 2016), 23.
104 Simone Weil, *The Need for Roots: Prelude to a Declaration of a Duty Towards Mankind* (London: ARK, 1987 [1949]), 41.

Bibliography

Abdulla, Danah. "Only Icons." In *Being Palestinian: Personal Reflections on Palestinian Identity in the Diaspora*. Edited by Yasir Suleiman, 22–24. Edinburgh: Edinburgh University Press, 2016.

Abulhawa, Susan. *Mornings in Jenin*. New York: Bloomsbury, 2010.

Abu-Lughod, Lila. "Return to Half-Ruins: Memory, Postmemory, and Living History in Palestine." In *Nakba: Palestine, 1948, and the Claims of Memory*. Edited by Ahmad H. Sa'di and Lila Abu-Lughod, 77–104. New York: Columbia University Press, 2007.

Abu-Lughod, Lila. "Return to Half-Ruins: Fathers and Daughters, Memory and History in Palestine." In *Rites of Return: Diaspora Poetics and the Politics of Memory*. Edited by Marianne Hirsch and Nancy K. Miller, 124–135. New York: Columbia University Press, 2011.

Abu Sitta, Salman. *Mapping My Return: A Palestinian Memoir*. Cairo: The American University in Cairo Press, 2016.

Ali, Zarefa. *A Narration without an End: Palestine and the Continuing Nakba*. Birzeit: Birzeit University Press, 2013.

Al-Jahdali, Samar H. "Venturing into a Vanishing Space: The Chronotope in Representing Palestinian Postcoloniality." *Journal of Postcolonial Writing* 50, no. 5 (2014): 216–229.

Allan, Diana. *Refugees of the Revolution: Experiences in Palestinian Exile*. Stanford: Stanford University Press, 2014.

Bardenstein, Carol. "Trees, Forests, and the Shaping of Palestinian and Israeli Collective Memory." In *Acts of Memory: Cultural Recall in the Present*. Edited by Mieke Bal, Jonathan Crewe, and Leo Spitzer, 148–168. Hanover: University Press of New England, 1999.

Benvenisti, Meron. *Sacred Landscape: The Buried History of the Holy Land since 1948*. Translated by Maxine Kaufman-Lacusta. Berkeley: University of California Press, 2000.

Dabbagh, Selma. "Me (the Bitch) and Bustanji." In *Qissat: Short Stories by Palestinian Women*. Edited by Jo Glanville, 61–77. London: Saqi, 2006.

Dabbagh, Selma. *Out of It*. London: Bloomsbury, 2011.

Davis, Rochelle A. *Palestinian Village Histories: Geographies of the Displaced*. Stanford: Stanford University Press, 2010.

DeKoven Ezrahi, Sidra. "'To What Shall I Compare You?': Jerusalem as Ground Zero of the Hebrew Imagination." *PMLA* 122, no. 1 (2007): 220–234.

Doumani, Beshara. "A Song from Haifa." In *Seeking Palestine: New Palestinian Writing on Exile and Home*. Edited by Penny Johnson and Raja Shehadeh, 17–21. Northampton, MA: Olive Branch Press, 2013.

El-Youssef, Samir. *The Illusion of Return*. London: Halban, 2007.

Elmusa, Sharif S. "Portable Absence: My Camp Re-membered." In *Seeking Palestine: New Palestinian Writing on Exile and Home*. Edited by Penny Johnson and Raja Shehadeh, 22–41. Northampton, MA: Olive Branch Press, 2013.

Erni, Fiorella Larissa. *Tired of Being a Refugee: Social Identification among Young Palestinian Refugees in Lebanon*. Geneva: Graduate Institute Publications, 2014.

Fischer, Nina. *Memory Work: The Second Generation*. Houndsmills: Palgrave Macmillan, 2015.

Fischer, Nina. "Seeing and Unseeing the Dome of the Rock: Conflict, Memory, and Belonging in Jerusalem." In *Spatialising Peace and Conflict: Mapping the Production of Place, Sites*

and Scales of Violence. Edited by Annika Björkdahl and Susanne Buckley-Zistel, 242–264. Houndsmills: Palgrave Macmillan, 2016.
Glanville, Jo, ed. *Qissat: Short Stories by Palestinian Women*. London: Saqi, 2006.
Green, David B. "A Conversation with British-Palestinan Writer Selma Dabbagh." *Haaretz*, October 1, 2012. http://www.haaretz.com/jewish/books/a-conversation-with-british-palestinian-writer-selma-dabbagh-1.467660. Accessed June 6, 2016.
Halbwachs, Maurice. *On Collective Memory*. Translated by Lewis A. Coeser. Chicago: University of Chicago Press, 1992.
Hartmann, Andreas. "Geschmack in der Kulturwissenschaft." In *Gedächtnis und Erinnerung: Ein interdisziplinäres Lexikon*. Edited by Nicolas Pethes and Jens Ruchatz, 231–232. Hamburg: Rowohlt, 2001.
Hiller, Mischa. "Onions and Diamonds." In *Seeking Palestine: New Palestinian Writing on Exile and Home*. Edited by Penny Johnson and Raja Shehadeh, 178–186. Northampton, MA: Olive Branch Press, 2013.
Hiller, Mischa. *Sabra Zoo*. London: Telegram Books, 2010.
Hiller, Mischa. *Shake Off*. London: Mulholland Books, 2011.
Hirsch, Marianne. *Family Frames: Photography, Narrative, and Postmemory*. Cambridge, MA: Harvard University Press, 1997.
Hirsch, Marianne and Nancy K. Miller, eds. *Rites of Return: Diaspora Poetics and the Politics of Memory*. New York: Columbia University Press, 2011.
Jacobs, Keith. *Experience and Representation: Contemporary Perspectives on Migration in Australia*. Farnham and Burlington: Ashgate, 2011.
Jarrar, Randa. *A Map of Home*. New York: Penguin, 2008.
Jayyusi, Lena. "Iterability, Cumulativity and Presence: The Relational Figures of Palestinian Memory." In *Nakba: Palestine, 1948, and the Claims of Memory*. Edited by Ahmad H. Sa'di and Lila Abu-Lughod, 107–133. New York: Columbia University Press, 2007.
Johnson, Penny. "Introduction: Neither Homeland nor Exile are Words." In *Seeking Palestine: New Palestinian Writing on Exile and Home*. Edited by Penny Johnson and Raja Shehadeh, IX–XVI. Northampton, MA: Olive Branch Press, 2013.
Johnson, Penny and Raja Shehadeh, eds. *Seeking Palestine: New Palestinian Writing on Exile and Home*. Northampton, MA: Olive Branch Press, 2013.
Karmi, Ghada. *In Search of Fatima: A Palestinian Story*. London: Verso, 2002.
Karmi, Ghada. *Return: A Palestinian Memoir*. London: Verso, 2015.
Khalidi, Ismail and Naomi Wallace, eds. *Inside/Outside: Six Plays from Palestine and the Diaspora*. New York: Theatre Communications Group, 2015.
Khalidi, Rashid. *Palestinian Identity: The Construction of Modern National Consciousness*. New York: Columbia University Press, 1997.
Khalili, Laleh. *Heroes and Martyrs of Palestine*. Cambridge: Cambridge University Press, 2006.
Levitt, Peggy and B. Nadya Jaworsky. "Transnational Migration Studies: Past Developments and Future Trends." *The Annual Review of Sociology* 33 (2007): 129–156.
Mason, Victoria. "Children of the 'Idea of Palestine': Negotiating Identity, Belonging and Home in the Palestinian Diaspora." *Journal of Intercultural Studies* 28, no. 3 (2007): 271–285.
Matar, Dina. *What It Means to be Palestinian: Stories of Palestinian Peoplehood*. London: I.B. Tauris, 2010.
Muaddi Darraj, Susan. *The Inheritance of Exile: Stories from South Philly*. Notre Dame: University of Notre Dame Press, 2007.

Neslen, Arthur. *In Your Eyes a Sandstorm: Ways of Being Palestinian*. Berkeley: University of California Press, 2011.

Nora, Pierre. "Between Memory and History: Les Lieux de Mémoire." *Representations* 26 (1989): 7–25.

Peteet, Julie. *Landscape of Hope and Despair: Palestinian Refugee Camps*. Pittsburgh: University of Pennsylvania Press, 2005.

Read, Peter. *Returning to Nothing: The Meaning of Lost Places*. Cambridge: Cambridge University Press, 1996.

Reisz, Mathew J. "Samir el-Youssef: At Home with the Heretic." *The Independent*, January 18, 2007. http://www.independent.co.uk/arts-entertainment/books/features/samir-el-youssef-at-home-with-the-heretic-432650.html. Accessed June 5, 2015.

Sa'di, Ahmad H. and Lila Abu-Lughod, eds. *Nakba: Palestine, 1948, and the Claims of Memory*. New York: Columbia University Press, 2007.

Said, Edward. "Invention, Memory, and Place." *Critical Inquiry* 26, no. 2 (2000): 175–192.

Said, Edward. *Out of Place*. New York: Knopf, 1999.

Said, Edward. "Reflections on Exile." In *Altogether Elsewhere: Writers on Exile*. Edited by Marc Robinson, 137–149. Boston: Faber & Faber, 1994.

Said, Edward. *The Question of Palestine*. New York: Times Books, 1979.

Said, Najla. *Looking for Palestine: Growing up Confused in an Arab-American Family*. New York: Penguin, 2013.

Said Makdisi, Jean. "Becoming Palestinian." In *Seeking Palestine: New Palestinian Writing on Exile and Home*, edited by Penny Johnson and Raja Shehadeh, 160–177. Northampton, MA: Olive Branch Press, 2013.

Said Makdisi, Jean. *Teta, Mother, and Me: Three Generations of Arab Women*. New York, London: W.W. Norton & Co. 2005.

Sayigh, Rosemary. "Palestinian Refugee Identity/ies: Generation, Region, Class." In *Palestinian Refugees: Different Generations, but One Identity*. Edited by Ibrahim Abu-Lughod Institute for International Studies, 13–28. Birzeit: Birzeit University Press, 2012.

Schama, Simon. *Landscape and Memory*. New York: HarperCollins, 1995.

Shapira, Anita. *Land and Power: The Zionist Resort to Force, 1881–1948*. Oxford: Oxford University Press, 1992.

Sharabi, Hisham. *Embers and Ashes: Memoirs of an Arab Intellectual*. Translated by Issa J. Boullata. Northampton, MA: Olive Branch Press, 2008.

Snajie, Olivia. "The Many Lives and Languages of a Palestinian Novel." *Publishing Perspectives*, March 21, 2012. http://publishingperspectives.com/2012/03/the-many-lives-and-languages-of-a-palestinian-novel/. Accessed September 13, 2015.

Suleiman, Yasir, ed. *Being Palestinian: Personal Reflections on Palestinian Identity in the Diaspora*. Edinburgh: Edinburgh University Press, 2016.

Uris, Leon. *Exodus*. New York: Bantam, 1958.

Weil, Simone. *The Need for Roots: Prelude to a Declaration of a Duty towards Mankind*. London: ARK, 1987 [1949].

Wieviorka, Annette. *The Era of the Witness*. Translated by Jared Stark. Ithaca, London: Cornell University Press, 2006.

Yuval-Davis, Nira. "Belonging and the Politics of Belonging." *Patterns of Prejudice* 40, no. 3 (2006): 197–214.

Zaidan, Ismat. *Palestinian Diaspora in Transnational Worlds: Intergenerational Differences in Negotiating Identity, Belonging and Home*. Birzeit: Birzeit University Press, 2012.

Part 2: **Writing the Homeland**

Regina Range
Worlds, Words, and Womanhood: Gina Kaus and the Formation of a Spiritual Homeland

The life and work of the Austrian-Jewish novelist, playwright, essayist, and scriptwriter Gina Kaus, who fled her home country to escape the Nazis, touches, inter alia, on the themes of homeland and exile. Born Regina Wiener, Kaus was a successful novelist and dramatist during the 1920s and 1930s. She moved in the literary and intellectual circles that would frequent the coffeehouses of Vienna and Berlin, and regularly interacted with famous and well-known litterateurs, artists, and psychologists, such as Franz Blei, Robert Musil, Milena Jesenská, Alma and Franz Werfel, Alfred Adler, Carl Sternheim, and Hermann Broch. Although well known in these circles and noted for her plays and novels, as a woman, Kaus struggled to have her work taken seriously like that of her male contemporaries.

Kaus's later transnational film work in Germany and Austria in the mid and late 1950s exemplifies how her texts – spanning more than a half century, and which include a variety of genres and a change in medium – present more than just a cultural critique, dissent, or protest of the current political and social situation. They are a call for agency, and show Kaus's belief in the possibility of change and betterment. A focus on Kaus, the exile, and her work, not only aids in broadening our perspective on the context of exile, *Wahlheimat*, and spiritual homelands, but also contributes to the growing body of research on the generally less visible female émigrées.

This chapter explores the significance of marginalization for Kaus's life and work, which was manifested on several levels: first, as a Jew living in Austria and Germany in the early twentieth century. Kaus's coming of age during the Habsburg monarchy, its dissolution, and the subsequent creation of successor states – an atmosphere that became increasingly and openly antisemitic and resulted in the annexation of Austria in 1938 – is pertinent to the analysis of her literary as well as film oeuvre. Second, the present chapter investigates Kaus as a female writer in the Viennese and Berlin literary circles, where she had to fight for recognition. Unable to achieve recognition among the male-dominated literati circles, she was labeled and marketed as an "*Unterhaltungsautorin*" (popular fiction author) and thus relegated to the ranks of writers of women's literature.[1] Third, as an émigrée

---

[1] The translation of the term *Unterhaltungsautorin* is not without complication. Whereas "*Unterhaltung*" means "entertainment" and could also be translated using the word "popular,"

in Hollywood, where she began her work as a scriptwriter. In a culture focusing almost exclusively on film directors and stars, scriptwriters would often remain invisible, and Kaus, as an émigré female writer, was no exception.

Denied financial and social stability by her repeated marginalization, Kaus utilized writing as a refuge that enabled the creation of a spiritual home independent from any physical home. Kaus's outlook on the concept of *Heimat*, and her perception of the United States, more specifically Hollywood, as a *Wahlheimat*, illustrates how the act of writing provided her with the opportunity to create a spiritual homeland through authorship, a process that began already prior to her exile in France and the United States.

1 Kaus in Interwar Vienna and Berlin

Gina Kaus's experience and aspirations as a female Jewish writer in the interwar period of Austria and Germany are paramount to understanding her sentiments about the concept of *Heimat*. Examining the historical contexts within which Kaus – who neither explicitly self-identified as Jewish nor addressed "Jewish topics" – wrote and published, provides a more thorough grasp of the topics central to her work.[2] Though one might encounter an absence of Jewishness in her writing, the presence and persistence of the muted boundaries and limitations she encountered as a Jew in interwar Austria, remain evident.

Marsha Rozenblit provides a key insight into understanding Kaus's perception of nationality and belonging. She argues that Habsburg Austria proved most receptive to Jewish ethnic identity. It was in particular the multinational, supranational character of the state that provided a relatively congenial atmosphere for the Jews, therefore "allowing them to retain their ethnic attachments even as they adopted the culture of one or another nation."[3] The supranational state, according to Rozenblit, "permitted the Jews to develop a tripartite identity that suited them very well. They could adopt German (or Czech or Polish) culture without having to join the German, Czech, or Polish nation."[4] This tripartite identity distinguished Habsburg Jewry from the Jews of ethnically monolithic countries such as Germany

---

we cannot help but notice a value judgment. This becomes even more apparent when attempting to use the terms "highbrow and lowbrow" literature or culture.
2 Even though Kaus lived in Vienna, she would often travel to Berlin during the 1920s and 1930s, and move in the literary and intellectual circles that would frequent the coffeehouses in both cities.
3 Marsha L. Rozenblit, *Reconstructing a National Identity: The Jews of Habsburg Austria during World War I* (New York: Oxford University Press, 2001), 9.
4 Ibid., 9.

and France. Furthermore, it played an important role in the identity of Viennese Jews, male and female, and influenced their political, cultural, and other activities.[5] Moreover, their "political loyalty to the Habsburg dynasty, their German ... cultural identity, and their Jewish ethnic identity allowed them a certain latitude in making choices to be as Jewish as they chose."[6] For Kaus and a number of other Jews, Habsburg Austria, or more specifically Habsburg Vienna, was a sufficiently cosmopolitan environment in which they did not have to assert their Jewishness.

The dissolution of the monarchy and creation of successor states eradicated the foundations of the comfortable tripartite Jewish identity. Nonetheless, Jews responded to the crisis by hoping to preserve as much of the old multilateral identity as possible, even if it was no longer politically realistic to do so.[7] Even though such an identity would have been more suited to a multinational or multiethnic society than to the nation-state of the First Austrian Republic, as Rozenblit points out, the "Austrian Jews clung to it because it best conformed to their deeply held convictions."[8]

Even more insightful in regard to Kaus's ongoing concern with overcoming boundaries and limitations in terms of gender, is Alison Rose's extension of Rozenblit's three-way idea to a quadripartite identity for Austrian Jewish women, as, "the images of them, and their cultural contributions were shaped by the various cultural, ethnic, political, and gender loyalties and pulls."[9] As the discussion of Kaus's autobiographical narrative in the context of nationality will show, the experience and self-understanding of the female émigrée also appears to conform to a similar model, namely one that allows more latitude and self-determination in terms of identity and belonging.

During the Austrian interwar period, female writers benefited but were also limited by the increasing numbers of Jewish men who were in charge of newspapers and publishing houses.[10] On the one hand, fellow Jewish publishers and filmmakers (regardless of their degree of Jewish self-identification) would often support Jewish women, on the other they would also circumscribe the content and scope of their work.[11] Kaus is no real exception in this regard. Originally married to the musician Josef Zirner who died in 1915 during World War I, Kaus

---

5 Alison Rose, *Jewish Women in Fin de Siècle Vienna* (Austin: University of Texas Press, 2008), 220.
6 Ibid., 220.
7 Rozenblit, *Reconstructing a National Identity*, 10.
8 Ibid., 160.
9 Rose, *Jewish Women*, 220.
10 Lisa Silverman, *Becoming Austrians: Jews and Culture between the World Wars* (Oxford: Oxford University Press, 2012), 88.
11 Ibid., 93.

was "adopted" at age twenty-three by the fifty-eight-year-old Joseph Kranz.[12] It was through this industrialist and well-known figure in Viennese circles that Kaus's financial situation improved. Kranz's patronage allowed her to concentrate on her career as a writer. During her relationship with Kranz, Kaus wrote her first play, *Diebe im Haus* (Thieves in the House), which was staged by the Vienna Burgtheater in 1919.[13] Additionally, Kaus founded the magazine *Die Mutter* (The Mother) in 1924.[14] This magazine's objective was to educate mothers on pregnancy, hygiene, family planning, and parenting. She regularly interviewed doctors, lawyers, social workers, and psychologists and then edited the information to make it more accessible for her readership. Kaus's concern and engagement went far beyond that of writing and editing the magazine; she also volunteered at counseling centers to provide practical help and advice to mothers.

Faced with financial pressure after a separation from her patron Kranz in 1920, and a failed marriage with Otto Kaus that ended in 1926, Gina Kaus attempted to sell the rights of *Die Mutter* to the Jewish-owned publisher Ullstein, located in Berlin. The publisher, however, did not buy *Die Mutter* but instead offered Kaus advance money to write a novel for them. This novel would become her first. *Die Verliebten* (The Lovers) was published in 1928, and provides an excellent example of marketing strategies and the limitations of female writers at the time.[15] Kaus wrote the novel slating it for publication with Propyläen Verlag, Ullstein's subsidiary, which targeted a more sophisticated readership accustomed to works by eminent writers such as Bertolt Brecht, Lion Feuchtwanger, and Heinrich Mann.[16] Instead of being placed among these authors, the novel appeared in the "light entertainment" section and was marketed as a fiction genre novel among the *Frauenromane* (women's novels).[17] This placement and categorization of Kaus's first novel consequently denied her a place among the writers who were considered highly refined, and rendered her invisible to an entire readership segment.

Despite her initial disappointment with Ullstein's treatment of *Die Verliebten*, Kaus began to consciously work with the limited possibilities presented to her. Rather than rebelling against the marketing strategies, she embraced the

---

[12] The adoption helped to cover up the fact that Kranz was Kaus's lover and enabled them to live together.
[13] Gina Kaus, *Diebe im Haus: Komödie in 3 Akten* (Berlin: Arcadia Verlag, 1929).
[14] Gina Kaus, *Die Mutter – Halbmonatsschrift für alle Fragen der Schwangerschaft, Säuglingshygiene und Kindererziehung* (Vienna: Offizielles Organ des Bundes für Mutterschutz, 1924–1926).
[15] Gina Kaus, *Die Verliebten* (Berlin: Verlag Ullstein, 1928).
[16] Gina Kaus, *Von Wien nach Hollywood. Erinnerungen* (Frankfurt am Main: Suhrkamp, 1990), 145.
[17] Luisa Afonso Soares, "Vicky Baum and Gina Kaus: Female Creativity on the Margins," in *Practicing Modernity: Female Creativity in the Weimar Republic*, ed. by Christiane Schönfeld and Carmel Finnan (Würzburg: Königshausen, 2006), 334.

situation. This is clearly reflected in her second novel *Die Überfahrt* (*Luxury Liner*), which became a bestseller and was purchased by Paramount and made into a film directed by Lothar Mendes in 1933, a year after its publication.[18] Kaus's novel *Die Überfahrt*, a *Zeitroman* (novel of the times), is exemplary in its exposition of the limitations, pluralism, and polarity her readership experienced daily. The novel presents a fictionalized version of 1920s Weimar society. Like a seismograph, it records a short historical moment, around October 1924, before the economic crash of 1929. The readership of *Die Überfahrt* is presented with a variety of passengers from varying social backgrounds who all wish to immigrate to America and begin a new life. Kaus's writing style, which is representative of New Objectivism, her choice of time, and the setting for her novel, were all in sync with and tapped into the quintessential narrative genre of the period. She manages to offer a non-moralist perspective on the limitations of prevailing class and gender hierarchies. *Die Überfahrt* was followed by her novel *Morgen um Neun* (*Tomorrow We Part*) in 1932.[19] Here Kaus deconstructs the image of the New Woman, and shows the harsh divide between social classes, while also revealing the limitations and challenges of marriage in connection with gender stereotypes. *Die Schwestern Kleh* (*Dark Angel*) appeared less than a year after, in 1933.[20]

Die Schwestern Kleh, much like *Die Verliebten*, deals with societal expectations of gender roles that both women and men faced.[21] More importantly, Kaus's choice of topics, such as the struggles of single motherhood, abortion, miscarriage, adoption, and the harsh limitations imposed on women with career aspirations, illustrate the fictionalization of topics gleaned from the psychologist Alfred Adler. An ardent feminist, Kaus was an avid follower of Adler, and discussed his work in her journal *Die Mutter*.

In 1935, Kaus published *Katharina die Große* (*Catherine the Great*).[22] This biography focuses on the Russian Empress's early life. Kaus emphasizes the parents' disappointment about Katharina being a girl rather than a boy. She contextualizes the empress's upbringing, socially, culturally, and historically. Kaus

---

18 Gina Kaus, *Die Überfahrt* (Munich: Knorr, 1932).
19 Gina Kaus, *Morgen um Neun* (Berlin: Ullstein, 1932).
20 Arnold Pressburger used Kaus's novel and produced *Conflit* in Paris. He wanted to remake the film in the United States, but could not secure the approval of the industry censors, as the story contained elements that were considered unacceptable for US audiences at the time. Pressburger gave the American rights to the film to his brother-in-law, Heinz Brasch, who hired Edgar G. Ulmer to direct Anne Green's screenplay, which was credited as an adaptation of *Dark Angel*. The new film, *Her Sister's Secret*, was released in 1946. A brief discussion of *Her Sister's Secret* can also be found in Isenberg's *Edgar G. Ulmer*, 160–64.
21 Gina Kaus, *Die Schwestern Kleh* (Amsterdam: de Lange, 1933).
22 Gina Kaus, *Katharina Die Große: Biographie* (Frankfurt am Main: Ullstein, 1991), 15.

therefore offers potential explanations for why Katherina was perceived and extensively criticized as power hungry, articulating the inadequacy of stereotypical approaches and understanding of gender roles. The biography also shares similarities with Kaus's play *Toni: Eine Schulmädchen-Komödie in zehn Bildern* (*Toni: A Schoolgirl Comedy in Ten Pictures*), published in 1927. In the latter, the audience follows the titular precocious teenage protagonist as she develops into a "New Woman."[23] The play revolves around Toni's coming of age during the Weimar period, providing a female perspective to the emerging tension and anxiety that both women and men encountered at the time.[24] In it, Kaus plays with the audience's inhibitions and violates social conventions, creating a compelling reflection on the promises and failures of social change during the Weimar Republic. Through the character of Toni, the playwright points to the limited social mobility of young women during the 1920s and illustrates just how little equality women had actually gained. Kaus extends this criticism further in *Katharina die Große* and also returns to the perceived problem of female ambition. Kaus portrays the empress "as a strong-willed, untamable woman who is willing to go to any length to overcome what was regarded as a femininity stigma."[25] The stigma of wanting "to be a man, as good as a man and better than a man."[26]

Characters are never judged or condemned in Kaus's works. Instead, they aid in the representation of a variety of ideas and models of "femininity," which all coexisted in the 1920s and early 1930s in Austria and Germany. This simultaneity of wide-ranging ideas and concepts also applies to the coexistence of highly diverse discourses regarding gender roles. Kaus's presentation of these notions complies with the vision of a pluralist culture, which was also shared by the fathers of the Weimar constitution and – as previously indicated – the Habsburg monarchy.[27] Although Kaus was initially upset about her experiences with Ullstein, she also saw the situation as an opportunity, not hesitating to make use of the mass market which she now had access to, since the fictionalization and novelization of these topics could reach a much larger readership than she had been accustomed to.

As becomes apparent, Kaus as a Jewish female writer was caught in the web of marketing strategies and genre expectations on the one hand and the liberal-leftist tendency and desire for changing the status quo on the other. The development of a fast-growing mass cultural market also brought about new possibilities, but

---

23 Gina Kaus, *Toni: Eine Schulmädchen-Komödie in zehn Bildern* (Berlin: Propyläen-Verlag, 1927).
24 Range, "Positioning Gina Kaus," 12.
25 Soares, "Vicki Baum," 337.
26 Gina Kaus, *Von Wien*, 15.
27 Range, "Positioning Gina Kaus," 20.

to participate, Kaus had to work within the liminal spaces to even try to influence it one way or the other. She adapted, found her niche, and crossed over into a different genre, and once in exile, into a different medium, rather than completely shying away from such a switch, or considering herself too refined for it. The need to survive and support her family, as will become apparent, played no unimportant role in this decision. Through her experience with Ullstein, Kaus learned to navigate the literary market, just as she learned to operate within the Hollywood production code later in her work for the Hollywood studios. She was able to use her talent for creating dialogue and narrative frames that spoke to thousands of people, while also developing them in a way that challenged those of her readers who were willing to take part in such a reading. She readily participated in a sector that would receive little serious attention and whose subversive potential was mostly ignored by those who favored a more bourgeois understanding of literature.

2 Exile Experience and Perception

The National Socialist agenda to cleanse German culture of Jewish and foreign influences, including pacifist and so-called "decadent" literature, placed Kaus's career and family at risk. In the years building up to and following the *Anschluss* of 1938, Austria became increasingly and openly antisemitic. It was in this atmosphere, that "Austrians found themselves defined as Jewish not according to invisible categories, but by Nazi racial policies."[28] As Rozenblit points out, "The anti-Semites regarded the Jews as dangerous foreigners, or worse, as racial enemies, who sought the destruction of the nation, defined by blood."[29] Kaus experienced this persecution first-hand when the National Socialists burned her books, an act that helped expunge her from the memory of the German-speaking public.

Along with her family – her two sons Otto and Peter and partner Erich Frischauer – Kaus fled Vienna in March 1938 on the very day of Austria's annexation.[30] First, they fled to Switzerland, then to France, and finally to the United States in 1939. It was during her exile in France that Kaus had her first experiences with the film industry. It was Kaus's agent George Marton, who introduced her to Austrian-Jewish film producer Arnold Pressburger, who also resided in Paris at the time.[31]

---

28 Silverman, *Becoming Austrians*, 173.
29 Rozenblit, *Reconstructing a National Identity*, 21.
30 Frischauer used to work as lawyer prior to his exile and later became a contract-bridge player and Hollywood real-estate broker.
31 Arnold Pressburger would later produce *Hangmen Also Die* with Fritz Lang as the director.

Pressburger bought Kaus's 1937 play *Gefängnis ohne Gitter*.[32] This became the highly successful *Prison sans barreaux*.[33] Along with the brothers Eis, Kaus also helped develop the story.[34] Kaus offered Pressburger her 1933 novel *Die Schwestern Kleh*, which became the film *Conflit*.[35] Pressburger appreciated Kaus's work and would later hire her to write "the big scenes."[36] Her cooperation on these films laid the foundation for her future work in Hollywood and established a relationship with Pressburger that later proved crucial for her flight from Paris to the United States.[37]

The American adaptation of *Conflit*, *Her Sister's Secret* (1946), was directed by Edgar G. Ulmer. In addition to her film work, Kaus also wrote a new novel during this time, *Der Teufel nebenan* (The Devil Next Door), for her publisher in the Netherlands, but it was not published until 1940.[38] Like *Die Überfahrt*, *Der Teufel nebenan* was also turned into a film titled *Teufel in Seide* (*Devil in Silk*) by director Rolf Hansen in 1956.[39]

In August 1939, Kaus and her children received visas for the United States and found themselves on the *Ile de France*, the last ship to leave Europe before war was declared. Kaus spent her first two months in the United States in New York City. While staying in a hotel, she wrote serialized articles for the magazine *True Story* to finance her trip to Hollywood.[40] Kaus finally arrived in Los Angeles in November 1939 and quickly acclimated herself to Southern California. With help from her friend and agent George Marton, Kaus immediately started collaborating

---

32 Gina Kaus, *Gefängnis ohne Gitter, Stück in 8 Bildern* (Vienna: Georg Marton, 1936).
33 Gina Kaus helped the brothers with the story development for *Prison sans Barreaux*, which was directed by Pressburger and adapted by Léonide Moguy. The movie, which featured Annie Ducaux, Roger Duchesne, Ginette Leclerc, Corinne Luchaire, and Marthe Mellot, premiered in France in 1938.
34 The brothers Otto and Egon Eis were both Austrian-born Jewish scriptwriters.
35 *Conflit* was based on Gina Kaus's novel. The script was written Charles Gombault, Léonide Moguy, and Hans Wilhelm. Kaus, as discussed, was not officially credited. Léonide Moguy directed the film, which starred Corinne Luchaire, Annie Ducaux, Raymond Rouleau, Roger Duchesne, Pauline Carton, and Jacques Copeau, and premiered in France in 1938.
36 Kaus, *Von Wien*, 180.
37 Cf. Capovilla, *Entwürfe*, 221.
38 Gina Kaus, *Der Teufel nebenan* (Amsterdam: de Lange, 1939).
39 *Teufel in Seide* was directed by Rolf Hansen, starring Winnie Markus, Curd Jürgens, and Lilli Palmer and premiered in Germany in 1955.
40 Kaus, *Von Wien*, 197.

on a screenplay with Ladislaus Fodor,[41] which was then sold to MGM. This was the beginning of Gina Kaus's career as a Hollywood script and storywriter.[42]

After leaving Austria in 1938, Gina Kaus never returned to live in Europe. Apart from smaller trips and conferences, she remained in the United States. She deliberately chose America as a *Wahlheimat*, an elected home. When she reflects in her autobiography about her visit and offers to participate in more transitional film projects after the war, she recounts: "I could have easily gotten a new contract, I was a highly-paid writer, but I simply had enough. I had no friends, neither in Munich nor in Berlin. The emigrants had dispersed into different cities, or had returned disappointedly to America."[43] Kaus no longer considered returning to Vienna or Berlin for good, but instead was looking forward to going home to her *Heimat*, her *Wahlheimat* America. She reemphasized her statement by writing: "Yes indeed – home ... I feel how right that is. I was very indebted to America, of course, that it took me in when my Fatherland abandoned me."

Kaus's autobiography offers a rather uncommon outlook on ideas of *Heimat*, *Wahlheimat*, nationality, and her feelings of belonging and identity as an exile writer. It further offers an alternative perspective on exile, one that constructs a counter-narrative to the widespread depiction of exile as a paralyzing, sad, or lonely experience. Moreover, Kaus's portrayal differs tremendously from many of her well-known, often male, fellow emigrés.[44] In her memoir, Kaus fashions exile as an opportunity and suggests that she tried to make the best out of the situation she was confronted with.[45] At first sight, her account of her experiences in France and the United States bears no resemblance to what Renato Camurri describes as the twentieth-century meaning of exile: an "experience of fracture,

---

41 Ladislas Fodor (1898–1978) was a Hungarian novelist, playwright, and screenwriter.
42 She further collaborated on scripts for such Hollywood productions as *The Red Danube* (directed by George Sidney, 1949), *Three Secrets* (directed by Robert Wise, 1950), *All I Desire* (directed by Douglas Sirk, 1953), and *The Wife Takes a Flyer* (directed by Richard Wallace, 1942). Kaus also developed stories and worked on adaptations or additional dialogue for other films, including *They All Kissed the Bride* (directed by Alexander Hall, 1942), *Blazing Guns* (directed by Robert Emmett Tansey, 1943), *Whispering City* (directed by Fyodor Otsep, 1947), *Julia Misbehaves* (directed by Jack Conway, 1948), *We're Not Married* (directed by Edmund Goulding, 1952), and *The Robe* (directed by Henry Koster, 1952). Kaus's film contributions were not limited to her work in Hollywood; she also worked transnationally, writing scripts for German and Austrian productions, namely *Das Schloss in Tirol* (Castle in Tyrol, directed by Géza von Radványi, AT, 1957) and *Wie ein Sturmwind* (Tempestuous Love, directed by Falk Harnack, DE, 1957), and the television movie *Der Tag danach* (The Day After, directed by Rudolf Jugert, 1965).
43 Kaus, *Von Wien*, 233.
44 For a more in-depth discussion of this topic, see Range, "Everyday Life."
45 For more information on Kaus's description of exile, see Range, "Positioning Kaus."

of displacement from the motherland, of alienation lived as a loss, an injury."[46] Kaus's experience also appears to diverge from Edward Said's notion of exile as "the unhealable rift forced between a human being and a native place, between the self and its true home: its essential sadness can never be surmounted."[47] To be sure, her portrayal of exile as opportunity does not mean that she did not experience it as a rift or suffer from loss; she simply refused to portray it as such in her autobiography. Instead, she decided to construct a retrospection of a female exile that was able to adapt quickly to any situation she encountered, whether it was to new circumstances, geographically, politically and socially, or the publishing and market demands during her time in Germany to secure her employment as a writer and playwright, or the Hollywood film industry. Kaus's self-image does not correspond with Said's description of the exile's "crippling sorrow of estrangement" either.[48] According to her portrayal, there was no time to overcome any form of estrangement, either during her time in France or in the United States. She had to start working the minute she arrived in the United States, as she was the family's sole breadwinner.[49]

Even Kaus's perception and portrayal of Southern California differs from most other exile writers, composers, actors, and the like, who left Europe under political pressure during the 1930s and 1940s.[50] Neither in her autobiography nor in any interviews did Kaus ever admit to having experienced such a shock. On the contrary, Kaus tended to find familiarity in her new surroundings. Her autobiographical narrative about her time in Hollywood focuses on the friends and allegiances she made. It further provides insight into her own and other exile writers' experiences with and attitudes toward the Hollywood studios. With respect to a

---

[46] Renato Camurri, "The Exile Experience Reconsidered: A Comparative Perspective in European Cultural Migration during the Interwar Period," *Transatlantica* 1 (2014): 6.
[47] Edward Said, "Reflections on Exile," in *Out There: Marginalization and Contemporary Cultures*, ed. Russell Ferguson, Martha Gever, Trinh T. Minh-ha, and Cornel West (Cambridge, MA: MIT Press, 1990), 357.
[48] Ibid., 357.
[49] Kaus and her family belonged to the "105,000 Germans (mostly but not exclusively Jewish) who managed to immigrate into the US between 1933 and 1941." (Fear and Lerner, *Screens*, 23). More specifically, Kaus belonged to the 10–15,000 German-speaking refugees, roughly 70 percent of whom were Jews, who landed in Southern California between 1933 and 1941. (Bahr, *Weimar*, 3–4). As Deborah Dash Moore points out, "Jewish enthusiasm for the City of Los Angeles surpassed that of other Americans in the post war era" (23). The Jewish population in L.A. almost doubled; "from 130, 000 before the war to over 300,000 in 1951" (Fear and Lerner, *Screens*, 23).
[50] Jarrell Jackman has noted that despite repeated experiences of exile, in Southern California Jews still experienced culture shock. See Jarrell C. Jackman, "Exiles in Paradise; German Emigres in Southern California, 1933–1950," *Southern California Quarterly* 61, no. 2 (1979): 183.

couple she befriended in Hollywood, she states in her autobiography: "You could visit them anytime without being formally invited or prior notification; it was like a coffee house."[51] While Jackman assumes that "exile in southern California ranged from mild discomfort to sheer agony, depending upon the individual in question,"[52] Kaus's autobiographical writing indicates that she does not wish to fit into any of these categories.

Moreover, Kaus's constant literary output seems hardly to have been affected by her exile in France and the United States, certainly when we consider the large number of film scripts, stories, treatments as well as translations she wrote. Again, as a female émigrée, Kaus deconstructs widespread ideas about exile. Even though Kaus was well into her forties when she switched from novelist to scriptwriter, and at roughly the same time from writing in German to English, her productivity level never faltered. Both Kaus's autobiography *Von Wien nach Hollywood* and *Die Unwiderstehlichen*[53] (The Irresistible) offer potential answers to why exile seems to not have impeded her output as writer.[54] Her experience as a female writer during the 1920s and 30s had prepared her for exile, for as noted, she had been exiled and marginalized in numerous ways: first, in the male-dominated Vienna and Berlin literary circles she had to battle in order to gain recognition as a female writer. Second, when she finally received attention as a writer, she was marginalized by being labeled as an "*Unterhaltungsautorin*," and thus relegated to the ranks of writers of women's literature. Third, when the National Socialists annexed Austria, they burned Kaus's books, which aided in the forgetting of Kaus by the German-speaking public. Regardless, of the circumstances and hardship, Kaus fashioned an image of herself that emphasized her relentless attempt to make the most of these situations. Through writing, she managed to fight against the patriarchal, nationalistic, and marginalizing tendencies she saw herself as well as others confronted with. It was Kaus's understanding of the author's role that made a particular physical homeland unnecessary; it was a constant and could be taken along wherever she went and enabled her to fashion a spiritual homeland based in writing itself.

---

51 All translations are my own, unless otherwise noted.
52 Jackman, "Exiles in Paradise," 183.
53 Gina Kaus, *Die Unwiderstehlichen: Kleine Prosa*, ed. by Hartmut Vollmer (Oldenburg: Igel-Verl. Literatur, 1926 & 2000).
54 *Die Unwiderstehlichen* contains a variety of Kaus's articles and essays stemming from the mid-1920s to the 1930s that were published in journals and magazines, such as *Vossische Zeitung, Die Arbeiter-Zeitung, Die Dame, Die Literarische Welt, Deutsche Zeitung Bohemia,* and *Prager Tageblatt.*

3 Writing For Hollywood

Kaus's exile in the United States, and more specifically Hollywood, represented a break with her familiar environment culturally, socially, linguistically,[55] and geographically. This meant finding another line of work, another medium through which to express herself. However, just as Kaus had managed to work successfully within social and gender boundaries prior to her exile, she pursued her feminist agenda in her scriptwriting for Hollywood productions through the narratives and characters she created for her film scripts portraying non-cliché, non-stereotypical women. Kaus succeeded in this agenda by working as a female scriptwriter, which was a rarity in the male-dominated Hollywood film industry.

Writing provided the physically exiled Kaus with a constant, a spiritual homeland that was mobile, that could be taken with her wherever and in whatever situation she found herself. Kaus, who was used to being denounced and marginalized, for once found herself at an advantage over many of her fellow male exile authors, as she sought to establish herself in the Hollywood industry. In her autobiography, Kaus recalls conversations with three fellow Jewish authors – Friedrich Torberg, Leonhard Frank, and Alfred Neumann – who like Kaus, did not belong to the *Nobelemigranten* and therefore found themselves confronted with less fortunate economic circumstances.[56] Kaus herself coined the expression *Nobelemigranten* and used it to refer to a group that consisted of "Thomas Mann, Lion Feuchtwanger, Franz Werfel, the musicians Schönberg, Strawinsky, and dozens of other famous people". Kaus recalls Torberg, Frank, and Neumann's inability to reorient themselves: "It was heartbreaking to see how these highly talented men faced this unfamiliar challenge ... The hidden contempt which these literati had for film work might have played a role in their failure."[57] Kaus was in no position to have an attitude as to whether it was good or bad for her reputation to work in the film business, as she had a family to support.[58]

---

[55] Kaus did not speak English well enough to write her scripts in English. Her son helped her translate during the first few months in the United States. After that, Kaus no longer needed his help. Quite the contrary, Kaus translated a variety of works by other German-speaking authors.
[56] Kaus uses the term to refer to the "distinguished," affluent, and predominately male émigrés. Her term also carries the meaning of "gentry." Kaus thus points to class system among the German-Jewish community in Hollywood. According to Kaus, they would not mingle with the less fortunate émigrés and would only speak German and did not work in the studios (206). Whereas the *Nobelemigranten* were capable of continuing their writing careers due to their fortunate financial independence, people like Kaus or the three authors mentioned above could not.
[57] Ibid., 205, 207.
[58] Ibid., 209.

The same drive to unmask and undermine oppressive forces and limitations that clearly underpinned her own life trajectory remained at the core of her writing.[59] Hamid Naficy's concept of accented cinema is based on the idea of a binary opposition between the dominant "Hollywood cinemas, whose films are realistic and intended for entertainment only, and thus free from overt ideology or accent" and the "alternative or marginalized cinemas," which "derive ... [their] accent from [their] artisanal and collective production modes and from the filmmakers' and audiences' deterritorialized locations."[60] Naficy provides a useful theoretical framework and vantage point from which to shed light on Kaus's film work, even if Kaus was a screenwriter working within the Hollywood establishment. Unlike Naficy's Iranian filmmakers, Kaus did not long "to move out of marginal cinema niches into the world of art cinema or even popular cinema."[61] She was hired immediately to work for the Hollywood industry upon her arrival in the United States. Nonetheless, her "double consciousness" constituted both "by the structures of feeling ... as displaced subject" and by the "exilic and diasporic traditions" permeates her writing for Hollywood.[62] Even though Kaus wrote for the Hollywood apparatus, she still managed to make creative and excellent use of the multiple narrative and potential interpretative levels of the filmic medium. Kaus created opportunities to critique the dominant cinema and its ideologies from within the dominant cinema, Hollywood, itself.

Just as Kaus's novels like *Die Verliebten*, *Morgen um Neun*, *Die Schwestern Kleh*, and *Katharina die Große* offered a channel for social commentary and a possibility to reflect upon repressive powers before her exile, her work as a film professional provided a similar opportunity once in America. Through her scriptwriting, story inventions and, in particular, her work on film dialogues, Kaus found herself in the position to not only critique the National Socialists, but also to intervene in the stereotypical gender discourses and constructions of "femininity" Hollywood provided for its audiences during the 1940s and 50s. Furthermore, Kaus's success in Hollywood also enabled her to work transnationally and to inscribe herself into the German and Austrian film landscape of the late 1950s and 60s.

As mentioned, Kaus was well aware of the social and political impact the medium of film and television could potentially exercise on the masses. Her anti-Nazi comedy *The Wife Takes a Flyer* (1942) presents one of the most explicit

---

59 See "Positioning Kaus" for a more thorough discussion of Naficy's theory and the implications for applying it to the film work of Kaus.
60 Hamid Naficy, "Situating Accented Cinema," in *Transnational Cinema: The Film Reader*, ed. by Elizabeth Ezra and Terry Rowden (London: Routledge, 2006), 119.
61 Said, "Reflections on Exile," 126.
62 Naficy, *Accented Cinema*, 22.

political criticisms during her career in Hollywood. Her work as a scriptwriter on this particular film can be seen as a response to and intervention in the Nationalist Socialist regime and ideology,[63] as she uses the genre's potential to indicate the limitations, preconceptions, and absurdities of social realities and discourses. With *The Wife Takes a Flyer*, she once again appears as a writer and a doer, but instead of addressing a German-speaking readership, she confronts her American viewers with the constraints, limits, and fragility of the safety of one's private sphere and life.

In the movie *Three Secrets* (1950), Kaus draws a portrait of a couple that suffers from the consequences of contrary gender expectations.[64] Phyllis, one of three female protagonists in the film, has just returned from her job as a war correspondent only to have to face her husband, Duffy, who wants a divorce. Duffy says: "I happen to be a sentimental guy that comes from a big family of twelve kids. I get lonely when the other eleven are not around – or even one." Phyllis responds: "What do you want me to do? Stay home and cook for you? Wash the dishes? No, Duffy. I am not that type. You knew that from the beginning." The dialogue reveals Kaus's own discontent with the discourses that position women as "natural" caretakers. Nonetheless, in an effort to save the marriage, Phyllis tries to conform to Duffy's expectations and gives up her job to become a stereotypical "homemaker." However, after accepting a tremendous job opportunity by her former boss, Duffy once again requests a divorce. When Phyllis asks him to at least try and understand the inner conflict she feels between wanting to please him and also wanting a career, he responds, "I do understand. I am sorry for you, Phyllis. You tried very hard to be a woman. You just couldn't make it." Not only is Kaus able to show the consequences of the government's political agenda that convinced white middle-class women to work outside the home for the nation's sake during wartime, she also exposes the psychological abuse involved in the reinforcement of traditional gender roles that persisted once women were expected to return to the home after the war was over. Kaus, who was responsible for and in control of the dialogue in *Three Secrets*, was therefore able to reveal that ideas of "femininity" or "masculinity" are constructions, exposing them as

---

63 Gina Kaus invented the story for *The Wife Takes a Flyer* and wrote the screenplay in collaboration with Jay Dratler. Richard Wallace directed the film, which starred Joan Bennett, Franchot Tone, Allyn Joslyn, Cecil Cunningham, Roger Clark, Lloyd Corrigan, and Lyle Latell, and premiered in the United States in 1942.

64 Kaus invented the story for *Three Secrets*. She also wrote the screenplay in collaboration with Martin Rackin. However, she was not credited for her work on the script. Robert Wise was the director of the movie that starred Eleanor Parker, Patricia Neal, and Ruth Roman, and premiered in the United States in 1950.

part of a patriarchal ideology and undermining the notion of women as "natural caregivers and homemakers."

Moreover, all of her films and movie collaborations point to the uneven power structures that were present during the 1940s and 50s in the United States. Similar to her literary works, Kaus represented a variety of ideas and models of "femininity," reflecting in many ways a vision of a pluralist culture and tripartite or, in Kaus's case, quadripartite experience that had been formed during the Habsburg monarchy.

Most importantly, Kaus provided her film characters with a voice, quite literally putting words into their mouths, and in so doing, exposing her audience to a multitude of situations and discourses, which both men and women could imagine themselves having to confront. In this, she continued the path of her pre-exile novels and plays, where she did not censor or dictate a certain perspective on social, political, or economic issues, but rather created opportunities for her readers and viewers to reflect on and question. In *Die Schwestern Kleh*, the narrator Eula provided insights into the hardships of a post-World War I era, and a variety of women and their newly developing roles. Through the conversations between Eula and Lotte, Kaus juxtaposes the generational views and allows both voices and perspectives to come to the fore. Similarly, in *Die Überfahrt*, Kaus manages to offer a non-moralist perspective on the limitations of class and gender hierarchies of the time by creating a microcosm of Weimar society through the characters aboard the luxury liner. Here, the author uses the fictive passengers as representatives of the various classes and presents them as both victims and perpetrators of the political and social tensions of the 1920s. Kaus's choice of an omniscient narrator not only for the main male character, Tomas, but also for all the other characters, making all of their ideas and thoughts transparent, allows the reader to learn about everyone's past experiences to pass their own judgment on them. Likewise, in *Gefängnis ohne Gitter* or *Toni*, through the interactions of a variety of characters from different backgrounds and levels of authority, Kaus presents a plethora of voices and opinions about the state of the educational system for young women, from conservative to progressive, and situates them in a dialogue with each other.

Kaus's critique of gender inequality, which often found expression in intense scenes in her film work as well, as illustrated in the above dialogue between Duffy and Phyllis, and especially those pertaining to war, marriage, divorce, the role of the state apparatus, abortion, adoption, motherhood, working women, and social inequality, to name only a few, created tension for the viewing audience. The tale of Duffy and Phyllis is but one of many stories, dialogues, and scenes created by Kaus that illustrate the consequences of the wartime mobilization of female workers and the post-war reassertion that middle class women should return to or remain in the house. Many of her other film collaborations such as *All I Desire*, *We're Not Married!*, *Julia Misbehaves* and *They All Kissed the Bride* include similar scenes in which the femininity of working women is questioned.[65] Like *Three Secrets*, *They All Kissed the Bride* (1942)[66] also features a working female protagonist, Margaret Drew, who runs a trucking company. The only way to actually be viewed as a "full-fledged woman," in particular by her own mother and doctor, is when she finally falls in love with a man.

Regardless of the particular outcome chosen by Kaus's fictive characters – often providing endings that would stay within the limits of the Motion Picture Production Code – the audience was introduced to the complexity involved in these themes and topics so typical for Kaus.[67] Like the author herself, Kaus's characters worked within the limits of the traditional expectations and rules imposed upon them, and exercised agency within the framework they were given.

Whereas Kaus's previously discussed oeuvre presented an intervention into a variety of discourses and incentives for her viewers to change the status quo, her 1957 transnational film *Das Schloss in Tirol* appears to have had an additional agenda.[68] This particular film illustrates how Kaus dispensed with a physical homeland. Her participation in the making of a "*Heimatfilm*" is especially intriguing, in that this genre has traditionally been framed in terms of its deliberate and elaborate use of nostalgia and wish for escapism from the recent history of the Third Reich.[69] During the mid-1950s, these types of films represented a successful genre in Austria and made up approximately about one-third of Austrian cinema.

---

[65] For *All I Desire* Gina Kaus teamed up with James Gunn and Robert Blees for the scriptwriting process. The director of the movie that premiered in 1953, was Douglas Sirk. *We're Not Married!*, a Twentieth Century Fox production directed by Edmund Goulding, featured such well-known actors as Ginger Rogers, Fred Allen, Marilyn Monroe, Zsa Zsa Gabor, and Louis Calhern, and was first screened in 1952. Finally, *Julia Misbehaves* was a collaborative adaptation by Gina Kaus and Monckton Hoffe, with Jack Conway as the director. The 1948 movie starred Greer Garson, Walter Pidgeon, Peter Lawford, Elizabeth Taylor, and Cesar Romero.

[66] Kaus provided both the story and the script for *They All Kissed the Bride*. She collaborated on it with Andrew Solt. Alexander Hall directed the film that was starring Joan Crawford, Melvyn Douglas, Roland Young, and Billie Burke and premiered in the Unites States in 1942.

[67] The Motion Picture Production Code is often also referred to as the Hays Code, named after Will H. Hays, the president of the Motion Picture Producers and Distributors of America during the early 1920s to 1945. The Production Code defined what was considered acceptable or unacceptable content for the American audience.

[68] For *Das Schloss in Tirol*, Gina Kaus, Fritz Eckhardt, Kurt Nachmann, and Géza von Radványi collaborated on the screenplay. Géza von Radványi directed the movie that premiered in Austria in 1957 and starred such well-known actors as Maria Andergast, Karlheinz Böhm, and Gustav Knuth.

[69] Well known examples of the genre during the 1950s are *Grün ist die Heide* (*The Heath is Green*, 1951, directed by Hans Deppe), or *Echo der Berge* (*Echo of the Mountains*, known abroad as *Der*

Through prolific use of imagery of natural settings, such as country landscapes, especially alpine mountains, filmmakers painted a picture of "an intact, guiltless, eternal Austria."[70] Kaus, as an exile, participated and reconstructed this genre, and the depiction of her (former) home country can be seen as the visualization of an idealized Austria, a materialization of an imaginary spiritual homeland.

The setting of *Castle in Tyrol* provided Kaus with the opportunity to remind her former fellow Austrians that they must take action and advantage of the country's situation following the Second World War. Yet, rather than merely imitating the genre, Kaus's *Heimatfilm* rewrites the concept of *Heimat*. *Castle in Tyrol* does not provide a nostalgic return to the "good old days" of the *Kaiserreich* and a life in the past but embraces a future filled with possibility. Kaus's participation in the making of this film can be seen as an attempt to contribute to the resignification of what has been tainted by the experience during National Socialism.

Kaus's main protagonist in *Castle in Tyrol* is once again a female character. The young woman, a countess, inherits an ancient castle as well as the debts of the old baron. Creditors immediately arrive to seize the castle along with its contents. The countess is thus faced with the need to find someone to rent the castle to pay off her creditors. A young engineer wishing to sell his latest invention – a small high-tech helicopter – desires to impress a potential client, an American, and leases the castle.

Whereas the traditional *Heimatfilm* demonizes the new and tries to provide stasis regarding the social and topographical geographies it focuses on, *Castle in Tyrol* deliberately invites progress. The film also reflects upon the current economic situation in Austria, which was clearly affected by the war. In Kaus's film, there is no idealized longing for pre-capitalist labor and romantic harmony between human beings and nature, which were typical for the genre. Furthermore, the presence of an American client as well as an American couple at the airport reminds the audience subtly of the occupation forces following the war.

Castle in Tyrol displays technology, in this case the helicopter, as exciting and an opportunity to encounter the new, the unknown, subverting the traumatizing memories of aircrafts and their deadly potential. The helicopter performs a minutes-long "dance" to the famous Vienna Waltz *An der schönen blauen Donau* by Johann Strauss. The aircraft is aestheticized and its meaning and potential re-signified and overwritten. Instead of only evoking feelings of nostalgia, the story also provides views of a possible future.

Förster vom Silberwald [The Forester of the Silverwoods], 1954, directed by Alfons Stummer), or *Heimatland* (1955, directed by Franz Antel), to only name a few.
70 Sonja Schachinger, "Der österreichische Heimatfilm als Konstruktionsprinzip nationaler Identität in Österreich nach 1945," M.A. thesis, University of Vienna, 1993, 91.

The film indicates a longing for interconnectedness and understanding; one that goes beyond physical and metaphorical borders. *Castle in Tyrol* presents ideas of mass production, technological advancements – in particular the small helicopter, which the engineer envisions will soon be available to the common people – as exciting and as an opportunity to encounter the new, the unknown; a topic all too familiar to the adventurous and ever-adapting émigrée Kaus. The film offers the German-speaking audience imaginative solutions and variations of the genre expectations. Once again, Kaus shows no reservation in using a popular genre and mass medium to reach her audience.

4 Seeking Refuge in the Spiritual Home of Writing

Throughout her lifetime, Kaus crossed not only physical and geographic borders, but psychological, metaphorical, social, and cultural ones too. As for so many exiles, this entailed being forced to leave the familiar, the *Heimat*, for the unfamiliar and, in the process, transform one's sense of self by exceeding and changing the discourses of either side. Kaus's choice of various concepts of homes, and her experiences in living in a variety of communities, circles, and cultures before and during exile, contributed to her ongoing self-formation and provided the base for her cultural critique. Rejecting the idea of just one home was a statement of her dissent and epitomized her anti-nationalist sentiment. Her understanding of writing and self-perception as an author were pivotal in enabling her to carve out for herself a spiritual home away from and independent of a physical home.

A closer look at Kaus's perception of the role of author, which can be traced back to her essay "Theater in der Kindheit" (Theater during Childhood),[71] helps elucidate the playwright, novelist, journalist, and eventual scriptwriter's self-assurance about writing for a mass audience and awareness of the potential impact of her work on her readership. In the essay, Kaus reflects on a formative childhood incident at age ten, when her grandfather gave her a tattered edition of Schiller's *William Tell*, but she had decided to read Schiller's *The Maid of Orleans*, a tale of Joan of Arc, instead. Kaus recounts that this reading experience "was an indescribable shock," and that the urge to write that struck her as a result "was not so much the desire to write something glorious, but rather to do something."[72] For Kaus, this was "less of an artistic than a heroic event" and created a "glowing and

---

[71] Gina Kaus, "Theater in der Kindheit," in *Die Unwiderstehlichen: kleine Prosa*, ed. Hartmut Vollmer (Oldenburg: Igel-Verlag Literatur, 2000 [1926]), 171.
[72] Ibid.

indescribable" longing that filled her with "enthusiasm and impatience,"[73] for she understood writing as a form of activism, as she concludes about this recollection, "beyond all words ... a female poet is an action."[74] Here Kaus stresses the duty and activist potential that accompanies the vocation of a female author. Writing itself presents Kaus with a sense of home in that the act of writing itself represents a moment of agency during which she can freely impose on the space left by homelands stolen from her. For Kaus, it was never much about a longing for a physical home – as she was already arguing prior to exile – so much as it was about creating a spiritual home – the wish to achieve recognition and a space for critical reflection and expression in a patriarchal world. Writing was, for Kaus, the way to actualize her full potential, even to the extent that she was indifferent to where she lived. Writing provided her with a place of belonging, a way to inscribe herself into the physical world, to leave a legacy that could overcome national, geographical, class, and gender boundaries. This is especially true when considering her scripts, which became films seen by thousands of people – even up to the present day.

More than a decade after writing that essay, after being "adopted" by the industrialist Kranz, Kaus finally found herself in a situation that enabled her to focus solely on her writing. When reflecting on moving into Kranz's house, she remembered a certain discomfort of not feeling quite at home. She wrote: "As strange as it sounds, at the Palais Kranz, there was no desk in the living quarters, my modern room had no desk either, and the other rooms were a museum. There was a secretary from the seventeenth century, however, but still no place where one could set up a typewriter – not to mention the many books that I kept buying uncontrollably."[75] It is thus not surprising that Kaus was overjoyed when she found a "studio apartment near the Palais Kranz" and was able to spend most of her day there.[76] She recalled: "Regularly I went right after breakfast. There I had my desk, my typewriter and my books. Friends came by sporadically."[77] The connection between a sense of home and the act of writing becomes even more evident in Kaus's description of having received her first advance to write a novel for the Ullstein publishing house. She recalls "My happiness was indescribable. I had found home ... I was a writer."[78] Writing was for her a kind of home, a spiritual home that provided her with a sense of belonging and purpose – even much more so than any physical homeland ever could.

---

73 Ibid., 172.
74 "[J]enseits aller Worte ... eine Dichterin eine Tat ist." Ibid.
75 Kaus, *Von Wien*, 42.
76 Ibid.
77 Ibid., 43.
78 Ibid., 124.

Equally significant to Kaus's idea of writing and authorship as home was her autobiographical reflection of nationality and belonging. In her autobiography, Kaus reconstructs a conversation between herself and Milena Jesenská, one of Franz Kafka's lovers, during a workers' uprising in the streets of Vienna shortly before the emperor's resignation. Jesenská is presented as overjoyed but trying to hide her good mood from her friend. Kaus tells her not to hold back, and then states: "I have no sense of nationality. I want to live in a country where the constitution suits me, but it does not matter to me whether it is large or small."[79] Defining herself without a sense of nationality also makes her independent of a need for a physical homeland, and enables her to fashion a spiritual home based in writing itself. The emphasis on a suitable constitution, a body of fundamental principles and established precedents is more important than national belonging. Flexibility, mobility, and the opportunity to impact the social and interpersonal level weigh more heavily than national identity and geographical rootedness. Furthermore, this anti-nationalist sentiment allows her to traverse a variety of barriers and even to overcome the language boundaries she encountered while in exile. Kaus's autobiography, and her overall body of work, allows insight into various discourses and opinions. Her statement reflects an attitude that Edward Said discusses in his essay "Reflections on Exile," where he argues that the "exile jealously insists on his or her right to refuse to belong."[80] Kaus portrays her early autobiographical self as having embraced this attitude long before it finds itself confronted with expatriation.

For Kaus, writing represented an opportunity to convey and unmask societal structures, a call for action that provided a wide variety of voices and opinions, and a way to make human interactions, discourses, and power structures more transparent. Kaus constructed herself as experiencing a sense of home only when and where she was able to write. Writing as a form of "doing," as a means for activism, transcends a particular location; it presents a spiritual home in which the author can seek refuge. It is a place where she can claim to be free of any sense of national belonging. The lure of writing for the Hollywood film industry, a mass medium with the potential to reach hundreds of thousands, and her previous familiarity with marketing strategies, helps explain why Kaus, in comparison to many of her fellow male exile writers, had no reservations about making the switch to film. More explicitly, Kaus appeared fully aware and convinced of the impact it had. In her autobiography, she states that it would be an idle question to ask what might have happened during the years 1930 to 1932 had the Weimar Republic presented Hitler with a worthy opponent and the Reichstag meetings broadcasted to the

---

79 Ibid., 64.
80 Said, "Reflections on Exile," 363.

German people via television. "They could not. There was no television yet. But I have witnessed America being saved from fascism by television."[81]

Flexibility, mobility, and the opportunity to impact the social and interpersonal level weigh more heavily than national identity and geographical rootedness. This sentiment allowed Kaus to traverse a variety of barriers and limitations she encountered while in exile.

Bibliography

Bahr, Ehrhard. *Weimar on the Pacific: German Exile Culture in Los Angeles and the Crisis of Modernism*. Berkeley: University of California Press, 2007.

Camurri, Renato. "The Exile Experience Reconsidered: A Comparative Perspective in European Cultural Migration during the Interwar Period." *Transatlantica* 1 (2014). http://journals.openedition.org/transatlantica/6920. Accessed June 2019.

Fear, Jeffrey R., and Paul Lerner. "Behind the Screens: Immigrants, Émigrés and Exiles in Mid Twentieth-Century Los Angeles." *Jewish Culture and History* 17 (2016): 1–21.

Isenberg, Noah W. *Edgar G. Ulmer: A Filmmaker at the Margins*. Berkley: University Press, 2014.

Jackman, Jarrell C. "Exiles in Paradise; German Emigres in Southern California, 1933–1950." *Southern California Quarterly* 61, no. 2 (1979): 183–205.

Kaus, Gina. *Der Teufel nebenan*. Amsterdam: de Lange 1939.

Kaus, Gina. *Die Mutter – Halbmonatsschrift für alle Fragen der Schwangerschaft, Säuglingshygiene und Kindererziehung*. Vienna: Offizielles Organ des Bundes für Mutterschutz, 1924–1926.

Kaus, Gina. *Die Schwestern Kleh*. Amsterdam: de Lange, 1933.

Kaus, Gina. *Die Überfahrt*. Munich: Knorr, 1932.

Kaus, Gina. *Die Verliebten*. Berlin: Verlag Ullstein, 1929.

Kaus, Gina. *Gefängnis ohne Gitter. Stück in 8 Bildern*. Vienna: Georg Marton, 1936.

Kaus, Gina. *Katharina Die Große: Biographie*. Frankfurt am Main: Ullstein, 1991.

Kaus, Gina. *Morgen um Neun* (Berlin: Ullstein), 1932.

Kaus, Gina. "Theater in der Kindheit." In *Die Unwiderstehlichen: kleine Prosa*. Edited by Hartmut Vollmer, 170–172. Oldenburg: Igel-Verl. Literatur, 2000 [1926].

Kaus, Gina. *Toni: Eine Schulmädchen-Komödie in zehn Bildern*. Frankfurt am Main: Propyläen-Verlag, 1927.

Kaus, Gina. *Von Wien nach Hollywood. Erinnerungen*. Frankfurt am Main: Suhrkamp, 1990.

Koerbner, Thomas. "'Auf der Alm, da gibt's koa Sünd'. Anmerkungen zum Heimatfilm." In *Heimat. Suchbild und Suchbewegung*. Edited by Fabienne Liptay, Susanne Marschall and Andreas Solbach, 103–131. Remscheid: Gardez Verlag, 2005.

Range, Regina C. "Positioning Gina Kaus: A Transnational Career from Vienna Novelist and Playwright to Hollywood Scriptwriter." PhD diss., University of Iowa, 2012.

---

81 Kaus, *Von Wien*, 219.

Range, Regina C. "Gina Kaus' Film Scripts and Autobiography as a Site of the Everyday Life in Exile." *Yearbook of the Research Centre for German and Austrian Exile Studies*. Amsterdam: Brill Rodopi, 2015.

Rose, Alison. *Jewish Women in Fin de Siècle Vienna*. Austin: University of Texas Press, 2008.

Rozenblit, Marsha L. *Reconstructing a National Identity: The Jews of Habsburg Austria during World War I*. New York: Oxford University Press, 2001.

Said, Edward. "Reflections on Exile." In *Out There: Marginalization and Contemporary Cultures*. Vol. 4. Edited by Russell Ferguson, Martha Gever, Trinh T. Minh and Cornel West, 357–366. New York: New Museum of Contemporary Art and MIT, 1990.

Schachinger, Sonja. "Der österreichische Heimatfilm als Konstruktionsprinzip nationaler Identität in Österreich nach 1945." M.A. thesis, University of Vienna, 1993.

Silverman, Lisa. *Becoming Austrians: Jews and Culture between the World Wars*. Oxford: Oxford University Press, 2012.

Silverman, Lisa. "Ella Zirner-Zwieback, Madame d'Ora, and Vienna's New Woman." In *Fashioning Jews: Clothing, Culture, and Commerce*. Edited by Leonard J. Greenspoon, 77–98. Indiana: Purdue University Press, 2013.

Soares, Luisa Afonso. "Vicky Baum and Gina Kaus: Female Creativity on the Margins." In *Practicing Modernity: Female Creativity in the Weimar Republic*. Edited Christiane Schönfeld and Carmel Finnan, 324–342. Würzburg: Königshausen, 2006.

Von Dassanowsky, Robert. *Austrian Cinema: A History*. North Carolina and London: McFarland & Company Inc., Publishers, 2005.

Filmography

All I Desire. Directed by Douglas Sirk. USA: Universal Pictures, 1953.
Blazing Guns. Directed by Robert Emmett Tansey. USA: Monogram Pictures, 1943.
Conflit. Directed by Léonide Moguy. France: Societé Parisienne de Distribution Cinématographique 1938.
Das Schloss in Tirol. Directed by Géza von Radványi. Austria: Rhombus Film, Wien-Film, UFA-Filmverleih, 1957.
Luxury Liner. Directed by Lothar Mendes. USA: Paramount, 1933.
Julia Misbehaves. Directed by Jack Conway. USA: Metro-Goldwyn-Mayer, 1948. MGM/UA Home Video, 1993.
Prison sans Barreaux. Directed by Arnold Pressburger. France: Les Films Osso, 1938.
Tempestuous Love. Wie ein Sturmwind. Directed by Falk Harnack. Germany: Central Cinema Company Film, 1957.
Teufel in Seide. Directed by Rolf Hansen. Germany: Fono Film, 1955.
The Red Danube. Directed by George Sidney. USA: Metro-Goldwyn-Mayer, 1949.
The Robe. Directed by Henry Koster. USA: Twentieth Century Fox, 1953.
The Wife Takes a Flyer. Directed by Richard Wallace. USA: Columbia Pictures, 1942.
They All Kissed the Bride. Directed by Alexander Hall. USA: Columbia Picture, 1942.
Three Secrets. Directed by Robert Wise. USA: Warner Bros. Pictures, 1950.
We're Not Married! Directed by Edmund Goulding. USA: 20th Century Fox Studios, 1952.
Western Mail. Directed by Robert Emmett Tansey. USA: Monogram Pictures, 1943.

Diego Rotman
Performing Homeland in Post-Vernacular Times: Dzigan and Shumacher's Yiddish Theater after the Holocaust

> On the way, the Jews became not only travelers but wanderers, immigrants, who travel to a faraway land ... they feel everywhere at home. Jews, wherever they travel, carry with them, thank God, their own home, their own ghetto with the exile itself.
> – Sholem Aleichem, *Kasrilevker Nisrofim* (The Burned-Out People of Kasrilevke)[1]

1 Theater as Destination

In 1927, the modernist Yiddish poet and playwright Moyshe Broderzon founded the avant-garde Yiddish theater Ararat in Łódź, Poland, serving as its director.[2] The name of the theater refers to its acronym (Artististisher revolutsioneter teater [Artistic Revolutionary Theater]), indicating the modernist and experimental aesthetics of the theater, and to a specific geographical location straddling Armenia and Turkey that symbolizes the mythical rebirth of humanity after the biblical flood.

Broderzon's understanding of the theater company as a territorial destination is stressed in Ararat's anthem, which was performed as the opening song in most of the theater's productions:

---

1 My translation.

״אין וועג זעען דעריבער ייִדן איז נישט נאָר ווי רייזנדער אַליין, נאָר ווי וואַנדערער, ווי ע מ י ג ר אַ נ ט ן, וואָס פֿאָרן אַריבער ערגעץ ווייטער אין אַ ווייטע מדינה [...] זיי פֿילן זיך דערפֿאַר אומעטום, ווי באַ זיך אין דער היים. ייִדן, וווהין זיי זאָלן נישט פֿאָרן, פֿירן זיי, ברוך־השם, מיט זיך זייער היים, זייער 'געטאָ' מיט זייער גלות״. שלום עליכם, ״כתרילעווקער נשרפים.״

2 Broderzon attempted to create a Yiddish *kleynkunst-bine* inspired by the Russian futurism and the European cabaret, as an alternative to the popular Yiddish theater of his time. On the history of Yiddish theater see, for example, Joel Berkowitz and Barbara J. Henry, *Inventing the Modern Yiddish Stage: Essays in Drama, Performance, and Show Business* (Detroit: Wayne State University Press, 2012). About Moyshe Broderzon, see Gilles Rozier, *Moyshe Broderzon: Un écrivain yiddish d'avant-garde* (Saint-Denis: Presses Universitaires de Vincennes, 1999).

https://doi.org/10.1515/9783110637564-005

> The world destroyed in a black shimmer/ The flood is coming to an end./ Young swimmers stroke through the water/ Looking for a beach!/ The air remains clouded,/ It is far from being calm... / Without an Ark, toward Mount Ararat/ We swim, we swim to the destination.³

According to the anthem, the group of young revolutionary actors go through Ararat-the-theater to reach Ararat-the-territory to fulfill their dream of cultural renewal. At a time of economic and social crisis, the experimental troupe became, or at least defined itself, both as a mythological and a physical destination. Broderzon, like the biblical Noah and Mordecai Manuel Noah (1785–1851),⁴ decided to fulfill a particular dream of renewal: to establish a revolutionary Jewish cultural autonomy in Poland that would, in this case, be a nomadic and sporadic territory, with its own language and aesthetics.

Ararat's first performance took place on October 25, 1927, at the Mount Eiffel Hotel in Łódź. This convergence of three different landmarks – the industrial Polish city of Łódź, known at the time as the Polish Manchester; the venue, a hotel whose name references the iconic French structure and the mountain in Canada named after it; and Ararat, a Yiddish theater troupe named after the mythical location of Noah's Ark – would mark not only the beginning of this experimental troupe but also the professional birth of the most important satiric Yiddish artists of the twentieth century, namely Shimen Dzigan (1905–1980) and Isroel Shumacher (1908–1961).

This article deals with the construction of temporary territories through language and performance, as these came into being in the artistic work of the Yiddish satirical theater of Dzigan and Shumacher, and of Dzigan's alone in post-WWII Poland (1947–1949) and the State of Israel (1950–1980). I introduce Dzigan and Shumacher's artistic background in the pre-war years with Ararat to delineate how Moyshe Broderzon's approach to the use of the vernacular language in

---

3 "פֿאַרגייט אַ וועלט אין שוואַרצן שימער,/ צום מבול נעמט אַן עק – / עס לייגן קלאַפּטער יונגע שווימער, / און זוכן אַ ברעג!/ דער חלל איז נאָך אַליץ פֿאַרכמאַרעט,/ עס איז נאָך ווייט פֿון רו [...]/אָן אַ תּיבה צו דעם בערג אַראַראַט/ מיר שווימען שווימען צו!"
Shimon Dzigan, *Dizgan-albom in vort un bild: 35-yor stsenishe tetykayt fun Shimen Dzigan* (Tel Aviv: Strud, 1964).
4 "Ararat" as a name for defining a revolutionary process of establishing a Jewish territory is reminiscent of the project of Mordecai Manuel Noah, a journalist, scriptwriter, and politician. In 1825, Noah decided to call his program of "revival, renewal and establishing a Jewish autonomy under the American constitution, in Grand Island, New York" Ararat. See Michael Weingrad, "Messiah, American Style: Mordecai Manuel Noah and the American Refuge," in *American Hebrew Literature: Writing Jewish National Identity in the United States* (New York: Syracuse University Press, 2011), 143–85; Jonathan D. Sarna, *Jacksonian Jew: The Two Worlds of Mordecai Noah* (New York: Holmes & Meier, 1981).

Yiddish theater influenced the artistic and political approach to language identity in Dzigan and Shumacher's theater in the post-War World II era, after the natural relationship between the Yiddish language and territory had been severed.

2 The Language of Autonomy

During its first years (1927–1930), Ararat adapted the Yiddish language to the dialect of the area where each performance took place, making Ararat's language site-specific. But from the first guest performances of Ararat in Warsaw in the early 1930s, the Łódź vernacular dialect became the troupe's preferred language, expressing a political and aesthetic decision that challenged the main trends in Yiddish theater of that time. If Ararat was a territory, the Yiddish dialect from Łódź would become the language of autonomy.

According to Dzigan's autobiography, it was in 1930 when Broderzon made the revolutionary decision and chose the local Łódź vernacular of Yiddish for his theater, thus challenging the standard Volhynia dialect used by the other Yiddish theaters of that period. The standardization of language in Yiddish theater was a collective attempt to find a language that would be understood by the entire Yiddish diaspora. In an essay on the Yiddish *bineshprakh* (the language of the Yiddish stage), published the same year Ararat was founded, the Yiddish linguist Noah Prilutsky examined the development of the *Deutsche Bühnenaussprache* and the domination of the Volhynia dialect in Yiddish theater as the common vernacular of the theater.[5] Broderzon opposed the standardization of Yiddish, and expressed a contrary approach: "When one asks, 'Dialect?' we answer, 'Why specifically Lithuanian Yiddish? Why specifically Volhynian Yiddish?' Why not Polish Yiddish, the dialect of a group of a couple of million speakers, with their abundance of juicy words, forthrightness, refreshing dialect, gushing forth like a spring, and more natural to our origins?"[6]

---

5 Noah Prilutsky presented the opposite view on the subject than that put forth by Broderzon. See Noah Prilutsky, "Di bine-shprakh," *Yiddish-teater* 1, no. 2 (1927): 129–44. On language and Yiddish theater see Mariana Sauber, "Le Téâtre yiddish et sa langue," *Temps Modernes* 41 (1984): 557–67.

6

„אַז מען פֿרעגט: דיאַלעקט? ענטפֿערן מיר: – פֿאַר וואָס דווקא ליטווישער? פֿאַר וואָס דווקא וואָלינער? און – פֿאַר וואָס נישט פּוילישער, דער פֿונעם עטלעך־מיליאָנדיק־באַרעדעוודיקן קיבוץ, דער קלינגענדיק־באַרעדעוודיקער, דער כאַראַקטערפֿולער, קוועלנדיק־אָפֿפֿרישנדיקער, און, פֿאַר אונדזער באַדן־נאַטירלעבערך?"

As quoted in Moyshe Pulaver, *Ararat un lodzer tipn* (Tel Aviv: Y.L. Perets, 1972), 14–15.

In his review of Ararat productions in Warsaw, the writer and poet Zusman Segalovitsh recognized and appreciated the use of the Łódź Yiddish vernacular and referred to the relationship between the dialect in which the actors perform and their body language on stage, both linked to the actors' city of origin – Łódź:

> It is no coincidence that the three of them [Shimen Dzigan, Isroel Shumacher and Shmulik Goldstein] come from the same city, Łódź, and perhaps even from the same alley. They bring with them a particular pronunciation of Yiddish speech. We would go so far as to say that they'll never be able to play a nobleman or baron. Dzigan only has to try to say "Ya" instead of "Yo," and the audience starts to crack up ... They come to the theater from the heart of Jewish society. They bring Jewish mimicry to the stage ... and the authentic Jewish joke.[7]

According to the review, these Yiddish actors play the folksy type of Łódź Jew – down-to-earth, unpretentious – because they would be incapable of portraying any "aristocrat figure." But their limitation of language, Segalovitsh goes on to say, can also be considered an advantage: their uniqueness is actually expressed through their specific dialect and body language.

In his analysis of Sholem Aleichem's literary work, Dan Miron argues that Sholem Aleichem decided to use the vernacular as a form of resistance to the tendencies of the Yiddish writers of his time.[8] According to Miron, the characteristics of marginality, splendor, and de-territorialization allow the application of Deleuze and Guattari's concept of minor literature,[9] to Sholem Aleichem's literary work. Sholem Aleichem adopted the sense of cultural-linguistic minority and marginality, delved deeply into it, and through it created a feeling of cultural and political independence. In so doing, he rejected the dominant Yiddish culture and subverted it.[10]

Following Miron's argument, it would seem that Broderzon, together with Dzigan and Shumacher, subverted the conventions of language politics in the

---

7

"נישט אומזיסט קומען אַלע דרײַ [דזשיגאַן, שומאַכער און גאָלדשטײן] פֿון אײן שטאָט, פֿון לאָדזש, און אפֿשר זענען זײ פֿון אײן געסל. זײ טראָגן אויף זיך דעם ספּעציפֿישן־ייִדישן קנייטש און וועגן זײ קאָן מען דרײַסט זאָגן, אַז קײן גראַפֿן, קײן באַראָנען וועלן זײ נישט קאָנען שפּילן, קײן מאָל נישט. זאָל דזשיגאַן פּרוון זאָגן 'יאַ' אַנשטאָט 'יאָ' ווטעט מען לאַכן [...] זײ זענען צום טעאַטער געקומען פֿון דער ייִדישער געדיכטעניש. זײ האָבן געבראַכט אויף דער סצענע די ייִדישע מימיק, נו [...] און דעם עכט־ייִדישן וויץ."

Zusman Segalovitsh, "Di 'samerodne' yatn ... vegn 'ararat'," *Der Moment* [Warsaw], October 14, 1934.
8 "While the Yiddishist establishment strove to ennoble the language and raise it from vernacularity and dialectism to the level of a genuinely referential language, he pulled it down into the bog of 'vulgarity.'" Dan Miron, "The Dark Side of Sholem Aleichem's Laughter," *Derekh Judaica Urbinatensia* 1 (2003): 42.
9 Deleuze and Guattari suggest that *minor literature* is a literature written in a language that is considered in an inferior position within the minority group to which it belongs. Gilles Deleuze and Félix Guattari, *Kafka: Toward a Minor Literature* (Minneapolis: University of Minnesota Press, 1986).
10 Miron, "The Dark Side," 16–55.

Yiddish theater. In a way, stage artists and poet continued the process Sholem Aleichem had started in his literary work, and brought it into a performative genre, as reflected in the critique of their performances.[11] Dzigan, Shumacher, and Broderzon brought the power of the Łódź vernacular of Yiddish – notably its marginality – to the Yiddish stage, using the language in unprecedented ways of expression and challenging the established convention of the Yiddish theater language of their time.

3 Two Bears Speaking Yiddish

In 1934, after six years in Łódź (1927–1933), a crisis in the troupe caused Dzigan and Shumacher, the main actors in the collective, to move to Warsaw. They performed with *Di yiddishe bande* (The Jewish Gang), and a year later succeeded in reestablishing Ararat in Warsaw together with some of the original actors from Łódź. In response to the political and economic reality on the eve of World War II, they abandoned modernist theater, focusing instead on satirical political theater. Their theater, which would play a key role in Eastern European Jewish culture, was characterized by sharp humor, witty political satire, and extraordinary acting. The renewed Ararat, in which Dzigan and Shumacher were both star performers and directors, became famous, and was later renamed the Dzigan and Shumacher Theater, with the actors' names becoming the moniker of a new destination.

The last show of Dzigan and Shumacher's satirical theater in pre-war Warsaw premiered on May 30, 1939, three months before the start of the war. In one of the skits, Shumacher speaks to the audience of the difficult living conditions of the Jews in Poland and informs the theatergoers of the sad fact that he must leave the country where he lives. He ends his speech with a farewell to all those present, including the mosquito he has caught buzzing around him: "Goodbye, mosquito! I leave [the country] and leave you here. Believe me, mosquito, I am jealous of you. You can fly freely wherever and whenever you want: you don't know about emigration difficulties, about passports, about visas, about any affidavits. Believe me, mosquito, I am weaker than you."[12] After Shumacher, the actor Josef Kamien comes on stage and

---

11 On comparisons to Sholem Aleichem see, for example, Chaym-Leyb Fuks, "Zikhere trit – dos drite 'ararat' program," *Lodzer veker*, January 30, 1928; Mordche Tsanin, "Ysroel Shumacher z'l," *Ilustrirte Velt-vokh*, May 31, 1961; "A bazukh fun Dzigan-Shumacher in di yiddishe tsaytung," *Di yiddishe tsaytung*, April 24, 1951; "Dzigan metachnen hatsagot beivrit," *Haaretz*, October 3, 1960.

12

"זײַ געזונט, פֿליג! איך פֿאָר אַוועק און לאָז דיך איבער. גלייב מיר, פֿליג, איך בין דיך מקנא. דו קענסט פֿרײַ פֿליִען וווּהין דו ווילסט און ווען דו ווילסט. דו וויסט ניט פֿון קיין עמיגראַציע־שוועריקייטן, פֿון קיין פּאַס, פֿון קיין וויזע, פֿון קיין אַפֿידייווויט. גלייב מיר, פֿליג, איך בין שוואַכער פֿון דיר."

confesses that he wants to become a cook. Shumacher then again appears together with Dzigan, but this time they are disguised as bears. They explain the reason: if the Jews in Poland can no longer live there as human beings, they should wear animal skins. Maybe this will enable them to save their own skins. Performing this change of identity, exchanging all cultural and human life for a wild existence – emigrating from a human body to an animal body – is presented as the last option for Jews in Poland in 1939. There was only one human quality the artists were unable to leave behind – the language: those two bears spoke *Lodzer Yiddish*.

After the German invasion of Poland and for the duration of the war, Dzigan and Shumacher found refuge in the Soviet Union, and, until the German invasion of the Soviet Union in June 1941, they worked as artistic directors and actors in *Der bialistoker melukhisher yiddisher miniatur-teater* (The Bialystok National Jewish Miniature Theater). Many of the reviews of their performance made specific mention of Dzigan and Shumacher's language. Regarding their presentations in Rostov and Yerevan,[13] reviews referenced the high level of the actors' expressiveness and the lightness of the program that allowed the public unfamiliar with Yiddish to enjoy the spectacle. In Baku,[14] the critic referred to this "language flexibility and lightness" and described the delight of the public in a Jewish theater where two-thirds of the audience were Russians, Azerbaijanis, and Armenians who did not understand Yiddish.

This internationalization, making the contents available to non-speakers, was interpreted by the critics as a central component of the theater's success, a means of "unifying different cultures." This process, this globalization of the language and culture of a specific ethnic group, was a stage in the deconstruction of cultural specificity in the Soviet Union.

Due to censorship committees and the pressure exerted on the artists, on the one hand, and the critics' discourse in the press, on the other, the sharp, highly critical Yiddish language that had characterized Dzigan and Shumacher's theater in Poland turned into a sound incapable of inflicting any damage. The actors had the freedom to perform in their language but it was a conditional freedom:

Moyshe Nudelman, "Kleynkunst- un marionetn-teaters tsvishn beyde velt-milkhomes," in *Yiddisher teater in eyrope tsvishn beyde velt-milkhomets (material tsu der geshikhte fun yiddishn teater): Poyln*, ed. Itsik Manger, Jonas Turkov, and Moyshe Perenson (New York: Alveltlekher Yiddisher Kultur-Kongres, 1968), 152–63.

13 Gregory Kats, "Workers of All Countries, Unite!" *Hammer [МОЛОТ[* (Rostov), March 22, 1941; N. Adamian, "Tours of the Bialystok Theater of Miniatures in Yerevan," *Kommunist* (Yerevan), April 12, 1941.

14 I. Samoilov, "'Singing and Dancing': Tour of the Bialystok Jewish Theater of Miniatures," *Baku Worker [Бакинский рабочий]* (Baku), September 10, 1940.

Yiddish was legal, or *kosher*, as theater language only when it lost its power, identity, and all the ways it could be intelligible to non-speakers. Universalism was the condition for particularism.

A few months after the group disbanded, the two actors were arrested for supposedly anti-Soviet activity. Dzigan and Shumacher spent four years in prison in the Oktyubinsk labor camp in Kazakhstan where they continued performing for the prisoners until their release in 1947.

4 Silence in *Lodzer* Yiddish: 1947–1950

One of the hardest periods in the life of the Jewish survivors in post-war Poland occurred between January 1946 and February 1947 with antisemitic attacks and killings of Jews in towns across the country. Between 1947 and 1948, two historical processes took place that would change the life of Polish Jews: the transition from a popular democracy to a communist regime and the establishment of the State of Israel.[15]

Dzigan and Shumacher returned to Warsaw in June 1947. On their first day in post-war Poland, they arrived late at night at the offices of the Central Committee of Polish Jews.[16] The night guard welcomed them and suggested they stay the night in the office. By morning, the arrival of the famous satiric artists from pre-war Poland was no longer a secret. Jews, thrilled to discover that both were alive and in Warsaw, flocked to the office to see them with their own eyes. Like miracle makers or saints performing before a big audience, Dzigan and Shumacher were expected to demonstrate that they were the original Dzigan and Shumacher: "They touched us in order to verify that we were real. I had to honor them with jokes from before the war, in order to convince them that we were really we, Dzigan and Shumacher."[17] Telling Yiddish jokes from pre-war Poland was, according to Dizgan, a sign of recognition, a code confirming that the teller and

---

[15] See Chana Shlomi, "Ha-hitargenut shel sridey ha-yehudim be-polin le-achar milchemet ha-olam ha-shniya, 1944–1950," in *Kium ve-shever – yehudei polin le-doroteyhem*, ed. Israel Bartal and Israel Gutman (Jerusalem: Shazar Center for Jewish History, 1997), 532–38.

[16] The committee was established in November 1944. It was supposed to be a mediator between the government offices and the Jewish community. At the beginning, Dr. Emil Zomershteyn was its president and the committee included representatives from different Jewish parties and organizations of that period. See Shlomi, "Ha-hitargenut shel sridey ha-yehudim," 523–48.

[17]

"מען האָט אונדז געטאַפּט צי מיר זענען אמתע. כ'האָב זיי געמוזט מכבד זײַן מיט אַ פּאָר פֿאַרמלחמהדיקע וויצן, זיי זאָלן זיך איבערצײַגן, אַז דאָס זענען מיר – דשיגאַן און שומאַכער."

the listener shared a common past; that they were alive, remembered, and still able to laugh. The joke became not only a humoristic interpretation of the present reality and a way to cope with it – it was also a document of the past. But it was not only the re-telling and the practice of remembering that became the main characteristic of Dzigan and Shumacher's theater in post-war Poland. In the formalization and aestheticization of their encounter with their public on stage, a long contemplative silence became the necessary ritualistic prologue. That was the beginning of the first skit of their first performance presented by the artists in each city in which they performed between 1947 and 1952, whether in Poland, Europe, Israel, or the United States.

Leon Leneman describes the skit, which bore the same name as the entire program "*Abi m'zet zikh*" ("The main thing is to see one another"), as follows:

> When the curtain went up, both Dzigan and Schumacher stood on the stage without saying a word, looking at the audience filling the venue to capacity. For a long time they remained watching the audience, "their audience," which sat quietly, understanding the significance of the silent look. Until together they said: "Abi m'zet zikh" [the main thing is to see one another] ... Those four words ... electrified the audience, and a storm of applause expressed, how much content those words possess ... "You are right! We are alive! ... We see each other, we live, we'll live!"[18]

The spectators "watched the Yiddish silence" stressed and stretched for an almost unbearable amount of time. Silence did not mean only stressing the absence of words to describe the tragedy; but also the symbolic and sonic expression of homelessness.

In those moments of silence, separating the tragedy from the continuity of life, history was split into two. Over the abyss separating past from present, life from death, silence from speech, floated these two mediators for whom the Yiddish word and the Łódź dialect functioned as a bridge constructed of the Yiddish saying "abi m'zet zikh" (the main thing is to see one another). Those words, more than simply stressing the act of seeing one another, brought life back

---

Shimon Dzigan, *Der koyekh fun yiddishn humor* (Tel Aviv: Gezelshaftlekhn komitet tsu fayern 40 yor tetikayt fun Shimon Dzigan oyf der Yiddisher bine, 1974), 288.

18

"ווען דער פֿאַרהאַנג האָט זיך אויפֿגעהויבן, זענען זיי ביידע, דשיגאַן און שומאַכער, געשטאַנען אויף דער בינע און נישט רעדנדיק גאָרנישט, געקוקט אויפֿן עולם, װאָס האָט פֿאַרפֿולט דעם זאַל. לאַנג האָבן זיי אַזוי געקוקט אויפֿן עולם, אויף 'זייער עולם','וועלכער איז געזעסן שטיל און גוט פֿאַרשטאַנען, װאָס דער שטומער בליק באַדײַט. ביז זיי האָבן ביידע צוזאַמען אַרויסגעזאָגט: 'אַבי מען זעט זיך...'. די דאָזיקע פֿיר ווערטער [...] האָבן ממש עלעקטריזירט דעם עולם און אַ שטורעם פֿון אַפּלאָדיסמענטן האָט געגעבן צו פֿאַרשטיין, וויפֿל זין און אינהאַלט די געציילטע ווערטער פֿאַרמאָגן אין זיך [...] 'איר זענט גערעכט! מיר לעבן! [...] מיר זעען זיך, מיר לעבן, מיר וועלן לעבן!'"

Leon Leneman, "Abi men zet zikh," *Keneder odler*, September 6, 1949.

Performing Homeland in Post-Vernacular Times — 89

Figure 1: Shimen Dzigan and Isroel Shumacher discussing their next theater program (staged photograph). From the Lydia Shumacher-Ophir z"l private collection.

to the stage, brought the audience to the present time, and rescued the listeners from the paralyzing abyss of the past.

Following the saying of "abi m'zet zikh," the performance would continue with a dialogue about the impossibility of speech, about the impossibility of action, anticipating the Beckettian tradition:

> Sh: Nu, why aren't you talking?
>
> D: Why aren't *you* talking?
>
> Sh: It doesn't talk. A strange feeling. Everything gets stuck in my throat.
>
> D: It's incredible.
>
> Sh.: It's actually not incredible at all. We waited so much for this moment. To be at home again, on the stage, like in the old days, with our public.[19]

For the artists, in post-war Poland, being back on the stage meant being home, being alive.

19

ש: נו, װאָס רעדסטו נישט?

ד: פֿאַרװאָס רעדסטו נישט?

ש: ס'רעדט זיך נישט, אַ מאָדנע געפֿיל אַלץ בלײַבט שטעקן אין האַלדז.

ד: ס'איז דען אַ װוּנדער.

ש: טאַקע נישט קײן װוּנדער, אַזױ לאַנג געװאַרט אױף דעם דאָזיקן מאָמענט. װידער זײַן אין דער הײם, אױף די בינע, װי אַמאָל, האָבן פֿאַר זיך אַן עולם.

5 In the Revival Was the Word

If, according to Dzigan and Shumacher's poetics in pre-war Poland, becoming a Yiddish-speaking bear was the necessary transformation for a Jew who wanted to survive, in post-war Poland a goat and a woman wearing a cross would be the closest visual representations, respectively, of a Hasidic man and a Jewish woman, one could expect to see. In this new world, where the Jewish body was transformed, translated, or in disguise, Yiddish speech would become the ultimate medium with the power of generating, recognizing, or recreating the vanished world as expressed by Dzigan: "We revived [the neighborhood of] Bałuty with our language ... The audience laughs, rejoices with happy, familiar-sounding words caressing the ears ... Again the Yiddish word and Yiddish song reminded him of his surroundings, his relatives, the most beautiful years ... for a moment you could think that nothing happened, that everything was a bad dream. This world was created by me and Shumacher, using the Łódź dialect."[20] The concept of revival became central in the post-war discourse, touching on the ideas of continuity, life, death, and survival. In this discourse of resurrection of Jewish life in post-war Poland, in those years when the "new Jew" in Poland was in an almost literal state of "homelessness," as reflected in the phrase *heymloze yiddn* (homeless Jews) often used in post-war years to describe the Jewish state of being,[21] Dzigan and Shumacher had, with their language, dialect, and body language, the miraculous power of bringing back to life the culture and the past, at least

---

20 "האָבן מיר אויפגעלעבט באַלוט מיט אונדזער לשון [...] דער עולם אין זאַל לאַכט, ער פֿרייט זיך מיט דעם באַקאַנטן ווערטער־קלאַנג, וואָס גלעט אזוי זיין אויער [...] ווידער האָט דאָס יידישע וואָרט, דאָס יידישע ליד, דערמאָנט יעדערן זיין סביבה, זײַנע נאָענטע, זײַנע בעסטע יאָרן [...] נאָך איין רגע און מען האָט געקענט מיינען, אַז ס'איז גאָרנישט געשען; אַז דאָס אַלץ איז געווען אַ בייזער חלום. אָט האָבן מיר, איך און שומאַכער, זיך פֿונאַנדערגערעדט מיט דער לאָדזשער אויסשפּראַך."

In Dzigan's monologue "Itshe Meyer," presented in Łódź in 1948, the Hasid Itshe Meyer tells the audience that he is looking for Jewish survivors, "with a *kapota*, with the Jewish hat, with a beard, a Jew from Nowolipki Street." He walks halfway across the city until he finds a beard, but it is not a real beard – just a *berdele*, a small beard, and not on a Jew at that, but on a goat. In this new reality, the Jew has changed his appearance, is in disguise, or has disappeared altogether. The closest reminder of a Jew is a goat. In post-war Poland, not only external appearances symbolized the disappearance of the (Hasidic) Jew from the human landscape of Poland, but the way to identify a Jewish woman was by ascertaining that she was wearing a cross:

ש: שאַ, דאַכט זיך גייט'ס אַ יידישע פֿרוי / ד: פֿון וואַנען ווייסטו אַז זי איז אַ יידישע?? / ש: זעסט דאָך, זי נײט אַ צלם.

Sh: Shush, it seems to me that this is a Jewish woman ... / D: How do you know that she is Jewish? / Sh: Look at her, she's wearing a cross.

21 See Isroel Efrat, *Heymloze yiddn* (Buenos Aires: Tsentral-farband fun poylishe yidn in argentine, 1947).

for the duration of the performance. That was their way of creating or staging *Yiddishland*, those temporary and independent sovereignties based on language, defined by the social and political thinker and one of the ideologists of Yiddishism and diaspora nationalism, Haym Zhitlowski (1865–1943): "[A] national spiritual territory ... whose atmosphere is the fresh and healthy air of the seashore, and in which every breath that is taken, every word that is spoken, upholds the living and their existence in the world as a nation."[22]

"For Zhitlowski," argues American scholar Jeffrey Shandler, "the tautology of language and people embodied in this term ... epitomizes the power of language to realize Jewish sovereignty in the face of the widespread perception of Jews as a people without a land."[23] According to Shandler, *Yiddishland* characterizes the linguistic practice of Yiddish after the Holocaust when Yiddish acquired a symbolic dimension beyond that of a language of communication.[24] If for George Steiner, the text is the Homeland, and for Czesław Miłosz, the mother tongue is his native land, for Dzigan and Shumacher, performing the Yiddish word and the specific Łódź dialect on stage was the act that allowed the artists to reconstruct the home, the territory.

The Yiddish poet Yankev Glatshteyn (Glatstein), developed the same idea, though he referred not only to speech itself but also to the gestures accompanying the actor's speech and his silences: "When Dzigan opens his mouth he is not only talking in *Lodzer Yiddish*. In his speech, Dzigan concentrates the entire music of Polish Yiddish." In Glatshteyn's words, Dzigan's post-war performance becomes a metonymic practice capable of reviving all the music of Yiddish uprooted from its natural European and Russian territory.

For Dzigan and Shumacher and for the Jewish survivors, post-war Łódź and Warsaw became non-places, or negatives of the cities in their pre-war state. In this reality, in which the cities were no longer what they had been, their representations on stage became more real, or closer to the original, than the actual Łódź or Warsaw. Warsaw and the Jewish neighborhood of Bałuty (Yid., Balut), in Łódź revived by Dzigan and Shumacher became Foucauldian heterotopias: counter-spaces, negatives, or better-expressed positives of the other spaces. The

---

22
"אַלװעלטלעכער גײַסטיק־נאַציאָנאַלער הײם [...] װאָס איר אַטמאָספערע איז די פרישע געזונטע לופט פון דער פֿאָלקס־שפראַך, װוּ מיט יעדן אָטעם װאָס מען אָטעמט, מיט יעדן װאָרט, װאָס מען רעדט אױס, האַלט מען אױף דאָס לעבן, דאָס זײַן אױף דער װעלט װי אַ פֿאָלק."
Haym Zhitlovsky, *Geklibene verk*, ed. Yudl Mark (New York: Tsiko, 1955), 321–23. The translation is quoted from Yael Chaver, *What Must Be Forgotten. The Survival of Yiddish in Zionist Palestine* (Syracuse: Syracuse University Press, 2004), xiv.
23 Jeffrey Shandler, *Adventures in Yiddishland: Postvernacular Language & Culture* (Berkeley: University of California Press, 2006), 37.
24 Ibid., 31–58, 126–53.

Yiddish language and the Łódź dialect no longer belonged to an existing geographical place, a landscape; they belonged to a group of dispersed speakers and dispersed survivors. The local place disappeared. The dialect became a sound without a place, a dialect in danger of extinction, containing the memory of a city and a culture, and a means to revive, for the duration of the performance, a world that had ceased to exist. The dialect, the language, became the territory, became the land, a faithful reconstruction of an original that no longer existed.

6 Performing in Hebrewland

In its first years, the issue of identity was of primary importance for Israeli society, and language was perceived as the central marker for defining the speaker's identity. If an actor or a citizen wanted to be absorbed into society, into the normative local Hebrew world, he had to give up the signs of the diaspora, first and foremost his or her diasporic language. With the establishment of the State of Israel, the state developed an official policy of supervising and controlling culture and language in an attempt to determine a new cultural order in which Hebrew was the exclusive national language of the Jewish nation. According to this new linguistic-cultural order, the Yiddish theater was perceived as a danger to the nation's cultural and linguistic character. The state assumed the role of defending the people from the Yiddish theater. In 1950, this gained a legal dimension when the Film and Theater Censorship Committee determined that it was forbidden to allow local troupes to perform in Yiddish. Through the attempts to repress Yiddish in Israel, permission to perform in Yiddish was given only to guest troupes and to actors from abroad.

In his book, *Der koyekh fun yiddishn humor* (The Power of Yiddish Humor), Dzigan recalls his arrival in Israel in 1950. He notes how surprised he was to find so many speakers of "juicy" Yiddish who remembered him and Shumacher from Łódź and Warsaw. "I had the impression," wrote Dzigan, "that I was back in Warsaw or in Łódź from before the war. I swam like a fish in water." But the water in which Dzigan swam was the water of exile.[25]

On March 13, 1950, Dzigan and Shumacher made their first appearance as guest actors in Israel. Their first program in Tel Aviv, "*Va-yisu va-yakhanu*" ("They Journeyed and They Encamped"), was a great success, both with the audience and with the theater critics in the Hebrew and Yiddish press. But Dzigan and Shumacher's rare and exceptional success in Israel intensified the perception on the part of the Israeli establishment that the Yiddish theater posed a threat to Hebrew

---

25 Dzigan, *Der koyekh fun yiddishn humor*, 304.

theater and culture, even though the theater was not yet local. This became the justification for plans to forbid their performance at the beginning of May 1950. As Azriel Carlebach, editor of the Hebrew daily newspaper *Maariv*, wrote: "The last performance by the actors Dzigan and Shumacher with the permission of the State of Israel will take place this evening. From tomorrow on, these performances will be forbidden. The reasons are highly important and convincing: these two people are – Jews. Even worse: they are Jewish refugees."[26] Carlebach, in an unusual show of support for the two guest actors, concluded his editorial in a sardonic tone that emphasized the purpose of the pressure employed against the actors: to make the transition into performing in Hebrew: "The trouble for Misters Dzigan and Shumacher is not so great. It's easy to help them. All they have to do is convert."[27] Two official reasons were given for forbidding their performance: first, the program was not submitted to the Films and Plays Censorship Committee (after the material was submitted to the committee, permission was again denied); second, the same committee enacted a new restriction that allowed guest actors to appear for a total of six weeks, a retroactively calculated limit, in all likelihood created as a result of Dzigan and Shumacher's success during the first six weeks of their stay.

Thanks to the intervention of Carlebach and Yosef Heftman, chairman of the Journalists' Union and one of the former editors of the Yiddish newspaper *Der Moment* in pre-war Poland, the two artists successfully managed to handle the Censorship Committee. They obtained a permit to continue to perform their program in Yiddish, but the permit was conditional on their plays including a Hebrew section that would fill at least one-third of the entire program. In order to meet these conditions, in a characteristic "trick," Dzigan and Shumacher hired a female singer who sang Hebrew songs in between the skits.

As a result of the social and political pressure created through their activity in Israel, and thanks to the Avraham Goldfaden Theater which continued to hold performances in Yiddish despite the prohibitions, at the end of 1951 the ban on local actors performing in Yiddish was repealed.[28] With the lifting of the ban, Israel's cultural policy became more sophisticated, and Yiddish changed from being "a language forbidden to Israelis" (at least in the field of the theater) to a "foreign language in Israel."[29] This was another expression of the policy of exiling Yiddish from the local cultural scene, and its significance was not only rhetorical

---

26 Azriel Carlebach, "Dzigan veShumacher," *Maariv*, May 2, 1950.
27 Ibid.
28 Rachel Rojansky, "Ben-Gurion's Attitude to Yiddish in the 1950s," *Iyunim bitkumat Israel* 15 (2005): 463–82 [Hebrew].
29 Yiddish changed its status from being "a forbidden language" in theater to the status of a "foreign language," although in the 1950s it was the only or first language for 33.3% of the Jewish

and cultural, but also economic: plays in the Yiddish theater, performed in a foreign language, were subject to higher taxes than plays in the Hebrew theater. This tax, and the withholding of budgets from theaters that did not perform in Hebrew, were justified as a means of supporting the transfer of actors in the Yiddish theater to the Hebrew stage. Thus, Dzigan and Shumacher had to continue dealing with the policy of discrimination against their theater in particular and against Yiddish theater in general.

Figure 2: Shimen Dzigan and Isroel Shumacher and their suitcases. From the Lydia Shumacher-Ophir z"l private collection.

Dzigan and Shumacher also had to overcome the pressure exerted on them by the critics' repeated demands to switch their language of performance to Hebrew. Most of the critics expressed expectations for "a Hebrew spirit in their plays," an urgent need for "their immediate switch to performing in Hebrew,"

---

population (524,000) and in 1961 for the 22.7% (446,200), see Joshua A. Fishman, *Yiddish: Turning to Life* (Amsterdam: John Benjamins Publishing Company, 1991), 407.

disappointment in "the insufficient amount of Hebrew in their shows," and in "their fanatical adherence to Yiddish." In 1953, the journalist Asher Nahor wrote the following in the newspaper *Herut*, published by the right-wing political party of the same name: "The large credit that was given at the time to the two actors when they were new immigrants, was given on condition ... the State of Israel was to serve as a place of refuge for their art, if this art would remove from itself its Diaspora cover and put on a uniform that is Hebrew in sound and style."[30] Two years later Nahor's words grew even more pointed: "Dzigan and Shumacher don't perceive that here is a matter of a national, cultural and even economic revolution, and therefore it is impossible to allow them to perform in Tel Aviv in the same way as they performed in Łódź and Warsaw. If they won't be with us, in the end they'll be against us, and a large part of their last program is against us."[31]

In the rhetoric of the Hebrew press, Dzigan and Shumacher were cultural delinquents – or at least linguistic transgressors – released on conditional probation. Dzigan and Shumacher's acceptance as Israeli artists depended, more than anything else, on their agreeing to change their language.

7 Conclusion

Language as an indicator of nationality is a common phenomenon in forming the modern nation-state. Language – like culture, race, or religion – was, as Elie Kedourie claimed, one of the signs in defining the national identity of communities and enabling the distinction between one national group and another.[32] Dzigan and Shumacher did not accept Israeli society's demand that they be "absorbed" into it by means of its language. They chose to maintain their identity, and as a result, their activities became activities of resistance, a linguistic and cultural heresy. The use of the Łódź dialect, the vernacular language, against the standard language in the Yiddish theater in Israel (as well as in Eastern Europe, the Soviet Union, Europe, North and South America), was a subversive political decision that characterized the discourse of the artists and defined them as "others." To speak in Yiddish allowed the artists, as well as the public, to be in another place. It stressed the non-belonging to the place and time where the performative practice was taking place. Yiddish speech on and off-stage was, for Dzigan and

---

30 Asher Naor, "Erev im Dzigan veShumacher," *Herut*, January 9, 1953.
31 Naor, "Dzigan veShumacher vehahumor haisraeli," *Herut*, October 14, 1955.
32 See Elie Kedourie, "Nationalism and Self-Determination," in *Nationalism*, ed. John Hutchinson and Anthony D. Smith (Oxford: Oxford University Press, 1994), 49–55.

Shumacher, a practice of an elective diaspora, a practice of their cultural and linguistic autonomy. This was especially poignant in Israel, where the paradigm of the "negation of exile" (*shlilat-ha-gola*)[33] considered Yiddish speech and Yiddish theater as a counter-practice to the Zionist project. To perform in Yiddish in Israel was to accept and affirm the diaspora, speaking as the equivalent to wandering. David Roskies described the Jewish inhabitants of Sholem Aleichem's world with the sentence "I talk, therefore I am." I would suggest a different version of that phrase to describe the world of Dzigan and Shumacher's performance in Israel: "I talk (in Yiddish), therefore I am (in exile)."[34] Dzigan and Shumacher's theater is the destination and the means to achieve it.

Since their return to Poland after World War II, Dzigan and Shumacher were in a virtual state of homelessness, a state in which identity, according to Gupta and Fergusson, becomes deterritorialized, or is in a constant flux between territories.[35] This literally was Dzigan and Shumacher's situation between the time when they left their Warsaw homes in September 1939 and bought their own homes in Tel Aviv nineteen years later. In the meanwhile, they lived in temporary homes, such as hotel rooms and short-term rental apartments in different countries. They finally did buy houses in Tel Aviv in 1958, but their only stable residence, their last refuge, was the stage, a Noah's Ark. An island in the territory of *Yiddishland* that continued to shrink around them.

Dzigan and Shumacher separated in 1960. Shumacher died in 1961 and Dzigan continued to appear with his satirical theater in Yiddish in Israel and abroad until his death in 1980.

Bibliography

Adamian, N. "Tours of the Bialystok Theater of Miniatures in Yerevan." *Kommunist* (Yerevan), April 12, 1941. [Russian]

Carlebach, Azriel. "Dzigan veShumacher." *Maariv*, May 2, 1950.

Dzigan, Shimon. *Dizgan-albom in vort un bild: 35-yor stsenishe tetykayt fun Shimen Dzigan*. Tel Aviv: Strud, 1964.

---

[33] See Ofer Shiff, ed., *Israeli Exiles: Homeland and Exile in Israeli Discourse I, Iyunim Bi-tkumat Israel*, vol. 10 (2015) [Hebrew].

[34] David G. Roskies, *Against the Apocalypse: Responses to Catastrophe in Modern Jewish Culture* (Cambridge: Harvard University Press, 1984), 163.

[35] James Ferguson and Akhil Gupta, "Beyond 'Culture': Space, Identity, and the Politics of Difference," *Cultural Anthropology* 7 (1992): 9–10.

Dzigan, Shimon. *Der koyekh fun yiddishn humor.* Tel Aviv: Aroysgegebn durkh dem gezelshaftlekhn komitet tsu fayern 40 yor tetikayt fun Shimon Dzigan oyf der Yiddisher bine, 1974.
Ferguson, James and Akhil Gupta. "Beyond 'Culture': Space, Identity, and the Politics of Difference." *Cultural Anthropology* 7 (1992): 9–10.
Fishman, Joshua A. *Yiddish: Turning to Life.* Amsterdam: John Benjamins Publishing Company, 1991.
Kats, Gregory. "Workers of All Countries, Unite!" *Hammer [МОЛОТ[* (Rostov), March 22, 1941. [Russian]
Kedourie, Elie. "Nationalism and Self-Determination." In *Nationalism.* Edited by John Hutchinson and Anthony D. Smith, 49–55. Oxford: Oxford University Press, 1994.
Leneman, Leon. "Abi men zet zikh." *Keneder odler*, September 6, 1949.
Miron, Dan. "The Dark Side of Sholem Aleichem's Laughter." *Derekh Judaica Urbinatensia* 1 (2003): 16–55.
Naor, Asher. "Dzigan veShumacher vehahumor haisraeli." *Herut*, October 14, 1955.
Naor, Asher. "Erev im Dzigan veShumacher." *Herut*, January 9, 1953.
Nudelman, Moyshe. "Kleynkunst- un marionetn-teaters tsvishn beyde velt-milkhomes." In *Yiddisher teater in eyrope tsvishn beyde velt-milkhomets (material tsu der geshikhte fun yiddishn teater): Poyln.* Edited by Itsik Manger, Jonas Turkov, and Moyshe Perenson, 152–163. New York: Alveltlekher Yiddisher Kultur-Kongres, 1968.
Prilutsky, Noah. "Di bine-shprakh." *Yiddish-teater* 1, no. 2 (1927): 129–144.
Pulaver, Moyshe. *Ararat un lodzer tipn.* Tel Aviv: Y.L. Perets, 1972.
Rojansky, Rachel. "Ben-Gurion's Attitude to Yiddish in the 1950s." *Iyunim bitkumat Israel* 15 (2005): 463–482. [Hebrew]
Roskies, David G. *Against the Apocalypse: Responses to Catastrophe in Modern Jewish Culture.* Cambridge, MA: Harvard University Press, 1984.
Samoilov, I. "'Singing and Dancing': Tour of the Bialystok Jewish Theater of Miniatures." *Baku Worker [Бакинский рабочий]* (Baku), September 10, 1940. [Russian]
Shiff, Ofer, ed. *Israeli Exiles: Homeland and Exile in Israeli Discourse I. Iyunim Bi-tkumat Israel* 10 (2015). [Hebrew]
Segalovitsh, Zusman, "Di 'samerodne' yatn … vegn 'ararat'." *Der Moment* (Warsaw), October 14, 1934.
Shandler, Jeffrey. *Adventures in Yiddishland: Postvernacular Language & Culture.* Berkeley: University of California Press, 2006.
Shlomi, Chana. "Ha-hitargenut shel Sridey ha-yehudim be-polin le-achar milchemet ha-olam ha-shniya, 1944–1950." In *Kium ve-shever – yehudei polin le-doroteyhem.* Edited by Israel Bartal and Israel Gutman, 532–538. Jerusalem: Shazar Center for Jewish History, 1997.
Zhitlovsky, Haym. *Geklibene verk.* Edited by Yudl Mark. New York: Tsiko, 1955.

Part 3: **Language in Exile**

Stefani Hoffman
The World as Exile and the Word as Homeland in the Writing of Boris Khazanov

> Emigration is like crossing the Red Sea, "glancing with horror and delight at the parting water."
>
> – B. Khazanov, *Mif Rossii* (Myth of Russia)

> Isn't emigration the ideal model of creativity, the ideal situation for a writer?
>
> – B. Khazanov, "Veter Izgnaniia" (Wind of Exile)

Exile once meant displacement from one's native land, but in modern times it has acquired multiple, occasionally positive, meanings with political, literary, and metaphysical dimensions. To some, humankind in the modern world exists in a state of exile from some primordial wholeness. After the collapse of the Soviet Union and Russia's reversion to a national state, former Soviet Jewish writers find that the issue of exile has become particularly complex. Is the person who left his homeland because of persecution still an exile if he remains abroad when circumstances permit return? On the other hand, if the individual returns, might he still feel like an exile in his original homeland, which, in effect, has become a different country?[1] Exile can thus turn into a borderline situation that provides insights into alienation and integration.

Jews are the archetypal people of exile: in the very first chapters, the Bible records Adam's expulsion from the Garden of Eden and continues through the book of Genesis with the patriarchs' wanderings to and from the Promised Land.[2] Here, too, the situation has become more complex. A third term, diaspora, or *tfutsot* in Hebrew, mediates between the Jews' ancient homeland – *Eretz Yisrael* – and exile as banishment – *galut*. Indeed, many modern commentators regard diaspora as the quintessential or preferred Jewish condition, positing it as a more enlightened, cosmopolitan state of being in contrast to what they perceive as a

---

[1] See Lisa Ryoko Wakamiya, *Locating Exiled Writers in Contemporary Russian Literature: Exiles at Home* (New York: Palgrave, Macmillan, 2009).
[2] For a sampling of contemporary writers' reflections on Jewish exile, see Alvin H. Rosenfeld, ed., *The Writer Uprooted: Contemporary Jewish Exile Literature* (Bloomington: Indiana University Press, 2008).

narrower nationalistic one tied to identification with the State of Israel.³ Some critics view the diaspora Jew as the paradigm of modern human existence.⁴

In this essay, I will examine the many interrelated themes of exile and homeland in the work of a contemporary Russian-Jewish writer, Boris Khazanov (pseudonym for Gennadii Faibusovich, b. 1928). His writing and life exemplify the many subtleties embedded in these terms and the transformations in meaning that they have undergone. Universal and specifically Jewish elements intertwine in his works. I will focus on his views concerning exile and homeland in relation to the Russian intelligentsia, language and creativity, and identity – Jewish and other – and his images and motifs as illustrative examples.

1 The Internal Exile of the Intelligentsia

Exile was a significant component of Khazanov's life even when he was growing up in the Soviet Union. The Soviet regime created internal exiles out of intellectuals who rejected the authoritarian *diktat*. While a student at the philological faculty of Moscow State University, he was arrested in 1949 for anti-Soviet behavior⁵ and sentenced to eight years in a strict regime labor camp. He was released in 1955 after Stalin's death. The physical exile left an indelible mark on his psyche: it deepened his alienation not only from the regime but also from the Russian *narod* (people) and from ethnic Russian intellectuals who worshiped the *narod*.

Fearing re-arrest because of his inherent antagonism to the regime, Khazanov decided to abandon the humanities and pursue a career that might be useful if he was sent back to the camps. He therefore studied medicine at a provincial university. While serving as a doctor in the provinces, he started "writing for the drawer" (in other words, composing works that could not be published in the

---

3 Daniel and Jonathan Boyarin, for instance, advocate "a privileging of Diaspora" in their essay "Diaspora: Generation and the Ground of Jewish Identity," *Critical Inquiry* 19, no. 4 (summer 1993): 693–725.
4 See, for example, Jean-Francois Lyotard's *Heidegger and "the jews,"* trans. Andreas Michel and Mark Roberts (Minneapolis: University of Minnesota Press, 1977) and a discussion of the topic in Vivian Liska, "Exile as Experience and Metaphor: From Celan to Badiou," in *German-Jewish Thought and Its Afterlife: A Tenuous Legacy* (Bloomington and Indianapolis: Indiana University Press, 2017).
5 He was arrested despite having already torn up a diary in which he had made unfavorable comments about Stalin. He notes they were four students, of whom three were Jews. The fourth, the informer, was the son of a member of the secret police ("Ponedel'nik roz," *Rodniki i kamni*, 72; http://imwerden.de/pdf/khazanov_rodniki_i_kamni.pdf).

Soviet Union because they would not pass the censorship). Upon his return to Moscow in the 1950s, he continued this clandestine activity while writing openly for medical journals.

In the 1970s, Khazanov participated in the most prominent Jewish *samizdat*[6] journal of that time, *Jews in the USSR*, contributing both fiction and essays. At that time, when many fellow Jews were leaving the USSR, which he compared to a sinking ship and an Augean stable with no Hercules to clean it out, Khazanov also contemplated emigration. In a notable article, "New Russia," published in 1974, he rejected that option because of his love for the Russian language, which he declared was his only homeland.[7] A few years later, however, when his *samizdat* activity entangled him with the KGB, he decided to leave the country rather than face another arrest and internal exile.

To the surprise of those familiar with his writing on various Jewish topics, in 1982, Khazanov chose to immigrate to Germany rather than to Israel. He alluded to his exposure from an early age to the German language, literature, and philosophy,[8] the desire to provide his son with a European education, and the possibility of finding work.[9] At the same time, he noted the special, complex aspects of a Jew living in Germany, "precisely here from whence destruction threatened me and those like me."[10] Having settled in Munich, Khazanov has continued to write fiction and essays in Russian. Some of his works have been translated into German and French, but very little into English. He has returned to Russia to visit and accept a literary award and has traveled to Israel and other places in Europe. In his writing, he has touched on the question of returning to live in Russia but firmly rejected it for reasons that I shall discuss later.

By identifying with the Russian intelligentsia, Khazanov embedded himself in a traditional Russian homeland/exile dichotomy. Just as their spiritual ancestors had felt alienated in the autocratic tsarist Russian Empire, so, too, the modern intelligentsia counterparts felt estranged in Soviet reality. In Khazanov's words, "I was an exile long before I left the country."[11] As advocates of individualism,

---

6 *Samizdat* works were primitively reproduced items that circumvented the official censorship.
7 Boris Khazanov, "Novaia Rossiia," *Evrei v SSSR*, no. 7 (May–June 1974), reprinted in *Evreiskii samizdat* (Hebrew University of Jerusalem, The Centre for Research and Documentation of East European Jewry, 1976), 10: 113.
8 John Glad, ed., *Conversations in Exile: Russian Writers Abroad* (Durham, NC: Duke University Press, 1993), 117; "Ponedel'nik roz," 93. He mentioned on several occasions that he attended a German-language kindergarten in Moscow.
9 Khazanov, *Mif Rossii* (New York: Liberty Publishing House, 1986), 160.
10 Ibid., 177.
11 "Ponedel'nik roz," 79. On the same page, he noted that even when he was happily at home with his family, he felt as if he were "on leave."

personal morality, and the rule of law, usually with an element of spirituality and a pro-Western or cosmopolitan outlook, the intelligentsia by their very nature represented a challenge to the regime whether or not they expressed open dissent. Clashes with the regime often resulted in arrest, meaning internal exile or exile abroad. In the nineteenth century, for example, the Western-leaning Alexander Herzen spent the last decades of his life in Europe, where he was free to publicize his socialist ideas in the hope they would attract a following in his homeland. In the Soviet period, Khazanov was one of several writers and poets whom the Soviet regime expelled, often after they had already served a term in Soviet prison camps.[12]

Khazanov's fiction abounds in intelligentsia figures who endure exile, often in the form of alienation within their society. In the novel *Nagl'far in the Ocean of Times*,[13] the enigmatic Tolia Baktarev, whose death is presaged in the opening chapter, represents a Soviet version of the nineteenth-century superfluous hero unable to find a meaningful role in society.[14] The writer mocks the traditional obsessions with the intelligentsia, the Jews, and the Russian Idea in depicting a card game at which the players pompously and vacuously discuss these issues.[15] In the novella "Antivremia" (Anti-time), the father of the anonymous youthful hero, himself an *intelligent* (individual member of the intelligentsia), former revolutionary, and Jew, launches into a tirade, berating the intelligentsia for supporting the Bolshevik revolution; Russia, he says, is merely another place of exile, and he urges his son to immigrate with him to the Jews' true homeland, Palestine.[16]

In certain prose works, Khazanov sharply negates the view often found among the intelligentsia that the Russian folk or *narod* constitute the very essence of the Russian homeland.[17] Interestingly, in the nineteenth century, a worshipful attitude toward the Russian people characterized not only those with Slavophile leanings such as Dostoevsky, who saw the *narod* as a "god-bearing" people, but also Westerners such as Herzen, who regarded the *narod* as potential precursors of a socialist commune. In the twentieth century, Alexander Solzhenitsyn stood at the head of a renewed "*pochvenniki*" [soil-based] and "village writers" movement

---

12 See, for example, the essays in Joseph Brodsky, *Less than One: Selected Essays* (London and New York: Penguin Books, 1986).
13 Khazanov, *Nagl'far v okeane vremen* (Moscow: Tekst, 1993).
14 Khazanov later wrote that the figure of Bakhtarev, originally conceived as the hero of the story, introduces "the undying, but always somehow subterranean, semi-existing order of the Russian intelligentsia" ("Ponedel'nik roz," 95).
15 Khazanov, *Nagl'far*, 88.
16 Khazanov, *Chas korolia. Antivremia* (Moscow: Slovo, 1991), 246–47.
17 See the essay "Russkaia intelligentsia" (1982), available on the site http://www.borischasanow.imwerden.de/. In later sections, I shall elaborate on Khazanov's cultural, linguistic approach to the concept of homeland and his equating of *intelligent* and Jew.

that glorified the Russian *narod* and its attachment to the land. The post-Soviet period, with its emphasis on Russian nationalism, has seen a resurgence of such views. Advocates of these views tend to espouse some degree of antisemitism, and regard Jews as rootless outsiders and usurpers who tried – and succeeded in the Bolshevik Revolution – in ruining the Russian motherland.[18] These attitudes bring to mind certain European-based fascist views or Heidegger's emphasis on the importance of the "soil" for the German people. Indeed, noting a similarity between German Romantic notions of the people and idealization of the peasantry with its Russian counterpart, Khazanov warns that a yearning for "the provincial, the soil, and national roots prepares the ground for the sin of fascist ideas."[19]

Khazanov's labor camp experience reinforced his abhorrence of this view of "homeland" and his disenchantment with the Russian *narod*.[20] In a work published after his emigration to Germany, *The Myth of Russia*, he faults the traditional intelligentsia for sacrificing its own values to a belief that only the *narod* possesses the truth about life.[21] Other intellectuals of Jewish origin similarly contested this glorification of the *narod* and, by extension, exclusion of the Jews from a deserved place in the Russian historical narrative. For example, in articles published abroad in the 1970s and in Russia of the *perestroika* period, Khazanov's friend Grigorii Pomerants, the essayist and scholar of religious thought, disparaged the land-based worship of the Russian *narod*, praising the Jews' diaspora model of rootlessness as more productive.[22] In his memoirs, Pomerants described the despair evoked in him by Solzhenitsyn's negative portrayal of Jews in *The First Circle*. The insinuation that Jews as a group were not truly patriotic, he wrote, made him feel that he had no future in the country.[23]

---

18 For a discussion of this topic in the late Soviet and post-Soviet period, see Judith Devlin, *Slavophiles and Commissars: Enemies of Democracy in Modern Russia* (London: Macmillan Press, 1999; and Vadim Rossman, *Russian Intellectual Antisemitism in the Post-Communist Era* (Lincoln and London: University of Nebraska Press, 2002).
19 Khazanov, "Pis'mo iz prekrasnogo daleka," *Iskusstvo kino* 5 (1990): 113.
20 See his article written while still in Russia, "Idushchii po vode" (Walking on water). In his review of Aleksandr Voronel's reflective memoir, *The Tremor of Judaic Concerns*, Khazanov harshly condemns worship of the *narod* and asserts that the Jews themselves became the intelligentsia after the disappearance of the Russian strain (Khazanov, "Idushchii po vode," *Evrei v SSSR* 11 [December 1975], reprinted in *Jewish Samizdat* (1977), 12: 209). For a further discussion of this topic see the section "Jewishness and Exile" in this essay.
21 Khazanov, *Mif Rossii*, 133.
22 Grigorii Pomerants, "Chelovek niotkuda," *Neopublikovannoe* (Frankfurt am Main: Posev, 1972), 123–75; Pomerants, "Problema Volanda," *Vykhod iz transa* (Moscow: Iurist, 1995), 146–202.
23 Grigorii Pomerants, *Zapiski gadkogo utenka* (Moscow: ROSSPEN, 2003), 226. See the article by Jonathan Frankel, "Solzhenitsyn and National Guilt" for an examination of Solzhenitsyn's ideas in his work *Two Hundred Years Together* about the Jews' negative role in the formation

2 Language as Homeland

In contrast to the soil-based Russian homeland model, Khazanov envisions "homeland" in terms of language and culture; in this context, however, his views evolved after his departure from the USSR. In the 1970s, when Khazanov rejected the idea of joining his fellow Jews in emigrating, he declared: "I cannot imagine myself in an environment where Russian speech is silent. For me, the Russian language is my sole fatherland. I can reside only in this invisible city."[24] He admitted, however, that such an attachment to language was typically Jewish.

Language, in Khazanov's exposition, not only forms the basis of a homeland, but it also underlies the foundation of the world itself. In a speech that he delivered upon receiving a literary prize in Heidelberg in 1998 (Hilde-Domin Preis für Literatur im Exil), Khazanov alluded to a kabbalistic postulate asserting that God created the world out of the twenty-two letters of the Hebrew alphabet. He added, however, that creation is a continuous act, suggesting that the writer participates in it: "From sentences and words, from letters of the alphabet, the world of our memory is constructed and the letters on the stone under which I shall lie will signify something larger than the name engraved on it."[25]

In the above speech, Khazanov briefly mentioned a hasidic legend that he had previously incorporated into a story written while he was still in Russia.[26] Notions of exile and language figure prominently in "The Besht or the Fourth Person of the Verb." The work features an anonymous main character called "the writer" – who shares certain biographical details with the author and the same initials, B. Kh. – but language itself is the real "hero" of the narrative. The story interweaves events in the life of the writer B. Kh. and a fable about the Besht, the legendary founder of the hasidic movement, known also as the Baal Shem Tov (from the Hebrew, literally, master of the good name), whose idealized picture hangs on the wall of the writer's communal Moscow apartment of the 1970s. The

---

of Bolshevik Russia (*Insiders and Outsiders: Dilemmas of East European Jewry*, ed. Richard I. Cohen, Jonathan Frankel, and Stefani Hoffman [Oxford and Portland, OR: Littman Library, 2010], 166–87). In an allusion to *Two Hundred Years Together*, Khazanov himself criticized Solzhenitsyn for thinking that he was justified in dividing guilt equally between Jews and Russians and for assigning collective guilt. "In fact, the principle of collective guilt and collective retribution is false, if not immoral," he declared ("Literaturnyi muzei: Iz devnika pisatelia," *Oktiabr*, no. 10 [2004], http://magazines.russ.ru/october/2004/10/ha14-pr.html).

24 Khazanov, "Novaia Rossiia," 114.
25 Khazanov, "Bukvyi," *Polnolunie* (Munich: ImWerdenVerlag, 2007; available on the site https://imwerden.de).
26 The story was published in the Israeli Russian-language journal *22*: "Besht ili chetvertoe litso glagola," *22*, no. 22 (1981): 78–107.

hasidic tale relates that, as punishment for his desire to hasten the coming of the Messiah, the Besht and his disciple are whisked away to a deserted island. Both have forgotten all words and thus are unable to say a prayer that would return them to their native town. The disciple, however, recalls the initial letters of the alphabet, and together the two men recall, first, all the letters, then words and phrases, enabling the Rebbe to piece together the incantation that returns them from exile to their home.

The omniscient narrator compares the figure of the writer in the story to the divine creator, facing the nothingness of the blank page from which he must create his own world. The writer, however, like the Besht, rebels against the existing order, and he too, suffers punishment. One morning, while he is working on a novella, KGB operatives burst into his apartment to search it, turning everything upside down, and "arresting" the novella in progress. The narrator suggests that the writer recognizes a deeper meaning behind the KGB's raid: it is retribution "for competition with God ... and ambiguity of creation ..." (106). When the narrator visits the writer later, he inquires whether the author remembers anything about his novella. He responds sharply, "Not a word" and adds after a questioning look, "Just the alphabet" (107).

In the intertwined hasidic and Moscow tales, man is exiled from his habitual world and deprived of language as punishment for rebellion – in the former case by the divine being and in the latter by the authoritarian regime that confiscates the writer's work. The individual preserves, however, the possibility of returning "home" as long as he retains the capacity to construct the world anew from its building blocks – language.

Of all the issues facing an exiled writer in a new country, language presents the greatest problem. Who is the readership? Separated from the source of one's native language, is the author destined metaphorically to run dry? An additional concern in the Soviet period was the regime's attempt to erase all traces of the disgraced exile: Khazanov wrote, "I no longer existed; therefore, everything, let's say, that I wrote was removed from the libraries; everything that I did was never done."[27]

From the time of his departure from the USSR, Khazanov's writing about language and exile is suffused with antithetical emotions conveying feelings of rupture and dislocation on the one hand and connection on the other. More than once, he compares emigration to jumping over a campfire or crossing the Red

---

[27] "Nemetskii epilog: neotpravlennoe pis'mo," *Rodniki i kamni* (Munich: ImWerden Verlag, 2008) (E-book *Rodniki odinochestva*, 2008), 164.

Sea, "with horror and delight glancing at the parting water."[28] Once he leaves Russia, he contends that there is no collective "we" representing the Russian emigration. Although united by a "feeling of loss and the great, sluggish language carried with you like a sack," now "you can represent only yourself."[29]

Whereas in the 1970s the Russian language anchored Khazanov in the Soviet Union, in the 1980s emigration offered the only possibility of remaining true to himself and to literature. After being stripped and deprived of all other valuables before departure, language was the sole treasure that he was able to take with him into exile. "The sole and ineradicable fatherland which the exile brings with him is language."[30] It has its dangers, however: "The blessing of the emigrant writer, his native tongue – is simultaneously his prison. He does not realize right away that he has dragged his cell with him."[31] Khazanov warns, moreover, of the danger of becoming a fossil. Almost every emigrant writer, he notes, tries to preserve the language he brought with him. "Involuntarily, he becomes a purist, and his readers (if, in general there are readers) receive food from him, so to speak, from cans. It seems to him that his native language in his motherland ... is becoming spoiled, decaying, vulgarized, and cheapened."[32]

Khazanov, nevertheless, finds benefits accruing to the exiled writer. Clearly taking a stand against the current Russian nationalist school, Khazanov asserts: "The Russian writer is not the one who is obliged to glorify the motherland; the Russian writer is the one who defends, no matter what the cost, the dignity of the Russian language."[33] In another article, he declares, "Taking into consideration what kind of country that was, you should be proud that they drove you out. They expelled you so that you could remain what you could not be in Russia: a Russian writer."[34]

Moreover, although Khazanov rejects Dostoevsky's contention that the Russian soul is inherently capable of universal understanding, he maintains that living and traveling in Europe, exposed him – and other exiled Russian writers – to broader horizons than those accessible to their counterparts in their former homeland, thus enriching their work.[35]

---

28 Khazanov, *Mif Rossii*, 154.
29 Ibid., 13.
30 Khazanov, "Veter izgnaniia," *Polnolunie*, 14.
31 Ibid.
32 Khazanov, "Literaturnyi muzei: Iz devnika pisatelia."
33 Ibid.
34 Ibid.
35 Khazanov, "Exsilium," *Novyi mir* 12 (1994), http://magazines.russ.ru/novyi_mi/1994/12/hazan.html. To bolster his arguments, he cites the work of Gogol in Rome, Turgenev in Paris, and Dostoevsky in Dresden ("Veter izgnaniia," 17).

Khazanov generalizes beyond the experience of a Russian emigrant: "The writer by his nature is a marginal being; the writer is an emigrant everywhere and hardly able to create anything worthwhile, while floundering in 'the thick of life.'"[36] From Munich, he wrote to his Moscow friend Grigorii Pomerants, "Evidently, I am to a great degree an individualist, to a great degree an 'emigrant,' no matter where I would live, in Russia or abroad."[37] In another essay, after remarking that Germany has become his home and that he realized "exile and bondage were my motherland," he adds, "Nevertheless ... exile is not our private theme, yours or mine. It is the topic of the twentieth century."[38]

The emigrant writer, living in an alien environment without a perceptible audience, experiences this universal condition of exile more strongly than any other individual does. Despite these hardships, however, the writer still feels the imperative to create.[39] Khazanov comments ironically: "Can one ask – or is it that same arrogance of outcasts [apostates] – can one turn the question upside down: isn't emigration the ideal model for creativity, the ideal situation for a writer?"[40]

3 The End of Exile?

The fall of the Soviet Union introduced new issues for writers in exile who were now able to return to Russia. Some, including famous authors such as Alexander Solzhenitsyn and Vasilii Aksenov, indeed, did return, but this often entailed encountering new problems of identity, belonging, and language.[41] Khazanov occasionally visited the new Russia, but he resolutely rejected the idea of returning to live there. For him, "exile is a life-time brand, there are such ineradicable stigmata. Exile, if you will, is an existential category."[42] In numerous articles, he emphatically reiterates his loathing of the grim totalitarian state that he left behind and the residual nightmares from his incarceration there. He told John Glad in an interview published in 2000, however, that his not returning was more

---

36 Ibid.
37 Cited by John Glad in "Iz besed," http/magazines.russ.ru/volga/2000/4/glad-pr.html.
38 Khazanov, "Literaturnyi muzei."
39 On a return visit to Moscow, Khazanov told an interviewer: "You [i.e., Khazanov himself] write in a language that no one understands. But all the same, I write" (*Literaturnaia gazeta*, April 19, 1995, 5).
40 Khazanov, "Veter izgnaniia," 18.
41 See Wakamiya, introduction to *Locating Exiled Writers in Contemporary Russian Literature*, 1–25.
42 Khazanov, "Veter izgnaniia," 13.

than just a matter of his lack of faith in Russian democracy.⁴³ For him, his former homeland had turned into "*chuzhbina*" (an alien land). The language of the street was no longer the Russian language in which he felt comfortable. During a visit to Moscow in 2010, an interviewer asked whether he longed for Moscow. He replied: "This city is a palimpsest for me. A manuscript written on some other old manuscript." Expressing amazement that the overburdened city still functions, he summed up: "In short, in the city where I grew up, I do not feel at home; I am a guest, a peripheral person."⁴⁴

Significantly, Khazanov, who emigrated when he was already in his fifties, did not try to write in the language of his new home, an option that has been successfully adopted by younger emigrants such as Gary Shteyngart, writing in English in the United States or Andreï Makine, writing in French in France. These writers generally are not properly "exiles," although constraining circumstances may have led to their departure. Rather, they may be seen as part of a transnational diaspora, often both Russian and Jewish.⁴⁵ In a work about Russian emigrant authors in France, Germany, the United States, and Israel who write in the local language, Adrian Wanner points out that their characters and settings tend to be Russian immigrant communities, the former Soviet Union, or post-Soviet Russia. Whereas exiled writers during the Soviet period tended to view themselves as preserving the true Russian culture, Wanner notes, "A more postmodern, self-conscious construction of Russianness for foreign consumption is characteristic of many members of the current post-Soviet diaspora."⁴⁶ Khazanov also comments on this paradoxical self-construct: "This fellow, the Russian writer, once he is abroad, most often no longer regards himself as a former outcast; on the contrary, 'here' he represents Russia or, at least, he imagines himself as a representative of Russia even though 'there,' he was a spiritual alien."⁴⁷

Although Khazanov, as noted above, never considered returning permanently or writing in a language other than Russian, nevertheless, his situation intersects with that of some of the above authors; the physical borders of exile

---

43 Glad, "Iz besed."
44 Maiia Bel'enkaia, "Boris Khazanov: Khoroshaia kniga utoliaet gorech' zhizni," *Novaia gazeta*, November 12, 2010, http://www.novayagazeta.ru/arts/876.html.
45 For works that discuss the transnational nature of Jews from the former Soviet Union/Russia, see Larissa Remennick, *Jews on Three Continents* (New Brunswick, NJ: Transaction Publishers, 2007; and Fran Markowitz, "Emigration, Immigration and Cultural Change: Towards a Transnational Russian-Jewish Community?" in *Jews and Jewish Life in Russia and the Soviet Union*, ed. Yaacov Ro'i (Ilford: Frank Cass & Co., 1995), 403–14.
46 Adrian Wanner, *Out of Russia: Fictions of a New Translingual Diaspora* (Evanston, IL: Northwestern University Press, 2011), 9.
47 Glad, "Iz besed."

have been effaced. He, too, is no longer in enforced exile but has chosen to remain in Germany and has absorbed some of the non-Russian attitudes there. In reacting to a Russian religious colleague who called him a "Western writer writing in Russian," Khazanov admits there may be some truth to that if he had in mind "irony, skepticism, religious indifference, distrust in pathos, something like that."[48]

Like his younger contemporaries abroad, Khazanov lauds the benefit of distance from his native land, asserting that it sharpens one's vision. Distance, can, however, also distort reality and time frames. Khazanov remarks that the emigrant writer no longer lives in the same present as his contemporaries in his native land; if he tries to remain in this actual time, he will run aground. Deprived of the present, the emigrant writer looks toward the past and memory: "Emigrant prose, like Lot's wife, is unable to turn its gaze from the past. The paradox, however, is that the past may turn out to be more long-lived than the present."[49] If, however, the writer seeks refuge in "internal" time, in memory, then he can turn the distortion of distance into something eternal and literary. In an approach that is both postmodern and exilic, time consists of subjective fragments that Khazanov pieces together – not necessarily chronologically – in his works.[50] One sees this in his fiction where dream and reality, past and present merge, often indistinguishably (as, for example, in "Anti-time," *Nagl'far*, "The Miracle Maker" ["Chudotvorets"], or "North of the Future" ["K severu ot budushchego"]).

Distance and alienation provoke issues of identity that can have a positive literary effect, as Wanner contends in his analysis of a work in French by Makine: "The double perspective of the person who is both an out- and insider, rather than leading to a schizophrenic alienation from reality, creates here a sort of stereoscopic vision, an enriched and fuller perception than the one accessible to the monolingual native speaker."[51] Even though he continued writing in Russian, Khazanov continually explored the theme of a double perspective in his works. In

---

48 Ibid.
49 Khazanov, "Veter izgnaniia," *Polnolunie*, 17. It is worth noting in this context that much of Khazanov's prose in the last five years is a mixture of literary and philosophical reflections interspersed with recollections of the Moscow of his youth. A return visit to Moscow sometimes stimulates these thoughts.
50 In an essay titled "Literary Museum: From a Writer's Diary" ("Literaturnyi muzei"), Khazanov wrote: "What I have written has the appearance of finished things. But if you take a good look – it's a pile of debris." Perhaps Khazanov, who was familiar with the works of Walter Benjamin, is alluding to Benjamin's essay "Angel of History," which offers an interpretation of Paul Klee's painting *Angelus Novus*. Benjamin comments that what the ordinary observer perceives as a connected chain of events, the backward-looking angel sees as a constantly growing heap of rubble.
51 Wanner, 33.

some cases, twin characters accentuate this duality. This is particularly noticeable in "Anti-time," where, as Khazanov notes "the principle of mirroring is carried out, perhaps too expressly, throughout the entire book."[52] Two of the main characters, both friends of the "hero-narrator" of the story, are male and female twins with the same name. The narrator, as Khazanov explained, has two fathers – a stepfather who raised him and represents the Russian side of his personality and a Jewish biological father who in his youth succumbed to the Russian revolutionary temptation but later meets his son and tries to win him over to his Jewish half.[53]

4 Return from Exile

Another facet of the writer-exile question is the case of writers who did, in fact, return to Russia. Does return to the homeland, either temporary or permanent, lead to a change in point of view, distinct from those who remained abroad and from those who never left the homeland?

In this context, it is worth comparing two novels – *Nagl'far* by Khazanov who, as already noted, chose to remain abroad after the collapse of the Soviet Union, and *Moskva Kva-Kva* by Vasilii Aksenov (1932–2009), who lived abroad after being deprived of Soviet citizenship in 1980 and decided, in the 1990s, to split his time between Russia and France. Certain striking similarities exist between the two works. Both deal with apartment buildings in Moscow in which the authors lived – Khazanov in the 1930s and Aksenov in the 1950s – and both have a distant mythic and ironic quality about them. The individuals in the tales represent Soviet types. In Khazanov's *Nagl'far*, the *intelligent*, the Soviet bureaucrat, the house informer, the peasant writer, the former villager, and so forth; at the same time, the author undercuts this typology by saying that each resident did not think he was a type but an exception.[54] In contrast to the average citizens in Khazanov's story, Aksenov's characters belong mainly to the Soviet elite and, symbolically, live in a building adorned with sculptures of the classical gods.[55] Aksenov emphasizes their unusualness by giving them names that derive from

---

52 Khazanov, "Ponedel'nik roz," 88. In this essay, Khazanov relates that some of the events in the novella were "plagiarized" from his own life, whereas others are borrowed from literary sources.
53 Ibid.
54 Khazanov, *Nagl'far*, 114–15.
55 Vasilii Aksenov, *Moskva Kva-Kva* (Moscow: Eksmo, 2006). A roman à clef describing Aksenov's life among the intellectual Moscow elite of the 1960s (the group referred to as the *shestidesiatniki* [the sixtiers]) was published posthumously, *Tainstvennaia strast'* (Mysterious passion) (Moscow: Sem' dnei, 2009).

mythology or whose meaning suggests artifice. The exemplary Soviet couple of the 1950s, for example, are Ariadna and Kseravii (Caesar) Novotkannoi (literally "newly woven"); their beautiful pro-Stalinist daughter is named Glikeriia, suggesting the German for good fortune. The pro-Stalinist poet is called Smel'chakov, a daring one.[56] Both works feature a young, initially innocent but sexually aroused girl around whom much of the action centers.

Khazanov describes a direct personal connection to the locus of his narrative: "The building and courtyard resemble the home of my childhood in Bol'shoi Kozlovskii Alley although a phantasmagoric sheen is thrown on it."[57] In *Moskva Kva-Kva*, Aksenov teasingly attributes facts of his own biography to the narrator who is a character in the story (he has parents who were arrested and spent time in labor camps and exile; he went to medical school, likes jazz, lives in exile outside Russia and returns to Moscow in the mid-1990s), but he changes other details – the narrator lived in Brazil and returns with a Brazilian wife. The narrator's name is a sarcastic allusion to his status as the son of "non-persons" – he calls himself Tak Takovskii (so and so). In both authors' works, the point of view alternates between a narrator who is omniscient and one who is part of the collective in the narrative. Although sometimes awkward, this strategy serves to convey both a mythic distance and the immediacy of a character in the thick of events.

Khazanov's story is replete with grimness and finality. The Islandic legend underlying *Nagl'far* foretells an apocalyptic time when a flood will unmoor the ship *Nagl'far*, constructed of the fingernails and toenails of dead people, and it will sail over the flooded land. There is no return; the *Nagl'far* of his Soviet world is doomed from the start. The book opens with the never fully explained death of the hero Baktarev[58] and the information that the building in the story, later described as a microcosm of the Soviet world, was totally destroyed by a bomb in World War II. The building-ship, constructed of dead matter, sails away into eternity. Individual personages also disappear, such as the girl's grandfather, the prototypical wandering Jew; her father already disappeared in the purges. In fact, the narrator states, "Along with the building, under its ruins, disappeared

---

[56] The name perhaps also contains an allusion to Iaroslav Smeliakov (1913–1972), a poet of proletarian origin, who fought in World War II, served the regime in various administrative positions, and was thrice awarded by it.
[57] Khazanov, "Ponedel'nik roz," 94.
[58] Khazanov later describes him as "the son of his country and epoch, the embodiment of impotence and disorder" ("Iz veshchestva togo zhe," *V sadakh za ognennoi rekoi* [2012], 78, http://imwerden.de/pdf/khazanov_v_sadakh_za_ognennoj_rekoj_2014.pdf).

the memory of its inhabitants, about everything that lived, trembled, dreamt and pottered around on the stairs, and in the apartments."[59]

In Aksenov's novel, in contrast, there is more continuity than rupture. In a short final chapter, the narrator not only returns to post-Soviet Russia, but he also revisits the towering building of his youth, which still stands, although commercialized in the manner of the 1990s. He paints the Soviet world of the 1950s in brighter, more glorious and majestic colors than Khazanov uses for the 1930s, but he exposes the hypocrisy of his supposedly patriotic heroes, and his depiction, especially of Stalin, is heavily laced with irony. Indeed, hypocrisy is part of the continuity of life that does not change: Ariadna, the seeming patriotic Soviet woman, in the 1990s has become a popular writer with a bestseller titled *Let's Dance in the Kremlin*; she spends most of her time in her Mediterranean villas. She and her nuclear scientist spouse now live respectively with the husband and wife team who worked in their home as housekeepers and spies. The female former spy now runs a private catering service. Perhaps Aksenov was acceding to a prevalent cynical post-Soviet mood; his novel was popular in Russia.[60]

The fictional narrator So-and-So, who hints at the author himself, by his very presence in the novel nevertheless suggests unease about the homeland that he and Aksenov left. His role in the story highlights a very unpleasant aspect of Soviet life – the world of arrests, camps, and orphaned children; his best friend, who is from the privileged caste, also winds up temporarily in the sordid prison world. This significant part of the Soviet past, and of the narrator's life, emphasizes a reality that present-day Russian society prefers to ignore.

Interestingly, in both authors' works, a mythical form of memory clothes the image of Moscow, the city of their youth; in some sense, the place is the main figure of both tales.[61] In a subsection entitled "*Bab'e leto*" (the Russian term means Indian summer, but the two words literally signify "an old dame's summer"), Aksenov writes, "But the chief dame, all the same, is Moskva Kva-Kva. She stands, spreading her colored skirts. She colors her mane on Lenin Hills, grows reddish, lily colored, and starts to turn cognac colored. Suddenly among the still warm streams, a Nordic reminder comes through with a thread of invisible silver."[62]

---

59 Khazanov, *Nagal'far*, 11.
60 In her book on returned exiles, Wakamiya notes the tricky task of "rhetorically constructing stable identities within a rapidly changing national imaginary" (*Locating Exiled Writers*, 1).
61 Khazanov wrote about *Nagl'far*: "As in 'Antivremia,' the superhero of the story is the city itself" ("Ponedel'nik roz," 94).
62 Vasilii Aksenov, *Moskva Kva-Kva* (Moscow: Eksmo, 2006), 224. The kva-kva in the title, while repeating the last syllable of the Russian word *Moskva*, also imitates a frog's croak, suggesting, perhaps, that life in the city rests on a swamp.

In the final sentences of *Nagl'far*, the postwar city of Moscow awakens to a new dawn that envelops the buildings in a tender, rosy, greenish hue. "For a moment, the city, singular and incomparable in its ugliness is improbably beautiful. Moscow, M-O-S-C ... a child reads the letters, the soul of the city arose from chaos at the moment when you first whispered that word: Moscow."[63] In both cases, city life goes on. The act of creative memory overcomes the exilic barrier of time and promises continuity in the future. Khazanov, the eternal alien, distances himself from the city he knew, but nevertheless, he envelops the site of his youthful experiences in a misty, possibly vibrant future. In keeping with Khazanov's belief in the creative power of language, it is a child reading the letters of Moscow that promises renewal.

In Aksenov's novel, the narrator, perhaps reflecting the author's own biography, returns to a transformed, brash city, but he too, remains distant. Takovskii seems to prefer the memories of his youth to the current crassness, and unlike Aksenov, he seems to be visiting, not coming back to live. Even in return, the exile seems to leave a part of himself behind.

5 One or Two Literatures?

At the time that Khazanov left the USSR in the 1980s, the Iron Curtain divided Russian-language literature into two parts: that produced in the Soviet Union and literature in exile. In the post-Soviet period, with the removal of censorship and barriers to physical movement and publishing, some critics have affirmed the existence of one transnational Russian literature that effaces the old boundaries.[64] In correspondence with fellow writer Mark Kharitonov, who remained in Russia and felt that two separate literatures had ceased to exist, Khazanov was more ambiguous, questioning whether such unity really existed.[65] He considered the question in more detail in an article, "'Fedot, but not that one': One or Two Literatures?"[66] At first, he emphasizes the cultural and linguistic differences

---

63 Khazanov, *Nagl'far*, 180.
64 For a discussion of this topic, see Inna Minaeva, "The Literature of the Russian Emigrants (the beginning of the 20th century – the beginning of the 21st century)," 75ff (in Russian), http://www.academia.edu/4134966/The_Literature_of_the_Russian_Emigrants_the_beginning_of_the_20th_century_-_the_beginning_of_the_21st_century_.
65 Mark Kharitonov, "Nam nuzhno vosstannavlivat' pamiat' (k 80-letiiu Borisa Khazanova)," *Vtoraia navigatssiia* 8 (2008): 310–11.
66 The title derives from a folk saying; the meaning here is that it, i.e., émigré literature, is the same as native Russian literature only different.

encountered by an emigrant who returns to Russia for a visit: "It turns out that over these years, without realizing it, from being a foreign Russian, he has turned into a Russian foreigner. ... Perhaps the new Russian language more than anything else reinforces the alienation."[67] He points, in particular, to the greater use of slang and swear words in speech and literature and the difference in daily experiences. He offers, however, another point of view, those who say that Russians writing abroad live in their own ghettos, barely mixing with the local population and publishing in Russia. Ultimately, he suggests the best solution is irresolution: "In the end, each Russian writer living outside of Russia resolves the question for himself. But it would be more correct to say that neither one nor the other answer – a single literature or two literatures – fully exhausts the topic. The truth lies in the middle. We are dealing with an outlandish literature. It has one body and two heads. Perhaps, that is for the best."[68]

6 Jewishness and Exile

Khazanov's attitude toward Jewry and Jewishness, as his views on other subjects, is both complex and, at times, contradictory. Here, too, motifs of exile and homeland figure prominently on the personal, theoretical, and fictional planes. Khazanov's Jewish identity was more profound than that of many typical Soviet Jewish *intelligenty* of his generation for whom its major significance was the fifth line on the Soviet passport (designating nationality) exposing one to various forms of discrimination and exclusion. Khazanov refers frequently to the presence of antisemitism in both the Soviet Union and the new Russia, but his Jewish identity encompasses many more elements than just a reaction to that phenomenon, as he noted in an article written while still in the Soviet Union. Whereas originally he had attached importance only to man's free will and independence, as he grew older, he became more aware of the national component in a person's make-up, more conscious of his own place in a chain of Jewish existence, and of his similarity to his immediate ancestors.[69] On a few occasions, he mentioned that his paternal grandfather, a tradesman living in a shtetl, was knowledgeable

---

[67] Khazanov, "'Fedot, da ne tot': odna ili dve literatury?" *Novyi zhurnal* 249 (2007), http://magazines.russ.ru/nj/2007/249/ha14.html.
[68] Ibid.
[69] Boris Khazanov, "Letters from Afar," *In Search of Self* (Jerusalem: Magnes Press, 1983), 235–38 (originally in *Sion* 20 [1977]: 43–50).

in Jewish law and from a line of adepts in Jewish learning.[70] From him, he claims, he inherited his love of the "Word, text, and writing."[71] Although Khazanov is not a religiously observant Jew, he consistently states that he does not consider himself assimilated. In the period before his emigration, he studied the Hebrew language[72] and read works of traditional Jewish sources, Jewish philosophy, and contemporary thinkers.[73]

In seeking to explain what he considers to be the essence of the Jewish people, Khazanov gives prominence to a diasporic concept of Jewry: "A certain ethnic group, a former nationality united by a common origin but dispersed around the world exists that upholds certain moral postulates in this world and the rituals that symbolize them – all of which is called culture – and in so doing, upholds itself. ... The Jews have no other bridgehead than their culture, they have no dry land, they float at sea in their little ships and carry all their possessions with them."[74]

Khazanov's views clearly resemble those of other figures in the West who regard the lack of "rootedness" as a salient feature of Jewry and even as a source of inspiration. In this respect, he is also a very typical representative of the Soviet Jewish intelligentsia of the mid-twentieth century. For example, Khazanov's friend Grigorii Pomerants, mentioned earlier in this essay, made a positive connection between the Jews' "rootlessness" (in other words, their life in the diaspora), and the rise of their unique monotheism that formed the cradle of Western religions.[75] In response to my question whether he considered the Jews as the people of exile par excellence, Khazanov wrote: "Well, the history of millennia literally affirms this. We are all descendants and inheritors of foreigners. As for

---

70 Recently, he discussed this in an interview published in the journal *Kreshchatik* in February 2016: http://magazines.russ.ru/kreschatik/2016/2/v-sumerkah-budushego.html. See also "Vzglyani na ieroglif," where he mentioned that his ancestry goes back to a contemporary of King David and the patriarch Jacob (Munich: ImWerdenVerlag, 2012, khazanov_vzglyani_na_ ieroglif_2012.pdf); also the opening of the essay "Ponedel'nik roz."
71 *Kreshchatik*, February 2016.
72 In later correspondence, he told a colleague that he had been studying Hebrew with an eighty-two year-old deputy designer of the Tupolev airliner, who descended from nine generations of rabbis (Kharitonov, "Nam nuzhno...," 303).
73 In an e-mail to this author from June 30, 2015, he mentioned, among others, the Old and New Testament, general knowledge of the Lurianic kabbalah, hasidic folklore as transmitted by Martin Buber and Elie Wiesel, the philosophy of Buber and Walter Benjamin, the poets Heinrich Heine, Paul Celan, and Vladislav Khodasevich, and Rabbi Adin Steinsaltz. He incorporates some midrashic and hasidic tales in several of his fictional works.
74 Khazanov, "Letters from Afar," 240.
75 Pomerants, *Zapiski gadkogo utenka*, 235, 248, 262, 279.

me personally, I must admit that my fate, too, impelled me to follow this ancient tradition."⁷⁶

Khazanov frequently equated the intelligentsia with the Jew in terms of attachment to Russian culture and alienation from the regime. In a review that appeared in the Jewish *samizdat* in 1975, for instance, he wrote: "I am convinced that being a Russian *intelligent* today almost inevitably means being a Jew."⁷⁷ In another essay written while still in the Soviet Union, he stated: "To me these two areas [*intelligent* and Jew] overlap each other like two circles as they are drawn in textbooks of formal logic, and I am inclined to place myself right in the shaded (overlapping) part."⁷⁸ In this respect, his views did not change in exile. He told interviewer John Glad that Russian nationalists regarded him as "a Jew without a country, who doesn't understand the sources of Russian life. ... In other words, not only do I belong to neither the Russian ethnic nor literary tradition, but I hate everything Russian as well." In response to those charges, he declared: "All I can say is that I couldn't care less whether people like that ... consider me to be Russian or not. ... I've already said that I am both a Jew and a Russian intellectual. For me there is nothing contradictory in those two terms. Such a synthesis seems very natural to me. It's even fairly traditional."⁷⁹

Khazanov's views on the diaspora have a corollary in his attitude toward Israel. In an essay from 1977, "Letters from Afar," he suggested that he was not entirely serious in his statement in "New Russia" about not wanting to leave Russia, but if one were to leave, "then, of course, it can only be to Israel."⁸⁰ All his subsequent statements, however, buttress his decision to immigrate to Germany, not Israel. In general, he speaks of practical considerations, but he applies to Israel the distrust of nationalism that he evinced in Russia. As he explains: "I, however, chose Germany as the country of residence because, on the one hand, I felt a closeness to German culture, and, on the other hand, without ceasing to be or feeling like a Jew, I did not sympathize with state nationalism anywhere, including in Israel."⁸¹ Despite his apprehension about Israeli nationalism, like many other diaspora Jews, he acknowledges the value of a Jewish state:

> For every Jew, no matter where he lives, the existence of a democratic Jewish state is at least a consolation. It is impossible not to sympathize with this state, not to take an interest in its fate, not to worry about its survival, not follow ardently its successes and failures. I do not

---

76 E-mail correspondence with the author, June 30, 2015.
77 Khazanov, "Idushchii po vode," 207.
78 Khazanov, "Letters from Afar," 237.
79 Glad, *Conversations in Exile*, 133.
80 Khazanov, "Letters from Afar," 240.
81 E-mail correspondence with the author, June 30, 2015.

feel sufficiently competent to discuss in detail the current situation of Israel, its ideology and the politics of its leaders. I can say only this: terror discredits, and in essence, abrogates any slogans. ... They become a smokescreen. On the banners of Palestinian terrorism, all phrases about national liberation, a struggle against Zionism, American imperialism and so forth, are nonsense.[82]

Khazanov does not, however, portray Germany as the ideal solution. Writing for the Israeli Russian-language journal *Nota bene*, he notes the many efforts in Germany to recount the Nazi crimes and commemorate the victims but admits that some antisemitism and neo-Nazi groups still exist. In response to the journal's question whether he felt at home in Germany, he stated, "What can you say, the fate of an émigré is not an enviable one. Perhaps it would have been more correct to say that in Germany, I feel less alien, less not at home than in Russia or any other place."[83] Perhaps, I would suggest this situation is optimal for an individual who considers that a writer not only is always an exile no matter his location, but who also needs the distance of exile in order to create. In such a case, Israel, in which he admitted he might feel more at home, could actually be an impediment to his creativity.

In the context of Khazanov's attitude toward Israel, it is interesting to look at the scene in "Anti-time" with the youthful hero and his Jewish biological father, who suddenly appears in his life. In a long, rambling speech, the father, who had been a socialist revolutionary and served time in Soviet camps,[84] denounces his own revolutionary past, the revolution itself, and, most sharply, the Russian masses. He tries to persuade his son that it is useless to remain in Russia, where the Jews are in exile, punishment for their futile messianic support of the revolution: the young man should seize the rare opportunity and join him in moving to Palestine. Incoherence rather than logic predominates: on the one hand, the father declares that the Jews are above history and above the usual signs of nationhood such as territory and a language, yet he blames Russian Jews for trying to leap out of history, and he insists that they could become free people and start a new life only in Palestine. Without engaging in a debate, the young man monosyllabically rejects the offer. Aware of the dangers he faces, he nevertheless returns home to his Russian stepfather. There he is promptly arrested by the secret police; in essence, he has chosen elective exile in Russia.

---

82 "Evrei v etoi strane," http://boris-chasanow.imwerden.de/evrej_v_etoj_strane.html.
83 Ibid.
84 Based on a real life acquaintance of Khazanov's in Moscow, Mikhail Baitalskii (pseudonym Domal'skii), who later supported the Jewish movement in the Soviet Union and participated in the Jewish samizdat. See John Glad's interview with Khazanov: "Iz besed."

Some critics have seen the biological father with his rumpled appearance, heavy Jewish accent, and disjointed speech as a completely negative figure.[85] Khazanov himself claimed that the father's views were "far from the author's credo."[86] I would argue, however, in favor of a more ambiguous approach. For one, in a conversation he described Baitalskii, the model for the father, as a "remarkable person."[87] Moreover, in some of his samizdat essays such as "Letter from Afar," Khazanov supported some of the same theories. It is important to keep in mind Khazanov's assertion that one must never take the views expressed in a work of fiction as those of the author.[88] He also stated that in all his writing, he discovered that, essentially, he was writing about himself.[89] In sum, it might be reasonable to conclude that the discourse itself and the participants in it represent certain ambivalent facets of the author's own personality.

7 The Holocaust and Exile

Khazanov, like many other diaspora Jews who see the essence of Jewry in its dispersion and cultural and moral tradition, not its bond to a national homeland, attaches great significance to the Holocaust, which he regards as a defining event in world history. He has commented on it in various essays and introduced the theme into several fictional works. In his opinion, as mentioned earlier, Germany has made great strides in acknowledging and repenting for its past. In contrast, he blames Russians for their silence.

Khazanov's fictional treatment of the Holocaust includes several variations on the story of the wandering Jew. In the basic plot, which takes place in the sixteenth century, Agasfer, or the wandering Jew, enters the study of the noted German philosopher and astrologer Agrippa von Nettesheim. Agasfer explains that because of his unwillingness to help Jesus on his way to the cross, Jesus had condemned him to wander until he himself returns to earth. Weary of his fifteen centuries as a homeless exile, Agasfer begs the astrologer to look into his crystal ball to predict when his wanderings will end. Agrippa is horrified when his

---

[85] Abram Kunik, "Boris Khazanov. Argument k cheloveku," *Sintaksis*, no 17 (1987): 135–36.
[86] Khazanov, "Ponedel'nik roz," 89.
[87] Glad, "Iz besed."
[88] Khazanov in conversation with Alla Latyna and Igor Kuznetsov, *Literaturnaia gazeta* (5547), no. 16, April 4, 1995, 5.
[89] "All my life I tried not to write about myself. All my life I wrote about myself. Indeed literature is self-exposure" (Boris Khazanov, "Dumaiu, mne povezlo...," interview by Boris Markovskii, *Kreshchatik*, no. 4 [2011], http://magazines.russ.ru/kreschatik/2011/4/ha28-pr.html).

crystal ball brings up an image of a line of Jews – both Agasfer and Jesus appear in the line with other men, women, and children whom the guards are forcing into the crematorium. Agrippa questions whether Agasfer has correctly identified the figure in the line as Jesus, "the son of God." "That's what you think," Agasfer replies. "He is the son of our people." When Agrippa repeats his experiment with the crystal ball, Agasfer does not return; he and Jesus perish with all the other Jews in the gas chambers.[90]

Khazanov sees the legend of the wandering Jew as representative of Christianity's centuries-long hatred and persecution of the Jews, of which the Holocaust was the culmination; "Christianity also perishes along with the Jews," he declares.[91] If Christianity thinks that after Auschwitz it can remain the same Christianity, "as if nothing in the world happened, that means that it truly is dead."[92]

Admitting that the Catholic Church had made some conciliatory moves toward the Jews, Khazanov criticizes the Russian Orthodox Church and Russians in general for refusing to face the issue and reconsider their attitudes. "Auschwitz is absent in the consciousness of the intelligentsia, and all the more so among the common people [in Russia]. Auschwitz is absent in the consciousness of the Church. ... Auschwitz is absent in the consciousness of our writers, not excluding, alas, the most famous and worthy."[93]

Precisely because of his focus on universal values and morality – and his belief that the diasporic Jewish people are the foremost bearers of this message to humanity – Khazanov sees the treatment of the Jews in the Holocaust as a litmus test that humanity failed. "We are all asthmatics of Auschwitz," he states, suggesting that humankind is suffocating from the smoke of the crematoria; it has polluted the moral as well as the physical atmosphere of those who are living and ought to evoke a universal reconsideration of values. He warns, "It is wrong to

---

90 A longer, more literary version, entitled "Khronika o Kartafile" appears in Khazanov's collection of short stories *Gorod i Sny* (The City and Dreams) (Moscow: Vagarius, 2001), 271–83. In this variation, the narrator gives the tale a supposed historical background and claims that a manuscript exists that describes the visit of the "Eternal Jew." The theme appears comically in the surrealistic novel *Nagl'far*, in the person of the heroine's grandfather, who lives in the basement, studies the kabbalistic book the *Zohar*, and regales his granddaughter with stories of Rabbi Akiva. In a denunciation against the grandfather, an informer in the building writes: "It's possible that under the guise of a Soviet citizen, a historically well-known international adventurist named Agasfer is hiding in the basement, having been sent into our country with a subversive task" (*Nagl'far*, 120).
91 Khazanov, "Vozvrashchenie Agasfera," in *Veter izgnaniia* http://imwerden.de/pdf/khazanov_veter_izgnaniya.pdf, 34.
92 Ibid.
93 Ibid., 35.

think that Auschwitz is the problem of the Jews or the problem of the Germans, or of someone else, but only not our problem. One must not forget that antisemitism is the universal school of evil and it is not for nothing that the many centuries of teaching in this school ended in the gas chambers and ovens."[94]

The story "The Miracle Maker" ("Chudotvorets"), published in the same volume with *Nagl'far*,[95] deals with the Holocaust in fictional form. At the same time, it poses broader existential questions about life itself and the life of the Jew in particular as an expression of exile. As in many of his other works, Khazanov plays with concepts of time and memory and erases the borders between dream and reality. He also inserts numerous biblical allusions into the narrative; for instance, a horse who addresses his driver recalls the story of the heathen prophet Bilaam and the donkey who talked back to him, revealing the truth.[96] The framework of "The Miracle Maker" is a grandfather's talk with his grandson; in the course of the grandfather's tale of his youth in a Polish shtetl on the eve of the Nazi invasion, however, the characters from the Polish tale are transported to Roman Judea at the time of Jesus.

The youthful narrator on one occasion accompanies his father who travels around the Polish countryside collecting items for his cluttered antique shop. The father turns into a Judean named Simon,[97] who tries to counter the Apostle Peter's claims of Jesus' divinity by – unsuccessfully – performing his own miracle of floating in the air.[98] Although the story debunks the New Testament version of events, the Jews, too, are incapable of transforming their deeds into miracles. Indeed, their twentieth-century fate is prefigured in the Judean period when Peter warns the Jews that those who do not believe the Messiah has come will burn in a fiery oven.[99]

The narrator-grandfather, who recounts episodes from his boyhood in the shtetl, often interjects midrashic tales and themes into his narrative. He relates that in the course of his apprenticeship as a painter, he painted a picture of the local Polish nobility's mansion licked by flames, a premonition of what occurred

---

94 Ibid.
95 The story is also available on the internet at http://mreadz.com/read186765, but, in my experience, these sites change over time and sometimes lead to other, undesirable sites. Citations refer to the internet version. An introduction to the story notes that it utilizes motifs from the movie script of Peter Lilienthal, "Simon der Magier," the book of Feliks Kandel, *Ocherki vremen i sobytii*, and stories of Bruno Shultz.
96 Khazanov, "Chudotvorets," 11.
97 In terms of possible allusions, Simon is the Hebrew name of the Apostle Peter; it is also the first name of Bar Kochba, the leader of the revolt against the Romans from circa 132–136 CE.
98 Khazanov, "Chudotvorets," 21.
99 Ibid., 20.

later during the war. He then says that the conflagration recalls the *midrash* of a traveler who sees a burning mansion alongside the road. A crowd is watching, but no one extinguishes the fire. The traveler asks whether there is an owner. "No," they reply. Suddenly a voice thunders from the heavens: "I am the owner of the mansion."[100] This *midrash* serves to illustrate the patriarch Abraham's realization that a divine being rules the world. There is, however, an exilic side to Khazanov's tale: the spectators see fire and chaos; they are passive, alienated, and seemingly homeless as they stand outside of the mansion. Some see in this tale a reference to man's original exile from the Garden of Eden. Khazanov links this *midrash* specifically to the world's indifference during the Holocaust.[101] A figure in the tale representing the Kotzker rebbe[102] predicts: "The castle is burning even though it has an owner ... when it catches fire, none of the servants raises a hand to extinguish it."[103]

The narrator's father, who refuses to escape in time, perishes in the Holocaust. He represents a naïve, cosmopolitan diaspora Jew who did not believe the rumors about German atrocities because "the Germans are most civilized people."[104] His antique-filled home, however, represents a repository of Jewish history. "My parental home," the narrator tells his grandson "was a home that was called history, and if at a given moment, we were not in the room, that meant only that we went into another room." Generations not only lived, fought, and procreated in this home but also they "recalled the passage from Egypt, the pharaonic chariots stuck in the sand, and the horsemen drowning in the sea; we lived in a home where in passing you could glance at a dim mirror and see in the murky depth the poor patriarch, barefoot king, or a semi-mad prophet." The recitation continues, and he concludes: "But now, this home burned down to the ground."[105]

Although the house and most of its inhabitants perish in the Holocaust, the narrator, who at the beginning acquires the skill of an artist, and another character who becomes his wife, manage to survive; the beneficiary is the young grandson who hears the tale. In a sense, the narrator's fictional telling of the tale to a younger generation and his weaving of the recent historical past and

---
100 Ibid., 6. The original source is Bereishit Rabbah 39:1. There is no crowd in the original.
101 As in the Agasfer stories, Jesus reappears in the tale, not as an affirmation of Christian doctrine, but to identify with the Jewish people.
102 The Kotzker rebbe (Menachem Mendel Morgensztern, 1787–1859), was an enigmatic but brilliant and outspoken hasidic rabbi who spent the final twenty years of his life in seclusion.
103 Khazanov, "Chudotvorets," 6.
104 Ibid., 24.
105 Ibid., 25.

more ancient history into an artistic fabric brings these events back to life and represent an answer to humankind's feeling of isolation and exile.

8 Conclusion

Khazanov's world is rife with aporias and paradoxes for which he offers partial resolutions on the artistic or metaphysical plane: the Russian *intelligent* is an exile in his own country, but on the moral and cultural level, he is its finest representative; the writer who has left Russia has endured a metaphorical shipwreck, but this catastrophe preserves him as a Russian writer; a writer in exile faces the danger of losing his native language, but with his distilled memory of his homeland, he can express its purest essence.

Khazanov describes the Jews as a people above history who best cultivate their talents and values in the diaspora; yet, I would suggest, history, including the author's own experiences, illustrates how the Jewish people have suffered most cruelly throughout the ages from lacking their own homeland. In the Soviet Union, as a Jew and *intelligent*, Khazanov felt that he was twice an exile. He would, he insists, feel equally alien in modern Russia, with its glorification of an ethnically Russian nationalist ideal and persistent antisemitic attitudes among intellectuals and common people. He is also wary of Israel because of its Jewish nationalist tendencies, but he can never be truly at home in Germany, although he tries to justify his stay there by praising their national repentance for the Holocaust.

Having opted out of geography, Khazanov chooses an attribute that is detached from a soil-based homeland and traditionally cherished by the Jews – language itself. In his retelling of Jewish legends, God created the world itself from the letters of the Hebrew alphabet. The creative individual retains the potential through language and literature to create new worlds.

These new worlds spring from a creative synergy between memory and time. According to Khazanov, time itself is paradoxical and subjective: "Time consists of two streams; it flows from the past into the future and from the future into the past."[106] An individual, looking at his past does not know whether his life was an accumulation of chance incidents or part of a plan. The creative individual, like the divine Creator himself, Khazanov suggests, can channel time and give meaning to this chaos: "Introducing meaning into meaningless-chaotic life is the task of art. One can compare the function of memory to the function of the novel-

---

[106] Khazanov, "Ponedel'nik roz," 88.

ist, but in a metaphysical perspective, to the function of God himself. Memory is not so much 'found time,' as the finding of reverse time."[107]

Khazanov's preoccupation with time, both in his fiction and as a literary critic, may well be related directly to his Jewish-Russian identity and exile in Germany. In writing about Franz Kafka, Gilles Deleuze and Félix Guattari develop a theory of a "minor literature," which they define as the literature "which a minority constructs within a major language."[108] The French philosophers posit deterritorialization of language as the most important attribute of a minor literature, ascribing revolutionary potential to it.[109] As Deleuze and Guattari note, Kafka was doubly a minority writer as a Jew writing in German in Prague. Khazanov, similarly, is twice deterritorialized, a self-defined Russian-Jewish *intelligent*, living and writing outside of Russia. His prose, however, is not subversive in a political sense nor is it linguistically revolutionary, although it employs a significant number of foreign words and often deals with specifically Jewish themes.

According to the above theory, the collapse of empire accentuates deterritorialization "and invites all sorts of complex reterritorializations – archaic, mythic, or symbolist."[110] One sees this process in various ways among Russian-language writers after the fall of the Soviet empire. As mentioned earlier, Aksenov, for example, introduced mythic elements into *Moskva Kva-Kva*. Khazanov, too, tends toward the mythic in his attempt to "reterritorialize" himself within the Russian tradition;[111] he deconstructs time in order to reconstruct and occupy place. In more than one story the narrator's watch stops telling time, but elderly Jewish craftsmen tell him that there is nothing wrong with his watch, meaning, time exists only in the imagination; therefore, one can fashion it as one wishes. In fact,

---

107 Ibid.
108 Gilles Deleuze and Félix Guattari, *Kafka. Toward a Minor Literature*. Theory and History of Literature 30 (Minneapolis: University of Minnesota Press, 1986), 16.
109 The other two characteristics are "the connection of the individual to a political immediacy and the collective assemblage of enunciation" (ibid., 18).
110 Ibid., 24.
111 Mikhail Krutikov discusses an interesting example of post-Soviet mythologization in the works of Oleg Yur'ev, a Russian-language writer living in Frankfurt. He writes that each work in Yur'ev's trilogy, *The Zhidiatin Peninsula* (2000), *The Golem or the War of the Elder and the Children* (2004), and *Vinet* "has its own set of myths on which a narrative about a certain segment of Soviet and post-Soviet history is constructed" (Mikhail Krutikov, "Jewish Memory and the 'Para-Soviet' Chronotope," *Novoe literaturnoe obozrenie* 3 [2014], http://www.nlobooks.ru/node/5154). An English version of Krutikov's article, "Four Voices from the Last Soviet Generation: Evgeny Steiner, Alexander Goldshtein, Oleg Yuryev, and Alexander Ilichevsky," can be found in *The New Jewish Diaspora: Russian Speaking Immigrants in the United States, Israel, and Germany*, ed. Zvi Gitelman (New Brunswick, NJ: Rutgers University Press, 2016), 251–65.

one watchmaker explains that the watchmaking profession is peopled mainly by Jews because the Jews are a nation not of space but of time – although, paradoxically, this time is fluid. In that work, *Look at the Hieroglyph*, an elderly narrator returns to today's Russia, but the subsequent narrative continually dissolves and shifts time frames, moving between dream and reality, between the narrator's Moscow childhood, the war period, prison camp, contemporary Germany, and the end of his life.[112] By playing with time in this work, in *Nagal'far*'s mythic Moscow of the 1930s, and in other works, Khazanov reasserts his claim to the city and country that he left because it still exists in his fiction. Although Khazanov employs many modern techniques – a polyphonic narrative style, a refusal to posit absolute truths or absolute reality, a confusion of time and place, and an acute concern with language itself – his faith in literature as such, endows his work with an old-fashioned hue. Life is bleak; the writer is an exile no matter his location and "the house has burned down, there's nowhere to return." Despite all that, the young girl in *Nagl'far* and the young grandson in "The Miracle Worker" hint at renewal. There is a temporary haven for humankind – "that eternal refuge where there is a place for all of us – Russian literature."[113]

Bibliography

Aksenov, Vasilii. *Moskva Kva-Kva*. Moscow: Eksmo, 2006.
Boyarin, Daniel and Jonathan. "Diaspora: Generation and the Ground of Jewish Identity." *Critical Inquiry* 19, no. 4 (Summer 1993): 693–725.
Glad, John, ed. *Conversations in Exile: Russian Writers Abroad*. Durham: Duke University Press, 1993.
Deleuze, Gilles and Félix Guattari. *Kafka, Toward a Minor Literature*. Theory and History of Literature. Vol. 30. Minnesota: University of Minnesota Press, 1986.
Kharitonov, Mark. "Nam nuzhno vosstannavlivat' pamiat' (k 80-letiiu Borisa Khazanova)." *Vtoraia navigatssiia* 8 (2008): 310–311.
Khazanov, Boris. "Besht ili chetvertoe litso glagola." *22*, no. 22 (1981): 78–107.
Khazanov, Boris. *Chas korolia. Antivremia*. Moscow: Slovo, 1991.
Khazanov, Boris. "Chudotvorets." In Boris Khazanov, *Nagl'far v okeane vremen*. Moscow: Tekst, 1993.

---

[112] Khazanov, *Vzglyani na ieroglif* (Munich: ImWerden Verlag, 2012). This and other works by Khazanov can be found on the internet site https://imwerden.de.

[113] Khazanov, "Veter izgnaniia," 82. Although Khazanov alludes to the specific world of Russian literature, Khazanov's writings display a vast familiarity with and respect for Western literature in general. In a certain way, his attitude is typical of the old generation of the Russian intelligentsia with its universalist self-image, that is, Russian literature perceived as a microcosm of the universal.

Khazanov, Boris. Interview by Boris Markovskii. "Dumaiu, mne povezlo…." *Kreshchatik* 4 (2011). http://magazines.russ.ru/kreschatik/2011/4/ha28-pr.html). Accessed August 2015.

Khazanov, Boris. "Evrei v etoi strane." http://boris-chasanow.imwerden.de/evrej_v_etoj_strane.html. Accessed July 2016.

Khazanov, Boris. "Exsilium." *Novyi mir* 12 (1994). http://magazines.russ.ru/novyi_mi/1994/12/hazan.html. Accessed June 2016.

Khazanov, Boris. "'Fedot, da ne tot': odna ili dve literatury?" *Novyi zhurnal* 249 (2007). http://magazines.russ.ru/nj/2007/249/ha14.html. Accessed July 2016.

Khazanov, Boris. "Letters from Afar." In *Search of Self*. Edited by David Prital, 235–238. Jerusalem: Magnes Press, 1983. (Originally in *Sion* 20 [1977]: 43–50).

Khazanov, Boris. "Literaturnyi muzei: Iz devnika pisatelia." *Oktiabr* 10 (2004). http://magazines.russ.ru/october/2004/10/ha14-pr.html. Accessed August 2015.

Khazanov, Boris. *Mif Rossii*. New York: Liberty Publishing House, 1986.

Khazanov, Boris. *Nagl'far v okeane vremen*. Moscow: Tekst, 1993.

Khazanov, Boris. "Novaia Rossiia." *Evrei v SSSR* 7 (May–June 1974). Reprinted in *Evreiskii samizdat* 10 (1976): 109–115.

Khazanov, Boris. "Ponedel'nik roz." *Rodniki i kamni*. http://imwerden.de/pdf/khazanov_rodniki_i_kamni.pdf. Accessed March 2008.

Khazanov, Boris. "Veter izgnaniia." *Polnolunie*. Munich: ImWerdenVerlag, 2007.

Khazanov, Boris. *V_sadakh_za_ognennoi_rekoi* [2012]. http://imwerden.de/pdf/khazanov_v_sadakh_za_ognennoj_rekoj_2014.pdf. Accessed September 2016.

Khazanov, Boris. *Vzglyani_na_ieroglif*. Munich: ImWerdenVerlag, 2012. khazanov_vzglyani_na_ieroglif_2012.pdf.

Krutikov, Mikhail. "Evreiskaia pamiat' i 'parasovetskii' khronotop: Aleksandr Gol'dshtein, Oleg Iur'ev, Aleksandr Ilichevskii." *Novoe literaturnoe obozrenie* 3 (2014). http://www.nlobooks.ru/node/5154.

Liska, Vivian. *German-Jewish Thought and Its Afterlife: A Tenuous Legacy*. Bloomington and Indianapolis: Indiana University Press, 2017.

Lyotard, Jean-Francois. *Heidegger and "the Jews."* Translated by Andreas Michel and Mark Roberts. Minneapolis: University of Minnesota Press, 1977.

Markowitz, Fran. "Emigration, Immigration and Cultural Change: Towards a Transnational Russian-Jewish Community?" In *Jews and Jewish Life in Russia and the Soviet Union*. Edited by Yaacov Ro'i, 403–413. Ilford: Frank Cass & Co., 1995.

Pomerants, Grigorii. *Zapiski gadkogo utenka*. Moscow: ROSSPEN, 2003.

Remennick, Larissa. *Jews on Three Continents*. New Brunswick, NJ: Transaction Publishers, 2007.

Rosenfeld, Alvin H., ed. *The Writer Uprooted: Contemporary Jewish Exile Literature*. Bloomington: Indiana University Press, 2008.

Wakamiya, Lisa Ryoko. *Locating Exiled Writers in Contemporary Russian Literature: Exiles at Home*. New York: Palgrave, Macmillan, 2009.

Wanner, Adrian. *Out of Russia: Fictions of a New Translingual Diaspora*. Evanston, IL: Northwestern University Press, 2011.

Judith K. Lang Hilgartner
Uncovering Accent and Belonging in Juan Gelman's *Dibaxu*

When Argentinian poet and intellectual Juan Gelman was forced into political exile in 1976 he began a process of self-examination, struggling to define himself as a first-generation Argentinian Jew.[1] Although Gelman never returned to his birth country for more than a brief visit, he found creative ways to deepen his connection to Argentina from afar. Following his exile, Gelman spent time in Spain, Italy, France, and the United States; ultimately, he chose to remain in Mexico until his death in 2014. Gelman's exilic trauma was inextricably linked to his perception of how being a Jewish poet effected his experience of language.[2] But it would take some time for this to congeal. Although by 1994, Gelman had become an acclaimed writer, activist and journalist, and a socially engaged poet, his published work had not yet explicitly addressed the purview of his Jewish identity.[3]

A decisive moment came when Gelman discovered the existence of the Ladino language through Clarisse Nikoïdsky's poetry, which inspired him to write his

---

[1] Gelman was forced into political exile following the military coup in Argentina, which began what is known as the Dirty War. See Shari Jacobson's discussion of how the trauma of the Dirty War affected the Ashkenazic community in Argentina in "Body and Soul: Therapeutic Dimensions of Jewish Ultra-Orthodoxy in Neo-Liberal Argentina," in *The New Jewish Argentina. Facets of Jewish Experiences in the Southern Cone*, Jewish Latin America 2, ed. Adriana Brodksy and Ranaan Rein (Leiden: Brill, 2012), 341–64. Particularly of note, Brodksy discusses the term "cultural citizenship" to describe how these events created a sense of solidarity within the Jewish community of which Gelman was not a part. From his papers, it seems like Gelman's family was not particularly religious on his father's side, but his mother maintained many of the traditional feasts and holidays.

[2] In private diary entries, he described the culture shock of interacting with each country's language as a "wound" that "hit him hard." Princeton University, Juan Gelman papers, Box B-000724 (hereafter, Gelman papers).

[3] Ilan Stavans's estimation of Gelman's view of exile as described in *Singer's Typewriter and Mine: Reflections on Jewish Culture* (Lincoln: University of Nebraska, 2012), is only partially accurate because it takes into consideration Gelman's views on the universal role of the poet as a person intrinsically and necessarily of exile. But Stavans does not take into consideration Gelman's affiliation with Argentina or his desire to be considered in the line of Argentinian writers like Gerchunoff and Borges. Stavans writes, "*Dibaxu* captures Gelman's central motif: the conviction that no matter who, where, or with whom he is, the poet – and this poet in particular – lives in permanent exile" does not reflect the whole picture (ibid., 75). While Gelman does care deeply about the ubiquitous role of the poet, that alone is not the full story.

own collection with side-by-side versions in Ladino and Argentinian Spanish.[4] Poignant journal entries reveal that years of study and introspection influenced the writing process of his bilingual collection.[5] The publication of *Dibaxu* marked an important development in Gelman's definition of himself as a writer in relation to his Jewish Argentinian heritage.[6] Although his angst regarding language, identity, and belonging was never completely resolved, through the writing process of *Dibaxu*, Gelman attempted to heal from the past and solidify his identification as a Jewish Argentinian poet.

Gelman's fascination with language was evident from a young age. His first linguistic exposure, beyond Spanish, was to Yiddish and Russian. During adolescence, he attempted some Yiddish to Spanish translations. After he was exiled from Argentina, he began to experiment with language once again as a means to explore his heritage.[7] *Dibaxu*, half-written in a Nikoïdsky-inspired version of "*sefardí*," became in Gelman's conception, a metaphor for the bond that he maintained with Argentina while in exile.[8]

---

[4] Monique Balbuena's perspective on Gelman's affiliation with Argentina puts much more emphasis on his participation with a universal Jewish culture as opposed to a nation-specific Jewish culture. Although she affirms that Gelman "interweaves his Jewishness and his Argentinian-ness, reading and reaching through the other," Balbuena believes that *Dibaxu* actually distances him from Argentina, more than it draws him near. See her valuable discussion of *Dibaxu* and Gelman in her book, *Homeless Tongues: Poetry and Languages of the Sephardic Diaspora* (Palo Alto: Stanford University Press, 2016), 154–56.

[5] Having read through all of the correspondence between Gelman and his editor Ricardo Ibarlucía at Seix Barral, it is clear that Gelman was reticent to introduce his collection at all.

[6] Juan Gelman, *Dibaxu* (Buenos Aires: Seix Barral, 1994). For the purpose of this paper, I will use "sefardí," [var. sephardi] "Jewish Spanish," and "Ladino" interchangeably. "Sefardí" is the term that Gelman used in all of his correspondence and in the prologue itself.

[7] In his papers, Gelman frequently mentioned that when he was twenty years-old, he translated a poem, "Tea with Bread" from Yiddish to Spanish: "Traduje a los 20 años un poema del idish: 'Tea with Bread.' 'Hay sólo té con pan y pan con té de nuevo, ¡Ay de esta vida a té con pan que llevo! Entonces, Dios, no quieres que coma? ¿Tan enojado estás que me haces esa broma?'" (At twenty years old, I translated a poem, "Tea with Bread" from Yiddish. "There is only tea with bread and bread with tea again. Oh, this tea and bread life that I lead! So then, God, you don't want me to eat? You are so angry with me that you play this joke?").

[8] There is controversy about how to name the language of the contemporary Sephardim. Remy Attig in his article, "Did the Sephardic Jews Speak Ladino?" *Bulletin of Spanish Studies* 89, no. 6 (2012): 831–88, discusses that Ladino originally referred to the act of copying sacred texts into Hebrew script. The term "Jewish Spanish," is the more accepted in sociolinguistic circles, while the term "Ladino" has now become commonly used among the Sephardim. One example of this common usage is *Ladinokomunita*, an online forum founded by Rachel Amado Bortnick only for those who correspond in the language. Other names for the language include Judeo-Spanish, Djudio, and Djudezmo. It is worth noting that Gelman refers to the language as "judeo-español"

The juxtaposition of Ladino and Spanish poems in *Dibaxu* reflects Gelman's struggle for belonging with an eye to the distant past – the expulsion of the Sephardim from Spain in 1492. Using Sephardic history as a metaphor for his own banishment, he employs the trope of permanent exile and nostalgia for *Sepharad*. *Dibaxu* is not merely a collection of poetry based on Ladino; it is a presentation of the concept of dialogue between words, languages, times, geographies, and identities. An examination of Gelman's private papers reveals that the poems collected in *Dibaxu* was the working out of many years of an identity crisis under which Gelman continually suffered while in exile. In *Dibaxu*, the opposition between modern-day Spanish and Ladino serves as a platform for Gelman's poetic voice to demonstrate that his exile enhanced his felt belonging to Argentina as a homeland.[9] For Gelman, Ladino was the language of exile *par excellence*, and therefore, by making it his language of choice, Gelman was able to nuance his own poetic voice, adopting an accent that, at least from his perspective, deepened his connection to Argentina.

Playing with accent and language as a means to examine bonds of identification is not an unusual topic in today's sociolinguistic scholarship. Ilan Stavans's soul-searching journey as represented in his memoir *On Borrowed Words: A Memoir of Language*, provides one recent example. Similar to Gelman, Stavans grew up in a Yiddish and Spanish-speaking home in Mexico. Although Stavans's roots are Ashkenazic (just like Gelman), he begins his memoir by citing a poem by Henry Wadsworth Longfellow which references the "foreign accent" of the first Sephardic Jews who arrived in North America.[10] The Sephardic Jews' historic affiliation with Spain has become an apt comparison for the more universal Jewish experience of inheriting a multilingual voice. In a similar way, in *Dibaxu* Gelman seeks some way to explain (more to himself than to anyone else) the complicated terms of belonging he experiences toward his Ashkenazic heritage, birth country, understanding of exile, and his poetic writing process.

In recent years, there has been a surge of interest in the complex narratives of identity in the Jewish Argentinian community. A collection of essays, *The New*

---

in his prologue to *Dibaxu*, but Clarisse Nikoïdsky uses the term Ladino. Clarisse Nikoïdsky was a Bosnian poet whose book *Lus ojos, las manos, la boca* (1976), inspired Gelman in writing his own. Dina Rot, a well-known Argentinian singer, introduced Gelman to Nikoïdsky's work. From reading his personal papers, it seems that although Gelman never actually met Nikoïdsky in person, he communicated with her through Rot.

9 Gelman frequently uses the word *"patria"* in Spanish to refer to Argentina. "Patria" can be translated as "fatherland" or "homeland." It is a feminine word in Spanish, but "patria" comes from the Latin word *"pater,"* which means father.

10 Ilan Stavans, *On Borrowed Words: A Memoir of Language* (New York: Penguin Books, 2001), 361.

Jewish Argentina: Facets of Jewish Experiences in the Southern Cone, set the stage for scholarship to begin to problematize the stereotypes of Argentinian Jews as merely victims of xenophobia, multi-generational poverty, and religious marginalization.[11] Most recently, Adriana Brodsky, in the introduction to her book, *Sephardi, Jewish, and Argentine*, argues that Jewish diasporic identity must be interpreted in light of what she calls "realized lands" and not just the "Promised Land."[12] She argues that in the history of the Jewish people, different geographical locations tied to varying degrees of affiliations have always been in flux, lending, in some cases, to a sense of multi-nationalism.[13] In the case of Gelman, his banishment from Argentina allowed him the space (both literally and figuratively) to evaluate these "realized lands" and to ultimately attempt to re-affirm his belonging to Argentina. While Gelman couched his national affiliations in poetic smoke and mirrors, it is important to recognize, in the words of Brodsky: "the ways in which *lo nacional* (the national) wove itself into this multi-diasporic story, creating new belongings and strengthening old ones ... identity was never a given, an a priori essence, it was always in the making, in flux, a choice, and a strategy."[14] An argument could be made that *Dibaxu* is an attempt to show the universality of exilic trauma in light of poetic expression. The collection is an expression of resilience that transcends Gelman's personal circumstances. *Dibaxu* can be read as a poet's search for belonging; the collection is replete with discursive strategies that attempt to forge belonging while at the same time never achieving consummation of those attempts.

1 Uncovering His Accent: Gelman's Self-Sephardization

Interpreting the poems from *Dibaxu* in light of Argentinian literary history and his personal papers helps to illuminate the multifaceted logic behind Gelman's fascination with Sephardic history. Through "self-Sephardization," Gelman attempted to regain a linguistic essence that he felt he had lost since birth, but his choice

---

[11] Adriana Brodsky and Raanan Rein, eds., *The New Jewish Argentina: Facets of Jewish Experiences in the Southern Cone* (Leiden: Brill, 2012), 5. This collection won the Latin American Jewish Studies Association Book Prize in 2013.
[12] Adriana Brodksy, *Sephardi, Jewish, Argentine* (Bloomington: Indiana University Press, 2016), introduction, esp. 6.
[13] Ibid.
[14] Ibid., 207.

to appropriate a Sephardic tongue was not without controversy.[15] *Dibaxu*'s brief prologue reads like a half-obfuscating justification of his language choice, as if Gelman anticipated the backlash in the Jewish community – a push-back which he indeed did receive to an extent from certain Sephardic readers.[16] On *Ladinokomunita*, an online forum for Ladino and Sephardic culture, the question was posed: "For what purpose would an Ashkenazi write in Ladino?"[17] This comment was later removed by its author, but it sparked a thread of conversation in which some members of the forum discussed whether or not the Sephardic community would receive Gelman's poetic collection favorably. This critique of his work implied that an Ashkenazic Jew did not have the right to use the language of the Sephardic community, particularly for the promotion of his literary career.[18] In defense of Gelman, another *Ladinokomunita* member replied: "I have no intention of stopping writing in Ladino, despite the fact that *Baruch Hashem*, I am Ashkenazi."[19] According to this post, writing in Jewish Spanish may be an inexplicable, but necessary choice for some Ashkenazim.

Gelman states that he is not even certain why he desires to write in the language: "I can't explain it even to myself."[20] His tentativeness implies awareness that he is crossing cultural and linguistic boundaries by writing in Ladino. The prologue conveys the idea that despite his concern of over-stepping, the comfort and tenderness Gelman finds in *sefardí* moves him to use it for his own emotive expression. The prologue explains that upon finding himself alone, isolated, and uprooted from his Argentinian homeland, Gelman sought a sense of grounding in the exilic language of the Sephardim.

Understanding the context of how and why the prologue to *Dibaxu* was written helps explain why this short text is in some senses more confounding than

---

15 In *Homeless Tongues: Poetry and Languages of the Sephardic Diaspora* (Palo Alto: Stanford University Press, 2016), Monique Balbuena used the term "self-Sephardize" to describe Gelman's comparison of himself with the Sephardic condition.
16 During summer 2015, when I was conversing with poet Matilda Koen Sarano, I asked her what she thought about Gelman's Ladino poetry. She did not respond to my question directly, answering instead, "Clarrise Nikoïdsky era la última poeta sefardí" (Clarrise Nikoïdsky was the last Sephardic poet; my translation). This dismissal speaks volumes about Gelman's appeal to a "purist" Sephardic audience.
17 "Deke eskrive en ladino un ashkenazi?"
18 Since this thread, *Ladinokomunita* members have repeatedly cited *Dibaxu* and praised the collection; thus the apparent consensus online is positive, but still the concern over the inappropriate usage of Sephardic language and tropes is an occasional topic of concern.
19 "Yo ... no tengo intisyon de aretar de eskrivir mis eskritas en Judeo Espanyol. Malgrado ke *Baruh Ashem* so Ashkenazi."
20 "Yo tampoco me lo explico."

illuminating. The quote from the prologue, "I can't even explain it to myself" is an accurate reflection of his feelings in so far as Gelman also expressed a similar sentiment in a letter to his editor, Ricardo Ibarlucía, in December 1993: "I don't think that it is necessary to add a prologue – at least not one from me – I would not and could not know how to explain the interplay between current Spanish and the other from centuries ago that accompanies the poems."[21] On the occasion of this letter and several others, Gelman expresses to his editor that he is not sure how to describe the feelings that have compelled him to write in Jewish Spanish.[22] After he finally conceded and sent Ibarlucía the text of the prologue, Gelman referred to it as a "*prologuito*," a tongue-and-cheek allusion to his reticence at having written one in the first place.

What remains evident from the prologue itself is that Gelman's feelings of displacement caused him to begin to reflect upon poetry as a means to return to the country of one's origin. For him, the poetic "word" itself is the key to return: Gelman's promised homeland is found through unearthing the "subsoil" of the Spanish language.[23] Gelman describes his writing process like a root trying to dig deeper in the soil: "to search for roots in the deepest and most exiled parts of language,"[24] showing that through his poetry in Jewish Spanish, Gelman consciously invents his own type of metaphysical return to a homeland by playing with language – and with his accent. His role as a translator allows him the flexibility to evoke new sounds – for example, the eliding difference between "*dibaxu*" and "*debajo*."[25] Even the title of the collection confirms the downward direction that Gelman contemplates because "*dibaxu*" means "underneath" in Ladino. The answer to belonging and origin is found through digging into the past, but not as a historian or archaeologist who is bound by time period or geographical location. Instead, Gelman creates "roots" through the writing process, finding a way to connect the past to the present.

In the years preceding the publication of *Dibaxu*, Gelman's search for his "roots" led him to undergo deep introspection about his childhood, particularly related to language. His physical exile from Argentina seems to have provoked in him a desire to understand how this banishment was not in fact his first encounter

---

[21] "No creo que haya que agregarle un prólogo, no por lo menos mío: no sabría, ni podría, explicar el juego entre el castellano actual y el otro de hace siglos que acompaña a los poemas." See Gelman, *Dibaxu*, 819.
[22] In one of his letters to Dina Rot, Gelman references the "enigmatic need" he felt to write in *sefardí*.
[23] Gelman, *Dibaxu*, 815.
[24] "[B]uscar raíces en las más profundas y exilidas de la lengua," ibid.
[25] In Jewish Spanish to this day, the "x" has maintained the sound "ʒ" according to the IPA.

with exile. In some of his writings, he described exile as an inherited condition from his Jewish parents and the trauma that they suffered back in Russia and the Ukraine.[26] Gelman's private papers and correspondence show that his use of Ladino was an attempt to regain a sense of homeland. In periodic journal entries starting in the late seventies, Gelman began to reflect on the fact that he was born into a home that was governed by the silence of past trauma and exile. Mystery and secrecy had characterized Gelman's relationship with his parents. In the 1970s, Gelman learned from his brother Boris that they had an older half-brother who had died in Russia when his father had tried to leave the country. In an interview with the literary magazine *La Nación* in 2014, Gelman commented that memories of his father had only in the past years become more frequent: "Once when I was twelve years old, I got sick and my dad sat next to me on the bed and read stories from Sholem Aleichem in Yiddish. I remember this, but for me, he was a man of silence, distant ... I don't know. Family secrets were always afoot."[27]

Over the course of his exile, Gelman wrote many deeply personal reflections on his childhood, including his memories of seeing his father sit alone in a dark dining room. In an undated journal entry labeled by archivists as dating to the late 1990s, Gelman reconstructed memories of his father brooding over memories of Russia: "Am I exiled since birth? Was the portrait of my grandfather on the wall of my parents' bedroom always looking at me like that because of this? Did he understand me because he was in his own exile in his land, a holy rabbi only eating tea with bread? Only from this sadness can I finally enter into his gaze that dogged me my whole life."[28] It seems that Gelman not only equated his own exile with that of his parents and of the Jewish people, but also, in this journal entry, he appears to realize that he had been living his entire life under an unidentifiable shadow, one that started to become clear only after he was exiled from Argentina. It was only when he was in exile that Gelman realized that his Argentinian accent was one of the defining features that made him feel a sense of belonging to his birth country. Yet, that was only the first layer of belonging as he continued to dig – "*dibaxu*" – underneath the surface.

---

26 Hernán Fontanet, *Gelman: Un poeta y su vida* (Buenos Aires: Alguilar, 2013), 27.
27 "Una vez estuve enfermo a los doce años, se sentó al lado de mi cama y me leía cuentos de Scholem Aleijem en idish. Me acuerdo de eso, pero era un hombre de silencio; para mí, distante ... No sé, el secreto familiar siempre anda por ahí," (cited in ibid., 29).
28 "¿Soy exiliado desde mi nacimiento? ¿El retrato de mi abuelo en una pared del dormitorio de mis padres me miraba así por eso? ¿O me comprendía en su propio exilio de la tierra, rabino santo que sólo comía té con pan? Sólo desde esta tristeza puedo entrar por fin en su mirada, que me siguió toda la vida como perro" (Gelman papers, Box 000717).

Right before publishing *Dibaxu*, Gelman wrote in his diary that the subliminal air of secrecy that pervaded his childhood caused a rupture from which he never could recover. The idea that he was the only Argentinian in his family (born in Buenos Aires in 1925) made him question how he could still carry around a subconscious feeling of exile. At some point, Gelman discovered that within his own Argentinian accent lay the potential to be Jewish, and that indeed, being Jewish and being Argentinian could fulfill each other. When Gelman visited Israel for the first time in March 2001, he explained his feelings in this way:[29] "I never had conflict with the Jewishness in me. Perhaps for that reason, I never had a conflict with the Argentinian-ness in me."[30]

By reimagining his poetic voice as Sephardic while writing *Dibaxu*, Gelman was simultaneously becoming (in his mind) more deeply Argentinian. As he wrote elsewhere: "The virtue of a true homeland is that it creates its exile."[31] For

---

29 Gelman's visit to Israel occurred during the beginning of March 2001. His sister, Teodora, a resident of Jerusalem, had recently passed away from cancer. When Gelman arrived at Ben Gurion Airport, he and his wife, Mara, had an unpleasant experience with the Israel Border Control. He later wrote about this experience in an essay called, "El Estado del Estado de Israel" – "The Condition of the State of Israel." In Princeton's Gelmanian archive, there are numerous letters and correspondences leading up to the publication of that article in *El molino de Pimienta* in addition to many letters and emails either supporting or decrying Gelman's sentiments. There are also numerous letters back and forth from Gelman to the Argentinian ambassador to Israel, Edwin Yabo. This incident caused a stir in the Argentinian-Israeli community. When I attended a lecture by Monique Balbuena about *Dibaxu* at the Hebrew University during the 17th World Congress of Jewish Studies in the summer of 2017, Gelman's visit to Israel was a polemical topic of conversation among those present.

30 "[N]unca tuve conflicto alguno con mi judío de mí. Tal vez por eso nunca tuve conflicto alguno con mi argentino de mí" (Gelman papers, Box 000724).

31 Gelman papers, Box 000724. The quote from Gelman's notes in the original Spanish text reads as follows: "La virtud de la patria verdadera es que crea su exilio." It is a paraphrase of María Zambrano's larger quote which reads: "El exilio es el lugar privilegiado para que la Patria se descubra, para que ella misma se descubra cuando ya el exiliado ha dejado de buscarla … Cuando ya se sabe sin ella … cuando ya no se recibe nada, nada de la patria, entonces se le aparece. No la puede definir, pues que tan siquiera la reconoce … Mas es reconocible en una sola palabra de su idioma, de su propio idioma, la que le da esa presencia impositiva, imperante, inesquivable. Tiene la patria verdadera por virtud crear el exilio" (Zambrano, "El Exiliado" in *Los bienaventurados* [Madrid: Siruela, 1990], 43). "Exile is a privileged place in order that the Homeland be discovered, so that it would discover itself, so that it would be discovered when the exiled person has already stopped searching for it … When you realized that you are without it … receiving nothing, nothing at all from the homeland, only then does it appear. [The homeland] is not able to be defined even if it is recognized … But it is recognizable by only one word from its language, just one word from its own language, one that gives [the homeland's] imprecise, demanding, unequivocal, presence" (my translation). Gelman was reading Zambrano's work, *Los bienaventurados*, and inserted paraphrases from her writing into his own. The page on which

Gelman, his experience of nostalgia during exile confirmed his affiliation with his birth country. In an undated manuscript also dated by the archivists from late 1990s, Gelman concludes: "How much less could I deny that I was born in Argentina, that the Argentinian society and culture of a certain class in Argentina have left a deep mark upon me, that I belong to a great motherland of the Castilian language, to her vision, her sounds, her silences, her continents, and her islands, her manner of exploding in hatred and in love."[32] This passage reflects Gelman's idealization of Argentina as a country of which the Spanish language is a source of both love and hatred. Later in the passage, Gelman references the homogenizing effect that Argentina had upon immigrants who come with their own languages; however, this disglossic instability does not seem to apply to him personally because he was born in the land. While Gelman acknowledges his diverse cultural and linguistic past, he strongly identifies with Argentina as his ultimate homeland. It is worth noting that Gelman wrote this passage while in exile, and he often used the Sephardic trope as a bridge between his strong identification with his Hispanic heritage and his Jewish one.

Nostalgia is a commonly accepted Sephardic trope in Argentinian literary history. Gelman was not the first Ashkenazic intellectual to adopt a Sephardic literary persona in an attempt to identity with the Argentinian mainstream.[33] In

---

these notes were found is undated, but it came from a folder of documents that were dated from 1987 and 1988.

32 "[M]enos puedo negar que nací en la Argentina, que la sociedad argentina y la cultura de una clase en la Argentina han dejados marcas profundas en mí, que pertenezco a la gran patria de la lengua castellana, a su visión, su sonido, sus silencios, sus continentes y sus islas, su manera de estallar en el odio y el amor" (Gelman papers, Box 000732).

33 The term "self-Sephardize" is related to a series of terms including the concept of "Sephardization," which refers to the usually literary process whereby Ashkenazic intellectuals appropriate Sephardic themes and tropes to facilitate cultural assimilation. While largely falling outside the scope of this paper, Carsten Schapcow and John Efron's work on the German Sephardizing trends during the German *Haskalah* movement are invaluable. In Russia, the *Haskalah* movement was later than the German one; its leaders defined themselves in contrast to the former German *maskilim*. Although a widespread trend toward philo-Sephardism is not documented, there are several authors and works that point to the consciousness of elevation of the Sephardic figure on the part of the Germans. In general, both *Haskalah* movements attempted to work out a version of assimilation either by aligning themselves to the Sephardic ideal or by rebutting it. Scholarship also shows that the Russian authors, including Pushkin, were swept up by Sephardism's close cousin, Orientalism, as part of their exploration of Romanticism. Litvak argues that the Jewish *Haskalah* movement in Russia was more contingent upon Romantic ideals than Jewish ones, it does not seem implausible to suggest that Gelman's romanticism of the Sephardic figure and his own rhetorical positioning as a noble, worthy-of-assimilation Jew, could have come about in part due to his own literary, social, political, and personal *milieu*, particularly in so far as his literary idols, Borges and Gerchunoff, belonged to a cosmopolitan literary arena.

particular, the early twentieth-century literary work of Alberto Gerchunoff served to solidify the Sephardic culture as part of mainstream Argentinian culture. The Sephardim were the first among the Jewish population to come to Argentina in 1888.[34] After World War II, the Jewish immigrants who came to live in Argentina were overwhelmingly European, and yet the first settlers were actually non-Ashkenazim from Morocco.[35] Among Ashkenazic Jews, who accounted for the majority of the community, a Sephardic identity was harnessed in order to justify their inclusion into Argentinian society. Gerchunoff's *Los gauchos judíos* published in 1910, used Sephardic themes to help create a sense of belonging in a predominantly Spanish-speaking country. During a time when Jews were marginalized not only in Europe, but also in the lands of the diaspora, Gerchunoff tried to connect his own Jewishness to the ancestral language of Jewish Spanish in order to show that even Ashkenazim could find commonalities with their Spanish-speaking neighbors. The logic of comparing the Russian immigrants to medieval Sephardim may seem strange at first. In an article, "Los gauchos judíos de Alberto Gerchunoff en su centenario" James A. Hussar clarifies Gerchunoff's reasoning behind his self-Sephardizing cause: "Argentinians are the descendants of the Medieval Spanish, while the Russian Jews, despite being Ashkenazic represent the heirs of the Sephardic culture that flourished in the Iberian Peninsula during the Middle Ages. The meeting of these two groups in the Americas presents an opportunity to repair the abuses of the past."[36]

Gerchunoff's project to integrate the Jewish community into Argentinian culture relied upon establishing that while Jews were culturally and religiously different from other Argentinians, there was no reason why they could not contribute to the richness of their new milieu. According to Gerchunoff's line of reasoning, making the connection between the new Russian immigrants and the expelled Jews of *Sepharad* gave the Argentinian government a chance to retroactively address the injustices of Spain. The implication is that the newly independent nation of Argentina should not commit the same mistakes as her mother country. If Argentina were to make the same errors, perhaps there would be negative ramifications just as Spain had experienced during the Latin American wars of independence. Gerchunoff's project of Jewish assimilation into mainstream Argentinean culture shows faith in his non-Jewish compatriots. As Stavans

---

34 Stephen Sadow, Annette H. Levine, and Natasha Zaretsky, *Landscapes of Memory and Impunity: The Aftermath of the AMIA Bombing in Jewish Argentina* (Leiden: Brill, 2015), 103.
35 Edna Aizenberg, *On the Edge of the Holocaust: The Shoah in Latin American Literature and Culture* (Waltham, MA: Brandeis University Press, 2016), 33.
36 My translation. James A. Hussar, "Los gauchos judíos de Alberto Gerchunoff en su centenario," *Hispanófila* 163, no. 163 (2011): 41.

explains in ¡Oy, Caramba! An Anthology of Jewish Stories from Latin America, that Gerchunoff's elected homeland was Argentina: "The province of Entre Ríos and the cosmopolitanism of Buenos Aires remained for him a diasporic Promised Land where the contribution of Jews would always be welcomed in the shaping of Argentine culture and where all manifestations of antisemitism would ultimately vanish."[37]

Mónica Szurmuk, in "Home in the Pampas," argues that the publication date of Gerchunoff's *Los gauchos judíos* coinciding with the centennial of Argentinian independence from Spain is significant for understanding his political motivations.[38] The historical fact that Jewish people who spoke a form of "Spanish" were the original immigrants to Argentina worked toward creating a rhetorical argument that Ashkenazic Jews could not only be integrated in the mainstream culture, but also contribute to the wholesome values on which the country was founded.[39] Judith Laikin Elkin points out that a common theme in Argentinian literature is the complexity of identity and multiculturalism, and thus these works contributed to the general interest in the effects of immigration on Argentina as a whole.[40]

From Gelman's perspective, the Sephardic Argentinian assimilation was "successful" because it offered a common Hispanic heritage between the Sephardim and their Spanish-speaking countrymen. In contrast, Gelman criticized his Russian father's attempt to assimilate into Argentinian society as merely copying or mimicking an authentic-sounding accent. Gelman grew up with the opinion that he was the only real *porteño* in his family, and that his father was in some way a hypocrite. Gelman's latent insecurity about his relationship with his father clarified as he began to write the poems that would later become *Dibaxu*. Gelman wrote about negative recollections from his childhood, including the memory of seeing his father sit alone in a dark dining room. Gelman surmised that his father must have been brooding over his memories of Russia. Gelman could not help feeling like his Ashkenazic background left him at a disadvantage in some way. Directly underneath this diary entry about his father's accent and Borges's perfect Spanish, Gelman wrote notes to continue reading María Zambrano's work on exile, the Lurianic Kabbalah, and in parenthesis, he wrote "escolio

---

[37] Ilan Stavans, *Oy, caramba!: An Anthology of Jewish Stories from Latin America* (Albuquerque: University of New Mexico Press, 2016), 11.
[38] See Mónica Szurmuk, "Home in the Pampas: Alberto Gerchunoff's Jewish Gauchos," in *Jews at Home: The Domestication of Identity*, Jewish Cultural Studies 2, ed. Simon J. Bronner (Liverpool: Liverpool University Press, Littman Library of Jewish Civilization, 2010), 245.
[39] Ibid.
[40] See Judith Laiken Elkin, *The Jews of Latin America* (New York: Holmes and Meier, 1998), 4.

de *dibaxu*," which linked his train of thought to *Dibaxu*, which he was in the process of drafting at the time.[41]

In an untitled and undated document, likely from 1987, Gelman wrote the following critique of his father's attempt to assimilate into the Argentinian culture, even as it was modeled on none other than Jorge Luis Borges: "I imagine my father, having left Russia definitely to make a home in Argentina. He spoke Argentinian Spanish, according to Borges – without an accent, and today I believe that is what truly indicated his perfect other-ness. He who so completely seems like the other is the other. The only thing that unites us is our differences."[42]

Scholarship from Brodksy, Ludmer, Sosnowski, and others has shown that Borges was considered a patriarchal figure in Argentinian culture during the twentieth century. According to Mariana O'Ryan in *The Making of Jorge Luis Borges as an Argentine Cultural Icon*, Borges had a role in twentieth-century Argentinian self-fashioning; his figure was instrumental in defining their cultural identity.[43] A canonical Argentinian writer *par excellence*, Borges and his literary oeuvre was one of the single-most influential factors in determining what was considered Argentinian. Gelman thought that his father not only wanted to be considered just as Argentinian as Borges was, but also as sophisticated and erudite. Before the Latin American Boom era, Borges had made Argentina famous worldwide by paving the way for a new era of cosmopolitan writers who did not want to be shackled by pejorative conceptions of Latin America as rural and backwards.[44]

Gelman thought that his father's perfect mastery of Argentinian Spanish revealed only more clearly how much he did *not* belong in Argentina. His father's attempt to assimilate and "pass" for a true Argentinian presented a contrast to Gelman's mother, who never could overcome her unassimilated immigrant status.[45] His father's perfect accent bespoke the subliminal silence of repressed memories

---

41 An "escolio" refers to a small annotation or clarification that appears next to a body of text. It seems that he is making a note to himself that everything he had mentioned before is at the root (Gelman papers, Box 000724).
42 "Imagino a mi padre, a los 41 de edad, abandonado Rusia para instalarse definitivamente en la Argentina. Hablaba el castellano el argentino, según Borges- sin acento y hoy creo que eso verdaderamente señalaba su perfecta ajenidad. Quien tanto se parece al otro es otro. Lo único que nos une son nuestras diferencias" (Gelman papers, Box 000724).
43 Mariana O'Ryan, *The Making of Jorge Luis Borges as an Argentine Cultural Icon* (Cambridge: Modern Humanities Research Association, 2014), 3.
44 Edna Aizenberg, *Borges and His Successors: The Borgesian Impact on Literature and the Arts* (Columbia: University of Missouri Press, 1990).
45 The daughter of a Ukrainian rabbi, Gelman's mother suffered the loss of her sister during a fire caused by a pogrom: "Y por qué esa imagen del pogrom en que mi madre perdió entre las llamas a una hermanita de dos años que mi abuela no alcanzó a rescatar pervive en mí?"

and trauma. Gelman's critique of his father goes beyond a mere judgment of his father's "passing;" his writings imply that his father was actively repressing his own Jewishness by imitation, thereby missing the fact that Borges could actually be considered a Jewish icon. Gelman was undoubtedly ahead of his time in his reading of Borges as a Jew. Only in 2016, Stavans published a book controversially titled *Borges the Jew*.[46] Stavans describes Borges as an honorary Jew – even though the writer had no demonstrable Jewish heritage. Borges professed to having "thought of himself as Jewish" without knowing whether or not he had the right to do so.[47] When he was accused of having Jewish heritage by political enemies, he accepted the adjective as a compliment.[48] Gelman's judgment of his father's Borges-quality accent implies that his father did not understand that what made Borges truly Argentinian was indeed his mutable multiculturalism.

On yet another undated document from his personal papers, Gelman wrote that Borges was an Argentinian by sheer will – having two layers to his patriotism to Argentina: the first was simply expressed in the short story, "El hombre de la esquina rosada" published in English as "Streetcorner Man."[49] Set in the slums of Buenos Aires, this short story, published early in Borges's career, is known for giving a realistic representation of Argentinian street slang. Gelman compares Borges's ability to accurately recreate the Argentinian speech patterns with his

---

(Gelman papers, Box 000724). "And why does that image live inside of me – the pogrom in which my mother lost her little sister that my grandmother wasn't able to save?" (my translation).

46 See Stavans's preface: "My principle argument is that Borges found Jewishness to be a key to entering and exiting the world, a way of reading, or better, a relentless desire to translate other literature in order to make them feel like home."

47 See Federico Finchelstein, "An Argentine Experience? Borges, Judaism, and the Holocaust," in *The New Jewish Argentina*, Jewish Latin America 2, ed. Adriana Brodsky and Raanan Rein (Leiden: Brill, 2014), 147–78, esp. 147.

48 It is interesting that the contemporary Sephardic community recognizes Borges's interest in Sephardic culture in a positive light, but as we have seen, Gelman's reception by his Jewish audience was not unequivocally positive. Borges incorporated both Ashkenazic and Sephardic historical elements into his works. As seen in the poem, "Una Llave de Salonika," Borges was inspired to write about the nostalgia that the Sephardim held for *Sepharad*: "Abarbanel, Farias o Pinedo, / Arrojados de España por impía Persecución, / conservan todavía / una llave de una casa de Toledo." "Abarbanel, Farias or Pinedo / Cast away by the evil Inquisition / still keep a key / to a home in Toledo" (my translation). Borges's connection to the Sephardic world is still remembered today in Sephardic articles and literary magazines. One example of interest in Borges was a Spanish radio show in 2013 that featured Sephardic studies scholar Matilda Barnatán. He also wrote extensively about the Ashkenazic Jewish experience. See Finchelstein, "An Argentine Experience?"

49 In his essay "Borges o el valor," Gelman praised Borges the writer for his courage to admit that he had been wrong in the past to remain politically silent and disconnected from the dangers of fascism.

patriotism, but he argues as well that the writer also had a "deeper" (or perhaps what could be translated as "fundamental") patriotism: Borges's elected Jewishness.[50] For Gelman, Borges's fundamental patriotic quality stemmed from his ability to flee parochial disagreements and, in the kabbalistic sense of the word, create new worlds. Borges cited his friend, Saúl Sosnowski's fundamental work, *Borges y la Cabalá*, as an example of how Borges's acquired Jewishness defined him and his essentially Argentinian character: "Borges was an Argentinian by sheer willpower and he achieved a fame to which he never aspired. From his superficial Argentinian-ness remained a few patriotic verses, among other texts, 'Streetcorner Man' … From his deep(er) Argentinian-ness was born the necessity to flee from local cannibalism, the invention of logical worlds, and even problems, the delirium of the universal library, time outside of time, and the sensation that we are all dreamers."[51] That fact that a figure as influential as Borges celebrated an acquired "Jewishness" gave Gelman the framework by which he too could be essentially Argentinian, by reinventing his accent through exploring Jewish Spanish.[52] Gelman realized that just as in the case of Borges, there could be something inextricably Argentinian about his Jewishness, and in a way, Gelman followed in Borges's footstep by "acquiring" a Sephardic poetic voice in *Dibaxu*.

In "Lo judío y la literatura en castellano" published by *Hispamérica* in 1992, Gelman elaborates on how he had grown to view his identity as a Jewish writer in terms of Latin American heritage. In this article, Gelman lists both Alberto Gerchunoff and Jorge Luis Borges as the most eminent Jewish writers of the twentieth century in the Spanish language. This article implies that the only author absent from this list is Gelman himself. Keeping in mind that until 1994 with the publication of *Dibaxu* Gelman's oeuvre did not specifically reference his own Jewish heritage, his article in *Hispamérica* could be viewed as Gelman's first step toward revealing his Jewish background.

One of the fundamental motivating factors for Gelman's fascination with Jewish Spanish was that he felt compelled to recover what he considered to be an

---

50 Borges often found literary inspiration from Jewish philosophy, and traditions as well as kabbalist themes and Lurianic mysticism.

51 "Borges fue argentino por pura voluntad y alcanzó una fama mundial que no se propuso. De su argentinidad de superficie quedan unos versos patrióticos y, entre otros textos, 'El hombre de la esquina rosada…' De su argentinidad profunda deben hacer nacido la necesidad de fuga de la antropofagia local, la invención de mundos ilógicos y aun problemas, el delirio de la biblioteca universal, el tiempo fuera del tiempo, la sensación de que todos somos soñados."

52 Josefina Ludmer discusses how Borges is considered a father figure in her essay, "Cómo salir de Borges," in *Jorge Luis Borges, intervenciones sobre el pensamiento y la literatura*, ed. William Rowe, Claudio Canaparo, and Annick Louis (Barcelona: Ediciones Paidos Iberica, 2000), 289–300). She uses the term "patricide" to refer to what it would be like to cut off his influence.

"authentic" accent. Gelman writes, "He who appears so much like the other is the other. The only thing that unites us are our differences." Gelman did not want to fall into what he considered his father's trap of attempting to belong by merely passing for the "other." According to Gelman's papers, he thought that if he truly wanted to belong to Argentina, he needed to recover his heritage and the unique Jewish accent that exposed the ostensibly most "authentic" part of himself.[53] Following this line of reason, Gelman grew to doubt the idea that language could make you belong to a place; instead he theorized that at the root of language itself was an ultimate form of exile: "Who knows. And the language of the other is a like a previous wound and even more so, an exile that was imposed like what happened to my parents. This happened to me in exile. Italian, French, the Spanish from Spain, like hard blows to the inside of my tongue, which sticks to the roof of my mouth."[54]

The fact that Gelman was put off by all of the other languages including Castilian Spanish is perhaps another reason why he was motivated to discover the Jewish language that came before.

While in exile, Gelman began to equate having an accent with truly belonging to a place, as if a "foreign" accent could be the only defining factor to prove an authentic affiliation with a particular country. The reference to Psalm 127 implies that in order for the Jewish people to be considered faithful among their enemies, they could never lose the linguistic markers of their lack of belonging. Their inherited Jewishness was defined by exile: "Language is so much more than a worldview. It has an unconscious depository of the centuries. It is perhaps the womb that holds us even still and continues to feed us and we feed on after being expelled from the mother's belly. We pass from the mother's womb to the mother tongue, from a material uterus to a spiritual one that will not abandon us until our death."[55]

---

53 In his private writings, Gelman criticized his father for inauthenticity, but seemingly failed to notice the similarities between them. Both of them made painstaking attempts to belong to Argentina by means of language. Gelman used the appropriation of the Ladino language to approximate himself to his homeland of choice, in the same way that his father attempted to pass for Argentinian. The appropriation of language (whether it was Ladino or modern-day Spanish) aided both of them in their attempts to belong. Despite these efforts, it is clear that a sense of "authentic" belonging would forever remain elusive for Gelman.
54 "Quién sabe. Y el lenguaje del otro como herida anterior y además, la lengua del exilio sobre impuesta como ocurrió con mis padres. Me ocurrió a mí en el exilio. (no antes salvo del modo dicho) Me hirieron el italiano, el francés, el español de España, como golpes duros al interior de mi lengua, esa que se pega al paladar" (Gelman papers, Box 000724). Gelman, "Testimonio: lo judío y la literatura en castellano," *Hispamérica* 21, no. 62 (1992): 83–90. This allusion to "which sticks to the roof of my mouth" is a quote from the iconic Psalm 137: "If I forget you, Oh Jerusalem."
55 "La lengua es mucho más que una cosmovisión. Tiene un inconsciente, depósito de siglos. Será además una matriz que aún nos contiene y con tenemos, aún nos alimenta y alimentamos,

According to Gelman, *Sepharad* was the symbol of the womb that birthed its child into the world. The only thing that the Sephardim could hold onto going forward was their maternal tongue, a veritable linguistic "depository of centuries" of successive exiles and traumas. After this "expulsion" from the womb, when a child begins to learn to speak, he is confounded by his lack of ability to express himself even in his "mother tongue." The difference between the reality of emotions and the child's inability to speak is the first universal form of exile: Gelman believed that the role of a poet is to attempt to recover a child's nascent emotions before attempting speech: "Como un niño, el poema busca nombrar lo que no puede."[56] In this same article, Gelman makes reference to both Yiddish and *sefardí*, the language of the Sephardic Jews expelled from Spain.[57] In Gelman's private notes about *Dibaxu*, he makes a direct connection between his linguistically repressed childhood and Poem XIII in Jewish Spanish:

eris	eres	you are
mi única avla	mi única palabra	my only word
no sé	no sé	I don't know
tu nombri[58]	tu nombre	your name

The language of Ladino, and indeed this specific poem, was at the nucleus of his theory of language, trauma, exile, and belonging. This little poem could be read in different ways. One way is that the poetic voice speaks directly to the poem

---

después de ser expulsados del vientre materno. Pasamos del vientre materno a la lengua materna, de una matriz material a otra espiritual, que no nos abandonará hasta nuestra muerte." Ibid., 84.

56 Gellman papers.

57 Gelman, "Testimonio: lo judío y la literatura en castellano," 83.

58 "[Y]ou are / my only word / I don't know / your name" (my translation). Interestingly, in all of Gelman's diary entries, letters, and notes about *Dibaxu*, he never quotes the Castilian Spanish version. It is unclear which he wrote first, but based on the way that he would cite his own work, it is my estimation that he wrote the Jewish Spanish versions first and that he considered them to the most important. On the other hand, every time he corresponded with a native Spanish-speaker about the collection (whether it was his editor or someone else), he always explained the existence of the Jewish Spanish from the perspective of the Spanish version and the "other." He also writes this way in his prologue when he says, "el otro para escuchar." It is my opinion that Gelman was not very invested in writing a prologue to begin with and for that reason, he practically quoted himself and the things he had written other people while drafting the prologue. Perhaps Gelman did not want to explain the reasons undergirding *Dibaxu* because they were far more personal than anyone would actually realize, until of course, his personal papers were showcased posthumously. For all of these reasons, this time I am quoting only the Jewish Spanish because instead of citing the published version of the collection, I am citing his private notes.

itself, saying "you are my only speech/word/poem." Another way of reading Poem XIII is that perhaps the "you" is an object of love that would indicate that through this dedication the interlocutor addressed becomes poetry itself.

By addressing a nameless "you," Gelman not only invokes his own feelings, but also those of a people historically voiceless – a people whose stories, experiences, fears, and dreams have disappeared along with the dying-out of the language. One of the themes of his notes and his poetry is silence that comes from trauma of his childhood, and indeed the trauma of losing his son, Marcelo, and daughter-in-law, Claudia, during the Videla dictatorship.

XII	XII	XII
lu qui a mi dates	lo que me diste	what you gave me
es avla qui timbla	es palabra que tiembla	is a word that trembles
mila manu del tiempu	en la mano del tiempo	in the hand of time
aviarta para bever /	abierta para beber/	open to drink /
cayada	callada	silent
esta la caza	está la casa	is the house
ondi nus bezamus	donde nos besamos	where we kissed
adientru dil sol /	adentro del sol /	beneath the sun /

Gelman realized that writing in Jewish Spanish was not just an optional literary adventure: *Dibaxu* was the most fundamental expression of his identity as a Jewish Argentinian poet. *Dibaxu* represented the fact that the exile that Gelman inherited by birth, the exile into which he was forced by the Videla regime and ultimately the exile that he chose as a poet all came together to create a multifaceted, but integral identity, all of which came to bear in this collection of poems. Instead of viewing exile as a punishment, Gelman came to see that exile and exilic travel were essential to creativity. In Poem XIV, the figure of the bird effectively bridges the gap between the languages, cultures, times, and even the spatial arrangement of the stanzas themselves. This little bird is a symbol of hope and resilience despite incredible difficulties:

XIV	XIV	XIV
lu qui avalas dexa cayer	lo que hablas deja caer	what you say lets fall
un páxaru	un pájaro	a bird
qui li soy nidi /	y le soy nido /	and I am the nest /
il páxaru caya adientru di mi /	el pájaro calla en mí /	the bird hushes inside of me
veyi	mira	look
lu qui faze di mi /	lo que hace de mí /	what it is making me /

This poem shows how the poetic voice has been able to fashion a personalized version of exile by turning it into a creative experience. This time it is the speech of the apostrophized "you" who lets a bird fall into the nest. The poetic voice says that he is the nest that provides a home for the bird. It is fascinating that in this poem we have an almost identical word pair, "*cayar*" and "*cayer*." Although the sounds of the words are similar, they have divergent meanings in the poem. In Ladino, "*cayar*" means "to be silent" and "*cayer*" means to "fall," thus rendering the stanza: the bird (through speech) falls into the welcoming nest of the poetic voice. Once in the nest, the bird goes quiet, as if comforted and nestled into the twigs. One interesting aspect is that due to the similarity of the sound and common phraseology, the line, "adientru di mi" almost reads that "the bird falls inside of me," instead of what it actually says, that the bird, "quiets down or hushes inside of me." This sound similarity is important to the interpretation of the poem in that the aural pattern is proven integral to interpreting the poem because we also have an additional potential sound confusion in the last line.

"Lu qui faze di mi" literally reads "what the bird does of me." "Faze di mi" or "hace de mi" usually mean making something of someone or something. This phrase could be used to talk about a cake that is made of flour, for example. But in the poem, the bird is hushing (not falling) inside of the poetic voice. Then the bird is making something with the poet or making something out of the poet, instead of making something inside of the poet. The prepositions "*adientru*" and "*di*" have contrasting meanings which subtly change the reading of the poem. This little bird traverses the space between the two stanzas, falls from the "you" through the "*avla*" and makes something with/of the poetic voice. These details imply that the travel from stanza one to stanza two allows the bird to inspire change in the poet himself. In this way, when the bird nestles down inside of the poet, he is actually transforming the poet's qualities or capabilities. A final intriguing aspect about this poem is the second address toward the apostrophized "you" in the second stanza. "*Veyi*" is an informal command that means "look" or "notice." This poem's familiarity with the apostrophized "you" seems to imply causality. Thanks to the "*avla*" that was unleashed by the "you," this brave little bird travels down to the poetic voice and creates something new inside of him: poetry, identity, belonging.

2 The "True" Homeland and the *terra ignota:* A Conflictive Romance

Gelman professed love for Argentina until the end, and yet he never returned to live there. Instead, he chose to remain in Mexico, the same place where his ashes were later scattered in a river by his wife, Mara.⁵⁹ In a prosaic poem entitled "Exile," Gelman referred to Argentina as if she (the country) were a woman that he loved:

> It is fair that I miss her. We always loved each other like that: her asking more of me, me asking more of her, both racked with pain that the other one caused, the strength of love that with which we loved each other. I love you, *patria*, and you love me. Through this love, we burn off imperfections, lives.⁶⁰

"Exile" is the most straightforward declaration of Gelman's affection for Argentina. He speaks to his country directly using the informal Argentinian dialect, *"vos"* that Gelman always employed in his personal correspondence with anyone who was born in Argentina regardless of the level of formality of the letter's content. The *"vos"* colors the sound of his voice and establishes a familiar, even playful connection with the interlocutor: "I love you, *patria*, and you love me." Gelman speaks about Argentina as if they both felt the same pain, the same love, and ultimately the same longing to be reunited once more. But why could they not be brought back together? After the dictatorship ended, Gelman could have returned to his beloved patria, but he chose not to. In *Dibaxu*, Gelman leaves clues that help shed light upon his rationale. In particular, Poem XXIV can be read as a direct address to Argentina – an attempt to explain why despite Gelman's desire for his beloved country, he could never return permanently:

amarti es istu:	amarte es esto:	loving you is this:
un avla qui va a dizer /	una palabra que está por decir /	a word that is yet unsaid /
un arvulicu sin folyas	un arbolito sin hojas	a tree without leaves
qui da solombra /	que da sombra /	that gives shade /

Gelman's notes about *Dibaxu* reveal that he was fascinated by silence that comes from a word that has not yet been spoken. The word remains between the mind and the mouth in the liminal space between conception and articulation. In his notes about Poem XXIV, Gelman described this silence like a *terra ignota* that lies

---

59 Gelman's ashes were scattered at a river near Nepantla, Mexico, the town where seventeenth-century poet Sor Juana Inés de la Cruz was born.
60 "Es justo que la extrañe. Porque siempre nos quisimos así: ella pidiendo más de mí, yo de ella, dolidos ambos del dolor que el uno al otro hacía, y fuertes del amor que nos tenemos. Te amo patria y me amás. En ese amor quemamos imperfecciones, vidas" (Gelman papers, Box 000732).

between the imagination and written word.⁶¹ Writing in Jewish Spanish allowed Gelman to play with this idea of silence because as he said in his prologue, there is "something" – a silence – that trembles between the two versions of the poem.⁶² In Gelman's work, "silence" is often a metonym of trauma, as evidenced here in his notes about Poem XXIV:

> I don't know what I am listening to when I write. Perhaps the silences of the imagination from where the least interrelated or connected things happen. It would seem as though the imagination is different from the silence of the word. Between the two, opens up or exists a *terra ignota* that I tend to feel like an emptiness. But this emptiness is not nothingness, it is alive, and in it tremble thousands of faces that I will never see ... like a shadow without a body?⁶³

What has a shadow without a body, but a tree without leaves? The empty space between branches can be understood as the rupture that characterizes that condition of exile – still belonging to the life-source, but separate; space figured by absence. And yet, the *etz hayim* depicted here in Poem XXIV is not without hope.⁶⁴ Just as the word that resides in the mouth waiting to be spoken, the tree in winter waits patiently to give forth leaves once more. One of the notes that can be found in Gelman's personal effects is the following dictum: "The journey toward the poem is necessary, the poem is not."⁶⁵ Gelman grew to believe that poetry was more about the process than the result, more about the journey than the destination, and for that reason, by remaining in exile, by choosing to die in exile,

---

61 According to the holdings at Princeton's Juan Gelman Archive at the Firestone Library, Gelman only wrote explicitly about two poems in *Dibaxu*: Poem XXIV "Amarti es istu" and Poem XIII "Eris mi unica avla."
62 Gelman, *Dibaxu*, 895.
63 "No sé qué escucho cuando escribo. Tal vez los silencios de la imaginación, por donde pasan atadas las cosas menos relacionadas entre sí. Pareciera que el silencio de la imaginación es diferente del silencio de la palabra. Entre ambos se abre o existe una terra ignota que suelo sentir como vacío. Pero ese vacío no es la nada, es un vacío que está vivo y en él agitan millones de rostros que nunca veré. ... ¿cómo sombra sin cuerpo?"
64 The "*etz hayim*" or Tree of Life is a kabbalist symbol of the divine emanations. See Gershom Scholem's discussion on the creation and Lurianic thought in his book, *Kabbalah* (Salinas: Meridan Publishing, 1978), 128–35. From his notes and personal papers, it is clear that Gelman was reading about Isaac Luria preceding the publication of *Dibaxu*. In particular, he read the fourth volume of a book in Spanish called, *Apócrifos del Antiguo Testamento* by Alejandro Diez Macho published in Madrid in 1984. There is a photocopy of pages of this book with Gelman's underlining and marginal notes.
65 "El viaje hacia el poema es más importante que el poema. El viaje es necesario, el poema no" (Gelman papers, Box 000717).

Gelman chose to characterize his path as that of a poet: one of eternal wandering, searching for a home through words.

Dibaxu was the culmination of the process by which Gelman tried to make sense of his feelings of rupture and displacement. By adopting a Sephardic accent in *Dibaxu*, Gelman tried to uncover an essence that he felt he lost during his repressed childhood. The way he conceived of the Sephardic condition of exile became an apt metaphor by which Gelman could approximate himself to his chosen homeland, Argentina. Gelman's choice to remain in Mexico until his death becomes less surprising upon making the realization he never felt more "Argentinian" than when he was away from his patria. As he commented in an interview in 2004: "Here I exercise my foreignness with a great deal of propriety."[66] Gelman went on to explain to the interviewer all of his late-night escapades involving the famed Mexican "vitamin T" – Tequila, Tacos, Tamales. Although remaining in Mexico made him feel more Argentinian than ever, his work as a poet never allowed him to rest. Gelman's private papers reveal that many nights after such adventures around the Mexican countryside, he would return to the stillness of his home, slip a piece of paper into the typewriter, and begin to write in a tender and inquisitive voice. *Dibaxu* ... underneath the bravado of "exercising of his foreignness" on Mexican soil pervaded a longing to comprehend the subliminal feeling of loss: "cayada esta la caza ..." and in that silence, Gelman would write.

Bibliography

Aizenberg, Edna. *On the Edge of the Holocaust: The Shoah in Latin American Literature and Culture*. Waltham, MA: Brandeis University Press, 2016.

Aizenberg, Edna. *Borges and His Successors: The Borgesian Impact on Literature and the Arts*. Columbia: University of Missouri Press, 1990.

Alazraki, Jaime. *Borges and the Kaballah: And Other Essays on His Fiction and Poetry*. Cambridge: Cambridge University Press, 1988.

Balbuena, Monique. *Homeless Tongues: Poetry and Languages of the Sephardic Diaspora*. Palo Alto: Stanford University Press, 2016.

Bortnick, Rachel Amado, ed. *Ladinokomunita*. Yahoo Forum Messages. Accessed July 19, 2008.

Brodsky, Adriana M. *Sephardi, Jewish, Argentine community and national identity*. Bloomington: Indiana University Press, 2016.

Elkin, Judith Laikin. *The Jews of Latin America*. New York: Holmes and Meier, 1998.

Finchelstein, Federico. "An Argentine Experience? Borges, Judaism, and the Holocaust." In *The New Jewish Argentina: Facets of Jewish Experiences in the Southern Cone*. Edited by Adriana Brodsky and Raanan Rein, 147–178. Leiden: Brill, 2014.

---

66 "Yo aquí ejerzo mi extranjería con muchísima propiedad." Ibid.

Fontanet, Hernán, and Osvaldo Bayer. 2015. *Gelman: un poeta y su vida*. Aguilar.
Gelman, Juan. *Between Words: Juan Gelman's Public Letter*. Translated by Lisa Rose Bradford. San Francisco: Coimbra Editions, 2010.
Gelman, Juan. *Dibaxu*. Buenos Aires: Seix Barral, 1994.
Gelman, Juan. Papers. Department of Rare Books and Special Collections. Princeton University Library, Princeton.
Gelman, Juan. *Poesía Reunida: 1956–2010*. Barcelona: Seix Barral, 2012.
Gelman, Juan. "Testimonio: lo judío y la literatura en castellano." *Hispamérica*. 21 (62): 83–90.
Hussar, James A. "Los gauchos judíos de Alberto Gerchunoff en su centenario." *Hispanófila* 163 (2011): 39–52.
Ludmer, Josefina. *A propósito de íconos nacionales: Borges*. New Haven: Yale University, 2001.
Naar, Devin. "In Search of Uncle Salomon." University of Washington. Kane Hall, Seattle, WA. January 6, 2013. JewDub Talks. Internet resource.
O'Ryan, Mariana. *The Making of Jorge Luis Borges as an Argentine Cultural Icon*. Modern Humanities Research Association, 2014.
Sadow, Stephen, Annette H. Levine and Natasha Zaretsky, eds. *Landscapes of Memory and Impunity: The Aftermath of the AMIA Bombing in Jewish Argentina*. Leiden: Brill, 2015.
Stavans, Ilan. *Oy, caramba!: An Anthology of Jewish Stories from Latin America*. Albuquerque: University of New Mexico Press, 2016.
Stavans, Ilan. *Singer's Typewriter and Mine: Reflections on Jewish Culture*. Lincoln: University of Nebraska Press, 2012.
Sosnowski, Saúl. *Borges y la cábala: la búsqueda del verbo*. Buenos Aires: Ediciones Hispamerica, 1976.
Szurmuk, Mónica. "El Viaje a Europa de Alberto Gerchunoff." *Hispamérica* 41, no. 121 (2012): 25–35.

Part 4: **Multiple Exiles, Contingent Homelands**

Jeffrey A. Grossman
France as *Wahlheimat* for Two German Jews: Heinrich Heine and Walter Benjamin

In 1844, Heinrich Heine published an obituary for the recently deceased scholar of Jewish religion and history, Ludwig Markus. Like Heine himself, Markus had twenty years earlier been a member of the short-lived Society for the Culture and Science of the Jews, and like Heine, he had ultimately settled in France. While the obituary is devoted to Markus's life and work, it becomes of necessity, Heine claims, an obituary for the society itself as well – providing an account of the society's members, their achievements and, more to the point, the society's ultimate failure.[1] That failure, Heine claims, resulted from the general post-Enlightenment decline in Jewish spirit, and was aided by the failed emancipation of Jews in the German lands.[2] Indeed, Heine begins his dual obituary by turning to the unhappy condition of Germans, Jewish or otherwise, living in France, asking specifically: "What is the reason that, of the Germans who come over to France, so many succumb to insanity?" "The number," he adds, "of those who, apart from a few more or less lucid moments, suffer from this dark malady is very great, and one would almost like to claim insanity as the national disease of the Germans in France."[3]

I begin with Heine's somber remark – which grows only darker when one learns that Markus himself went insane two weeks before his death in 1843 – because it underscores the peculiar situation of the German, and perhaps especially German Jewish exile – in France – living, that is, in the place of refuge, which, whatever its own political and social problems, has crossed so to speak to "the other side" of the question of emancipation and embodies hope for the future – the bitterness of which only grows when one casts an eye on conditions in the actual German homeland.

In the following, I explore this dynamic in the case of two German intellectuals of Jewish extraction – Heinrich Heine and Walter Benjamin. Born a century apart – Heine in 1797, Benjamin in 1892 – and both dying mid-century in exile, though from different causes and under very different conditions, Heine and Benjamin may initially appear to make for an odd pairing. Heine was known for the

---

[1] Heinrich Heine, "Ludwig Markus," in *Heinrich Heine: Historisch-kritische Gesamtausgabe der Werke*, ed. Manfred Windfuhr et al., 16 vols. (Düsseldorf: Hoffmann und Campe, 1973–1997) 14.1: 269; further references to this edition of Heine's work are abbreviated as DHA.
[2] DHA 14.1: 270–71.
[3] Ibid., 265; all translations, unless otherwise noted, are my own.

popularity of his poetry and prose and his many literary provocations, political and otherwise, but was also criticized by influential twentieth-century intellectuals like Brecht and especially Karl Kraus – both of whom Benjamin admired and responded to in his own work.[4] Hence, Benjamin, who admitted to having read the poetry only in passing and without ever developing a taste for it, retained at best a detached view of Heine.[5] He read with interest Heine's *Französische Zustände* (*French Conditions*, 1832), a collection of the articles Heine wrote from Paris in the aftermath of the 1830 revolution in France, but also echoed Kraus by referring to Heine along with Börne as the "creator of German feuilletonism" – a backhanded compliment, since Benjamin seems to have accepted Kraus's criticism of especially Heine's feuilletons as a trivializing form of journalism.[6]

Alternatively, Benjamin, whose work is perhaps more familiar or at least more broadly discussed in academic circles today, and to whom no brief characterization can do justice, is widely recognized for his theoretical complexity, his almost uncanny ability to draw from aesthetic theory and philosophy, art and literature, from Marxist theory (often mediated second hand – through thinkers as different as Lukács, Karl Korsch, Asja Lacis, Brecht, and Adorno, among others)[7] and aspects of Jewish mysticism, about which Gershom Scholem was the most important, if not sole, interlocutor – and to weave them into a single, if multivalent, narrative. With his often elliptical, often seductive critical inquiries into literature and allegory, society and change, culture and commodity, into the translation and transmission of texts and artworks, their production and reproduction under changing conditions – technological and otherwise – Benjamin's inquiries are often cited for their vividly suggestive language and provocative theses. At the same time, a certain quality about Benjamin has, as the late Michael André Bernstein noted, prompted observers to frequently adopt a reverential attitude toward him – the result perhaps of a combination of intellectual and personal

---

[4] Karl Kraus, *Heine und die Folgen* (Munich: Alberg Langen, 1910); Bertolt Brecht, "Profane und pontifikale Linie der Lyrik," in *Werke: Große kommentierte Berliner und Frankfurter Ausgabe*, ed. Werner Hecht et al. (Berlin, Weimar, Frankfurt am Main: Aufbau and Suhrkamp, 1994), 26: 416–17.
[5] Dietmar Goltschnigg and Hartmut Steinecke, introduction to volume 2 of *Heine und die Nachwelt*, ed. Dietmar Goltschnigg and Steinecke, 3 vols. (Berlin: Schmidt, 2006–2011), 2: 56.
[6] Walter Benjamin, "Juden in der deutschen Kultur," in *Gesammelte Schriften*, ed. Rolf Tiedemann and Hermann Schweppenhauser, with Theodor Adorno and Gershom Scholem (Frankfurt am Main: Suhrkamp, 1972–1991), 2.2: 811–12; references to Benjamin's collected writings in German are henceforth given as GS.
[7] Howard Eiland and Michael W. Jennings, *Walter Benjamin: A Critical Biography* (Cambridge, MA: Belknap Press of Harvard University Press, 2014), 204–7, 320–26, 640.

characteristics as well as circumstances:[8] the demand for philosophical rigor, melancholy observation, left-wing political criticism, longing for messianic redemption, failed academic career (though he was a highly successful independent cultural critic and journalist), difficult personal life, and tragic ending of his life by morphine overdose in the small Pyrenees town of Port Bou while in flight from the Nazis.

Still, whatever the difficulties with this pairing, I want to argue that for both Heine and Benjamin, France served in figural and practical terms as a particular kind of *Wahlheimat*. If the connections between the France, or more precisely Paris, of Benjamin and Heine are not exactly parallel, their points of contact *together* with their differences – different periods in history, their different approaches to writing, culture and society, and their varying relationships to the place of their exile – can also shed light on the idea of *Wahlheimat*, the forms it might take, and the roles it might assume in one's life. Paris and France as *Wahlheimat* could, for both, serve as a point of projection. For Heine, it signaled, among other things, enlightenment and with it emancipation for Jews and indeed universal human emancipation. For Benjamin, in ways more complex, France held out the potential for future emancipation, or redemption, though this potential would have to be revealed by rigorous analysis and inquiry into French culture and society, and especially of (nineteenth-century) Paris as a modern city, as, that is, the place in which the most intensified confrontations and conflicts of modernity became most visibly manifest and had potential to illuminate.

Yet, precisely because France loomed so prominently in both Heine and Benjamin's writing and lives, there seems to be no one clear point of entry into this subject. In seeking that entry, I will focus here on points where an idealized or at least partly idealized image of France confronts disillusion and explore the ramifications of that encounter. This approach seems warranted because both Heine and Benjamin had an even deeper interest in and acquaintance with France than many of their contemporaries – in a period when among progressive German intellectuals it was standard practice, perhaps even a sine qua non, that one follow developments there, both cultural and political.

This approach, the focus on moments of disillusion, seems additionally warranted because, whatever the pull that France exerted upon them, both Heine

---

8 Michael André Bernstein, "Walter Benjamin: Apocalypse and Memory," in *Five Portraits: Modernity and the Imagination in Twentieth-Century German Writing* (Evanston, IL: Northwestern University Press, 2000), 79–98; despite Heine's devotees, especially among the German New Left, this is not a claim one can by any means broadly make for the controversial poet, ample evidence for which is found in the three-volume reception history and documentation *Heine und die Nachwelt*, compiled by Goltschnigg Steinecke, cited in n. 3.

and Benjamin ultimately moved to or, at least, chose to remain in France in times of duress. To be sure, the threat to Benjamin after 1933 was far greater, but Heine's own fear of arrest prompted his departure even as his remarks on insanity as the national disease of Germans in French exile should also give pause.

1 Heine's Troubled *Heimat*en

Heine went into French exile in 1831, remaining there, except for two visits to Germany in 1843 and 1844, until his death in 1856 from a mysterious illness that, from 1848 onward left him partially paralyzed and confined to what he called his "mattress grave."[9] After his move, Heine frequently wrote – both essays and journalism – about France for German audiences and, if less frequently, nonetheless memorably about Germany, especially German literature and thought, for French audiences. Yet, his connection to France dates to far earlier than 1831, and suggests why the France of his imaginings, a France perhaps less of the spirit at times than of the flesh, long preceded France as an actual adoptive homeland. Born in Düsseldorf on December 13, 1797, Heine lived until 1802 and again beginning in 1806 in a city under French administration, something that continued until the final defeat of the French forces and the Vienna Congress in 1815. In 1811, the then thirteen-year-old Heine witnessed Napoleon's arrival in Düsseldorf, an event memorialized in what many consider Heine's best work of prose – the partly fictional, partly autobiographical *Ideas: The Book Le Grand* of 1826 – although Heine would later adopt a more critical view of Napoleon and his imperialist aspirations. With the defeat of the French and occupation of Düsseldorf by Russian troops in 1813 and with the installation of Prussian rule at the Vienna Congress of 1815, the rights granted to Jews under Napoleon were largely rescinded there.[10] Jews were prohibited from entering the civil services, which included university professorships, a factor that played a role in Heine's later decision to undergo baptism, an act he experienced as deeply humiliating.[11] That situation no doubt influenced Heine's view of both Prussia and France, as did his inheritance of Enlightenment views of emancipation as a universal goal.

---

9 The best biographies of Heine in German and English, respectively, are Jan-Christoph Hausschild and Michael Werner, *"Der Zweck des Lebens ist das Leben selbst": Heinrich Heine-Eine Biographie* (Cologne: Kiepenheuer and Witsch, 1997), and Jeffrey Sammons, *Heinrich Heine: A Modern Biography* (Princeton, NJ: Princeton University Press, 1979).
10 Hausschild and Werner, *"Der Zweck des Lebens": Heine-Biographie*, 32–33.
11 Jan Scheithauer, *"Land der Philister" – "Land der Freiheit": Jüdische, deutsche und französische Identitäten beim jungen Heine* (Bielefeld: Aisthesis, 2013), 255–69.

Heine's move to France in 1831 came nine months after the July revolution of 1830, an event that galvanized a generation of Germans, Heine included – the disappointing developments that followed notwithstanding. Yet, the motives for his move are multiple. As he followed events in France, Heine continually struggled with the censorship of his own writing, which, in turn, affected his economic situation. Shortly before his decision to leave, he had received warning that his situation in Germany was unsafe – precipitating his move to Paris in April and May 1831.[12] The image of France as a place of liberation was, however, not merely political or a matter of *Geist* (that is, of spirit or intellect). Drawn to the political philosophy of Saint-Simon, especially to its support for alleviating human suffering by improving material conditions and the rejection of a repressive Christianity, Heine found at least as appealing that wing of Saint Simonians that preached the emancipation of the flesh, something Heine intended to live out first hand.[13]

Yet, Heine's generally enthusiastic response to France eventually met with severe disillusion in 1840, rooted in a deeply unsettling event that indeed relates to politics. It specifically amounted for Heine to a sudden collision – after neglecting the subject for much, if not all, of his life – with how Jews were perceived at a given moment in France and elsewhere. To gain the sense of that collision, it would help first to consider a text that Heine published in February of 1840 as the second chapter of his book *Ludwig Börne, A Memorial* (*Ludwig Börne: Eine Denkschrift*) devoted to his letters from Helgoland whose genesis and content attest to Heine's enduring positive response to France in his initial decade there.[14] The letters bear the dates from the summer of 1830, the first dated July 1, the last August 19 – with the revolution, which occurred on July 27–29, falling more or less in the middle.

---

12 Hausschild and Werner, *"Der Zweck des Lebens": Heine-Biographie*, 174–90.
13 Heine's turn to Saint Simonian thought points not so much to a marked transformation; rather, the Saint Simonians seem to have re-awakened sympathies and provided terms by which he could express thoughts he had long been developing, in part under the influence of Hegel, Spinoza, and Goethe (e.g., the emphasis on universality, material progress, and pantheism). Many scholars believe that the authoritarian turn in the movement after Saint Simon's death in 1825, especially under the influence of Prosper Enfantin, must have put Heine off, although Heine knew Enfantin and remained a long-term friend of Michel Chevaliar. All seem to agree that Heine rejected outright the reactionary turn, exhibited, e.g., in Amand Bazard's exposition of the movement – which blamed the Reformation and the Enlightenment for the abhorrent "critical" epoch dominant in the society of their time. Sammons, *Heine: A Modern Biography*, 159–68; Georg Iggers, "Heine and the Saint Simonians: A Re-Examination," in *Comparative Literature* 10, no. 4 (1958): 289–309; Nigel Reeves, "Heinrich Heine: Politics or Poetry? Hegel or Enfantin? A Review of Some Recent Developments in Research," Modern Language Review 75, no. 1 (1980): 109–13; Hausschild and Werner, *"Der Zweck des Lebens": Heine-Biographie*, 219–25.
14 DHA 11: 35–57.

Although bearing these dates and based partly on diary entries from the period, Heine revised the "letters" in significant ways, so that they only acquired their mature, published form much later, probably in 1839.[15] Not giving a contemporaneous report of those events, Heine nonetheless seeks with the "Letters" to convey the sense of epoch-making, liberating momentousness of the revolution. Hence, Heine begins his first letter from the British-ruled Helgoland and dated July 1, by expressing at the outset his longing for a sense of peace unavailable in Germany, since back there he cannot lay his head to rest without a German policeman coming to shake him so as to determine whether or not he is sleeping.[16] Seven weeks later, the mood in Germany has transformed radically. Now even in deeply Francophobic Hamburg he claims in mid-August to find great "enthusiasm for France" and declares: "Yes, everywhere, in all countries, people are very easily able to grasp the meaning of these three days in July and see in them a triumph of their own interests and celebrate it. The great deed of the French speaks so clearly to all people and all the intelligence, the highest and the lowest, and in the steppes of the Bashkirs the spirits will be as deeply shaken as at the heights of Andalusia."[17] Heine's celebratory mood is palpable here, even if he may have composed these lines retrospectively in 1839–40. That he praises German enthusiasm suggests his continual hope for a future emancipation in Germany that will draw upon and live up to the French model. Heine's own enthusiasm would, however, soon collide with the Damascus blood libel of February 1840 and the troubling responses within his adoptive France, all of which came to Heine's attention in March of that year, just after the publication of the "Letters" in the *Börne* book.

To recall briefly: After the disappearance of an old, Catholic monk in Damascus, rumors began to spread that Jews had murdered him to use his blood for Passover. The French consul in Damascus, Ratti-Menton, supported the charge, and the French government – mindful, not least, of its own imperialist designs – refused to protest the affair, while press coverage of the incident, especially in the sensationalist and ultramontane Catholic press, repeated the accusation.[18] The accusation led to arrests, torture, and forced confessions, while feeding hostility toward Jews in the Middle East and continental Europe. The event itself was shocking enough to Heine, along with many other Jews and heirs of the Enlightenment;

---

15 Ibid., 251–56.
16 Ibid., 35.
17 Ibid., 54; Heinrich Heine, *Ludwig Börne: A Memorial*, trans. with commentary and introduction by Jeffrey L. Sammons (Rochester, NY: Camden House 2006) 47; translation slightly modified.
18 Jonathan Frankel, *The Damascus Affair: "Ritual Murder," Politics, and the Jews in 1840* (Cambridge: Cambridge University Press, 1997): 65–78, 88.

the response in France troubled him even more deeply.[19] Unlike Ratti-Menton, the Austrian consul in Damascus disbelieved the rumor, exposed the evidence as tainted, and protested the persecutions.[20] In other words, it was reactionary Austria – which had previously joined Prussia in the censorship and persecution of Heine and other writers of the progressive Young German movement – that now came to the defense of Jews, even as the more liberal France remained complicit in the kind of antisemitic charge thought to have disappeared with the Middle Ages. In his first published article on the affair, dated May 7, 1840 and published in the *Augsburger Allgemeine Zeitung* on May 13, Heine remarked acerbically:

> Today's Paris newspapers present a report of the Imperial Royal Austrian [*k.k. österreichischen*] Consul of Damascus to the Imperial Royal Austrian General Consul in Alexandria, in regard to the Damascus Jews, whose martyrdom recalls the darkest times of the Middle Ages. Whereas we in Europe rework this same [kind of thing] into poetic material for fairytales and amuse ourselves with those terrible, naive legends with which our ancestors frightened themselves not a little; whereas for us there is talk only in poems and novels of those witches, werewolves, and Jews who need the blood of pious Christian children for their Satanic ritual[s]; while we laugh and forget [about it], people in the orient are beginning to very sadly remember the old superstition and to put on faces so serious – faces of the darkest fury and despondent agonizing torment. ... The French Consul in Damascus, Count Ratti-Menton, must bear the blame for things that provoked here a general cry of terror. He is the one who injected this occidental superstition into the Orient and circulated a tract to the rabble, in which the Jews are accused of the ritual murder of a Christian.[21]

Apart from his own journalistic interventions, which included a misguided and later regretted attack on wealthy members of the Jewish community for purportedly failing to support the victims or criticize the government, Heine responded by reworking and publishing as a fragment his uncompleted novel *The Rabbi of*

---

19 Jonathan Frankel incisively describes Heine's response to the crisis, which was especially critical of wealthy and well-positioned Jews; Frankel situates Heine's response in the broader context of Jewish responses to the affair, noting what Heine got wrong and what he got right: Heine's criticism of the limited Jewish response and willingness to act was too extreme, failing to give recognition where it was due. Still, it did contain insights – the response was indeed more limited than one would have hoped, and Heine was right to heap praise on Adolphe Crémieux who did more than anyone else to refute the charge; Frankel, *Damascus Affair*, 234–36, 243; among Heine biographers, Yigal Lossin gives one of the most detailed accounts in his *Heinrich Heine: Wer war er wirklich?* trans. Abraham Melzer (Neu Isenburg: Melzer Verlag, 2006), 354–80, esp. 371.
20 Frankel, *Damascus Affair*, 90–105.
21 DHA 13.1: 46–47; Heine later included the article in *Lutezia* (1854), a volume of his articles on France dating from 1840 on; although he had been aware of the blood libel since March 1840, anti-Semitism inflected much of the initial coverage in the French press; only with Crémieux's publication of part of the Austrian consul's report in early May did Heine find the kind of judicious treatment he could rely on, whereupon he intervened in the public debate; DHA, 13.1: 921.

Bacherach (1824/40), depicting a blood libel in the small idyllic town of its title. Heine's inability to complete the novel, which, among other things, suffers the contradiction of trying to make a hero of its rabbi-protagonist who, together with his wife, abandons his community when under threat only to learn soon thereafter of its massacre, is perhaps less important than the signal Heine sought to give by taking up the subject again, after having dealt only very occasionally with Jews in his writings, and scarcely at all for more than a decade.[22]

While Heine's work by no means turned wholly or even predominantly toward Jewish subjects at this point, the Damascus affair had a profound impact on him as it had for many Jews at the time in France, Germany, and elsewhere.[23] Heine appears to have worked together behind the scenes with James Rothschild in responding to the affair as well as with Adolphe Crémieux, from whom he obtained the Austrian consul's original report, which he sent together with his article for publication in the *Augsburger Allgemeine Zeitung*.[24] The affair seems also to have triggered an increased concern with the situation of Jews in Heine's poetic works, which began to include more references, often in unexpected places, as when, in the long satirical poem *Germany, A Winter's Tale* (1844), he produces the ghost of Friedrich Barbarossa only to have the medieval king ask about the welfare of his subject Moses Mendelssohn.[25] While this increased attention to Jewish subjects is worth noting, the further question is how, if it all, the Damascus affair affected in the long term Heine's view of France, particularly in its role as his adoptive homeland? Critics have noted, for instance, an increased turn to radical left politics in Heine in the 1840s, though his biographer Jeffrey Sammons attributes this radicalization to various increased pressures. Besides the decline in his health in the early 1840s, the German governments discontinued censorship of Young German writers who took a loyalty oath *if* they lived in Germany – a measure Heine (rightly) believed to be aimed at him; additionally, they banned all products by his publisher Hoffmann and Campe. That ban was lifted, to be sure, after the great fire that befell the publisher's home city Hamburg in 1842, but Heine's mother also lived in Hamburg, and though she survived, her home was burned out; finally, in September 1844, Prussia issued an order to arrest Heine, along with Karl Marx and his circle, at the border.[26]

---

22 DHA 5: 602–9; see also Sammons, *Heine, A Modern Biography*, 94–96, who views the fragment as testimony to Heine's serious concerns with Jewish suffering while finding it to have failed as a novel.
23 Frankel, *The Damascus Affair*, esp. parts III and IV; Frankel focuses especially on the French and German Jewish responses, in part because they provide the most evidence; he does also note at least some other responses, e.g., from Poland, Russia, and England.
24 See the discussion in DHA 13.1: 921–22, which reprints letters by both Heine and James Rothschild regarding the affair.
25 DHA 4: 126.
26 Sammons, *Heine: A Modern Biography*, 251–52.

Figure 1: Heinrich Heine in 1841. Lithography by Ernst Harder, based on the portrait by Ernst Benedikt Kietz. Courtesy of the Heinrich-Heine-Institut, Düsseldorf.

Despite – or perhaps also owing to – these unhappy developments, Heine continually fixed his gaze on Germany, however much attention he also paid to events in France. He did so even while also exhibiting ambivalence about those on the far left (among others) with whom he was often affiliated.[27] Heine hated the aristocracy, but believed in constitutional monarchy, nullifying any potential alliance with the Republicans; he opposed the puritanical streak found in much of the left – so at odds with his celebration of the senses; and he remained ambivalent about social revolution, the possibility of which he doubted, save in the form of "social Armageddon," a fear perhaps related to his memory of past mob violence directed at Jews, as in the Hep Hep riots of 1819, as well as his belief that the communists and masses would sooner tread upon than read or esteem his poetry or any other art for that matter.[28]

---

[27] Ibid., 171, 188; see also Sammons's provocative essay, "Who Did Heine Think He Was?" in *Heinrich Heine's Contested Identities*, ed. Jost Hermand and Robert Holub (New York: Lang, 1999), 1–24, esp. 13–16; on Heine's ambivalence, see the preface to the French version of the volume of collected articles on France, *Lutezia/Lutèce*, in DHA 13.1: 166–67.

[28] Sammons, *Heine: A Modern Biography*, 261–64; Heine had friendly relations with the Marxes in the 1840s, but despite their shared values (opposition to tyranny, economic deprivation, and social inequality), Heine lacked Marx's rigorous critical analysis of capital and political economy; his stance toward puritanism and sexual repression constituted the core of Heine's (infamous) attack in the *Börne* book; see Holub, "Heine's Sexual Assaults: Towards a Theory of the Total Polemic," *Monatshefte* 73, no. 4 (1981): 415–28.

Rather than try to resolve the often vexed issue of Heine's various and fluctuating allegiances – whether social, political, or spiritual – it might prove more instructive to return to Heine's obituary for both Ludwig Markus and the *Cultur Verein*, composed only four years after the Damascus affair, in 1844. There, one finds in Heine's discussion of his subjects the kind of criticism of German states' refusal to grant emancipation one might expect. Heine, however, also chastises proponents of Jewish emancipation who do not, to his mind, conjoin that project to an overall project of human emancipation. This second, broader project ultimately remains for Heine embodied in a liberal, if at times also flawed, post-revolutionary France. It remains embodied, that is, in the side of France ultimately expressed during the Damascus affair by the freedom of its press as well as by the jurist Adolphe Crémieux whose intervention on behalf of the Jews at the time had a profound impact despite the fact of his own Jewishness, and who would, two years later in 1842, become minister of justice. France, in other words, would appear to remain Heine's elective, perhaps even spiritual homeland. And yet, returning to Heine's reflections on insanity, the Markus text troubles this perspective in another way. For if France had become Heine's *Wahlheimat*, or true "spiritual homeland," one would not expect the Germans and German Jews living there to suffer from their state of exile. The fact that they do so, and Heine clearly means to reflect on his own condition as well, points to yet a further ambivalence in Heine's own attachments, to, that is, a continual and profound connection to Germany, or even a longing for Germany, but one transformed in ways that would allow to thrive the freedoms (e.g., of the press) and liberties he finds in France.

Indeed, this troubled attachment of Heine's finds expression in his writings. He set *The Rabbi of Bacherach* in a small German town on the Rhine, and famously declared in the thirteenth poem of his cycle *Die Heimkehr* (The Homecoming) "Ich bin ein deutscher Dichter, / Bekannt im deutschen Land" (I am a German poet/ Renowned in the German land). One might describe this attachment to language and culture, which was anything but nationalistic, as something as personally and deeply felt as the dejection resulting from the ongoing censorship, in force since 1835, and the prohibitions noted above. Hence, his famous melancholy lines of "Ich hatte einst ein schönes Vaterland" (I once had a lovely fatherland) in which the second strophe reads:

Das küßte mich auf deutsch, und sprach auf deutsch
(Man glaubt es kaum
Wie gut es klang) das Wort: "ich liebe dich!"
Es war ein Traum.

It kissed me in German and spoke in German
(Hard to believe
How good it sounded) the words: "I love you."
It was a dream.

Yet, more intimately, he begins the poem *Nachtgedanken* (Night Thoughts): "Denk ich an Deutschland in der Nacht / dann bin ich um den Schlaf gebracht" (If I think of Germany in the night, then I am robbed of sleep), only to undercut nationalistic connotations, by devoting the remaining lines to his concerns about his mother's well-being there.

My point is not that France therefore ceased to be a "*Wahlheimat*" for Heine, but rather that the term has, it seems, more than one referent. It becomes fragmented for Heine – one particular elective *Heimat* can fulfill certain longings, but not others. As a fragmented concept, it becomes dispersed across different countries, lands, and regions – defying Heine's efforts to latch solely onto one *Heimat*. The question this leaves us with is whether such a notion amounts to exile? Or does it rather point to the need in Heine's case for multiple reference points, multiple *Heimaten*.

2 Benjamin's Homelessness

If in Heine's case one cannot restrict the idea of a *Wahlheimat* to one particular place or country, the concept becomes in Benjamin's case arguably even more complex. In gazing from France, as adoptive homeland, to Germany, from which he is exiled, Heine expresses a mix of bitterness, wit, and melancholy. In contrast, Benjamin's overall view of modernity seems conditioned by an expression of melancholy, with wit at least in his published writings generally absent, and bitterness largely sublimated in theoretical reflection as well as a longing for redemption, conceived in largely apocalyptic, or *weak* messianic terms, as he would call it in his final essay "On the Concept of History."[29] That a melancholy affect can easily lend itself to longings for the *Heimat* is something connoted even more strongly by the German "*Heimweh*" than by the English "homesickness" – with its literal suggestion of an ache ("-*weh*") or a pining for the homeland. In Benjamin's case, however, such feelings go hand in hand with an intellectual intensity and tendency to philosophical abstraction as well as a rejection of – and indeed alienation from – history understood as a gradual

---

[29] Walter Benjamin, "On the Concept of History," trans. Harry Zohn, *Selected Writings*, 4 vols., ed. Howard Eiland and Michael W. Jennings (Cambridge, MA: Belknap, 2004–2006), 4: 390.

process of unfolding and often quotidian experience in favor of an apocalyptic view of sudden, radical transformation.[30] This combination, I will argue, results first in an unstable view of the idea of "*Heimat*," which, in turn, suggests a view of *Wahlheimat* strongly inflected by Benjamin's otherworldly intellectualism.[31] Moreover, this combination of qualities, paradoxically perhaps, had no less profound an impact on Benjamin's image of Paris, where he would spend most of his years in exile, than it had on his response to the politics of Nazi Germany, which had compelled this exile in the first place and would ultimately send him into the (frustrated) flight from occupied France to Spain that led to his suicide. How, though, do such factors contribute to an understanding of the role of *Wahlheimat* in Benjamin's case?

In order to address this question, I need to take a somewhat more circuitous route than in the case of Heine, who, for all his own elusiveness, tended to address himself more directly to the events of the day. Hence, I will first explore Benjamin's complex relationship to history and thought more broadly, then briefly consider his view of the notion of *Heimat*, and finally return specifically to his relationship to Paris in his writings and own actual life. I begin by considering Benjamin's last known essay, "On the Concept of History" (February–May 1940), which, like Heine's obituary for Ludwig Markus a century earlier, responds from Paris to conditions in Germany, conditions, however, unlike those of 1844 insofar as they were by then engulfing much of Europe and increasingly posing a direct threat to Benjamin's life.

The essay "On the Concept of History" provides one of the most potent expressions of Benjamin's melancholy, apocalyptic view of history in the well-

---

[30] In this connection, Benjamin, as is well known, also rejected the idea of progress – one of the main targets of the "Concept of History" essay. That again distinguishes him from Heine who, though perhaps vague on the details, did seem to believe – at least before his last years in the "mattress grave" – that progress was possible. For these aspects of Benjamin's thought, see the excellent discussion in Bernstein, "Walter Benjamin," 79–98. In regard to this tendency toward abstraction, Bernstein notes how easily Benjamin's apparent changes in thought – e.g., his turn to Marxism – "recast into a different explanatory mold the same apocalyptic longings and compositional techniques on which his criticism had always relied" (97); Susan Buck-Morss makes a similar point when she notes that "it is remarkable how little the structure of Benjamin's thought was altered in accommodating his 'political radicalization'"; *The Dialectics of Seeing: Walter Benjamin and the Arcades Project* (Cambridge, MA: MIT Press, 1989), 14.

[31] Theodor Adorno was only one of Benjamin's friends and acquaintances to attest to this otherworldly (or "*weltfremd*") aspect of his personality; Adorno, "Benjamin as Letter Writer," *The Correspondence of Walter Benjamin, 1910–1940*, ed. Gershom Scholem and Theodor W. Adorno, trans. Manfred R. Jacobson and Evelyn M. Jacobson (Chicago: University of Chicago Press, 1994), xvii.

known image he invokes of the "angel of history." Inspired by Paul Klee's painting *Angelus Novus*, Benjamin describes the angel as being blown into the future but with his face turned toward the past, viewing all history as "one single catastrophe" that piles "wreckage upon wreckage": "The angel would like to stay, awaken the dead, and make whole what has been smashed. But a storm is blowing from Paradise and has got caught in his wings. ... This storm drives him irresistibly into the future, to which his back is turned, while the pile of debris before him grows toward the sky. What we call progress is *this* storm."[32]

There is much one can say about this passage, beginning with its seductive image lifted directly from the Klee painting and the elliptical formulations about the possibility and nature of redemption. Benjamin, for instance, describes the storm as one "blowing from Paradise" even as it *prevents* the angel's efforts to come to a standstill so as to "awaken the dead, and make whole what has been smashed"; he then proceeds to equate the storm with "progress." Even when one recognizes that Benjamin disparages the idea of "progress" throughout the essay, one is still left wondering why, if it is redemption he seeks, "progress" as storm should be blowing precisely from "Paradise"? This image becomes all the more elliptical when one notes that the essay calls for redemption in messianic terms. Interpreters of Benjamin have developed plausible explanations for this view, arguing that the Messianic in Benjamin arises not from an outside force but from within the empirical, immanent world, and that it depends on the ability to adopt an alienated perspective on the world even as one lives within it, such that one can read it allegorically or as parable.[33] In doing so, one learns to read the world in ways that release its messianic force. Such an understanding can explain, for instance, Benjamin's claims for the historical materialist approach to history later in the same essay:

> The historical materialist approaches a historical object only where it confronts him as a monad. In this structure he recognizes the sign of a messianic arrest of happening, or (to put it differently) a revolutionary chance in the fight for the oppressed past. He takes cognizance of it in order to blast a specific era out of the homogeneous course of history; thus, he blasts a specific life out of the era, a specific work out of the lifework. As a result of this method, the lifework is both preserved and sublated *in* the work, the era *in* the lifework, and the entire course of history *in* the era. The nourishing fruit of what is historically understood contains time in its *interior* as a precious but tasteless seed.[34]

---

32 Benjamin, "On the Concept of History," 4: 392.
33 Howard Eiland, "Walter Benjamin's Jewishness," in *Walter Benjamin and Theology*, ed. Colby Dickinson and Stéphane Simons (New York: Fordham University Press, 2016), 128.
34 Benjamin, "On the Concept of History," 396.

Accordingly, future and past are collapsed into and signified by the present moment, and Benjamin's historical materialist can pursue the redemption of the unredeemable by recognizing, in Howard Eiland's summary, "its [the unredeemable's] parable-character, its possible teaching and summary judgment."[35]

While this image exemplifies the nature of Benjamin's apocalyptic stance, which draws on both Jewish and Marxist terminology as well as a mix of poetic and cultural critical analysis, it also signals an alienated and indeed also alienating stance toward the world, and one has to wonder whether the articulator of such a view could find a "*Wahlheimat*" anywhere in the world.[36] Nor is this alienated and apocalyptic view one that begins only with Benjamin's exile or increasingly desperate situation at the time of the essay's writing in early 1940, although the essay does signal a loss of faith in the possibility of redemption through either political revolution or reform.

Heine, too, when crippled with illness, became far more pessimistic about the kinds of change possible. He nevertheless continued, as in his preface to the French edition of *Lutezia*, to declare the need to redress social injustice and everyday needs, like hunger, endured on a daily basis by the common people – even if voicing in the same context the kinds of concerns, for instance about communism, noted above.[37] Benjamin, in turn, dismisses in "The Concept of History" the ideas of gradual change found in Weimar-era social democracy, the primary political target for his disparagement of progress. He does so, while also arguing that such politicians "managed to erase the name" of the nineteenth-century revolutionary Louis-Auguste Blanqui, who had, however, as Benjamin himself also knew, ended his life on a note of utter resignation to forces beyond the control of such political actors.[38]

---

35 Eiland, "Benjamin's Jewishness," 128.
36 "Alienated" in the sense of neo-Marxian, neo-Freudian "*Entfremdung*," also central to members of the Frankfurt School, and alienating in the sense of "*Verfremdung*" (defamiliarization) as Brecht called it, though others – most notably the Russian formalists – also discussed it, arguing that its Russian equivalent (*ostranenie*) was an effect of all poetic language.
37 DHA 13.1: 166–68, 294–96; Heine had, at times, also been inclined to believe in grand gestures and grand figures (like Napoleon), but continued, as a child of the Enlightenment, to show more conviction about the possibility of gradual change as when he sought through his journalism to intervene in specific cases like the Damascus affair, or, in the earlier articles (especially the sixth and seventh) of the collection *Französiche Zustände* (*French Conditions*, 1832) to describe the impact he witnessed in Paris of the cholera epidemic of 1832 in the aftermath of the revolution – interventions, in other words, that sought to draw attention to present day events and thereby remedy them; DHA 12.1: 129–42, 152–72.
38 Benjamin, "On the Concept of History," 394, and "Paris, Capital of the Nineteenth Century (Exposé of 1939)," in *The Arcades Project*, trans. Howard Eiland and Kevin McLaughlin

Yet, the fact that Benjamin expressed such views in an essay completed in Paris – which he left only in the eleventh hour on or around June 14, 1940 – only adds to the complexity of the situation.[39] Likewise, adding to that complexity is Benjamin's attitude more generally to the notion of *Heimat*, a term that, to be sure, had become by the 1930s highly charged with Nazi ideology of "blood and soil." Hence, when discussing Baudelaire in the 1935 exposé "Paris, the Capital of the Nineteenth Century" for the never-completed *Arcades Project*, Benjamin describes the poet's intimate relationship to Paris but pointedly asserts that his poetry is *"keine Heimatkunst."*[40] In rendering the term as "no hymn to the homeland," the translators want, to be sure, to convey Benjamin's explicit distancing of himself from the language of Nazism.[41] Yet, even if the term *Heimat* were not so charged by then, Benjamin's view of history together with that quality of not quite living in the world, suggests that a concept like *Heimat* could never be for him anything but troubling – both personally and intellectually.

Others, like the writer Joseph Roth, could still use the term in the 1930s in less dismissive ways, even if Roth also invoked *Heimat* (and its loss) as a problem in modern life, as in his depiction of the (reluctant) Austrian military officer Carl Joseph von Trotta in the novel *Radetzky March* (1932). Von Trotta experiences a series of profound disappointments, culminating in both the command to have his troops suppress – and eventually fire on – a factory worker uprising in Galicia, and serious injury to himself. Disillusioned with the old ways of empire in pre-First World War Austro-Hungary, von Trotta finds himself utterly alienated by ossified social and military traditions.[42] He observes the Emperor Franz Joseph as

---

(Cambridge, MA: Belknap Press, 1999), 25–26; Benjamin omits reference to communism here, but his disillusionment with it and the Soviet Union is evident elsewhere; in a letter to his son Stefan several months earlier, Benjamin worries, e.g., about Stefan Benjamin's "isolation" in terms that prompt one to think of his own situation when he notes such isolation "belongs of course to the plagues that Hitler and, respectively, his social democratic and communist midwives unleashed on the world" ("Diese Isolierung gehört natürlich zu den Plagen, die Hitler bezw. seine sozialdemokratischen und kommunistischen Geburtshelfer in die Welt gesetzt haben."). Walter Benjamin, vol. 6, 1938–1940, of *Gesammelte Briefe*, ed. Christoph Gödde and Henri Lonitz [Frankfurt a. M.: Suhrkamp, 2000], 319; see also his letter to Gershom Scholem of January 11, 1940, *Gesammelte Briefe*, 6: 378–81).
39 Eiland and Jennings, *Walter Benjamin*, 668.
40 Walter Benjamin, "Paris, die Haupstadt des neunzehnten Jahrhunderts," in *Gesammelte Schriften*, ed. Rolf Tiedemann (Frankfurt am Main: Suhrkamp, 1982), 5.1: 54.
41 Walter Benjamin, "Paris, the Capital of the Nineteenth Century (Exposé of 1935)" in *The Arcades Project*, 10.
42 Joseph Roth, *Radetzkymarsch* (Munich: DTV, 2015), 274.

he approaches during an inspection, and takes note of his own indifference: "He had the feeling that he was neglecting his duty. The army had become foreign to him. The supreme commander of the military had grown foreign to him. Lieutenant Trotta was like a man who had not only lost his homeland [*Heimat*], but also the longing [*Heimweh*] for this homeland. He had sympathy with the white-bearded old man … The lieutenant had wished for that intoxication that had [once] filled him in all the festive hours of his military career."[43] In contrast to this personal expression of loss, made palpable by Roth, one might consider Benjamin's more cerebral *Berlin Childhood around 1900*, begun in 1932 but first published as a complete text only posthumously in 1950 and, again, in 1955 by Adorno and Tilman Rexroth.[44] The work presents itself as a memoir of childhood and includes reflections on Benjamin's early life, family home and outings, along with types and landmarks in the city, with section headings ranging from "Tiergarten" (Berlin's central park), "Das Telephon," "Loggien," and "Abreise und Rückkehr" (Departure and Return) to "Bettler und Huren" (Beggars and Whores) and "Krumme Straße" (Crooked Street). Yet, while focused on such objects, figures, and experiences, those images generally serve as occasions not for personal reflections on *Heimat*, homesickness, or their loss; nor does the memoir generally occasion portraits of his family members as manifest in childhood memory. In the discussion, for instance, of a family vacation (in "Abreise und Rückkehr"), we learn nothing of his family but receive rather an account of the disorienting changing images of the city upon departure, and of how, upon the eventual return, the family apartment – with its rolled up carpets, covered armchairs, etc. – always appeared transformed. With their footsteps making impressions like "those of thieves in the dust," Benjamin would feel upon their return like a person without a home ("*Heimatloser*").[45]

To be sure, there is a parallel here to Roth's von Trotta having lost both "*Heimat*" and "*Heimweh*." But where Roth's novel registers that impact as a symptom of decline of empire and the character's own scarring, Benjamin seems rather to want to suppress or perhaps sublimate such emotion, to subject the objects or moments that might evoke such emotion to

---

43 Roth, *Radetzkymarsch*, 274–75; the German text reads: "Er hatte das Gefühl, eine Pflicht zu versäumen. Fremd geworden war ihm die Armee. Fremd war ihm der allerhöchste Kriegsherr. Der Leutnant Trotta glich einem Mann, der nicht nur seine Heimat verloren hatte, sondern auch das Heimweh nach dieser Heimat. Er hatte Mitleid mit dem weißbärtigen Greis … Der Leutnant hätte sich jenen Rausch wieder gewünscht, der ihn in allen festlichen Stunden seiner militärischen Laufbahn erfüllt hatte."
44 GS 7.2: 691.
45 GS 4.1: 246.

re-description, resulting in detached but often suggestive and illuminating analyses and elaborations. The descriptions, both evocative and highly focused, ultimately also suggest an intense effort at cerebral detachment, as if the alternative would be personal collapse under the weight of the buried melancholy. In the opening paragraph of the first published version of *Berliner Kindheit*, for instance, Benjamin emphasizes the need to learn how to get lost in the city, in contrast to a forest. Only then would it be possible to register the city's images, from its street names to the undiscovered corners, in terms of its hidden meanings, to read the city – as he will several years later suggest of Baudelaire's Paris – in allegorical terms but not to recall it in those that would be personal.[46]

In this regard, the foreword to the final version of *Berlin Childhood* is revealing. Only discovered in the archives of the Bibliothèque Nationale in 1981 (by the Italian philosopher Sergio Agamben, Benjamin's Italian editor), this final handwritten manuscript of 1938 is in its significantly revised form now considered the definitive edition.[47] At the outset, Benjamin does invoke the feeling of "homesickness [*Heimweh*] in exile," but he cites it precisely in order to underscore the need to guard against it. In the chapter "Loggias," for instance, now both revised and moved from the latter half of the earlier text into the position of first chapter, he speaks openly of "*Heimat*," but does so in reference to a palm tree that – with the hanging of a clothesline in the family loggia – appears to become all the more homeless (*obdachloser*) "since it was clearly no longer the dark portion of earth but rather the neighboring living room that was perceived as its *Heimat*."[48] With this image Benjamin performs a double displacement of the experience of "*Heimat*," first from himself onto the palm tree, then from the palm tree itself, which appears as if further removed from its position neighboring the earth to one neighboring the salon. Significantly, this "removal" results not from an actual movement of the palm tree, but only from the change in visual perception – suggesting further that Benjamin projects onto it that sense of removal.

In the same period to which this manuscript dates Benjamin found himself pleased to receive a positive response from his sister-in-law, Hilde Benjamin, to a passage about "*Heimat*" she had recently read in his work. Benjamin had quoted the passage in his introduction to the eighteenth-century German revolutionary Georg Forster (1754–1794) in the volume *Deutsche Menschen*, an edited collection

---

46 Benjamin, GS 4.1: 238; "Paris, Capital (Exposé of 1935)," 10–11.
47 GS 7.2: 691–96.
48 GS 7.1: 387.

of letters by German intellectuals written between 1767 and 1883, which he published in 1936 under the pseudonym Detlev Holz. The passage reads: "I no longer have a homeland [*Heimat*], a fatherland, or friends; all those who were close to me have left me to form other attachments. And if I think of the past and still feel myself bound, that is merely my choice and my idea, not something imposed by circumstances. Happy turns of fate can give me much; unhappy ones can take nothing from me, except the satisfaction of writing these letters, should I be unable to afford the postage."[49] Forster's letter, also written from Parisian exile, appears to signal a complete abandonment of the idea of homeland of any sort. The fact of Benjamin's enthusiasm for it and its positive reception suggests the degree to which he, himself, shared in the sentiment.

Yet, these multiple efforts of appearing to contain, control, or even abandon the concept of *Heimat*, in turn, also point to an underlying attachment. For Benjamin, not so unlike Heine's account after all, that attachment would itself seem ultimately to pose a threat to one's well-being, or mental and emotional stability. When he proceeds therefore to describe his efforts to resist *Heimweh* in the 1938 foreword to *Berlin Childhood*, Benjamin reaches for medical terminology, stressing his previous positive experience with "inoculation" as a means of active immunization.[50] In setting out in 1932 to write *Berlin Childhood*, he tells us in 1938, he sought to apply this same principle by intentionally calling to mind the "the images that in exile most intensely foster the awakening of *Heimweh*." In that way, those feelings would no more become the "master of the spirit" (Herr über den Geist) than did the inoculated disease come to master the healthy body.[51] Throughout his text, he would keep this longing in check by concentrating his memory not on accidental biographical details but on the "inevitable social unrecoverability of that which has passed" (die notwendige gesellschaftliche Unwiederbringlichkeit des Vergangenen [sic]).[52] Benjamin's response to the loss of *Heimat* seems to lead less to renewed reflection on the personal than to an occasion in which he might again creatively attempt to redeem history.

As a last example, one finds Benjamin writing in a similar vein in a review of a novel titled *Jan Heimatlos*, written by a German Jew in French exile, a young friend of Benjamin's named Ernest Gustave Morgenroth who wrote under the pseudonym Stephan Lackner. Describing its depiction of two generations of an

---

49 The English is quoted in Eiland and Jennings, *Walter Benjamin*, 594; the German is found in Benjamin, GS 4.1: 160.
50 GS 7.1: 385.
51 Ibid.
52 Benjamin, *Berliner Kindheit*, 1938 edition, in GS 7.1: 385.

intermarried family headed by a Jewish father, Benjamin quotes the father's emphasis on his own family's German pedigree dating back to Roman times, and his insistence on remaining in Germany until the Germans return to their own senses, or else until he and his family are ruined (*"zugrunde gehen"*).[53] Noting that the second alternative is now on the verge of its realization, Benjamin finds that the novel offers a third response to the father's comments. The young protagonist had at one point traveled back to Germany from his own safe position in exile in order to save his lover. It ends ultimately with a "second journey home" (einer zweiten Heimkehr), one, however, no longer dedicated to the young lover, herself now in exile, but "to the struggle for the liberation of all the oppressed in the Third Reich."[54] To this, Benjamin adds a comment that no doubt suggests his own situation: "Lackner's book proves that the school of exile does not strike at a young writer so badly if only he brings to it decisiveness and talent."[55]

3 Parisian Phantasmagorias and the Bibliothèque Nationale: Benjamin's *Wahlheimat*?

If Benjamin's view of *Heimat* suggests an ambivalence toward the notion itself, it would seem to share with the essay "On the Concept of History" the directing of focus away from either personal or quotidian details of existence onto a historically broader, if less transparent, significance – presented in *Berlin Childhood* as the endeavor to recover "the inevitable social unrecoverability of that which has past" and in the "Concept of History" as a messianic intervention. Each work in its own way expresses the tendency in Benjamin noted above toward dissatisfaction with narrative history and gradual change and longing for a more radical, even apocalyptic transformation. If that is the case, however, it raises the further question of what we can learn from his writings about Paris as a possible *Wahlheimat*, whether he intended it to be or not. Here, too, one finds a profound ambivalence, but of a different kind. Benjamin's period of exile is in itself a complex story.

---

53 Benjamin, "Roman deutscher Juden," in GS 3: 547. Reprinted from *Die neue Weltbühne* 34 (1938), 1621–22 (No. 51; December 22, 1938), where the review appeared under the pseudonym Karl Gumlich.
54 Benjamin, "Roman," in GS 3: 548.
55 "Lackners Buch beweist, daß die Schule des Exils einem jungen Schriftsteller nicht so schlecht anschlägt, wenn er nur Entschiedenheit und Begabung mitbringt." Benjamin, "Roman," 3: 548.

Figure 2: Walter Benjamin at the Bibliothèque Nationale, Paris, 1937. (© Gisèle Freund/IMEC/Fonds MCC)." http://imecimages.imec-archives.com/5d1c6545ad9cdom8.html.

In the early years of his exile, beginning with his departure from Germany in March 1934, Benjamin moved around considerably, often dependent on the goodwill of others, often living on a pecuniary income, some of which he at one point also gambled away in the casinos of Monaco.[56] The difficulties, sense of displacement, and hardship of the first years eventually gave way to a more stable period, beginning in spring 1935, when he began to reside primarily in Paris and when the Institute for Social Research, which from its new location in New York had paid him a monthly stipend of 500 francs since spring 1934, doubled that income for four months and provided an additional 500 francs for relocation to Paris. Despite the improved situation, exile had taken a toll on Benjamin by the late 1930s, which according to reports by friends, acquaintances, and Benjamin himself left its traces in the form of premature aging and, by the end of the 1930s, a serious heart condition.[57] While he seems early on to have underestimated the brutality, if not the willfulness, of the Nazis, he would later linger too long before leaving Paris on or just before June 14, 1940. Indeed, it seems that Benjamin would also come to thrive there, even more so once he managed to finally move into his own apartment in January 1938 where he would also be able to eventually house

---

56 Eiland and Jennings, *Walter Benjamin*, 484–85.
57 Ibid., 581, 648, 656, 673–74.

his books.⁵⁸ The presence of his own books and, both before their arrival and thereafter, the resources of the Bibliothèque Nationale were central to his sense of well-being there. With such resources making it possible for him to work, he came to experience the time in Paris by the mid to late 1930s as one of the most productive and rewarding periods of his life.⁵⁹ Indeed, the visible shock he experienced when at the outbreak of the war the French interned him, along with thousands of other German and Austrian refugees, initially at the Stade Olympique Yves-du-Manoir in Colombes (a northwest suburb of Paris), only further suggests Benjamin's sense in Paris of otherwise having found a stable existence in the city.⁶⁰ If Paris therefore became for a time a *Wahlheimat*, rather than merely a place of exile, what was it that made possible such an experience? And: how, given Benjamin's repeated efforts to dispel and indeed even dismiss such attachments, might the notions of *Heimat* and *Wahlheimat* be said to nonetheless express themselves in his writing? What forms might their expression take? What tensions – resolved or unresolved – in Benjamin's writing might they give rise to?

When Benjamin turned to writing specifically about France, his primary focus was not on current or recent events, though he did in this period review books – some of which addressed the present situation – and sent reports in the late 1930s to the Institute for Social Research on intellectual trends in France.⁶¹ Benjamin, that is, typically addressed the present in theoretical terms that may at times have reflected the impact of the changing political conditions, but his major projects – unlike those of Heine – did not generally address themselves directly to the specific details of the current situation. He invoked revolution at times but did not describe how it might occur or what it might look like.⁶² An idea of revolution, though without all too specific details, remained for him a way out of the present.⁶³ Primarily,

---

58 Ibid., 574, 622.
59 Ibid., 483–575.
60 The displacement resulted in an almost complete withdrawal and loss of ability to act or adapt. Were it not for the help of a young acquaintance there named Max Aron, Benjamin may not have survived; for an account of the internment, see ibid., 647–53.
61 Ibid., 582–89, 630–31.
62 Benjamin, himself, suggested as much to Adorno; see "Benjamin as Letter Writer," xvii.
63 Bernstein, "Walter Benjamin," 82–83; indeed, even sophisticated scholars committed to the Marxist view of Benjamin (while incorporating the Jewish Messianic aspect of this thought) present his revolutionary thrust in terms that can be verbally seductive and perhaps theoretically suggestive, yet remain highly abstract in terms of actual revolutionary praxis: "he describes … his task as the historical materialist who 'blasts apart' the continuum of history, constructing 'historical objects' in a politically explosive 'constellation of past and present,' as a 'lightning flash' of truth" (Buck-Morss, *Dialectics of Seeing*, 241); beyond the written word revolutionary praxis assumes here the form of a "Messianic promise" – one viewed, to be sure, as historically

though, his major intellectual project, besides the ongoing revisions to *Berlin Childhood*, took the form of the vast set of notes and materials recorded for his never-completed *Arcades Project* (*Das Passagenwerk*), along with the exposé written for the project in 1935 – with a revised French version in 1939 – entitled "Paris, the Capital of the Nineteenth Century" ("Paris, Hauptstadt des XIX. Jahrhunderts"). Separate from, but closely related to *The Arcades Project*, were the long essay "Paris of the Second Empire in Baudelaire" (1938), as well as the two other essays he composed as part of a projected book on the poet whom Benjamin both deeply admired and considered central to understanding the changes and contradictions of his age.

With these projects Benjamin undertook what amounted to a series of philosophical, historical, and critical explorations of past moments, events, historical figures, and expressions of Parisian culture and civilization, with the aim of uncovering "primordial history" (*Urgeschichte*), all of which were, however, to be conveyed in a literary montage and to be understood, ultimately, dialectically.[64] At the methodological center of *The Arcades Project*, notes Benjamin scholar Max Pensky, stood the "dialectical image" (it was central to related works as well).[65] Yet, Pensky continues, the term remains elusive since Benjamin never managed to provide "a coherent, intelligible account of what dialectical images were."[66] For my purposes, it is important to note the centrality of the concept and that,

---

immanent rather than mythical, but one never really clarified – beyond the claim of a "Messianic break from history's course," or of a "rupture of tradition [that] now frees symbolic powers from conservative restraints for the task of social transformation, that is, for a rupture of those social conditions of domination that, consistently, have been the source of tradition" (279); or, in Irving Wohlfarth's discussion of Benjamin's essay on Eduard Fuchs: "This materialist critique, or would be destruction, of so-called culture and cultural history again points up the political radicalism of Benjamin's project. It operates in the name of a liberating Marxian dialectic between the forces and relations of production ... It would, in other words, have taken nothing less than a political revolution to dissipate the phantasmagorias of the nineteenth century. The kaleidoscope [mirroring 'the concepts of the rulers ... by which the image of an "order" came about'] would have to be smashed"; "Smashing the Kaleidoscope: Walter Benjamin's Critique of Cultural History," in *Walter Benjamin and the Demands of History*, ed. Michael P. Steinberg (Ithaca: Cornell University Press, 1996), 204; see also 190 for the "kaleidoscope" reference.

64 Uwe Steiner, *Walter Benjamin* (Stuttgart and Weimar: Metzler, 2004), 153–63; Eiland and Jennings, *Walter Benjamin*, 288–93.

65 Pensky, "Method and Time: Benjamin's Dialectical Images," in *Cambridge Companion to Walter Benjamin*, 178.

66 Ibid.; Pensky quotes, for instance, an oft-cited passage: "It's not that what is past casts its light on what is present, or what is present its light on the past; rather, image is that wherein what has been comes together in a flash with the now to form a constellation. In other words, image is dialectics at a standstill" ("Bild ist die Dialektik im Stillstand"); Benjamin, GS 5.1: 577, Konvolut N 2a, 3; *The Arcades Project*, 462; Pensky adds that despite "a good deal of dedicated scholarship" "at the heart of the Arcades Project, the 'lightening flash' of the dialectical image

while elusive, it is indebted on some level to Hegel, Marx, and perhaps especially Lukács's essay "Reification and the Consciousness of the Proletariat," as well as to Surrealism and Freud – because of their focus, in these last two cases, on unconscious forces and dream imagery as means to clarify – or for the Surrealists – transform the human world.[67]

Beyond dialectical images, the Marxist literary theorist Terry Eagleton has suggestively likened Benjamin's approach in his explorations to a Foucauldian archaeology *avant la lettre*.[68] In doing so, Eagleton underscores the importance for Benjamin of his extensive excavations of the past, combined as they often were with his reflections about the materials, ideas, and forces that went into shaping that past. Indeed, one of Benjamin's main points is to present analysis that will, so to speak, undo or escape from history – something similar to what he claims of historical materialism in "On the Concept of History." In the introduction composed for the revised *Arcades Project* exposé of 1939, Benjamin therefore rejects a "conception of history … that corresponds to a viewpoint according to which the course of the world is an endless series of facts congealed in the form of things."[69] He rejects what he calls the "making [of] an inventory … of humanity's life forms and creations" undertaken by the "History of Civilization," which "amasses" these "riches … in the aerarium of civilization [so that they] henceforth appear as though identified for all time" ("Paris, Capital" [exposé 14]).

In aiming to find an alternative to this conception of history, which would also avoid its reifying tendencies ("facts congealed in the form of things," "identified for all time"), Benjamin seeks to uncover a broad range of material – whether on *flâneurs* and bohemians, painted panoramas and photography, or the use of iron and glass in modern architecture (e.g., the arcades), etc. – to be theoretically worked through. Yet, this view also has a more basic and direct relevance for thinking about the role that Paris could play for him as *Wahlheimat*. Submerging himself deeply within the cultural archive of nineteenth-century Parisian history, Benjamin, in particular, shows the city of Paris to be a world of illusions, or what he calls "phantasmagoria."

---

has, to this day, remained far more a dark start, indeed a kind of methodological black hole"; Buck-Morss seems less troubled by this elusive term, but her own prose can at times be elusive: "In the traces left by the object's after-history, the conditions of its decay and the manner of its cultural transmission, the utopian images of past objects can be read in the present as truth" (Buck-Morss, *Dialectics of Seeing*, 219).
67 Margaret Cohen, "Benjamin's Phantasmagoria: The *Arcades Project*," in *The Cambridge Companion to Walter Benjamin*, ed. David S. Farris (Cambridge: Cambridge University Press, 2004), 200–5.
68 Terry Eagleton, *Walter Benjamin or Towards a Revolutionary Criticism* (London: Verso, 1981), 56.
69 "Paris, Capital," 14 (Exposé of 1939); "congealed in the form of things" is in Benjamin's German notes for this introduction "verdinglicht" (GS 5.2: 1255).

The term "phantasmagoria" originally referred to a device for creating optical illusions first used in the eighteenth century. In the *Arcades Project*, Benjamin seeks with this term to refer to a phenomenon that manifests itself as real, and may have real effects, while being at the same time illusory in nature. As literary and media scholar Timo Skrandies notes, for Benjamin "everyday existence appears ... as the commodity-shaping of life, as a life embedded in the matrix of a *phantasmagoria*," which he conceives of "not 'ideologically' in the strict Marxist sense, but in the form of sensuous phenomenality [or appearance]."[70] One can analyze phantasmagoria as congealed formations, so to speak, in order to disclose the hidden forces or energies in modern, industrialized society that have given rise to their form, while also tracing the effects of any such phenomenon of this kind. In such phantasmagoria, which constitute, so to speak, the stuff of modern Parisian life, one cannot ultimately find oneself settled, on stable ground, at home. At the same time, Benjamin seems here, as in "On the Concept of History," to equate certain kinds of historical writing to the reifying process of more powerful historical forces (e.g., of capital, modern technology, etc.) themselves.[71] Or how else does one explain the complex referent of the following: "as a consequence of this reifying *representation* of civilization, the new forms of behavior and the new economically and technologically based creations that we owe to the nineteenth century enter the universe of a phantasmagoria. ... *They are manifest as phantasmagorias*"?[72] The reference to actual historical events or figures, beyond their representation in historical writing, may be somewhat opaque here. It becomes less opaque if one considers certain key examples Benjamin cites in the exposé. In the section "Haussmann and the barricades," for instance, he argues that the massive re-design of Paris undertaken by George Eugène Baron Haussmann resulted in large-scale demolition, leading to higher rents and forcing the working class into the *faubourgs*, while it in the meantime "estranges their city from the Parisians."[73] At the same time, with the development of the grand boulevards of Paris, Haussmann sought to advert civil war by preventing the erection of revolutionary barricades like those of 1848 – an endeavor whose failure becomes manifest with the Paris Commune where "the barricade is resurrected ... stronger and better than

---

[70] Timo Skrandies, "Unterwegs in den Passagen-Konvoluten," in *Benjamin-Handbuch: Leben, Werk, Wirkung*, ed. Burkhardt Lindner et al. (Stuttgart: Metzler, 2006), 279; emphasis added.
[71] See, among others, Wohlfarth, "Smashing the Kaleidoscope," 196–200, and Buck-Morss, *Dialectics of Seeing*, 218–21; in this sense, Benjamin prefigures certain poststructuralist challenges to the traditional Marxian base-superstructure model.
[72] "Paris, Capital," (Exposé of 1939), 14, emphasis added.
[73] Ibid., 12; GS 5.1: 57.

ever."[74] In the first instance, Haussmann presents himself as someone who will improve the city of Paris, but his expenditures and new designs, while perhaps visually impressive, actually harm the lives of the many Parisians, themselves reduced to mere objects of those designs; in the second instance, Haussmann's attempt to defend the interests of his class – by adverting revolution – actually helps undermine those interests, creating even better conditions for revolution (with the boulevards serving as a new space for barricades). The phantasmagorias of modern Parisian life mean that ultimately the forms and forces of this life elude even those best positioned to exercise power over them.

For the Benjamin of this period, these nineteenth-century phantasmagoria coincide with a change in the place of literary and artistic production in the world. Now subject to the world of commerce, works of literature and art "linger on the threshold" at "the point of entering the market as commodities."[75] As "residues of a dream world," these works help give rise to "dream images," a term Benjamin uses for "dialectic images."[76] They help make possible "dialectical thinking," itself the "organ for [the] historical awakening" necessary to resist the reifying processes of history. In *Berlin Childhood*, Benjamin had sought to inoculate himself against *Heimweh* by engaging in a socially relevant, if also somewhat paradoxical, perhaps impossible form of remembering (of the "inevitable social unrecoverability of that which has past"). In the same way, he now positions literary and artistic works as "residues of a dream world" perched on the "threshold" to commerce, something that in turn leaves them somehow unsettled, not at home in their world, and hence precisely for that reason able to give rise to "the historical awakening" he seeks.

The figure whose poetry would for Benjamin best exemplify this threshold position – unsettled between "dream world" and "commodity" and precisely therefore able to unsettle and historically awaken – is Baudelaire, especially in his work *Les Fleurs du Mal*. In the exposé, Baudelaire appears in a transmogrifying dimension, characterized as poet, allegorist, *flâneur*, and ultimately *bohème* – in roles that will themselves become socially, culturally, and politically manifest in different ways at different moments in Benjamin's presentation. At the same time, Benjamin seeks to describe how Baudelaire's deeply ambivalent excavation of the modern metropolis Paris both reveals and participates in the city's modern ambiguities and dilemmas. Benjamin refers to Baudelaire's "genius" as "allegorical

---

74 Ibid.; Ibid., 58.
75 Ibid., 13; Ibid., 59.
76 Ibid.

genius [nourished on melancholy]."[77] As allegories, Baudelaire's images allow present and past, city surface and city depths to interpenetrate, much like a palimpsest.[78] Describing him as the first poet to make Paris itself the subject of his poetry – the claim that prompts Benjamin's dismissal of the term "*Heimatkunst*" – he adds that Baudelaire reveals the alienation of "big-city dwellers" from the modern metropolis Paris. Viewed from another angle, one might say that Benjamin's Baudelaire describes a Paris that can *no longer* serve as "*Heimat*." Quite literally, he notes in "The Paris of the Second Empire in Baudelaire" that Baudelaire's efforts to evade his creditors sent him in flight to cafés, reading circles, and the occupying of at least two residences at once: "So he roamed about in the city, which had long since ceased to be a home (*Heimat*) for the *flâneur*."[79]

Yet, precisely for this reason, Baudelaire as *flâneur* is positioned like the lyrical and artistic works themselves on a "threshold," from which he can comprehend the world of the bourgeoisie and marketplace, or of the modern metropolis. He can recognize and embrace the "modernity" of Paris, but in so doing also gaze incisively – "with the gaze of the allegorist" and "the alienated man" – through it, such that his poetic images also refer allegorically to the "chthonic elements" that underlie the city – "the old abandoned bed of the Seine."[80] In the poems of "Spleen et Idéal," Baudelaire's vision "fractures [*zerspellt*] the ideal" – including any idealized image of the modern metropolis.[81] Yet, decisive for his poetry is precisely Baudelaire's capacity to dwell in ambiguity. Amidst the "death-fraught idyll" (*totenhaften Idyllik*) of Paris he rediscovers "a social, a modern substrate," even as beneath glittering arcades and marketplaces (and "allegorized" by them), he discovers the sunken, chthonic element.[82] Yet, for all its enthusiasm, Benjamin's description of Baudelaire also retains its own ambiguity: it figures Baudelaire as the poet who can reveal the contradictions of modern Parisian life, but also as someone enmeshed within them, unable, for instance, to take the revolutionary stance Benjamin himself would frequently invoke.

---

[77] "Exposé 1935," 10; GS 5.1: 56; Bernstein, among others, has noted Benjamin's self-description as melancholic and his "spiritual kinship with writers like Baudelaire, Proust, and Kafka," all three of whom he wrote about brilliantly; Bernstein, "Walter Benjamin," 93.

[78] In a letter to Max Horkheimer in spring 1938, Benjamin would clarify his understanding of "allegory" by reference to modern film and photography, as "dissolve" or "superimposition" (*Überblendung*); *Gesammelte Briefe*, 6: 65–66; cited in Eiland and Jennings, *Walter Benjamin*, 618–19.

[79] Walter Benjamin, "The Paris of the Second Empire in Baudelaire," trans. Harry Zohn, *Selected Writings*, ed. Howard Eiland and Michael W. Jennings (Cambridge, MA: Belknap Press, 2003), 4: 26; *Gesammelte Schriften*, 1.2: 550.

[80] "Exposé 1935," 10; GS 5.1: 55.

[81] Ibid.

[82] Ibid.

If ambiguity occupies such a privileged position in his thought about Baudelaire and Paris in the nineteenth century, there seem as well to be parallels between Benjamin's observations of Baudelaire and his own relationship to Paris as *Wahlheimat*. Whatever connection he had to present-day Paris – and, beyond the city's inherent pull, he was apparently professionally and intellectually well-connected by the late 1930s[83] – Benjamin first and foremost submerged himself for long hours in the library holdings of the Bibliothèque Nationale, excavating the "submerged" past and contradictions of the city, and the various ways these became manifest in the nineteenth century. Theodor Adorno notes that it was because of the Bibliothèque Nationale with its resources for the *Arcades Project* that Benjamin knowingly lingered in Paris long after it became dangerous to do so.[84] Perhaps more than the city itself, the Bibliothèque Nationale became for him a true *Wahlheimat*, since although he rejected history as inventory, Benjamin as "collector" sought in great detail the "life forms and creations" of the past.[85] At the same time, the city was not irrelevant to Benjamin who felt isolated, for instance, when temporarily residing relatively near to Bertolt Brecht in the Danish countryside, but able to meet with people only in the evenings for gatherings at the Brecht home.[86] Noting Charles Dickens's complaints about the "lack of street noises" when away from London, he quotes the novelist: "It seems as if they [the streets] supplied something to my brain, which it cannot bear, when busy, to lose."[87]

In seeking to move beyond mere inventory, the historical materialist apostle of weak messianism wanted to dislodge the past "life forms and creations" from traditional historical narrative ("the History of Civilization"), seeking out the potential to redeem history. Yet, Benjamin could not pursue his task without oscillating between the depths of the Bibliothèque Nationale and the Parisian street – between "the intoxication to which the *flâneur* abandons himself in the crowd" and the search for nineteenth-century riches to subject to dialectical thinking in pursuit of "historical awakening."[88]

---

[83] Eiland and Jennings, *Walter Benjamin*, 574–75, 579, 582–84.
[84] Adorno, "Benjamin as Letter Writer," xxii.
[85] On Benjamin as "collector," see his "Unpacking My Library," in *Illuminations*, ed. Hannah Arendt, trans. Harry Zohn (New York: Schocken, 1969) 59–67; to be sure, Benjamin also conceived the *Arcades Project* in revolutionary terms, and hence as a response to the present but at the expense of actually registering with any real accuracy the dangers of the present.
[86] Eiland and Jennings, *Walter Benjamin*, 451–52, 462–63.
[87] Benjamin, "Paris of the Second Empire," 28.
[88] Ibid., 31.

4 Conclusion: Divided Attachments

In the first part of this paper, I argued that one can best think of Heine as having not one but two "*Wahlheimaten*," making use in the process of a German linguistic rarity (the plural form of "*-heimat*"), in part to underscore its peculiarity. In Benjamin's case, the notion of Heimat is in itself problematic, placing further pressure on the question of whether *Wahlheimat* exists at all for him – even as Paris clearly served him as refuge from Nazi Germany when threatened as leftwing intellectual and, even more thoroughly, as a Jew. If Heine gazed at France and Germany, Benjamin, while conditioned by events in Germany, would appear to have gazed variously from Parisian archive to Parisian street, and back again. This remains the case even as one remains suspicious of employing for Benjamin a term containing the component "*-heimat*," even when that term clearly designates "election" rather than something organically or essentially given. It also, though, prompts one to ask whether the capacity to experience a place as a *Wahlheimat* presupposes a capacity for attachment to or uncomplicated experience of a *Heimat* in the first place. Does the inclination, which seems almost reflexive in Benjamin, to swiftly supplant any feeling of "*Heimweh*" with intellectual explorations of the "inevitable social unrecoverability of that which is past" render impossible an unqualified response to the (quasi-)elective place of residence? Or are the divided sentiments, expressed at times by both Heine and Benjamin, to the Parisian *Wahlheimat* ultimately different only with respect to the objects of the divided attachments – Paris vs. Germany, street vs. archive? And if so, might that be a tendency more generally endemic to post-Enlightenment German Jewish intellectuals in exile?

Bibliography

Adorno, Theodor. "Benjamin the Letter Writer." In *The Correspondence of Walter Benjamin, 1910–1940*. Edited by Gershom Scholem and Theodor W. Adorno. Translated by Manfred R. Jacobson and Evelyn M. Jacobson, xvii–xxii. Chicago: University of Chicago Press, 1994.

Benjamin, Walter. *The Arcades Project*. Translated by Howard Eiland and Kevin McLaughlin. Cambridge, MA: Belknap Press, 1999.

Benjamin, Walter. *Gesammelte Briefe*. Edited by Christoph Gödde and Henri Lonitz. Vol. 6. Frankfurt am Main: Suhrkamp, 2000.

Benjamin, Walter. *Gesammelte Schriften*. Edited by Rolf Tiedemann and Hermann Schweppenhäuser. 7 vols. Frankfurt am Main: Suhrkamp, 1972–1991.

Benjamin, Walter. *Selected Writings*. Edited by Michael W. Jennings, Howard Eiland et al. Translated by Harry Zohn, Edmund Jephcott, Howard Eiland, et al. 4 vols. Cambridge, MA: Belknap, 2004–2006.

Benjamin, Walter. "Unpacking My Library." In *Illuminations*. Edited by Hannah Arendt. Translated by Harry Zohn, 59–67. New York: Schocken, 1969.

Bernstein, Michael André. "Walter Benjamin: Apocalypse and Memory." In *Five Portraits: Modernity and the Imagination in Twentieth-Century German Writing*. 79–98. Evanston, IL: Northwestern University Press, 2000.

Brecht, Bertolt. "Profane und pontifikale Linie der Lyrik." In *Werke: Große kommentierte Berliner und Frankfurter Ausgabe*. Edited by Werner Hecht et al. Vol. 26: 416–417. Berlin, Weimar, Frankfurt am Main: Aufbau and Suhrkamp, 1994.

Buck-Morss, Susan. *The Dialectics of Seeing: Walter Benjamin and the Arcades Project*. Cambridge, MA: MIT Press, 1989.

Cohen, Margaret. "Benjamin's Phantasmagoria: The *Arcades Project*." In *The Cambridge Companion to Walter Benjamin*. Edited by David S. Ferris, 199–220. Cambridge: Cambridge University Press, 2004.

Eagleton, Terry. *Walter Benjamin or Towards a Revolutionary Criticism*. London: Verso, 1981.

Eiland, Howard. "Walter Benjamin's Jewishness." In *Walter Benjamin and Theology*. Edited by Colby Dickinson and Stéphane Simons, 113–143. New York: Fordham University Press, 2016.

Eiland, Howard and Michael W. Jennings. *Walter Benjamin: A Critical Biography*. Cambridge, MA: Belknap Press of Harvard University Press, 2014.

Frankel, Jonathan. *The Damascus Affair: "Ritual Murder," Politics, and the Jews in 1840*. Cambridge: Cambridge University Press, 1997.

Goltschnigg, Dietmar and Hartmut Steinecke, eds. *Heine und die Nachwelt*. 3 vols. Berlin: Schmidt, 2006–2011.

Hausschild, Jan-Christoph and Michael Werner. *"Der Zweck des Lebens ist das Leben selbst": Heinrich Heine-Eine Biographie*. Cologne: Kiepenheuer and Witsch, 1997.

Heine, Heinrich. *Heinrich Heine: Historisch-kritische Gesamtausgabe der Werke*. Edited by Manfred Windfuhr et al. 16 vols. Düsseldorf: Hoffmann und Campe, 1973–1997.

Heine, Heinrich. *Ludwig Börne: A Memorial*. Translated with commentary and introduction by Jeffrey L. Sammons. Rochester, NY: Camden House 2006.

Holub, Robert C. "Heine's Sexual Assaults: Towards a Theory of the Total Polemic." *Monatshefte* 73, no. 4 (1981): 415–428.

Iggers, Georg. "Heine and the Saint Simonians: A Re-Examination." *Comparative Literature* 10, no. 4 (1958): 289–309.

Kraus, Karl. *Heine und die Folgen*. Munich: Alberg Langen, 1910.

Lossin, Yigal. *Heinrich Heine: Wer war er wirklich?* Translated by Abraham Melzer. Neu Isenburg: Melzer Verlag, 2006.

Pensky, Max. "Method and Time: Benjamin's Dialectical Images." In *The Cambridge Companion to Walter Benjamin*. Edited by David S. Ferris, 177–198. New York: Cambridge University Press, 2004.

Reeves, Nigel. "Heinrich Heine: Politics or Poetry? Hegel or Enfantin? A Review of Some Recent Developments in Research." *Modern Language Review* 75, no. 1 (1980): 109–113.

Roth, Joseph. *Radetzkymarsch*. Munich: DTV, 2015.

Sammons, Jeffrey L. *Heinrich Heine: A Modern Biography*. Princeton, NJ: Princeton University Press, 1979.

Sammons, Jeffrey L. "Who Did Heine Think He Was?" In *Heinrich Heine's Contested Identities*. Edited by Jost Hermand and Robert Holub, 1–24. New York: Peter Lang, 1999.

Scheithauer, Jan *"Land der Philister" – "Land der Freiheit": Jüdische, deutsche und französische Identitäten beim jungen Heine*. Bielefeld: Aisthesis, 2013.

Skrandies, Timo. "Unterwegs in den Passagen-Konvoluten." In *Benjamin-Handbuch: Leben, Werk, Wirkung*. Edited by Burkhardt Lindner et al., 274–283. Stuttgart: Metzler, 2006.
Steiner, Uwe. *Walter Benjamin*. Stuttgart and Weimar: Metzler, 2004.
Wohlfarth, Irving. "Smashing the Kaleidoscope: Walter Benjamin's Critique of Cultural History." In *Walter Benjamin and the Demands of History*. Edited Michael P. Steinberg, 190–205. Ithaca: Cornell University Press, 1996.

H. Esra Almas
The Girl from the Golden Horn: Kurban Said / Lev Nussinbaum's Vision of Home and Exile in Interbellum Berlin

Set against a backdrop of three empires devastated by World War I – the Austro-Hungarian, the Russian, and the Ottoman – the work of Essad Bey and Kurban Said, both pen names of Lev Nussinbaum (1905–1942), a Jewish Azerbaijani who settled in Germany, insinuates a world where people and borders are in flux, and home is, above all, an imaginary space. Lev Nussinbaum, scion of a Jewish oil tycoon from Azerbaijan, was one of the thousands of Russians who fled following the Bolshevik takeover of the country, and settled in Weimar Germany. Nussinbaum became an acclaimed writer, first as Essad Bey, and then as Kurban Said, before his Jewish connection became public. He died in Italy in hiding in 1942, unable to get treatment for a mysterious blood disease.[1] The unusual affinities of Nussinbaum and his prolific oeuvre were forgotten until they became the subject of Tom Reiss's bestselling biography, *The Orientalist: In Search of a Man Caught between East and West*; his life has eclipsed his work ever since.

Nussinbaum's trajectories bear witness to a time when Turkish presence in interwar Germany and Austria was a regular feature of the cultural landscape, and when East and West, home and exile, and Islam and Judaism converged in unusual ways. As opposed to the mostly biographical studies on Nussinbaum, this chapter traces Nussinbaum's unusual predicament through his last published work, *The Girl from the Golden Horn* (1938), a lesser-known novel on Ottomans in exile in post-imperial Europe, which has curiously been left out of Reiss's work on Nussinbaum.[2] Evoking the trajectories of the writer himself, the novel provides

---
1 Gerdien Jonker, "In Search of Religious Modernity: Conversion to Islam in Interwar Berlin," in *Muslims in Interwar Europe*, ed. Bekim Agai, Umar Ryad, Mehdi Sajid (Leiden: Brill 2016), 18–46. Tom Reiss, *The Orientalist: A Man Caught between East and West* (London: Vintage, 2006). Sascha Talmor, "Ali and Nino – A Treasure from Azerbaijan," *The European Legacy: Toward New Paradigms* 6, no. 6 (2001): 793–811. The multiplicity of names and the controversy around the identity of Lev Nussinbaum make the choice of name a challenge. Both Jonker and Talmor refer to the writer as Lev Nussinbaum and Nussinbaum/Essad Bey. In Reiss's extensive biography, the writer is referred to as Lev. This article prioritizes the given name, adding the pseudonym according to the text in question.
2 Lev Nussinbaum/ Kurban Said, *The Girl From the Golden Horn* (*Das Mädchen vom goldenen Horn*) trans. Jenia Graman (New York: Overlook Press, 2001).

insight into questions surrounding its authorship, but also as a meditation on exile, home, filiations, and affinities.

The appeal of Nussinbaum's *Girl from the Golden Horn* has to do not just with the feeling of discovery that reading an obscure novel by a mysterious writer evokes; it also relates to the metonymic reference to Istanbul, especially in relation to the period. The reference to Istanbul, the demoted metropolis turned into a locus of exile in a novel written in Nazi Germany, evokes the plight of Jewish scholars, a significant number of whom escaped Nazi persecution by accepting posts in Istanbul. The most notable of these was Erich Auerbach whose *Mimesis*, the founding work of comparative literature, is a product of his exile in Istanbul.[3] This article uses the city as a bridge between the two writers; it ends by introducing Auerbach's letters to Walter Benjamin from Istanbul, which recount the former's early impressions of the city, in order to propose an affinity around "the problem of man's self-orientation," a question posed in different ways by both Nussinbaum and Auerbach in their aforementioned works.

1 The Many Names and Trajectories of Lev Nussinbaum

The concurrent dismemberment of the Russian and Ottoman Empires at the end of World War I, and the policies of the states that superseded them, initiated major flux in the territories over which these centurial powers stretched. For the minorities living within these empires, notably the Jewish, the empires' demise meant the reconfiguration of political and cultural identities in search of a home to strive for and dream of. Abraham Nussinbaum, a Jewish oil magnate from Baku, and his young son Lev were among the hundreds of thousands of refugees who fled the country following the Bolshevik takeover.[4] Like many, their destination was Germany. Indeed, more than 1,500,000 refugees flooded Germany at the end of World War I: of these 500,000 were from the Russian Empire, of whom approximately 360,000 settled in Berlin, temporarily transforming the city into

---

[3] Erich Auerbach, *Mimesis: The Representation of Reality in Western Literature* (Princeton, NJ: Princeton University Press, 2003).
[4] The situation of Jewish minorities in the European states that emerged after the fall of the Austro-Hungarian, Russian, and Ottoman Empires was a concern in the United States as well. A notable study that dates from the period is Oscar Janowsky's *The Jews and Minority Rights, 1898–1919* (1933), a prominent argument for Jewish political and cultural autonomy in postwar Eastern Europe.

"Russia's second capital."[5] During the Nussinbaums' detoured escape through Georgia, Persia, and the Ottoman Empire, young Lev became enthralled by Islam and the waning Empire. What made Lev extraordinary was that after settling in Weimar Germany, he put this fascination into effect: he converted to Islam in the Ottoman embassy in Berlin on August 4, 1922, while the Empire had officially ceased to exist.[6] As the first refugee crisis of the twentieth century quickly elicited public anxiety regarding the *Ostjuden*, the Jews from Eastern Europe, Lev changed his name to Essad Bey and attended the Seminar for Oriental languages at the Friedrich-Wilhelms-Universität to learn Turkish and Arabic; he also visited clubs where Muslim émigrés frequented in order to cultivate his oriental persona.[7]

Lev Nussinbaum's interest in the Orient was remarkable, but not entirely idiosyncratic, especially in the Weimar period. Indeed, the extent of Nussinbaum's life and work suggests the convergence of multiple political, ideological strands that marked the period. His orientalism likewise spoke to an idiosyncratic, albeit mostly forgotten culturescape and points to the peculiarly Jewish case of cultivating an oriental identity. Indeed, for many renowned orientalists of Jewish descent in the nineteenth century, oriental identity was not simply an intellectual pursuit; it was a means of reconciling with Jewish difference.[8] For the Jews in the Austro-Hungarian Empire, Ottoman affinity was a privilege. The Ottoman Jewish community in Vienna was allowed to build a synagogue in 1887.[9] In a similar manner, in Germany, Jews constituted a large part of the Ottoman migrants, and in Berlin, Ottoman Jews came together around the Sephardic Jewish Association, established in 1905.[10] The privileged status of the Ottomans in Austria and Prussia during the Weimar period also related to Wilhelm II's ambitions in the

---

5 Anne Marie Sammartino, *The Impossible Border: Germany and the East, 1914–1922* (Ithaca: Cornell University Press, 2010).
6 Gerdien Jonker, *The Ahmadiyya Quest for Religious Progress. Missionizing Europe, 1900–1965* (Leiden: Brill, 2015), 141–42.
7 Reiss, *The Orientalist*, 193–95.
8 See Paul Mendes-Flohr's *Divided Passions. Jewish Intellectuals and the Experience of Modernity* (Detroit: Wayne State University Press, 1991), 77–93, for a brief introduction to Friedrich Arndt-Künberg, who converted to Islam in Istanbul in 1886 and continued his life as Omar al Rachid Bey in Bedouin attire in Munich, and influenced, among others, Paula Buber. On the role of Islam in German-Judaic studies as a means of "purifying" Judaism, see Susannah Heschel, "German-Jewish Scholarship on Islam as a Tool for De-Orientalizing Judaism," *New German Critique* 117 (Fall 2012): 91–109. For an overview, see Martin Kramer "Introduction," in *The Jewish Discovery of Islam: Studies in Honour of Bernard Lewis*, ed. M. Kramer (Tel Aviv: The Moshe Dayan Center for Western and African Studies, 1999), 1–48.
9 Marc David Baer, "Turk and Jew in Berlin: The First Turkish Migration to Germany and the Shoah," *Comparative Studies in Society and History* 55, no. 2 (2013): 331.
10 Ibid.

Middle East, especially to his endorsement of pan-Islamist movements. In this, an unusual mixture of Zionists, Pan-Islamists, and enthusiasts of Aryanism such as Baron Max von Oppenheim assisted Wilhelm.[11]

Muslim identity was very much in vogue during the Wilhelmine and Weimar periods, for very different reasons. German pan-Islamism culminated in the disastrous collaboration during the Great War between the Ottoman Empire and Germany. One of its relatively unknown results was some 20,000 Muslim prisoners of war in Berlin; these were mostly Indian, Tatar, and Arab revolutionaries who were trained by German and Ottoman officers to inspire insurgencies against the British, French, and Russians/Soviets. In addition, during the Weimar period, in a manner not unlike the *turqueries* that swept continental Europe in the eighteenth century, it was fashionable for the elite "to turn Turk."[12] The aristocratic converts to Islam and Jewish orientalists made Islam a coveted intellectual pursuit especially in Europe. One of Nussinbaum's many aristocratic friends from Vienna, Baron "Umar" Rolf von Ehrenfels, was an active member of the Muslim community.[13] Jewish converts to Islam were also prominent in these circles.[14] The most renowned Jewish convert was probably Leopold Weiss (Muhammad Asad), who converted to Islam in 1926 in Berlin, but he was not the only one. The career of "Hamid" Hugo Marcus, who led the Wilmersdorfer mosque in Berlin until the mid-1930s, is equally telling.[15] The visitors to this mosque included Albert

---

11 Sean Mc Meekin, *Berlin-Baghdad Express: the Ottoman Empire and Germany's Bid for World Power* (Cambridge, MA: Belknap Press of Harvard University Press, 2012). Lionel Gossmann, *The Passion of Max von Oppenheim: Archaeology and Intrigue in the Middle East from Wilhelm II to Hitler* (Cambridge: Open Book Publishers, 2014). Accessed April 3, 2017.
12 Eve R. Meyer, "*Turquerie* and Eighteenth-Century Music," *Eighteenth-Century Studies* 7, no. 4 (1973): 474–88. Meyer extensively covers the Turkish vogue in the eighteenth-century art and music. See also, Reiss, *The Orientalist*; Jonker, "In Search of Religious Modernity." Reiss and Jonker both provide detailed descriptions of the Muslim vogue in Weimar Germany and Austria.
13 Umar Ryad, "Salafiyya, Ahmadiyya, and European Converts to Islam in the Interwar Period" in Agai, Ryad, and Sajid, *Muslims in Interwar Europe*, 47–88. A convert to the popular Ahmadiyya sect, Baron "Umar" Rolf von Ehrenfels helped found the Islamische Kulturbund (Association of Muslim Culture), was appointed co-editor of the *Moslemische Revue*, and wrote several articles for the journal (77–79).
14 Baer, "Turk and Jew in Berlin." Baer discusses the story of the Behars, a Jewish family from Istanbul, whose Turkish citizenship was renounced and were hence prosecuted by the Nazis.
15 Marc David Baer, "Muslim Encounters with Nazism and the Holocaust: The Ahmadi of Berlin and the Jewish Convert to Islam Hugo Marcus," *American Historical Review* 120, no. 1 (February 2015): 140–72. Hugo Marcus (1880–1966), the scion of a Jewish industrialist, studied at the Friedrich-Wilhelms-Universität in Berlin. Already a writer and activist of gay rights and pacifism of repute, he converted to Islam in 1925, and became its leading figure, as Baer illustrates: Marcus "edited Berlin Mosque's German-language publications and served as the chief editor of and the

Einstein, Martin Buber, and Hermann Hesse. This European, and in particular German, interest in Islam with Ahmadiyya backing also related to a larger international appeal, as Hollywood blockbusters like *The Sheikh* and Rudolf Valentino's ensuing stardom made the nomadic Muslim a dazzling figure.[16]

Increased Muslim presence on German soil and Prussian ambitions made Germany the perfect home for Nussinbaum's oriental personas, which soon became a professional one. From 1926 onward, he became a regular contributor in *Die Literarische Welt*, the prestigious literary review of the period. Writing under the name Essad Bey, "the expert on the East," he published more articles for the journal than Walter Benjamin.[17] With his first book *Blood and Oil in the Orient*, an autoethnographic account of his life as the scion of a Muslim oil baron in Baku and the remains of that life in Europe, published in 1929, Nussinbaum became a writer with international renown.[18] His characters are caricatures, including oriental cosmopolitans like the Bukharan princess at an artists' ball in Hotel Adlon in Berlin, and a former oil baron living on the Ku'damm complaining about "barbaric Europe."[19] Essad Bey's early books are not mere entertainment; they playfully resist the stereotypes of the exiled, homeless, the oriental, or the westerner in favor of a cosmopolitan identity. Occasionally, there are affirmations of Jewish identity, as in this passage from *Twelve Secrets of the Caucasus* (1931), the sequel to *Blood and Oil*: "All Caucasian peoples without exception have taken over some legacy from the Jews ... here an *Old Testament* word used by them in their prayers, there some custom, such as levirate marriage ... Many Caucasian races confess their Jewish origin with pride and are considered honorably distinguished by it."[20]

---

major contributor to the *Moslemische Revue* (1924–1940), which had a circulation of at least 1,000, and in which he published nineteen articles between 1924 and 1933 ... He was also the editor of the Ahmadi German Quran translation and commentary, published in 1939 in several thousand copies. Marcus was the chairman of the German Muslim Society from its founding in 1930 to 1935. He gave dozens of lectures at the society's 'Islam Evenings' at the mosque, which attracted between 250 and 400 attendees, including two of his acquaintances from homosexual rights and literary circles, Thomas Mann and Hermann Hesse, and other German intellectuals" (156). Marcus was interned in Sachsenhausen concentration camp in 1938, and once released with the help of imam Dr. Sheikh Muhammad Abdullah (1889–1956), he left for Switzerland.

16 Jewish identification with *The Sheik* may have been a commonplace tactic at the time. In the first chapter of Art Spiegelman's *Maus I: A Survivor's Tale* (New York: Pantheon, 1991), entitled "The Sheik," the young Vladek Spiegelman proudly attributes his appeal to young women to his looks reminiscent of *The Sheik*.
17 Reiss, *The Orientalist*, 206–11.
18 Lev Nussinbaum/Essad Bey, *Blood and Oil in the Orient* (New York: Overlook Press, 2008 [1929]).
19 Ibid., 154, 35.
20 Lev Nussinbaum/Essad Bey, *Twelve Secrets of the Caucasus* (Freiburg: Bridges Publishing, 2008 [1931]), 147–48.

Nussinbaum's fantastic world of fabulous Caucasians introduces the audience to a faraway world where, despite volatile affinities and violent politics, Jewish origins serve as a means of self-recognition. In a time of violent identity politics and rampant antisemitism, these early narratives reveal a young writer proudly claiming Judaism as a basis of cultural identity in Weimar Germany.

Nussinbaum's literary output was prolific; in addition to his articles and public speeches, his numerous books included biographies, with titles ranging from *Mohammad* (1932), to *Stalin* (1932), and to the last Tsar *Nicholas II* (1935).[21] Following the success of his work, Nussinbaum and his ambiguous cultural identity received extensive media coverage, albeit not always in a favorable light. Azeri nationalists and Muslim refugees condemned his writings for their stereotypical representations of the peoples of the region.[22] The "Western" audience also condemned Nussinbaum's Jewish heritage. By the same token, his tumultuous divorce from the Viennese socialite and poetess Erika Loewendahl, who eloped to the United States with a fellow writer from the same circle in 1937, was featured in tabloids, which told of the disillusioned wife's frustration on finding out that her husband was not of "princely Arabian lineage, but plain Leo Nussinbaum."[23] A Jewish background, in this case, was considered an impediment to a genuine understanding of the East.

The confluence of the upheavals in his private life with Nazi policies put an end to Essad Bey's publications in 1937. Nonetheless, Nussinbaum continued to write, albeit under a different pseudonym: Kurban Said.[24] The two subsequent novels published in German, *Ali and Nino* (1937) and *The Girl from the Golden*

---

[21] Lev Nussinbaum/Essad Bey, *Mohammed* (Berlin: Gustav Kiepenheuer Verlag, 1932); *Stalin* (Berlin: Gustav Kiepenheuer Verlag, 1931), and *Nikolaus II: Glanz und Untergang Des Letzten Zaren* (Berlin: Hole& Co Verlag, 1935).

[22] Zaur Gasimov and Wiebke Bachmann, "Transnational Life in Multicultural Space: Azerbaijani and Tatar Discourses in Interwar Europe" in *Muslims in Interwar Europe: A Transcultural Historical Perspective*, ed. Agai, Ryad, Sajid, 205–25, esp. 211–13. Another Berlin based Azerbaijani anti-communist, Hilal Munschi (1899–?), published in 1930 *Die Republik Aserbaidschan: Eine Geschichtliche und Politische Skizze* (The Republic of Azerbaijan: A Historical and Political Outline), a monograph on the history and culture of Azerbaijan. In the monograph, Munschi denounces Essad Bey's bestselling *Blood and Oil in the Orient* for its stereotypical representations of the peoples of the region.

[23] Reiss, *The Orientalist*, 293–95, presents a detailed coverage of the episode and its treatment in the international media.

[24] Wilfried Fuhrmann, "Gesellschaftliche, ökonomische und politische Aspekte im Werk von Essad-Bey," Potsdam 2008, Anhang: Quelle B-2, www.essadbey.de. Accessed April 2017. Fuhrmann, an economist with Azerbaijani specialization, recounts the following anecdote: "Nussinbaum's choice of Kurban Said as pseudonym is linked to meeting a stranger in Istanbul in 1936, on the vigil of the Muslim feast of the Sacrifice (Kurban). The stranger, not knowing Arabic,

Horn (1938), are his most enduring pieces. In these novels, the themes that mark Essad Bey's work and Nussinbaum's life converge. On account of Nussinbaum's multiple name changes, this intersection has mostly been disregarded, if not completely ignored. The English edition of the novel, as well as recent studies on the period and Reiss's biography, ascribe authorship to Lev Nussinbaum; in Azeri and Turkish circles however, the novel is attributed to an Azeri author, Yusuf Vezir Cemenzamanlı. A further source of confusion was the copyright: both novels were registered under Baroness Elfriede Ehrenfels, one of Nussinbaum's aristocratic friends from Vienna. The Baroness was no stranger to Islam thanks to her husband, Baron "Umar" Rolf von Ehrenfels.[25]

2 Ottoman Exiles in Berlin and Vienna

Nussinbaum/Kurban Said's final novel, *The Girl from the Golden Horn* is an oriental fantasy about Ottoman aristocracy in exile.[26] The novel connects many of the personal tribulations of Nussinbaum with his longing for the multicultural atmosphere of the Ottoman Empire, through characters that cross cultural and geographical boundaries. The novel tells the story of Asiadeh Anbari, a member of the Ottoman aristocracy, who lives in exile in Berlin with her father, Achmed-Pasha, following the dismemberment of the Empire. We first meet Asiadeh studying Turkic languages in the Oriental institute in Berlin as a means of overcoming nostalgia and connecting to her distant ancestors:

> [A] thousand years separated her from her robust ancestors who had once come from the deserts of Turan to overrun the gray plains of Anatolia ... During these thousand years' empires, towns, and vowel dislocations had arisen. One of her ancestors had conquered, founded, and lost cities and empires. What remained was a small oval face, light gray wistful eyes, and an aching memory of the lost empire, the sweet waters of Istanbul, and the house on the Bosphorus with its marble courtyards, slender columns, and white inscriptions over the entrances.[27]

---

mistakes the salute 'Kurban-Said' (Happy Feast!) for Nussinbaum's name: 'nice to have met you, Mr. Kurban Said,' he said to me. And it was thus that this became a surname."
25 Umar Ryad, "Salafiyya, Ahmadiyya, and European Converts to Islam in the Interwar Period" in Agai, Ryad, and Sajid, *Muslims in Interwar Europe*, 47–88.
26 Lev Nussinbaum/Kurban Said, *Haliçli Kız*, trans. Bilgin Adalı (Istanbul: Everest Yayinlari, 2005). The book is currently out of print. Despite the presence of Ottoman characters in an international setting and a favorable, if not nostalgic representation of the Empire, the novel is mostly unknown to Turkish audiences.
27 Kurban Said, *The Girl from the Golden Horn*, 4.

Asiadeh's longing is not simply for a city and a fallen empire, but also for Turan, the mythical motherland in Central Asia.[28] In her mind, homeland is an idiosyncratic blend of Istanbul's imperial culturescape and the warring spirit of the Turks. The loss of the city is intermingled with the loss of the original spirit of conquest, resulting in a wistful pain of exile. Similarly, her motivation to learn Turkic languages derives not from the nostalgia for an empire that is no more, but from the nomadic spirit of the warlike Turks. The fabulous past of the nomadic Turkic tribes echoed in an exilic present are not unlike Nussinbaum/Essad Bey's earlier portrayals of the Caucuses in his accounts of the region.[29] As the novel progresses, Asiadeh finds that stories of the past inform the future, and give her the strength to bring about the changes she wants.

On a visit to a hospital to treat her sore throat, Asiadeh makes friends with her laryngologist, Alexander Hassa. A Viennese man in self-imposed exile in Berlin, Hassa is melancholic as his wife has just eloped with a fellow doctor and abandoned him. Hassa's predicament here is not unlike Nussinbaum's own later abandonment by his wife Erika in favor of a fellow poet from their circle of friends. Asiadeh, however, is interested in the lovelorn laryngologist because she notes in Hassa's surname a distant Turkic ancestry. Apart from the surname, however, Dr. Hassa bears no traces of his Bosnian roots. To the contrary, Hassa introduces her to the ways of the West, from swimming to psychoanalysis, to pragmatic thinking. Opposites attract, and Asiadeh falls under the charms of this "exotic animal."[30] They decide to get married, and after their honeymoon in Bosnia, an episode during which Hassa becomes acquainted with his distant Muslim roots in Europe, the couple moves to Vienna. Asiadeh's longing is not only for the lost homeland, nor is it for Hassa. Her heart is with Abdulkerim, the Crown Prince she was promised to as a child but has never met. She writes a letter to the prince, asking to be set free from this childhood pledge. Yet, Abdulkerim has long ago shed his imperial identity; he is now John Rolland,

---

28 Jacob Landau, *Pan-Turkism in Turkey: A Study of Irredentism* (London: C. Hurst, 1981). Nussinbaum/Said's work also relates to Turan, the nineteenth-century Pan-Turkist political theory promoting cultural and political unity between lands inhabited by Turkic speaking peoples. Conjoining Timurlane's Mongolians and the Ottoman Turks, the extent of geography made Turan a challenge at best, a project that lost its popularity with the end of the Russian and Ottoman Empires.
29 Lev Nussinbaum/Essad Bey, *The Twelve Secrets of the Caucasus* (Freiburg: Bridges Publishing, 2008), provides one of the many examples in the writer's texts where the "barbaric" peoples of mysterious origins in the Caucasus are portrayed commendably: "For there is one thing certain: these illiterates who go about armed to the teeth, these brutish barbarians, are by no means savages, and by no means virgin wax upon which Europe can set its imprint. An ancient culture has held sway over many of these races, and it rules over them still" (24).
30 Nussinbaum/Said, *The Girl from the Golden Horn*, 47.

a Hollywood screenwriter based in New York. Torn between the exhilaration of adapting to the vertical life in New York, and the yearning for his old life in Istanbul, the former prince prefers to drown the occasional upsurge of memory in whiskey. In this, he is aided by his friend and manager Perikles, a Greek from Istanbul, or Sam Dooth, as the latter has rechristened himself. Despite their effective stratagems for forgetting their past, Asiadeh's letter sets into motion a series of events, including journeys across Europe and North Africa, in search of their roots, and prospective routes, before Abdulkerim and Asiadeh can build a home together.

The Girl from the Golden Horn does not only provide a panorama of exotic locales; it also presents a panorama of stereotypes; a hilarious array of exiles and locals, their prejudices and clichéd imageries serve as ways of asserting that despite cartographies in flux, cultural identities may be continuous and comical. The encounters between the Ottoman exiles and the Viennese provide humorous lenses to contemplate the notions of home and identity. Hassa and his friends, the Viennese doctors, are excessively academic. They categorize forms of behavior they meet according to their specialization. Hassa's friend Kurz, the psychoanalyst, playing with the notion that Vienna was known for psychoanalysis due to the presence of Sigmund Freud, is perhaps the most clichéd caricature: he considers even seduction a particular form of scientific research, and a logical result of the proximity of women with beautiful necks, such as Asiadeh.[31]

In diametrical opposition to the Austrian doctors and men of science, we have a parade of dreamy exiles of the Ottoman Empire. Asiadeh's father, Achmed Pasha, a descendant of the governors of Bosnia, works in a carpet store and frequents the Café *Watan* (homeland), a club where he meets exiled imperialists to share his memories of bygone days of glory. This café is not unlike the Café Oriental that Nussinbaum frequented in his early days in Berlin. Similarly, Asiadeh and Achmed Pasha read like characters featured in Nussinbaum's early works, *Twelve Secrets* and *Blood and Oil*. Achmed Pasha is keen to kill anyone who lays eyes on his daughter unless it is the president of the United States, who can send warships to Istanbul to claim it for the father-daughter pair. Yet, the character who best exemplifies the cosmopolitanism of the empire is Perikles. Originally from Phanar, the ancient Greek neighborhood in Istanbul, he has taken on the moniker Sam Dooth and helps the crown prince by exercising a variation of the ancient practice of dragoman, or translator, and by extension serving also as a matchmaker (both practices traditionally associated with the Greek population of Istanbul).

---

31 Ibid., 193.

Figure 1: "Lev Nussinbaum as Essad Bey"

Hassa's predilection for Asiadeh and his curiosity and openness for the "East" make him into an intermediate figure – bridging East and West. For Hassa, the East is sick and decayed, "at the mercy of the elements unlike Europe, which has conquered nature."[32] Yet, he also admits that his understanding is a personal observation and that from Asiadeh's eyes "they are just barbarians who know about medicine,"[33] thereby confirming the relativity of cultural norms. The caricaturized differences between the Ottomans and the Westerners, also confirmed through Hassa, provide humorous snapshots of the clichéd European from a clichéd Ottoman perspective, and vice-versa. Through the observations on the difference between Europeans and Ottomans, the narrative "turns the tables," to borrow Azade Seyhan's words, "on [its] Western reading public by exoticizing the Occident through the eyes of [its] storytellers."[34] Seyhan's remarks address contemporary diasporic writing, which she calls "writing outside the nation," also the title of her study on transnational writers working outside their mother tongue. Nussinbaum/Said's novel extends the timespan of Seyhan's argument, confirming that the imaginary character of homeland and identity is a common concern for diasporic writers of different times. Identities, if not in flux, are situated in-between: in between empires, countries, past and present, East and West.

---

[32] Ibid., 227.
[33] Ibid., 91.
[34] Azade Seyhan, *Writing Outside the Nation* (Princeton, NJ: Princeton University Press, 2001), 27.

3 Kaleidoscope of Affinities

In a tone unexpected from a novel replete with German Turcophilia, *The Girl from the Golden Horn* makes clear that the absence of fixed markers of identity is not exclusive to the exiled, or to an ethnic group. The ambiguity of cultural filiations becomes a leitmotif, marking the novel and the writer. The main characters change names, identities and affiliations, building their identities on the move, and in the void, providing subtle parallels with Nussinbaum's own multiple connections. Early in the novel, when Asiadeh proudly notes in Hassa's surname a distant Turkic ancestry, Hassa's response reveals the fluidity of cultural identities, in a manner not unlike the crown prince, and by extension, Nussinbaum. Hassa affirms: "If Kara Mustapha had conquered Vienna, or the Peace of San Sebastian had turned out differently, my name would be Ibrahim-Bey-Hassanovic, and I would wear a Turban. But Kara Mustapha did not conquer Vienna, so I have become a good Austrian, and my name is Dr. Alexander Hassa."[35] Cultural identifications are neither permanent nor fixed; they are shaped primarily by power and politics. Hassa's personal alliances, seemingly built on scientific methods, are no different.

Asiadeh's unflinching dedication to her Turkic roots stands in diametrical opposition to Hassa's understanding of identity in relation to the present. The Ottoman princess reaches an understanding of her roots through the ancient texts of nomadic Turkic tribes in Central Asia. The stories in the ancient Orkhun inscriptions feel as if they are "the story of her own dreams, desires, and hopes."[36] Asiadeh's innermost emotions seem to be a part of a communal, albeit highly nationalistic, memory. We are told very little about her life in Istanbul. Nonetheless, the novel makes clear that Asiadeh's allure as well as her defining traits reside in "the real Istanbul polish" with which she has been raised while growing up in a palace by the Bosphorus, without any further explanation. The strait, a prominent image used almost interchangeably in the novel with the Ottoman lifestyle, functions as a metaphor that captures the flux at the core of the book and its main characters. Indeed, even though Asiadeh is portrayed as a nationalist character, her name suggests otherwise: Asiadeh is an invented Turkish name, popularized through the eponymous heroine of the best-selling belle époque writer Pierre Loti's *Aziyadeh* (1879).[37] The acclaimed French exoticist's debut novel – set in Istanbul, the seat of the crumbling Empire – recounts his life and love *alla turca*: a naval officer settles in the ancient quarter of the city, assumes a Turkish

---

35 Nussinbaum/Said, *The Girl from the Golden Horn*, 28.
36 Ibid., 51.
37 Pierre Loti, *Aziyadeh* (Paris: Folio/Gallimard, 1991).

identity, and conducts an affair with a young Muslim woman. This oriental dream is also one of double deceptions: the name Aziyadeh is not really a Turkish name, but a coinage of Loti, which he admits to have made up so as to protect the identity of his beloved, disguising not only the identity of his lover, but also that of the writer. Behind the pseudonym Pierre Loti stood the naval officer Julien Viaud, whose many journeys to exotic lands served as the basis of his oeuvre. Nussinbaum/Said's choice of an invented name for an Ottoman princess throws doubt on the authenticity of this novel, which despite its fictional framework placed substantial emphasis on the history and the variations of Turkish language. A subtle marker of Asiadeh's multiple connections, the name also hints at the complex issues of authorship, language, and identity, turning the female protagonist into a kaleidoscope of ambiguous filiations.

An unusual echo of Nussinbaum's trajectory resonates in the multiple names and careers of the male protagonist of the novel. The crown prince Abdulkerim Effendi (1906–1935), on whom the main character is loosely based, has a story the tragic complexity of which rivals that of Nussinbaum. The grandson of the pan-Islamist Abdulhamid II, Abdulkerim Effendi was exiled following the abolition of the Empire, and settled in Beirut with his family. In 1933, the crown prince was invited to Tokyo to help found an Islamic state in the Japanese occupied regions of Manchuria. The campaign proved unsuccessful and the prince left for New York City, where he was found dead in a hotel room in 1935.[38] Moreover, very much like Nussinbaum, Abdulkerim Effendi's plight has faded from the annals of history, with the exception of occasional and passing references to his visit to Japan. In *The Girl from the Golden Horn*, this tragic yet minor character is given new life as John Rolland, a creator of illusions and alternative identities, including his own. Abdulkerim/Rolland's decision to shed one identity in favor of a more convenient one, the willingness to adapt to his surroundings, and yet feed from his dreamy past when crafting new identities, albeit fictional ones, is not unlike that of Nussinbaum himself. In a manner reminiscent of Nussinbaum's accounts of his travels in Europe and the Middle East, the prince travels the former lands of the Ottomans as well as European metropolises, unable to avoid seeing Ottoman traces everywhere. Through the story of the prince and Asiadeh, the narrative takes the reader on a grand tour ranging from Western metropolises to exotic locations, from Libyan deserts to Asian steppes, from Berlin to Bosnia and New York, tracing the trajectories of the main characters in search of a home. Asiadeh and the prince encapsulate kaleidoscopic identities that not only dramatize but also poeticize the need to belong.

---

[38] Hiroaki Kuromiya and Andrzej Pepłoński, "Between East and West: Gaiaz Iskhaki and Gabdulkhai Kurbangaliev," *Nowy Prometeusz* 3 (December 2012): 89–105.

4 Inhabiting Movement

A story of cultural, political, and geographical crossings, *The Girl from the Golden Horn* shows the idea of home as a shifting space of imagination. Within the period of intense upheaval, in which the novel is set, millennial traditions like the caliphate were overthrown overnight. In this context, Asiadeh's devotion to the stories of the past is a survival strategy not only for herself, but also for her imaginary homeland. What remains are thoughts and stories. This is made explicit through an epigram which Asiadeh notes down and keeps in her pocket only to discover it months later in Vienna: "Everything which this world holds must end and vanish. Only the written word remains."[39] Writing is a means of not only preserving the past, but also of bridging the past and the future. Narratives of bygone glory and perseverance provide roots to connect to, and possible routes to pursue, as well as an awareness of the fictionality of all affinities and affiliations.

Home and self make sense only when one can identify their others or locate a difference between the local and the strange, the savage and the civilized, the past and the present. Asiadeh notes: "This world was not a bad world; perhaps there was no such thing as a good or bad world. Any world could make its people happy. But all differed from the others, divided from one another since the beginning of time, strong and immovably rooted in their own individuality."[40] Asiadeh's words demonstrate that the difference between the old and the new, the East and the West, the good and the bad are ultimately points of view. After all, as Asiadeh points out, "any world could make its people happy," as long as one can appreciate each world in its particularity. These remarks foreshadow Auerbach's emphasis, in *Mimesis*, on the necessity of "making oneself at home without fixed points of support."[41] But they also articulate it as a predicament for, as well as the privilege of the exiled. Surviving in a world without hinges points to the possibility of making *any* place a home.

The crown prince, having lost all points of orientation, travels in pursuit of fiction. In Gadames, a village of caravanners in a remote town in Libya, where he shoots a Hollywood movie, the prince meets an imam who informs him that in Gadames "each of us carries his homeland in his heart or in his head. It is always there. A man can lose a foot, an arm, an eye – everything – but not his homeland."[42] Transitions, as the words of the imam point out, do not necessarily entail points of departure and destination. Inhabiting the in-between is part of

---

39 Ibid., 263.
40 Nussinbaum/Said, *The Girl from the Golden Horn*, 229.
41 Auerbach, *Mimesis*, 311.
42 Nussinbaum/Said, *The Girl from the Golden Horn*, 217.

the human predicament and can be invested as sources of new meaning. Nomads keep their homes in their hearts. Thanks to the caravanners he meets in Libya and to Asiadeh, the crown prince ultimately makes peace with his past and present, concluding with an identity built in transit. With that discovery, the prince goes to Vienna, to claim Asiadeh as his home. In the final encounter between Hassa, the prince, and Asiadeh, the predicaments of exile and in particular of being an Easterner in the Western world are resolved. In response to Hassa's question on bridging the gap between Eastern origins and Western lifestyle, the prince's response reveals the main theme of the book: in-between is a productive and inhabitable space of meaning:

> "The home," he said, "that is the bridge. As long as you have that, there is no contrast between the outer being and the inner consciousness. Home is not the bathroom you use every day, nor the cafe you go to every day. Home – that is the structure of the soul, formed by the earth of the homeland. Home is always there, always in man's heart. As long as he lives, man is within the magic circle of his home, regardless of where he happens to be. An Englishman goes to the African bush, and his sleeping tent is England. A Turk goes to New York, and his room in Manhattan is Turkey. Only he who never had a home or a soul can ever lose it."[43]

Abounding in images of oppositions, this passage reveals a complex understanding of home. It is a structure, a conduit, a feeling, and foremost, a human condition. A major claim of the novel is that for those who live in the West but carry Asia in their soul, home is the movement between in and out, East and West. Yet, there is more to the idea. Calling the bridge a home is to inhabit movement, in the sense that a bridge is a structure that links but does not belong to either of the sides it connects. Inhabiting the bridge means inhabiting the space of detachment as well as attachment between the two sides the structure of the bridge aims to link. Georg Simmel in his essay "The Bridge and the Door," posits the bridge as a structure that can exist only because the mind that designs it sees the two parts it connects as separate.[44] A bridge does not simply join; it also separates. The aesthetic value of the bridge is to make this ambiguous act of separation and relation visible. Simmel's conceptualization of bridging, which relates visibility to aesthetics, provides insight into the exceptional space of habitation that Prince Abdulkerim invokes. The bridge-as-home does not only carry one across; it is not simply a conduit that enables passers-by to move between two points: it is the space where affinities are materialized, providing the locus of identity,

---

[43] Ibid., 268.
[44] Georg Simmel, "The Bridge and the Door," in *Simmel on Culture*, ed. David Frisby and Mike Featherstone (London: Sage, 1997).

transforming movement into space, bridges into homes. Abdulkerim's response ultimately encapsulates the plight of not only the protagonists but also the writer: living in homelands carried within. The story suggests that the predicament can be overcome; through bridges in the form of a constant dialogue between the mythic past, an alien present, and a utopian ideal, temporal and spatial distances collapse into moments of being at "home."

The novel ends with Asiadeh's letter to her father detailing her separation from Hassa, her union with the crown prince, and extending an invitation to the Pasha to join them in New York to build a new home. Asiadeh and the prince, already masters at electing their home and identity, work together to create their Istanbul of the mind, to adapt Salman Rushdie's phrase on diasporic nostalgia for the forsaken home.[45] Just like the idea of home, the lifestyle along the Bosphorus can be transposed, albeit in part, to other stretches of water: the novel ends with the promise that the Ottoman lifestyle by the Bosphorus is to be continued by the shores of the Hudson River. The fairytale world of *The Girl from the Golden Horn* ends with a wishful thought. The timing of the publication at the end of Nussinbaum's career turns it into a manifesto of his staunch belief in the possibility of self-orientation in a world without hinges, as well as his swan's song to a world of multiple affinities.

5 Letters from Istanbul: Home and Exile

The setting of Istanbul as a lost home adds further layers to this palimpsestic last novel. Istanbul of the 1910s, the city Lev Nussinbaum visited and to which he felt attached, was a city with non-Muslims constituting half of its population.[46] The shift from the Ottoman Empire to the Turkish Republic, and the move of the capital to Ankara left the city desolate and dilapidated. With the nationalist cultural policies of the Republic, the city as well as the country, was above all deserted by its non-Muslim inhabitants in the following decades.[47] For the German-Jewish scholars in 1930s Germany, Istanbul, by contrast, offered a sanctuary from the antisemitic policies of Nazi Germany. For Erich Auerbach, who

---

45 Salman Rushdie, *Imaginary Homelands: Essays and Criticism, 1981–1991* (London: Penguin/Granta, 1991).
46 Stefanos Yerasimos, "Kozmopolit Yapıdan Milliyetçiliğe" (From Cosmopolitanism to Nationalism), in. *Istanbul 1914–1923: The Capital of a Lost World or the Death of Old Empires*, ed. S. Yerasimos (Istanbul: Iletişim, 1992), 12.
47 Ibid.

accepted a teaching post at Istanbul University in 1936 to flee Nazi persecution, Istanbul was already a locus of exile, as well as a refuge. The glimpses of Istanbul that peek through his letters to Walter Benjamin are their attestations. In a letter dated December 12, 1936, Auerbach notes an insurgent nationalism in his new locale: "The situation here is not exactly simple, but it is not without charm. They have thrown all tradition overboard here, and they want to build a thoroughly rationalized – extremely Turkish nationalist – state of the European sort. The process is going fantastically and spookily fast: already there is hardly anyone who knows Arabic or Persian, and even Turkish texts of the past century will quickly become incomprehensible since the language is being modernized and at the same time newly oriented on "Ur-Turkish."[48] These remarks, obviously referring to the language reforms of the new Republic, contain Auerbach's silence on Istanbul. This bleak image of the country's culturescape points to the complexity of the period of Auerbach's stay.[49]

Auerbach's ambiguous stance concerning Turkey and the country's cultural policies extends to its inhabitants. In a letter dated January 3, 1937, Auerbach refers to Anatolian Turks as "a naïve, distrustful, honest, somewhat blunt and boorish, but also emotional race of men (who), (b)ecause they are accustomed to slavery and hard, slow work, are tougher and more unpolished, and also more rigid and more surly, than southern Europeans, but at the same time they are quite likeable and have much vital energy."[50] Such overgeneralized, critical, yet also compassionate depictions of his hosts are not unlike the caricatured representations in Nussinbaum's early work, with the exception of being sheltered in the privacy of personal correspondence. Auerbach's impressions of Istanbul, notably the Bosphorus, foreshadow some of the themes that resonate in *The Girl from the Golden Horn*; the views of the Bosphorus from the house are glorious, and the nineteenth-century palazzos of the sultans and pashas are mostly dilapidated. There are no records whether Auerbach's remarks were repeated in literary circles, but as Nussinbaum and Benjamin belonged to a similar milieu, dissemination of information is not entirely unrealistic.[51] Regardless, their faint echoes

---

48 Erich Auerbach, "Scholarship in Times of Extremes: Letters of Erich Auerbach (1933–46), on the Fiftieth Anniversary of His Death," Introduction and translation by Martin Elsky, Martin Vialon, Robert Stein, *PMLA* 122, no. 3 (2007): 749.
49 The government-enforced move from the use of Arabic letters to Latin alphabet in 1928 was followed by the language reform of 1936, which purged the Turkish language of its Ottoman vocabulary and syntax, introducing newly coined words from Turkic languages. These policies, accompanied by a new historical thesis that bypassed the Ottoman past, aimed to sever the remaining ties with Islamic heritage in order to facilitate processes of Westernization.
50 Auerbach, "Scholarship in Times of Extremes," 750–51.
51 Reiss, *The Orientalist*, 211.

can be heard in Nussinbaum's last novel, where Asiadeh points out that in Istanbul, there were no longer Osmans, and only Turks left.[52]

Auerbach's stay in Istanbul culminated in *Mimesis*, the magisterial survey of realistic representation in Western literature.[53] Auerbach started working on *Mimesis* in 1942 – almost five years after his letters to Benjamin – in the Dominican Monastery of San Pietro di Galata, to the library to which he was given access by Angelo Roncali, the future John XXIII.[54] In the epilogue to *Mimesis*, however, Auerbach refers to the time and place of writing as an apology for its scope as well as methodology: "the book was written during the war and at Istanbul, where the libraries are not well equipped for European studies."[55] The locale warrants the scope of the work, as Auerbach adds that the lack of resources mobilized him, suggesting that it "is quite possible that the book owes its existence to just this lack of a rich and specialized library."[56] In other words, absence creates presence, with Istanbul helping Auerbach bridge the canonical texts of Western Literature.

The links between Auerbach's magisterial work and Istanbul have been much explored.[57] Intellectual life in Istanbul during the 1930s, especially around Auerbach, was far livelier than he implied.[58] Auerbach's remark on Istanbul is notable because, as Edward Said notes, "to have been an exile in Istanbul at that time of fascism in Europe was a deeply resonating and intense form of exile from Europe."[59] For a scholar of medieval and classical literature like Auerbach, Istanbul as the seat of "the Turk," represents the antagonistic Other of Europe, evolving throughout centuries from "the scourge of Christendom" to the Oriental

---

52 Nussinbaum/Said, *The Girl from the Golden Horn*, 159.
53 Auerbach, *Mimesis*.
54 Auerbach "Scholarship in Times of Extremes," 743.
55 Auerbach, *Mimesis*, 557.
56 Ibid.
57 Emily Apter, *The Translation Zone: A New Comparative Literature* (Princeton, NJ: Princeton University Press, 2006); David Damrosch, *Meetings of the Mind* (Princeton, NJ: Princeton University Press, 2000); Kader Konuk, *East-West Mimesis: Auerbach in Turkey* (Stanford: Stanford University Press, 2010). Probably the most curious among these is David Damrosch's 2000 novel *Meetings of the Mind*. One character, a scholar from Istanbul, considers Auerbach's exile as an excuse for not doing bibliographical research, and not a compelling necessity. He adds: "Auerbach was exaggerating his exile in Istanbul ... He was not trapped in some tent on the edge of a desert after all" (53–57).
58 Apter, *The Translation Zone*, 50–52. Apter lists a literary journal published under Auerbach's editorship and a number of European politicians, intellectuals, and artists who either worked or sought refuge there during his residence, including Leon Trotsky, Hans Reichenbach, Paul Hindemith, and Steven Runciman.
59 Edward Said, "Secular Criticism," *The World, the Text, and the Critic* (Cambridge, MA: Harvard University Press, 1983), 6.

despot, the "sick man of Europe," and finally the "Eastern question." The old metropolis provides the vantage point from which Auerbach could reflect on the European literary tradition as a whole. Yet, the location complicates Auerbach's position as a humanist and scholar of European culture who, exiled by a product of that culture, now attempts to rescue it in the very city that has been for centuries represented as Europe's greatest enemy. In a city, which stands for exile and isolation, he turns to literature and establishes a mode of reading, however fleeting and un-academic it seems to him, as orientation. *Mimesis*, according to Edward Said, "owes its existence to ... not only a massive reaffirmation of the Western cultural tradition, but also a work built upon a critically important alienation from it."[60] Auerbach's achievement is therefore located in his alchemy of homelessness, where detachment turns into attachment as literary works representing the Western literary tradition become points of orientation.

The theme of writing as a solace, home, and a point of support, if not a bridge, resonates with Nussinbaum's final novel, albeit in entirely different ways. The overlapping trajectories of Auerbach and Nussinbaum show that not only filiations, but also the experiences of exile are kaleidoscopic. A reading of Auerbach with Nussinbaum in the context of Nazi Germany reveal self-orientation not only as the task of the modern man, but also as a form of bridge-building, an ambiguous act of separation and relation. The bridge-as-home provides the locus of identity, transforming movement into space, bridges into homes. In a world without hinges, Nussinbaum's alchemy of homelessness resonates with Asiadeh's realization that there is no such thing as a good or bad world: affinities, like homes are established foremost in the mind, and writing, in all its guises, is their only lasting manifestation.

6 Conclusion

Nussinbaum's story of cultural, political, and geographical crossings reveals the idea of home as primarily a space of imagination, one that resists intruders of all kinds. What stands out in his work and his person is the possibility of building affinities that transcend ethnic, religious, and political boundaries. In a similar vein, in the afterword to *Blood and Oil in the Orient*, Tom Reiss defines Nussinbaum/ Essad Bey/ Kurban Said's exceptional stance in the following words: "Essad Bey's books took readers into a somehow reassuringly strange world of the mysterious Orient at the darkest moment of the twentieth century. At a time when the borderlands of Europe and Asia were squeezed between totalitarian

---

60 Edward Said, *Culture and Imperialism* (London: Vintage-Random, 1994), 8.

ideologies ... his world promised that there were hills and valleys that could never be conquered."[61] Nussinbaum appealed to, even as he played with and upended, strong orientalist modes, ranging from characters reminiscent of *The Sheikh* to catering to the German reading audience's voracity for stories from the Orient – exotic, different, mysterious. Nussinbaum's orientalism however is not simply about representing the Orient for Western audiences, but about representing a world where Islam and Judaism, people of different beliefs and lifestyles are, to quote John Efron's words, "symbiotically linked."[62]

The Girl from the Golden Horn holds the same promise, not for hills and valleys, but for imagination and elections. Set in a world where cartographies and cultures are in flux, this obscure novel questions the parameters with which to define home and exile. Set in a world of changing boundaries and alliances between people as well as countries, Nussinbaum's last novel is an undeservedly understudied affirmation of the writer's identity beyond ethnic and religious divides. Marked with transformations of varying degrees and scopes, the myriad roots and routes of the writer, and of the main characters of his last novel link Judaism and Islam, Germans and Turks, East and West in a shared past, seeking a convivial future, but foremost in the shared longing for a home, wherever and in whatever form it might be located.

Bibliography

Apter, Emily. *The Translation Zone: A New Comparative Literature*. Princeton, NJ: Princeton University Press, 2006.

Auerbach, Erich. *Mimesis: the Representation of Reality in Western Literature*. Reprint. Princeton, NJ: Princeton University Press, 2003 [1953].

Auerbach, Erich. "Scholarship in Times of Extremes: Letters of Erich Auerbach (1933–46), on the Fiftieth Anniversary of His Death." Introduction and translation by Martin Elsky, Martin Vialon, Robert Stein. *PMLA* (2007): 742–762.

Baer, Marc David. "Muslim Encounters with Nazism and the Holocaust: The Ahmadi of Berlin and the Jewish Convert to Islam Hugo Marcus." *The American Historical Review* 120, no. 1 (February 2015): 140–172.

Baer, Marc David. "Turk and Jew in Berlin: The First Turkish Migration to Germany and the Shoah." *Comparative Studies in Society and History* 55, no. 2 (2013): 330–355.

Damrosch, David. *Meetings of the Mind*. Princeton, NJ: Princeton University Press, 2000.

Efron, John. *German Jewry and the Allure of the Sephardic*. Princeton, NJ: Princeton University Press, 2016.

---

[61] Reiss, "Afterword," in *The Orientalist*, 260.
[62] John Efron, *German Jewry and The Allure of the Sephardic* (Princeton, NJ: Princeton University Press, 2016), 229.

Fuhrmann, Wilfried (Hrsg.). "Gesellschaftliche, ökonomische und politische Aspekte im Werk von Essad-Bey"; Potsdam 2008. Anhang: Quelle B-2. www.essadbey.de. Accessed April 2017.

Gasimov, Zaur and Wiebke Bachmann. "Transnational Life in Multicultural Space: Azerbaijani and Tatar Discourses in Interwar Europe." In *Muslims in Interwar Europe: A Transcultural Historical Perspective*. Edited by Bekim Agai, Umar Ryad, and Mehdi Sajid, 205–225. Leiden: Brill Open, 2016.

Gossman, Lionel. *The Passion of Max von Oppenheim: Archeology and Intrigue in the Middle East from Wilhelm II to Hitler*. Cambridge: Open Book Publishers, 2014. Accessed April 3, 2017.

Heschel, Susannah. "German-Jewish Scholarship on Islam as a Tool for De-orientalizing Judaism." *New German Critique* 117 (Fall 2012): 91–109.

Jonker, Geraldine. "In Search of Religious Modernity: Conversion to Islam in Interwar Berlin." In *Muslims in Interwar Europe: A Transcultural Historical Perspective*. Edited by Bekim Agai, Umar Ryad, and Mehdi Sajid, 18–47. Leiden: Brill Open, 2016.

Konuk, Kader. *East-West Mimesis: Auerbach in Turkey*. Stanford: Stanford University Press, 2010.

Kramer, Martin. "Introduction." In *The Jewish Discovery of Islam: Studies in Honour of Bernard Lewis*. Edited by Martin Kramer, 1–48. Tel Aviv: The Moshe Dayan Center for Western and African Studies, 1999.

Kuromiya, Hiroaki and Andrzej Pepłoński. "Between East and West: Gaiaz Iskhaki and Gabdulkhai Kurbangaliev." *Nowy Prometeusz* nr 3 (grudzień 2012): 89–105.

Landau, Jacob. *Pan-Turkism in Turkey: A Study of Irredentism*. London: C. Hurst, 1981.

Landau, Jacob. *Tekinalp, Turkish Patriot 1883–1961*. Istanbul and Leiden: Nederlands Historisch-Archaeologisch Instituut, 1984.

Loti, Pierre. *Aziyadeh*. Paris: Folio/Gallimard, 1991 [1879].

McMeekin, Sean. *The Berlin-Baghdad Express: the Ottoman Empire and Germany's Bid for World Power*. Cambridge, MA: Belknap Press of Harvard University Press, 2012.

Mendes-Flohr, Paul R. *Divided Passions: Jewish Intellectuals and the Experience of Modernity*. Detroit: Wayne State University Press, 1991.

Meyer, Eve R. "*Turquerie* and Eighteenth-Century Music." *Eighteenth-Century Studies* 7, no. 4 (1973): 474–488.

Mufti, Aamir. "Auerbach in Istanbul: Edward Said, Secular Criticism and the Question of Minority Culture." *Critical Inquiry* 25, no. 1 (1998): 95–125.

Nussinbaum, Lev, as Essad Bey. *Blood and Oil in the Orient*. Freiburg: Bridges Publishing, 2008 [1929].

Nussinbaum, Lev, as Essad Bey. *The Twelve Secrets of the Caucasus*. Freiburg: Bridges Publishing, 2008 [1929].

Nussinbaum, Lev, as Kurban Said. *Ali and Nino*. London: Vintage, 2000 [1937].

Nussinbaum, Lev, as Kurban Said. *Ali ve Nino*. Translated by Semih Yazıcıoğlu, İstanbul: Hürriyet Yayınları, 1971.

Nussinbaum, Lev, as Kurban Said. *Haliçli Kız (The Girl from the Golden Horn)*. Translated by Bilgin Adalı. İstanbul: Everest Yayinlari, 2005.

Nussinbaum, Lev, as Kurban Said. *The Girl from the Golden Horn*. New York: Overlook Press, 2001 [1938].

Reiss, Tom. "Afterword." *Blood and Oil in the Orient*. Freiburg: Bridges Publishing Press, 2008.

Reiss, Tom. *The Orientalist: a Man Caught Between East and West*. London: Vintage, 2006.

Rushdie, Salman. *Imaginary Homelands: Essays and Criticism, 1981–1991*. London: Penguin/Granta, 1991.

Ryad, Umar. "Salafiyya, Ahmadiyya, and European Converts to Islam in the Interwar Period." In *Muslims in Interwar Europe: A Transcultural Historical Perspective*. Edited by Bekim Agai, Umar Ryad, and Mehdi Sajid, 47–88. Leiden: Brill Open, 2016.

Said, Edward. *Culture and Imperialism*. 1993. London: Vintage-Random, 1994.

Said, Edward. "Secular Criticism." *The World, the Text, and the Critic*. 1–31. Cambridge, MA: Harvard University Press, 1983.

Sammartino, Anne Marie. *The Impossible Border: Germany and the East, 1914–1922*. Ithaca: Cornell University Press, 2010.

Schorsch, Ismar. "Converging Cognates: The Intersection of Jewish and Islamic Studies in Nineteenth-century Germany." *Leo Baeck Institute Year book* 55 (2010): 3–36.

Seyhan, Azade. *Writing Outside the Nation*. Princeton, NJ: Princeton University Press. 2001.

Shissler, Holly A. *Between Two Empires: Ahmet Ağaoğlu and the New Turkey*. London: IB Tauris, 2003.

Simmel, Georg. "Bridge and Door." In *Simmel on Culture*. Edited by David Frisby and Mike Featherstone, 170–173. London: Sage, 1997.

Spiegelman, Art. *Maus I: A Survivor's Tale*. New York: Pantheon, 1991.

Talmor, Sascha. "*Ali and Nino* – A Treasure from Azerbaijan." *The European Legacy: Toward New Paradigms* 6, no. 6 (2001): 793–811.

Yerasimos, Stefanos. "Kozmopolit yapidan milliyetçiliğe. [From a cosmopolitan structure to nationalism]." In *Istanbul 1914–1923: The Capital of a Lost World or the Death of Old Empires*. Edited by Stefanos Yerasimos, 9–25. Istanbul: Iletişim, 1992.

Anna M. Parkinson
"In der Fremde zu hause": Contingent Cosmopolitanism and Elective Exile in the Writing of Hans Keilson

In 1944, philosopher and critical theorist Theodor W. Adorno began writing what was to become the collection of aphorisms published under the title *Minima Moralia: Reflections from Damaged Life*. An aphorism titled "Protection, Help, and Counsel" addresses life in exile, a topic salient for the German philosopher, Jewish intellectual, and *persona non grata* in National Socialist Germany, living in exile in the United States:

> Every intellectual in emigration is, without exception, mutilated, and does well to acknowledge it to himself, if he wishes to avoid being cruelly apprised of it behind the tightly-closed doors of his self-esteem. He lives in an environment that must remain incomprehensible to him, however flawless his knowledge of trade-union organizations or the automobile industry may be; he is always astray. ... His language has been expropriated, and the historical dimension that nourished his knowledge, sapped. ... All emphases are wrong, perspectives disrupted. Private life asserts itself unduly, hectically, vampire-like, trying convulsively, because it really no longer exists, to prove it is alive.[1]

Published in 1949, on occasion of the fiftieth birthday of fellow exile, friend, and colleague Max Horkheimer, Adorno's aphorisms emerge, often directly and in obvious ways, from his own experiences in exile in the land that produced the swift efficiency of the Ford assembly line and the guileless smile of Mickey Mouse, ambassador of mass popular cultural production in the USA.

The subtitle of Adorno's book, "Reflections from Damaged Life," captures his concern not only with the hollowness of life in forced emigration or exile that echoes through this aphorism, but, more broadly, with a world held in the thrall of the advanced stages of what he and Horkheimer called "the dialectic of

---

[1] Theodor W. Adorno, "Protection, Help, and Counsel," *Minima Moralia: Reflections from Damaged Life*, trans. E. F. N. Jephcott (London/New York: Verso, 2005 [1951]), 33.

Note: My gratitude goes to Marita Keilson-Lauritz for her openness, intellectual curiosity, fabulous sense of humor, and warmth. This article, and all else I have written on Hans Keilson's work, has been enriched significantly by the depth of knowledge and generosity that Marita extended to me, and for which I am thankful.

https://doi.org/10.1515/9783110637564-010

Enlightenment" in their eponymous book.[2] Caught in the historical backwash of the destructive dialectical movement between reason and myth, Adorno clearly sees the exile as a figure in transit and transition, Odysseus-like, always on her or his way back home from a foreign place. He depicts the exile as "mutilated" and diminished, caught in a vacuum inscribed with the hieroglyphics of a history, language, and culture that remains foreign and perplexing. Not only is the exile's knowledge "sapped," even the very modes of expression or familiar rhetorical styles are distorted, poorly timed, or unavailable to him: "all emphases are wrong" and "perspectives disrupted." This process of social alienation and distortion is given an expressionistic cinematic slant when Adorno captures the liminal state of the exile in the figure of the undead: "vampire-like, trying convulsively, because it no longer exists, to prove it is alive." The figure of the exile or political refugee as the undead is suggestive, not least because it brings into focus the precarious status of the exile in relation to the conditions of their nation state from which they seek refuge.

In Adorno's dark aphorism we are brought face to face with the truth of his hyperbolically negative claim: namely, the ambivalence upon which this type of forced emigration – even with its underlying potential for transformation into elective exile – is based. Another evocative trope associated with the liminal space of exile, the cosmopolitan, is productive in this context. A multivalent and increasingly ambivalent term, cosmopolitanism will be problematized as the point of departure for thinking through the dialectic between damage and reparation, and reality and utopia that constitutes the concept of "elective exile" and the concomitant search for a community in which one is at home, at least sometimes.

A citizen of the world, the cosmopolitan subject is simultaneously international and between nations, staging an ambiguous, if not also potentially disruptive relationship to the nation state. In this chapter, I intend to consider the relationship between the figure of the exile and the cosmopolitan expressed through the writing and in many ways also encapsulated in the biography of Hans Keilson. In this way, I hope to explore the proximity of – and important differences between – "elective exile" and what I am calling "contingent cosmopolitanism" that ostensibly serves as a precondition for elective exile in response to traumatic circumstances and their aftermath.

What if the émigré elects to stay in the land in which she or he has temporarily taken up residence? How might the foreign be made home without completely

---

[2] Theodor. W. Adorno and Max Horkheimer, *The Dialectic of Enlightenment: Philosophical Fragments*, ed. Gunzelin Schmid Noerr, trans. Edmund Jephcott (Stanford: Stanford University Press, 2002 [1947]).

abandoning the exiled subject's founding affiliations? What are the conditions that facilitate membership in a "spiritual homeland"? Adorno's dark parable of emigration, which depicts exile as a liminal space for the living dead ("vampires"), indexes forms of exile necessitated by political and existential causes (here, specifically, in response to the life-threatening antisemitism incessantly propagated by the so-called Third Reich). Although Hans Keilson, too, left Germany to go into exile in the Netherlands in 1936 when confronted with the antisemitic propaganda and social exclusions imposed on Jews in Germany by the National Socialist party, his work and life demonstrate a far less melancholic, and distinctly non-vampiric, dialectical relationship between different layers of time and space (or history and place) constitutive of what might be called "contingent cosmopolitanism." The category of contingent cosmopolitanism, I argue, reveals how, paradoxically, the radical and often painful deterritorialization or uprooting caused by forced exile is the precondition for any kind of *Wahlheimat*. As a precondition for forging new connections with non-indigenous places and communities, contingent cosmopolitanism is not necessarily a remedy or bandage for the experiences endured in the passage to and often also within the land of exile; rather, it is a concept that captures both the descriptive and normative aspects of the forging of new affinities while continuing to reflect on past affiliations. Significantly, this new state of belonging is achieved not by suspending or suppressing the past, but by radically and continuously working on loss and mourning (*aufarbeiten*, to use T. W. Adorno's term for the work of critical reflection in relation to one's past)[3] in the here and now. In this sense, painful experiences become the very foundation for the sense of being "In der Fremde zu Hause" (at home in the foreign/at home in a foreign place), to evoke a phrase Hans Keilson penned to describe his relationship to the Netherlands – his home of choice after World War II. This ongoing negotiation of time and space – that is, of the past in relation to the present place of dwelling – can be seen in (at least) two different modalities in Keilson's writing. The first is an ironic mode of relation to exile in the 1947 novella *Comedy in a Minor Key*; while the second, which can only be briefly touched on here, can be gleaned from Keilson's essayistic writing and poetry thematizing the trauma of exile and persecution and the subsequent embrace of the "foreign" as a psychological, existential, and affective dwelling: as one's home.

---

3 Theodor W. Adorno, "The Meaning of Working Through the Past," *Critical Models: Interventions and Catchwords*, trans. Henry W. Pickford (New York: Columbia University Press, 1998 [1963]), 89–103.

1 "Here Life Goes on in a Most Peculiar Way..."

Jewish-German psychiatrist, psychoanalyst, poet, musician, and author of three novels, Hans Keilson was born in Germany in the spa town of Bad Freienwalde an der Oder in 1909, and died in the Netherlands in 2011 at the generous age of 101.[4] Having studied medicine at the University of Berlin during the Weimar years, his career in medicine was essentially aborted before it began when, having attained his qualifications in 1934, National Socialist anti-Jewish legislation (given legal expression in the Nuremburg Laws of 1935) prevented him from practicing as a doctor. Instead, he supported himself by working as a physical education teacher at a variety of Jewish schools in Berlin and its environs, before immigrating to the Netherlands in 1936 on the insistence of his first wife, Gertrud Mainz.

Keilson's first novel, *Das Leben geht weiter* (*Life Goes On*), was published in 1933 by the Fischer Verlag. The book provides a strongly autobiographical account of the inexorable toll inflicted on a Jewish merchant family by the political and social upheavals of the volatile Weimar years. This book also had the dubious honor of being the last debut by a Jewish author at the Fischer publishing house before the National Socialists came to power; banned in 1934, its release was almost contemporaneous with its censorship.

Although Keilson and Mainz found refuge in the Netherlands in 1936, when National Socialist forces invaded and ultimately occupied the Netherlands in 1940, Keilson was forced into "hiding." In his particular case, this also meant working and traveling with forged identity papers – and not without risk to himself – for the clandestine Dutch resistance organization, the *Vrije Groepen Amsterdam*.[5] Keilson, Mainz, and their young daughter Barbara (born in 1941) survived the war. His parents, Max and Else Keilson, were not as fortunate, and were deported first to the Dutch internment camp Westerbork and then to Auschwitz-Birkenau, where they were murdered on arrival.

---

[4] The heading of this section is a citation taken from the title of an exhibition catalogue on psychoanalysis before and after 1933. *"Here Life Goes on in a Most Peculiar Way...": Psychoanalysis Before and After 1933*, eds. Karen Brecht, Volker Friedrich, Ludger M. Hermanns, Isidor J. Kaminer, Dierk H. Juelich, and Hella Ehlers, trans. Christine Trollope and Joyce Crick (Hamburg: Kellner, 1992), 2, 9. The citation is listed as having being taken from a letter by John F. Rittmeister to Alfred and Edith Storch, Müsingen, October 15, 1939. Appropriately enough, Hans Keilson was asked to write the introduction to the exhibition catalogue in the original German version. The exhibition was mounted in 1985 on the occasion of the first meeting of the International Psychoanalytic Association in Germany since the 1932 IPA congress in Wiesbaden.

[5] For a detailed account of Keilson's activities in the final war years in the Netherlands see Marita Keilson-Lauritz, "Vorwort," in Hans Keilson, *Tagebuch 1944 und 46 Sonette*, ed. Marita Keilson-Lauritz; "Afterword" by Heinrich Detering (Frankfurt am Main: Fischer, 2014), 7–20.

Having trained as a psychiatrist and a psychoanalyst in the Netherlands after the war, Keilson published in 1979 the first quantitative-statistical and qualitative-descriptive clinical analysis on the long-term effects of sequential traumatization of Dutch-Jewish child orphans of the Holocaust.[6] Keilson based his publication in part on his initial psychological evaluation and subsequent therapeutic analysis of Jewish child survivors provided by the non-government Dutch organization for Jewish orphans Le-Ezrat Ha-Jeled, of which he was a co-founder in 1945, directly after the war. Keilson's psychoanalytic writings on sequential traumatization of child orphans persecuted by the Nazis bear witness to a complex and polyvalent understanding of potential long-term effects of trauma initially inflicted through antisemitic persecution of Dutch-Jewish child orphans, and then through their postwar resettlement in Jewish families from the perspective of the orphans and their lived trajectories after thirty years. Specifically, he focused on cases of Jewish child survivors of concentration camps or children who went into hiding with families that were not their own in the Netherlands. The state of numbness, dislocation, and the at times seemingly futile attempts to create alternative, elective homelands in the wake of traumatic experiences demonstrates the lasting damage of the Holocaust in the lives of these more than one hundred individuals. For many of Keilson's patients the concept of a home, elective or otherwise, remained distinctly dystopian, if not entirely unobtainable due to their earlier experiences of persecution and dislocation.

On an adjacent plane, and in reference to his capacity as an author of fiction and poetry, Keilson's two postwar novels dramatize and explore by literary (and semi-autobiographical) means the experience of being in hiding and the psychological effects of persecution, respectively. The publication history of his books provides a study in untimeliness. The third and final work of prose fiction published by Keilson, *Der Tod des Widersachers* (*The Death of the Adversary*), was begun after he emigrated to the Netherlands in 1936, but went underground in 1940 (quite literally – it was buried in a garden in Delft), when the Nazi occupation of the Netherlands forced Keilson into hiding between 1943 and 1945.

Keilson's second book, *Komödie in Moll* (*Comedy in a Minor Key*), was his first post-war publication in 1947. Significantly, his novel was published by Querido, a publishing house in Amsterdam committed to the publication of German-language authors in exile. (Adorno and Horkheimer's *Dialektik der Aufklärung* was also published by Querido in the same year).[7] Keilson's recently published wartime

---

6 Hans Keilson, *Sequential Traumatization in Children: A Clinical and Statistical Follow-Up Study on the Fate of the Jewish War Orphans in the Netherlands* (Jerusalem: The Magnes Press, 1992).
7 For a history of the Querido publishing house, particularly its express role of publishing German language literature by German-speaking exiles after Hitler's assumption of power in

journal, written in 1944 during his time in hiding, and published posthumously with an introduction by his second wife, Marita Keilson-Lauritz, documents the flurry of fiction and poetry writing that took over Keilson's life during that eventful year. In addition to completing a draft of what was to become *Komödie in Moll*, he wrote at the same time a collection of forty-six sonnets in 1944, which, along with the aforementioned wartime journal, was published for the first time in 2014. In his journal, Keilson charted an intimate connection between events in his life and his frenetic and swift writing of the sonnets, which, according to Keilson himself, were inspired by his relationship with a young Jewish-German woman, Hannah Sanders, with whom he had a passionate affair while in hiding in Delft.[8] It may attest to the difficult thematic content of the novel *Comedy in a Minor Key* that this book was published in Germany by a German publishing house for the first time only in 1988.[9] The plot centers around a Dutch couple that clandestinely takes a Jewish man into their home, only to find themselves needing to dispose of his body when he dies of natural causes after living in hiding with them for more than a year. In the context of elective exile and contingent cosmopolitanism, this novella certainly warrants closer scrutiny, to which I will return below.

Keilson's third and final book, *Der Tod des Widersachers*, was released in Germany in 1957. A psychologically intricate and stylistically complex text with its theme of the Jewish narrator's apparent identification with the perpetrator offers dark insight into individual and mass identification with Hitler (although the latter is never directly named in the novel). It was no doubt equally perplexing to the German readership that the protagonist, who sees his counterweight (his "adversary") in Hitler, is clearly a young Jewish man, although this, too, is suggested obliquely rather than overtly specified in Keilson's text. By contrast, the 1962 English translation of the novel was recognized, in part for the same psychological complexity that appeared to irritate many German reviewers of *Tod des Widersachers*, as one of the ten best books of the year in the United States of America, alongside books by modernist authors of international stature, including Vladimir Nabokov and Jorge Luis Borges.[10] *The Death of the Adversary* then dropped from public view and went underground once again. In 2010, author

---

Germany from 1933 onwards, see publisher Fritz H. Landhoff's memoir: *Amsterdam, Keizersgracht 333, Querido Verlag: Erinnerungen eines Verlegers: Mit Briefen und Dokumenten* (Berlin: Aufbau Verlag, 1991).

8 Hans Keilson, *Tagebuch und 46 Sonette*.
9 See Roland Kaufhold, "'Das Leben geht Weiter': Hans Keilson, ein jüdischer Psychoanalytiker, Schriftsteller, Pädagoge und Musiker," *Zeitschrift für psychoanalytische Theorie und Praxis* 23, no. 1/2 (2008): 142–67, 150.
10 No author given, "Anatomy of Hatred," *Time*, September 14, 1962, 83–84.

and literary critic Francine Prose enthusiastically exhumed the English-language translation of Keilson's novel in a book review in the *New York Times*. Prose unreservedly hailed *The Death of the Adversary* as a "masterpiece" and Keilson as a modernist "genius."[11]

Arguably, *The Death of the Adversary* might be seen to be a fragmentary modernist novel detailing a powerful psychological profile of the extraordinary Jewish male protagonist who believes that he will be able to stave off persecution and hatred by thinking his way into the structure of antisemitism that consumes his adversary. Through his disavowed identification with his "adversary" – again, none other than Adolf Hitler – the unnamed protagonist attempts to understand and even dismantle the binds of this structure of hatred and, ultimately, to convince Hitler of the error of his attitude toward the Jews, even as his encounters with him, fueled by external circumstances, take place solely within the theater of the protagonist's mind. Indubitably, both *Comedy in a Minor Key* and *The Death of the Adversary* testify to the terrifying psychological costs to both victim and perpetrator inflicted by the prejudice and hatred of antisemitism.

This bold act of misrecognition in *The Death of the Adversary*, among other literary ploys in Keilson's fiction, serves to disrupt the more somber or even mournful pathos characteristic of canonical works by writers of Holocaust literature. Further, elements of dark satire and irony in Keilson's prose offer up what might be called a form of psychoanalytic grotesque characteristic of his late fiction. This provocative literary approach was echoed later, and in divergent ways, in writing by other Jewish-German fiction authors. Perhaps the best known of these writings is Edgar Hilsenrath's novel *Der Nazi und der Friseur* (first published as *The Nazi and the Barber* in English in 1971, because he was unable to find a German publisher until 1977).[12] Hilsenrath's book is driven by an unscrupulous protagonist in the shape of a former Nazi who assumes the identity of his murdered neighbor, a Jewish man, to the extent that he ultimately immigrates to Israel – his new *Wahlheimat* – to escape prosecution in Germany after the defeat of the Nazi regime. All this to indicate that Hans Keilson's fiction was clearly ahead of the normative curve defining what would come to be known as Holocaust literature.

---

11 Francine Prose, "As Darkness Falls," *New York Times*, August 5, 2010, n.p.
12 For an analysis of Hilsenrath's book and its reception history see Stephan Braese, "Wider den Mythos von der deutsch-jüdischen Symbiose: Edgar Hilsenraths 'Der Nazi und der Friseur' (1977)," *Die andere Erinnerung: Jüdische Autoren in der westdeutschen Nachkriegsliteratur* (Berlin/Vienna: Philo, 2001), 429–84; Erin McGlothlin, "Narrative Perspective and the Holocaust Perpetrator: Edgar Hilsenrath's *The Nazi and the Barber* and Jonathan Littell's *The Kindly Ones*," in *The Bloomsbury Companion to Holocaust Literature*, ed. Jenni Adams (London/New York: Bloomsbury, 2014), 159–77.

2 Interlude: Elective Exile and Contingent Cosmopolitanism

Returning for a moment to the title of this essay, what are we to make of the oxymoronic term "elective exile"? Both the ambiguity and the potentiality of elective exile may be illuminated productively from the vantage point of what I am calling "contingent cosmopolitanism." The word "contingent" has a fleet of competing meanings, ranging from: "depending on something else that might or might not happen," "likely, but not certain to happen," "not logically necessary" and, most significantly here: "happening by chance or unforeseen causes" or "not necessitated: determined by free choice."[13] Thus, "contingent" itself hosts a collection of ambivalent or even incommensurate meanings, enabling the co-existence of the concept of free choice along with the element of chance or uncertainty.

Similarly, the concept of "cosmopolitanism," which is often used loosely as shorthand for pluralism, tolerance, multiculturalism, and even worldliness, may also be read as a node of ambivalent identification that is nonetheless sufficiently capacious to offer space for speculative alternatives of dwelling in a world in which belonging is defined existentially and politically in terms of membership in a nation state. Immanuel Kant's positive understanding of cosmopolitanism as a normative ideal with the utopian outcome of a peaceful world federation with mutual respect of other cultures and ideas has been radically challenged in the wake of critiques of the uneven hierarchies of power constitutive of multiculturalism in the cultural debates around difference and the nation state in the 1990s and early twenty-first century.[14]

In the postcolonial, global context of the twenty-first century, cosmopolitanism has become a productively disputed hermeneutic turf.[15] The term's complex and wide-ranging history is characterized by tensions between claims of legitimacy based on the nation state in relation to those of citizenship (as found in cosmopolitan discourses on world citizenship, for example), and between liberal and democratic claims of legitimation. These tensions arise in the debates around cosmopolitanism in the work of political theorists with approaches

---

[13] All definitions are taken from: www.merriam-webster.com.
[14] The book that best embodies the movement from ideal to critique in relation to the concept of "cosmopolitanism" from a postcolonial perspective is, perhaps, *Cosmopolitics: Thinking and Feeling Beyond the Nation*, eds. Pheng Cheah and Bruce Robbins (Minnesota: University of Minnesota Press, 1998).
[15] See the recently published edited volume with contributions by Rosi Braidotti, Paul Gilroy, and Sneja Gunew, among others, addressing the concept and practices of "cosmopolitanism" with an eye to the historical moment and contemporary politics and ethics: *After Cosmopolitanism*, ed. Rosi Braidotti, Patrick Hanafin and Bolette Blaagaard (New York: Routledge, 2013).

ranging from the normative, such as that of Jürgen Habermas, that privileges processes of procedural rationality, to deconstructive critical theory that reveals how acts of violence are constitutive of foundational acts, such as the analysis of cosmopolitanism through the prism of speech act theory in Bonnie Honig's work on agonistic democracy. Recently, sociologist Ulrich Beck has argued that "cosmopolitanism" has moved beyond an abstract philosophical concept to become sociological reality, stating rather optimistically that social scientists can no longer take national organization as the point of departure for analysis as he draws questions of social inequality and climate change into the critical itinerary of processes and structures of cosmopolitanism.[16]

In the field of literary studies, theorist Galin Tihanov argues that cosmopolitanism should be seen as a contested discursive arena in which the politics of inclusion and exclusion is negotiated.[17] Tihanov views cosmopolitanism in the tradition of Kantian Enlightenment thought in its significance as "a marker / symptom of recalibration of the polis ... in the wake of significant historical events."[18] As we will see in Keilson's novel, although his writing may not lead directly to a reconfiguration of the polis, these texts are interventions in the complex political relationship between individuals and the putatively "normalcy" of the locus of the home. Keilson's work illustrates how disruptive events may also be staged or manifested in writing, be it through novels or poetry, psychoanalytic case histories or memoirs.

The common denominator of rigorous critical analyses of cosmopolitanism appears to be an antinomic, and thus irresolvable tension between instances of the particular and the universal. Narratives of cosmopolitanism, as with those invoking the pathos of exile, often seem to imply an optimistic or even utopian path, providing a redemptive moral interpretation of what might otherwise be seen as unstable, untimely, painful or even at times existentially untenable.[19] In

---

[16] Ulrich Beck, "Cosmopolitan Sociology: Outline of a Paradigm Shift," in *The Ashgate Research Companion to Cosmopolitanism*, ed. Maria Rovisco and Magdalena Nowicka (Surrey: Ashgate, 2011), 17–32. See also Ulrich Beck, *The Cosmopolitan Vision*, trans. Ciaran Cronin (Cambridge: Polity Press, 2006).

[17] Galin Tihanov, "Do Minor Literatures Still Exist? The Fortunes of a Concept in the Changing Frameworks of Literary History," in *Reexamining the National-Philological Legacy: Quest for a New Paradigm?*, ed. Vladimir Biti (Amsterdam: Rodopi, 2014), 169–90. Many thanks to Jamie Trnka for introducing me to Tihanov's work.

[18] Galin Tihanov, "Cosmopolitanism in the Discursive Landscape of Modernity: Two Enlightenment Articulations," in *Enlightenment Cosmopolitanism*, ed. David Adams and Galin Tihanov (London: Legenda, 2011), 133–52.

[19] Edward Said makes this point in relation to exile when he contrasts the ways in which exile is "strangely compelling to think about but terrible to experience"; in Said's experience, as might

this sense, "elective exile" and "contingent cosmopolitanism" share the quality of remaining critically, yet productively unresolved, with each adjectival modifier underscoring the dissonant, yet parallel trajectories of each concept.

3 Uncanny Dwellings: There's No Place Like Home

Hans Keilson's novel *Death in a Minor Key* offers a subtle, yet explicitly psychological account of the tensions and encounters intrinsic to the experience of both the "host" and the "guest" in the attenuated situation of hiding a persecuted individual in one's home – here, specifically, during the German occupation of the Netherlands (1940–1945). The slender text harbors three protagonists: a man of unspecified nationality (he is identified as Jewish only, and in this way is rendered "stateless" once again by the novel itself), a former traveling perfume salesman, who introduces himself with the pseudonym Nico; and the non-Jewish Dutch couple made up of the husband, Wim, who works in an office, and his wife Marie, a meticulous homemaker. Wim and Marie provide Nico with a hiding place and lodging for over a year in their home in German-occupied Netherlands during the German-Allied wartime bombing campaigns that provide the constant backdrop for the interpersonal events in the narrative.

It is important to note that Nico, who has been in hiding in various locations for an unspecified, yet lengthy period of time, has been declared stateless in the Netherlands under the Nazi-imposed ruling of 1941. Essentially, this makes an exile of Nico, even if the Netherlands is his home country, where he is no longer granted freedom of movement or at this point even the right to exist. This stateless status is certainly not an elective state of existence; Nico's disinherited national belonging that turns his homeland and most of Europe into a place of exile and persecution is incurred through circumstances beyond his control and volition. In this sense, Keilson's understated, yet dramatic story of Nico's destiny in hiding offers a hyperbolic, pointed account of exile as something that one does not elect or select for oneself. Rather, in this context exile is portrayed as a tragic mode of statelessness and forced displacement through violent, precarious or unlivable conditions arising or existing in one's place of origin. This example of

---

also be said of Keilson: "exile is a condition of terminal loss," even as the underlying pathos of many narratives of exile seems to suggest a move towards resolution through an appeal to humanism – or, for that matter – an ethics of cosmopolitanism. Edward Said, "Reflections on Exile," in *Reflections on Exile and Other Essays* (Cambridge, MA: Harvard University Publishers, 2000), 173–86, 173–74.

seeking shelter during World War II may seem dramatic or exceptional in terms of conceptions of elective exile. However, it is the passage through the state of homelessness to that of finding a home or becoming part of a new community that is dramatized (or even parodied) in Keilson's novel. Indeed, the narrative deftly illustrates how the status of statelessness is a necessary precondition for elective exile or the process of establishing new affiliations beyond those of national identity. This is a form of unwitting or even unwilling cosmopolitanism that harbors the contingencies of loss, and one that does not lose sight of the ambiguities, and even ambivalence, upon which a "*Wahlheimat*" may be founded.

When we first encounter Nico, the Dutch-speaking Jewish protagonist of the novel, it is by way of what at first blush appears to be an omniscient narrator. On closer examination, however, the voice and purview of the narrator reveals idiosyncrasies in tone and narrative blind spots, exhibiting both more transparency and sharper moral judgment in relation to the psychological life and motives of the couple than insight into the unhappy Nico, who remains for the most part strangely opaque to the reader. This slanted narratorial optics both exposes and satirizes the Dutch couple's attitude toward and perspective on Nico's dire situation in descriptions of even his most vulnerable moments, indicating the limits imposed on free choice in morally distorted or negatively circumscribed circumstances, in which minor individual decisions or acts may have ominous or even violent repercussions.

The narrator's failure to act as an impartial observer of the dynamics at work in the relationship between Nico and Wim and Marie, as well as the rhetorical strategies through which this "failure" to be impartial is expressed, signal to the reader – at the very least – the complex and precarious moral ground on which exile is founded. Even when the Dutch couple elects to provide shelter to Nico, based on what appears, at least on the surface, to be rational and humane decisions, this too remains unstable ground, less humane than all-too-human. For the couple's granting Nico harbor, the reader gleans from the text, is originally set in motion by a canny colleague clearly working for the resistance, who understands how to engage Wim on terms that will speak to his conscience and reflect his values as positive attributes: "Jop – an office colleague who, [Wim] assumed, often handled such things – had asked whether Wim ever thought about fulfilling his 'patriotic duty' and ...'Patriotic duty,' Jop had said, and the concept, which had never made the slightest impression on Wim before, much less been able to move him toward any action, sounded new and full of meaning, now that the Netherlands had been conquered and occupied."[20] This passage indicates that

---

[20] Hans Keilson, *Comedy in a Minor Key*, trans. Damion Searls (New York: Farrar, Straus & Giroux, 2010 [1947]), 25.

an individual's belief in a universal concept of "humanity," and her or his consequent reactions to the crisis of persecution, exile, and the need to provide shelter, often proceed by way of the particular. Here, the suggestion of facilitating Nico's survival by providing him with a place to hide – possibly a perverse version of exile in one's own country when one is made stateless – is seen by Wim to be an act of national pride, or even resistance, in response to the Nazi occupation. Wim, who otherwise has not thought of himself in nationalistic terms as a "patriot," is interpellated into the Dutch resistance by association through his relationship to the particularity of national belonging.

Just a few lines further on, the narrator shifts subtly from Wim's perspective to that of Jop to illustrate the cynicism – or pragmatics – of the ends justifying the means in this moment of danger by describing Jop's approach to recruiting helpers. He recruits individuals by speaking to them in the discourse that he thinks will be most effective in motivating each person to action: "Jop knew the people he approached: with one he talked about 'a purely humane act,' with another it was about 'Christian charity for the persecuted,' and to a third he spoke of 'patriotic duty.' This was how he achieved his goal, the same in each case."[21] Thus, the narrator disabuses the reader of the potential illusion of the singular altruistic selflessness of these acts or even a more universal moral adherence to a transcendent sense of humanism. Even in times of war and persecution – or perhaps precisely during these precarious times – rhetorical persuasion and an awareness of how political morals are to be manipulated are necessary to achieve one's aims. In this sense, Keilson's tale of shelter in the shadow of imminent persecution and death shows the many ethical, political, and interpersonal layers at play beneath notions of elective exile and the concept of cosmopolitanism. Rather than the more utopian concept of cosmopolitanism as a global form of ethical humanism beyond the nation state, Wim's decision appears to be based on the logic of patriotism and civil disobedience. In fact, these passages illustrate the complexity and the contingency constitutive of how individuals choose their alliances.

Departing from the humanist tone of compassionate identification and selfless engagement, or the trope of redemption that is used to give meaning and closure to events in order to console the reader, as is associated with much canonical literature on the Holocaust, Keilson's unusual story tells a slanted, far less optimistic tale of exile. Much of this ambiguity is conveyed through the tone of the narrative, which moves almost seamlessly between, on the one hand, apparently neutral descriptions of events and reflections that appear to originate with

---

[21] Keilson, *Comedy in a Minor Key*, 25.

the characters, and, on the other hand, a far more critical tone, where irony is used to destabilize possible redemptive expectations of Holocaust narratives by, for example, casting the sincerity of the characters into doubt. This fluctuation in tone has the effect of unmooring the reader's stable approach to the shifting sands of the narrative, alerting us to the ambivalence and instability at the heart of practices of exile and asylum, both for those extending – as well as the recipient of – shelter in precarious times.

As stated above, Keilson's novel explores the preconditions of – the "before" or the enabling passage toward – elective exile. It also demonstrates the psychological costs incurred by both parties in the process of experiencing one another in such close quarters. In this historical moment of Nazi occupation and antisemitic persecution, Nico represents an uncanny force in the life of the couple, Wim and Marie, as he is simultaneously the familiar (a human being, a man), as well as a foreigner to their way of life (a Jew living under the imminent threat of betrayal, persecution and death, unlike the non-Jewish Dutch couple). Prior to Nico's arrival at their house he is referred to in the novella as "a refugee" and "the stranger." Here, the narrator clearly takes up the couple's perspective of the circumstances, infusing the scene with their caution and awkward behavior vis-à-vis the situation: "Jop brought the stranger at night, in the dark, a little before eleven."[22] Based on exotic tropes and self-confirming projections about "Jews" and foreigners more generally, the description of the Jewish Nico on his arrival in their house demonstrates the tone of irony in which the narrator indulges at certain moments of the text, presumably with the aim of drawing attention to the couple's limited perception and feelings vis-à-vis their visitor: "He wore a winter coat and seemed to be hot from running through the city. There were beads of sweat on his forehead, and his face – dark-complexioned, with little wrinkles around the mouth, and eyes carved deep into his otherwise firm, clean-shaven skin – glittered in the light. His large, dark, somewhat melancholy eyes looked feverish and flickering. His hair was thick and smooth, low over his forehead. A Spanish type!"[23] Wim is mentioned both in the opening and closing lines of the paragraph in which this observation is embedded, and although it is not directly credited to him, it is suggested that this observation originates with him, and perhaps also Marie, who is also present at the initial meeting. The cliché "a Spanish type," and the unexpected emphasis of the exclamation mark at the end of the phrase, indicate an ambivalence and demonstrate an awareness of the prejudice or even ignorance informing the description of Nico, which is otherwise not in keeping

---

22 Ibid., 27.
23 Ibid., 28.

with Wim's attempts throughout the novel to remain sovereign in every situation, in spite of the obvious age gap between the older Nico and himself. In other words, here the choice of expressive or even hyperbolic punctuation appears to be in excess of the character's own consciously modulated voice and behavior, suggesting, as in many other passages throughout the novel, the limited perceptions, reactions, and feelings of the couple, and metonymically, the bourgeois milieu they represent. They are living in the face of a deadly racism that they do not support, yet from which they are unable to fully extricate themselves – and at times even embody. Even in the very process of offering Nico sanctuary in their home, Marie and Wim are riddled with an ambivalence that emanates as much from their own interpersonal dynamic with Nico – the abstract humanity his figure represents and his particularity as Jewish – as from the broader, more obvious circumstantial danger they feel themselves exposed to by having agreed to hide a Jewish man from the Nazi occupiers.

The ambivalence structuring this act of sheltering manifests itself after Nico has entered the strange house and stands before the threshold to the room in which Wim sits. On Wim's invitation, Nico enters the room: "The stranger stepped silently over the threshold."[24] The crossing of a threshold is often used as a literary trope to underscore the instability of the boundaries that are drawn between spaces such as the private and the public, or interiors and exteriors. The detailed description granted both this moment of crossover and Wim's welcoming Nico into the house, sealed by a handshake as if signing a contract, point to the centrality of this scene. By inviting Nico, "the stranger," into his home, Wim takes up the role of host vis-à-vis a visitor, who is also a stranger. As Jacques Derrida emphasizes in a discussion of the concept of hospitality, the Greek word "*xenos*" means both foreign and also a guest through a contractual form of friendship; likewise, the Latin term "*hostis*" can mean enemy, guest, or host.[25] Clearly, there is ambivalence at the root of this concept that is played out in these apparent antinomies of meaning that is also at stake in the situation of exile and hiding in which Nico finds himself of necessity. An enemy of the state, in legal terms, Nico is nonetheless simultaneously a guest, albeit in hiding, at the couple's home. Likewise the proximity of the word "hostis" as the root of both "host" and "hostage" points to an instability of power relations that are realized in Keilson's story by the eventual, ironic reversal of fortunes of the figures of the person in hiding and the host.

---

[24] Ibid., 29.
[25] Jacques Derrida, *Of Hospitality. Anne Dufourmantelle Invites Jacques Derrida to Respond*, trans., Rachel Bowlby (Stanford: Stanford University Press, 2000), 21, 157.

Likewise, the discussion between Marie and Wim as to whether they should give asylum to a persecuted individual, whom the narrator initially refers to as a "stranger," demonstrates their sense of Nico as a foreign and potentially destabilizing element of their own attempts at maintaining their equilibrium under occupation. Like the shifting semantics of the root of the word for host and stranger, this discussion prior to Nico's arrival also reveals what is at stake when electing to hide a persecuted, stateless person. Throughout the novel, leading up to and even after Nico's death in their home caused, ironically enough, by pneumonia, ongoing oblique references to Nico, descriptions of the day-to-day irritants of living together in close quarters, as well as Marie's sense of moral righteousness and Wim's slight paternalism toward the older Nico continue to undermine or thwart a potential interpretation of this narrative as an unambiguously humanist narrative of a cosmopolitanism, which would see the stranger or foreigner granted unconditional hospitality and, further, would offer the reader the relief of redemptive closure.

Through many subtle instances, particularly in exchanges between Wim and Nico, the narrator makes it clear that in spite of the German occupation, Wim views Nico with pity and assigns him the role of the Nazi's enemy and persecuted victim, in this way using Nico's example as a foil against which to stage his and Marie's exclusion from the dangerous category of the stranger/enemy. Only Nico is able to perceive this power imbalance proper to the figure of the exile and he attempts to address this relationship explicitly in the following exchange between the host and guest-in-hiding when they first meet one another:

> "... For your sake I hope it won't be too much longer." Wim stood up. "I think we'll go –"
> "Not just for my sake," Nico interjected, and grew serious. Now it was clear that he was much older than Wim ... "There are so many, so many ..." It sounded like the simple honest truth.
> Wim hesitated. He understood Nico's tone well.
> "You're right – for everyone who's in your situation, here or wherever –"
> "And it's not just Jews," Nico added. He stood up. He had said what needed to be said![26]

The relatively sheltered Wim does not understand that under German occupation he is not immune to Nazi aggression as a potential victim of nationalist fascist violence. Instead, Wim projects the danger, weakness, and fear onto the Jewish Nico. The disparity between their ages and their experience is captured through a subtle, understated economy of narration, which is representative of Keilson's writing style, and, in turn, reveals the proximity between psychoanalytic

---

26 Ibid., 32.

thought, with which he is very familiar, and how his own thinking and writing are structured by the same. This can be seen in a style of writing that implies that just as much is hidden as is revealed in the characters' dialogue and gestures, which are most productively read through a careful process of hermeneutics indebted to reading that which is expressed symptomatically and for psychological depth. Further, the novel teems with observations and details that indicate the author's familiarity with the premises of psychoanalytic theory and practice; for example, in the passage above, the exchange demonstrates how processes of projection act as self-protective defense mechanisms, where the self attributes to an Other those very qualities and aspects which they do not wish to or cannot acknowledge as their own. Some of the subtlety is conveyed minimally, as where Keilson places punctuation in the service of tone. The exclamation mark at the end of the quotation indicates Nico's psychological state of relief, as well as his belief that by asserting himself he has added layers of complexity to Wim's comprehension of the larger political picture, while also averting his own reduction to a Jewish victim – an Other produced through defensive projections driven by fear, warranting pity, but no longer on an equal footing as a stateless individual, representing the apotheosis of homelessness.

This form of exile, even within the borders of one's own nation, represents an unusual and extreme position on the spectrum of exilic possibilities – a paradoxical form of psychological exile, albeit with very real, crippling material effects. It might be considered a form of elective exile in the sense that one's physical relocation (in hiding) represents the persecuted individual's complete vulnerability in the face of an almost certain death, which would be the consequence of remaining at one's registered address. However, the very extremeness of Nico's exilic status, as it is represented in the narrow physical and psychological microcosm of Wim and Marie's domestic environment, emphasizes the costs and danger of exile constitutive to some extent of every decision to enter into exile that manages to outlive or live beyond its precarious original conditions to be considered, then, a form of "elected" exile.

Deploying an artful narrator and staging "a dark comedy of wartime manners,"[27] Keilson charts the destructive psychology that goes hand-in-hand with forms of exile based on trauma, whether experienced firsthand or by way of empathizing with the fate of others. As a stateless refugee, Nico is overwhelmingly aware of his own vulnerability, although he valiantly tries to shield Marie and Wim from his oftentimes perilous state of mind, mainly because he fears

---

[27] This comment is garnered from the incisive, uncredited description of the novel that graces the inner side of the dust jacket of the book. Ibid.

his eviction from the household should he become too great a burden. With characteristic psychological precision, Keilson, who himself spent the years 1943 to 1945 in hiding with a couple in Delft (Leo and Suus Reemtsma, to whom the book is dedicated – a somewhat ambiguous tribute in this context), describes Nico's flights of fear:

> The feeling came over him like some sort of feverish illness that he was a burden, that the others had had enough of him and wanted to be rid of him at last. Even though no one had ever given him the least indication of such a thing, these imagined thoughts of the others held him in their grip ... It is like a sickness affecting the thoughts of people in hiding, it destroys their naturalness and makes them rude or weak. Few are left unaffected.[28]

Once again, Keilson subtly shifts tone and perspective within the short space of a paragraph, as can be seen on either side of the ellipsis in the citation above. Nico's thoughts represent an expression of the psychoanalytic concept of projection, used here to describe the infinite mirroring of defensive paranoia provoked by the existential vulnerability of the person in hiding. When the narrator shifts from Nico's perspective to more general observations concerning the effects of the condition of being in hiding on individuals, it is testimony both to Keilson's own biography and the importance of psychoanalysis to him as hermeneutic template for understanding this particular mode of exile through the extreme affects that possess the disenfranchised, including intense irritation or even aggression toward the relatively unencumbered position of the at times guileless hosts.

Nico's fears are compounded by moments of utter dejection, where his imagination plagues him with hallucinations of anonymous masses of suffering people, who, unlike him, did not manage to find refuge:

> Then his room was filled with suffering faces – contorted, disfigured, beaten to a pulp – whose features he eagerly studied to see if they weren't perhaps known to him. He heard groaning, whimpering, sniveling, wailing, calling upon God, cursing God; saw men and women, very old and very young – they were endless, the images he heard and saw in these hours. ... When he breathed in deep, he tasted gas. Gas! His room was full of gas![29]

There is historical import to this disturbing sequence, which demonstrates that, at the latest in 1944 – if not well before this, the fate of Jews traveling to the camps in the East was common knowledge. In addition, this passage shows how the boundaries between self and other, which form a key interface of analysis in psychoanalytic practice as the fulcrum for the individual's relationship to

---

28 Ibid., 37–38.
29 Ibid., 63.

the outside world, become blurred here through an intense empathy that, rather than providing relief, produces anxiety and extreme guilt ("survivor's guilt" in the terminology of trauma studies in the wake of World War II, a field in which Keilson was also a pioneer). Clearly, the fate of other, less fortunate political exiles presses down on him during the many hours that stretch before and behind him: "He was turning into nothing. It was unbearable. It meant his annihilation, his human annihilation, even if it – maybe – saved his life. The little thorn that grows invisibly in anyone who lives on the help and pity of others grew to gigantic proportions, became a javelin lodged deep in his flesh and hurting terribly."[30] Here, in what might be called a phenomenology of the condition of exile-in-hiding, Keilson peels back the surface of mere existence to reveal the many complex psychological layers constitutive of this condition. The distinction between physical and psychological survival, or "life" and the "human," reveals itself as a fearful, gaping "unbearable" nothingness that cancels out those qualities that connect one to a broader sense of humanity. The "little thorn" that grows to be a javelin "lodged deep in his flesh and hurting terribly," objectifies the exile's human body so that it becomes amorphous "flesh," while at the same time revealing a net of conflicting emotions in which the exile finds himself caught. These are ambivalent, even paradoxical emotions, where pity and charity (modes of humanist conduct) become weapons of self-inflicting pain in the dialectic between resentment and gratitude. At the same time, the paradoxical logic of the relationship between the guest and host discussed earlier can be seen as the fragile psychological structure of this condition of exile.

This so-called "comedy of wartime manners" depends precisely on the narrator revealing the tension between the thoughts and behavior of the figures, as well as the discrepancy between the couple's sense, at times, of (self-) righteousness and their actual limitations, which remain invisible to them, or simply escape their narrow frame of reference. This distance is precisely what Nico attempts to bridge on the very first night in cautious conversation with the couple. Wim and Marie perceive their act of hiding the Jewish man as a variety of everyday heroism, and are relieved and even "happy" when he offers them a place in the noble pantheon the narrator acerbically terms "the brotherhood of all those who suffer" beyond Jewish suffering: "It had made them happy to hear those words; he didn't demand any special pity for himself. He stepped modestly back, so to speak, into the circle, the brotherhood of all those who suffer – the same as everyone else, one among many. It was a sympathetic gesture for him to make – a

---

[30] Ibid., 64.

gesture, but not the full truth."[31] By sublimating the particular ("Jewish") into the universal ("the brotherhood of all those who suffer"), Nico protects the couple by allowing them to keep their vision of humanism, even if Nico knows otherwise. The economy of the final sentence, where the perceptive narratorial voice moves from description to judgement, interrupts the false universal by comparing the (perhaps necessary) "gesture" with "the full truth," which is revealed only to the reader in passages such as the penultimate citation above.

Wim and Marie continue this conversation when Nico is absent, refuting and muddying Nico's claim with a remarkable lack of self-reflectivity. Wim states:

> "Actually they're all unlucky."
> "Who?"
> "The Jews."
> They were not in the habit of talking about "the" Jews. If someone was Jewish, that wasn't a problem for them.
> "They have had it hard," Wim said. "They're like rabbits, hunted. And now it seems like the off-season, when they're safe, is over."
> "Why do they let themselves be hunted?"
> "What else should they do?" Wim asked. "Run away or let themselves be caught …?"
> "And yet they want to keep on being rabbits," Marie said, "Can you understand that?"
> …
> In truth, even though they were helping to hide one, neither of them truly understood what it meant: a Jew. A human being like everyone else. But … But what?[32]

This exchange between Marie and Wim is striking for the consistent gaps in the logic of their statements, their choice of analogy, and their inability to reconcile the universal ("a human being like everyone else") with the particular ("the Jews") as they clumsily struggle, teetering on the precipice of antisemitism, to understand the particularity of Jewishness. Clearly, up until this point they have politely avoided thinking beyond decent, mildly humanist, middle-class conventions, where there is a vague awareness of the error of collapsing individuals into a category ("the" Jews). Keilson artfully compounds the hidden levels of prejudice when he allows the exchange to stand alone without any conclusive narratorial commentary. The conversation demonstrates a form of resistance to thinking through or even tolerating difference by refusing one's own implication in racist thought with a clichéd response that inadequately declares tolerance in place of interest or concern in this historically fraught moment: "If someone was Jewish, that wasn't a problem for them." In the next sentence, Wim draws a bizarre

---

31 Ibid., 109.
32 Ibid., 107–8.

analogy between rabbits and Jews, using the muted figure of rabbit hunting as a comparison to racial persecution. The clumsy choice of analogy, striking and almost even satirical because of its absurd inappropriateness, allows Jews to be compared to an animal species as common as it is defenseless. Likewise, the insidious conclusion that Jews "let themselves be hunted" and are thus, it is implied, responsible for their own persecution, emphasizes a form of persistent "everyday" antisemitism and the potentially dangerous ignorance of the interlocutors. Ultimately, the figure of the Jew represents a blind spot for the couple. The sentence fragments, the inability to think beyond the unfinished contingency of the word "but," the use of punctuation to indicate incomplete knowledge or understanding in the form of ellipses, and the final question mark at the end of the citation signal that the couple – and, by extension, the average, well meaning, middle-class Dutch citizen – have reached their logical and affective limits.

Perhaps what is most striking about this seemingly simple, yet psychologically complex exchange is the inability or even unwillingness of the conversation partners to move beyond the question of identity to analyze political and ethical questions addressing the persecution of the Jews, and the violence visited on them by their persecutors. The limits of understanding and empathy of those sheltering or living with individuals forced into exile is amply demonstrated through the couple's inadequate response to or even avoidance of directly addressing that which they feel to be foreign and alien. This couple represents a balefully underequipped version of the forms of community and the shrunken and contingent worlds available to those occupying the status of the stateless exile. Ironically, the couple's woefully inadequate attempt to find an appropriate understanding of the category of "Jewishness" mirrors the absurdity – the caveats and unclear contours – of a category of identity defined by the Nazis in invented racial terms then imposed upon diverse and variable individuals.

Comedy in a Minor Key certainly is a "comedy of wartime manners," in a dark vein. Might we also understand the novella as a satirical "drama of cosmopolitanism" or an exploration of the limits to the concept of cosmopolitanism, with its claim to accept the full multivalence of the Other? Likewise, has the term "cosmopolitan" retained any of its Kantian-tinged capacity as a term to represent a condition of perpetual peaceful co-existence of different cultures and people? In the previous section of this essay, the concept of contingency was brought into play with the idea of the "cosmopolitan" to consider in which ways "elective exile" might also be a form of "contingent cosmopolitanism," and what this might mean for the idea of belonging beyond the initial state of forced exile that is the precondition of "elective exile." In Keilson's case, Tihanov's definition of cosmopolitanism through a Kantian lens as "a marker/symptom of recalibration of the polis ... in the wake of significant historical events," seems apt in regard to how the concepts of humanism and community are thrown radically into question.[33] What is even more pertinent, though, is the ambivalence captured in the movement between the semiotic poles of these seemingly tautological, constantly oscillating concepts of "elective exile" or "contingent cosmopolitanism," which appear capacious enough to allow for the affective, political, and existential ambiguities captured in Keilson's fiction and psychoanalytical writings alike.

4 Conclusion: Speaking of Home

In concluding, I would like to turn to a publication from the final years of Hans Keilson's long life, where he addresses different facets of the ambivalence constitutive of elective exile and contingent cosmopolitanism alike. This kind of ambivalent cosmopolitanism, at the crossroads of politics, community, and writing, is encapsulated in Gilles Deleuze and Felix Guattari's notion of "minoritarian literature" as a site of historical and political contingency that is not identical with the nation state, instead offering a space of literature where de- and reterritorialization is played out.[34] In this dialectical movement between de- and reterritorialization, we discover the potential conditions of emergence for what might be called a "spiritual homeland." Taken from an edited collection of occasional memories that Keilson had written down over the years, the small booklet, auspiciously titled *Da steht mein Haus* (*There Stands My House*), defies generic definition by concluding with a conversation between Keilson and German literary scholar Heinrich Detering that was conducted shortly before Keilson's death in 2011. Keilson opens with the following observation: "Whoever has lived and survived as a Jew and a persecuted person on the run in the middle of Europe, is offered, in retrospect, only one single, unbroken continuity as the background of his existence: that of the calendar with its monotonous, recurring numbers of weeks and months, weekdays, Sundays, and holidays, printed in red ink and valid all over the world."[35] If this description of universal time provides the

---

33 Tihanov, "Cosmopolitanism in the Discursive Landscape of Modernity," 133–52.
34 Gilles Deleuze and Félix Guattari, *Kafka: Toward a Minor Literature*, trans. Dana Polan (Minneapolis: University of Minnesota Press, 1986 [1975]).
35 "Wer als Jude und Verfolgter auf der Flucht mitten in Europa gelebt und überlebt hat, dem bietet sich im Rückblick als Hintergrund seines Daseins nur eine einzige, ungebrochene Kontinuität an: die des Kalenders mit seinen eintönig, wiederkehrenden Zahlen der Wochen und Monate, Wochen- und Sonn- und Festtagen, mit roter Farbe gedruckt und gültig in aller Welt." Hans Keilson, *Da steht mein Haus: Erinnerungen* (Frankfurt am Main: Fischer, 2012), 9. All translations of citations from this publication are my own.

continuous existential backdrop for the uncertain and distorted temporality of persecuted individuals – time stretched out of shape or warped by years of hiding in other people's attics and crawl spaces; time jammed, telescoped, or caught in a repetitive loop after traumatic experiences – the penultimate paragraph of his text turns the reader's attention to the spatial and affective parameters of Keilson's life that enabled his embrace of the Netherlands as his *Wahlheimat*, where he received Dutch citizenship directly after the war in recognition of his participation in the Dutch underground during the years of Nazi occupation. Keilson writes: "At home in a foreign place – I have often been asked how I arrived at this seemingly paradoxical image. My answer was that here, in Holland, I had found my work after all, not just any work, rather my work, with children and adults, with survivors of the occupation, persecution, and deportation, with Jews and non-Jews."[36] The focus shifts here from the temporal landscape of the introduction to the spatial metaphor of home (the German "*zu Hause*," which implies both a spatial descriptor and an affective inclination). Yet, in Keilson's case this home is defined less by concrete spatial parameters or the boundaries of a nation state, instead it circumscribes the affective realm of work with those persecuted during the Third Reich, a rich and ambivalent dwelling indeed, in which boundaries between national and affective belonging are inextricably intertwined.

In conversation with Detering, Keilson states: "I am Dutch. I was German. I am a Dutch doctor, who publishes in German. When I heard of the death of my parents, I ceased to be German."[37] What Keilson points to in all of the citations above is the symbolic investments that bind the individual to place – the practices and processes of contingent cosmopolitanism in Keilson's life world. For Keilson, his choice to make his home in exile in the Netherlands is based on the exigencies of persecution, war, and murder motivated by racial hatred – and yet his ongoing extraterritorial tie to the German language he evinced through his writing demonstrates the palimpsest of affects and investments that make his *Wahlheimat* the Netherlands, but locate his spiritual homeland in a space of contingent cosmopolitanism between the written word of German and the spoken word of Dutch. The tension between his elected homeland and his affective and

---

36 "In der Fremde zu Hause – man hat mich oft gefragt, wie ich zu diesem paradox erscheinenden Bild gelangte. Meine Antwort war, dass ich hier, in Holland, schließlich meine Artbeit gefunden hätte, nicht irgendeine, sondern meine Arbeit, mit Kindern und Erwachsenen, mit Überlebenden der Besetzung, Verfolgung und Deportation, mit Juden und Nicht-Juden." Keilson, *Da steht mein Haus*, 98.

37 "Ich bin Holländer. Ich war Deutscher. Ich bin ein niederländischer Arzt, der auf Deutsch publiziert. Als ich vom Tod meiner Eltern gehört habe, habe ich aufgehört, ein Deutscher zu sein." Ibid., 112.

existential ties to the German language is captured in a neologism found in one of his poems: "*sprachwurzellos*" (being without the roots of language or the state of being in a language that remains rootless).

The example of Keilson (that in some ways could stand in metonymical relation to the lives and writing of many other Jewish exiles during the so-called Third Reich, such as Konrad Merz, Jakob Wassermann, and Stefan Zweig), demonstrates that a *Wahlheimat* may be chosen when one's hand is forced and at an enormous psychic cost. No straightforward instance of a chosen community, Keilson's attachments are forged at a price – namely through the mourning he never completed in face of the murder of his parents, who were deported from Amsterdam to Auschwitz in 1943. In part, Keilson established Amsterdam as his home of choice through the act of co-founding the organization Le-Ezrat Ha-Jeled. The intersubjective implications of founding a new home for these orphaned children of the Holocaust may be read as a therapist's symbolic adoption of a "community" of orphans (in some cases for up to thirty years).

These therapeutic practices of grief and empathy arguably allowed Keilson to work through his own bereft and orphaned status and to weave these losses into the fabric of his everyday life through his psychoanalytic practice. Indeed, his dedication in the book he published in 1979 on the long-term study of sequential traumatization of child orphans after the Holocaust reads: "in place of a *Kaddish*," indicating that Keilson's spiritual homeland went well beyond the geopolitical co-ordinates of national citizenship or religious affiliation. The host of psychic investments supported by his intimate relationship with the German language and literature carved out a space of potentiality in which to house memories, affect, identification with those dead and alive, and a lived sense of self. It could be said that Keilson's writing, both fiction and non-fiction, structures and contains what philosopher and literary critic Georg Lukács called the "transcendental homelessness," represented for Lukács by the form of the novel.[38] In this sense, perhaps Keilson's *Comedy in a Minor Key* constitutes a space where "transcendental homelessness" and "elective exile" resonate together, without forgetting the nation state that provides the modern individual with ironclad structures of belonging and exclusion.

Allowing Adorno the final word, I return to his reflections on damaged life in *Minima Moralia*, to cite the famous final sentence of aphorism 18, named "Refuge for the Homeless": "Wrong life cannot be lived rightly."[39] This holds true;

---

38 Georg Lukács, *The Theory of the Novel. A Historico-philosophical Essay on the Forms of Great Epic Literature*, trans. Anna Bostock (Cambridge, MA: The MIT Press, 1971 [1920]), 41.
39 Adorno, "Refuge for the Homeless," *Minima Moralia*, 38–39.

however, of necessity, wrong life is nevertheless lived time and again by individuals somehow and somewhere. What is important is how and to what extent the ambivalence and loss that accompanies Adornian "damaged life" is acknowledged, engaged with, and granted the space to coexist with new affinities and alternative paths.

Bibliography

Adorno, Theodor W. "Protection, Help, and Counsel" and "Refuge for the Homeless." In *Minima Moralia: Reflections from Damaged Life*. Translated by E. F. N. Jephcott, 33 and 38–39. London/New York: Verso, 2005.

Adorno, Theodor W. "The Meaning of Working through the Past." In *Critical Models: Interventions and Catchwords*. Translated by Henry W. Pickford, 89–103. New York: Columbia University Press, 1998.

Adorno, Theodor W., and Max Horkheimer. *The Dialectic of Enlightenment: Philosophical Fragments*. Edited by Gunzelin Schmid Noerr and translated by Edmund Jephcott. Stanford: Stanford University Press, 2002.

Anonymous. "Anatomy of Hatred." *Time Magazine*, September 14, 1962.

Beck, Ulrich. "Cosmopolitan Sociology: Outline of a Paradigm Shift." In *The Ashgate Research Companion to Cosmopolitanism*. Edited by Maria Rovisco and Magdalena Nowicka, 17–32. Surrey: Ashgate, 2011.

Beck, Ulrich. *The Cosmopolitan Vision*. Translated by Ciaran Cronin. Cambridge: Polity Press, 2006.

Braese, Stephan. "Wider den Mythos von der deutsch-jüdischen Symbiose: Edgar Hilsenraths 'Der Nazi und der Friseur' (1977)." In *Die andere Erinnerung: Jüdische Autoren in der westdeutschen Nachkriegsliteratur*. 429–484. Berlin/Vienna: Philo, 2001.

Braidotti, Rosi, Patrick Hanafin and Bolette Blaagaard, eds. *After Cosmopolitanism*. New York: Routledge, 2013.

Brecht, Karen et al., eds. *"Here Life Goes on in a Most Peculiar Way...": Psychoanalysis Before and After 1933*. Translated by Christine Trollope and Joyce Crick. Hamburg: Kellner, 1992.

Cheah, Pheng and Bruce Robbins, eds. *Cosmopolitics: Thinking and Feeling beyond the Nation*. Minneapolis: University of Minnesota Press, 1998.

Deleuze, Gilles and Félix Guattari. *Kafka: Toward a Minor Literature*. Translated by Dana Polan. Minneapolis: University of Minnesota Press, 1986.

Derrida, Jacques. *Of Hospitality. Anne Dufourmantelle Invites Jacques Derrida to Respond*. Translated by Rachel Bowlby. Stanford: Stanford University Press, 2000.

Kaufhold, Roland. "'Das Leben geht Weiter': Hans Keilson, ein jüdischer Psychoanalytiker, Schriftsteller, Pädagoge und Musiker." *Zeitschrift für psychoanalytische Theorie und Praxis* 23, nos. 1–2 (2008): 142–167.

Keilson, Hans. *Comedy in a Minor Key*. Translated by Damion Searls. New York: Farrar, Straus & Giroux, 2010.

Keilson, Hans. *Da steht mein Haus: Erinnerungen*. Frankfurt am Main: Fischer, 2012.

Keilson, Hans. *Sequential Traumatization in Children: A Clinical and Statistical Follow-Up Study on the Fate of the Jewish War Orphans in the Netherlands*. Jerusalem: The Magnes Press, 1992.

Keilson-Lauritz, Marita. "Vorwort." In Hans Keilson, *Tagebuch 1944 und 46 Sonette*. Edited by Marita Keilson-Lauritz, 7–20. Afterword by Heinrich Detering. Frankfurt am Main: Fischer, 2014.

Landhoff, Fritz H. *Amsterdam, Keizersgracht 333, Querido Verlag: Erinnerungen eines Verlegers: Mit Briefen und Dokumenten*. Berlin: Aufbau Verlag, 1991.

Lukács, Georg. *The Theory of the Novel. A Historico-philosophical Essay on the Forms of Great Epic Literature*. Translated by Anna Bostock. Cambridge, MA: The MIT Press, 1971.

McGlothlin, Erin. "Narrative Perspective and the Holocaust Perpetrator: Edgar Hilsenrath's *The Nazi and the Barber* and Jonathan Littell's *The Kindly Ones*." In *The Bloomsbury Companion to Holocaust Literature*. Edited by Jenni Adams, 159–177. London/New York: Bloomsbury, 2014.

Prose, Francine. "As Darkness Falls." *New York Times*, August 5, 2010.

Said, Edward. "Reflections on Exile." In *Reflections on Exile and Other Essays*. 173–186. Cambridge, MA: Harvard University Press, 2000.

Tihanov, Galin. "Cosmopolitanism in the Discursive Landscape of Modernity: Two Enlightenment Articulations." In *Enlightenment Cosmopolitanism*. Edited by David Adams and Galin Tihanov, 133–152. London: Legenda, 2011.

Tihanov, Galin. "Do Minor Literatures Still Exist? The Fortunes of a Concept in the Changing Frameworks of Literary History." In *Reexamining the National-Philological Legacy: Quest for a New Paradigm?* Edited by Vladimir Biti, 169–190. Amsterdam: Rodopi, 2014.

Part 5: **Of Other Spaces: Travel and Trauma**

Agnes C. Mueller
Israel as a Place of Trauma and Desire in Contemporary German Jewish Literature

"Cosmopolitan memory" emerges from the "historical link between the memories of the Holocaust and the emergence of a moral consensus about human rights."[1] This is how "cosmopolitan memory" is described in 2006 by Daniel Levy and Nathan Sznaider in *The Holocaust and Memory in the Global Age*. "Cosmopolitanism" here seems to be associated with an explicitly positive way of conceptualizing, or remembering, the specificity of a place or a history. Our ambiguity toward contemporary Holocaust memory might then be wrapped up in this imagination of a "cosmopolitan" memory culture – in that it suggests Jewish particularity as well as universalizing and normalizing attempts of German memorial culture. Of course, in 2006, "global" or "cosmopolitan" still meant different things than in 2018. And perhaps it means different things entirely for the memory of the Holocaust. Yet, all prejudice notwithstanding, it might today be useful to think about cosmopolitanism and the implications of "cosmopolitan memory." The very term "cosmopolitan memory" does suggest a universal dimension to memory, and one that might at first consideration eclipse the specificity of Jewish memory. But, for Sznaider, Jewish memory is simply an "instantiation" of Jewish memory, and hence not at odds with a larger, or "cosmopolitan," dimension.[2] There is, in other words, no hierarchy implied between different memory discourses. Therefore, we may be able to connect "cosmopolitan memory" easily with Michael Rothberg's concept of a "multidirectional memory," a way of remembering the Holocaust that connects it to other trauma discourses throughout history.[3] For Rothberg, still, the Holocaust is the "original memory." But Jewish memory, and Jewish cosmopolitanism, is still always also a particular memory and compared with other memories, perhaps a privileged form of both genocide and trauma memory and cosmopolitan memory. While the term "privilege" smacks of arrogant domination of one class, race, or sex over another, there might, on the other hand, be

---

[1] Daniel Levy and Nathan Sznaider, *The Holocaust and Memory in a Global Age* (Philadelphia: Temple University Press, 2006), 20.
[2] As pointed out by Stuart Taberner, "The Possibilities and Pitfalls of a Jewish Cosmopolitanism. Reading Natan Sznaider through Russian-Jewish Writer Olga Grjasnowa's German-language Novel *Der Russe ist einer der Birken liebt* (All Russians Love Birch Trees)," *European Review of History: Revue europeenne d'histoire* 23, nos. 5–6 (2016): 917.
[3] Ibid.; Michael Rothberg, *Multidirectional Memory. Remembering the Holocaust in the Age of Decolonization* (Stanford: Stanford University Press, 2009).

good historical reasons for such "privilege." Untangling some of these conceptual iterations of Holocaust memory will shed light on how and why Israel has become an important point of orientation for German Jewish Holocaust discourse, and how this is especially visible in recent German Jewish fiction.

"When Hamas threatened suicide attacks again a few days ago, it caused more worry in Germany than here [in Israel]. My friends wrote emails with the subject line 'Are you still alive?'"[4] Thus observes the first-person Russian German Jewish narrator and protagonist named Anja in Lena Gorelik's entertaining novel *Hochzeit in Jerusalem*. The idea that Israel's precarious situation might cause more worry in Germany than in Israel itself is an underlying theme of this narrative. Gorelik wrote a text that most German critics reviewed favorably, but received little attention outside of Germany. The plot concerns the love story between Anja, who invites her German and Jewish friend Julian to a family wedding in Jerusalem. Julian wants to explore his newly discovered Jewish roots, and Anja wants to help him to do so. Importantly, the simply constructed story establishes a *locus amoenus* where Anja, the novel's first person narrator, slowly falls in love with Julian, who had been courting her since their first encounter via an online dating site for Jewish singles. Their love flourishes, and seems vitally centered on the differences between German and Jewish identity. This particular – perhaps unexpected – setting, where Israel is portrayed as an imagined location of healing and overcoming German Jewish tension, is emphatically exposed as a place of nearly unambiguous positivity, where the encounters between Julian (who has only recently found out that his father was Jewish) and Anja's Jewish family are enriching and important for both protagonists. Curiously, Julian is able to fully realize his love for Anja only after a brief infatuation with an ultra-Orthodox Jewish woman whom he meets at the wedding in Jerusalem (hence the title of the novel). It seems that Anja and Julian, who are both depicted as exceedingly well integrated into German mainstream culture, are only able to explore their love when they are away in Israel, a setting that is personified in the figure of Julian's Orthodox love interest.

Such an apparently uncritical and affirmative stance toward Israel might be surprising were it not reflected in several additional contemporary German Jewish texts, mostly by younger Jewish writers who were born after 1970. Lena Gorelik, born in 1981, is exemplary for this generation. A journalist and writer, she has been living in Germany since she was 11, as a Russian refugee. Today she lives in Munich and, after receiving a literary prize in 2009, has published

---

[4] Unless otherwise noted all translations throughout this article are my own, ACM. Lena Gorelik, *Hochzeit in Jerusalem* (Munich: SchirmerGraf, 2007), 163.

two more novels. The ethnically diverse background of this author is typical especially for the younger generation of German Jewish identities. Recent works by younger German and Jewish writers frequently imagine Israel as a place of desire. It serves as a site for projection to address traumas of the past. Reflected in these narratives are individual and collective Holocaust memories, as well as other instances of ethnic persecution and genocide.[5] In all of these stories, Israel is embedded into the narrative as a specific place of reconciliation and working through the past. There are many important ways in which German Jewish reconciliation has been on public display in Germany and elsewhere, the extensive Holocaust memorial culture being the most visible. Yet, in the private and personal sphere, antisemitic images and tropes also persist, sometimes hidden even from those who harbor them. Given the difficult and multiply unsatisfactory history of German Jewish relations and the persistence of antisemitic speech in some of contemporary German literature,[6] how do we evaluate the positive stance that these young, new texts take toward Israel? Are we dealing with a return – or escape – to Israel from a German Jewish perspective, perhaps as a counterpoint to the specifically German context? How does the Jewish experience of diaspora, which especially the previous generations of Jews were significantly affected by, relate to this newfound positivity? In some, but not all fictional narratives, the contemporary reality of an Israeli-Palestinian conflict is imagined as a foil that can turn previous trauma into productive or at least reflective experiences, and thus help the German Jewish subject heal. Yet, considering the terror and violence that structure daily life in Israel, this seems paradoxical at the very least.

This apparent contradiction provokes further questions resulting from the tension between Israel as a place of love and friendship, of positive dealing with the past on the one hand, and as a contested place of terror and ethnic, political, and religious conflict on the other. Why and how exactly do culturally and ethnically diverse young German Jewish writers imagine Israel as a place for healing? How does this positive image of Israel bear on collective memories of the Shoah, both in Germany and beyond? What do the emotions that are expressed toward Israel mean for the self-consciousness of such authors (and their national and international reception)? How do the diverse, often migratory, fictional accounts of places of terror and mourning connect with the idea of healing and a *locus amoenus*? And,

---

5 The texts that fall into this paradigm but are not discussed here: Adriana Altaras, *Doitscha* (2015), Oliver Polak, *Der jüdische Patient* (2014), and Katja Petrowskaja, *Vielleicht Esther* (2014).
6 For a full discussion of this phenomenon in recent German literature, see my book *The Inability to Love: Jews, Gender, and America in Recent German Literature* (Evanston, IL: Northwestern University Press, 2015). Published in German as *Die Unfähigkeit zu lieben. Juden und Antisemitismus in der Gegenwartsliteratur* (Würzburg: Königshausen & Neumann, 2017).

finally, how do these newer texts relate to notions of "cosmopolitan" or "multidirectional" memory? Does the setting of Israel provide some kind of political or personal redemption within the German Jewish discourse?

Markus Flohr's entertaining narrative of 2011, *Wo samstags immer Sonntag ist*, is the only text by a non-Jewish author to be discussed here. It is also – perhaps not coincidentally – the one text that received the least attention from the German press of all the ones under consideration. In *Wo samstags immer Sonntag ist*, Flohr's first-person narrator explicitly comments on Israeli and German Jewish relations. Flohr, born in 1980 in Hanover, is a journalist who studied history and journalism in Hamburg and Jerusalem. Even though he recently published his second book *Alte Sachen*, he is mostly known as a journalist. The two literary publications of the author do not appear on www.perlentaucher.de for example. One reason for the relative invisibility of Flohr's debut might be the fact that its subtitle is "Ein deutscher Student in Israel" (a German student in Israel), which might give the impression that this is a travelogue rather than a novel. A closer look, however, reveals more of an affinity with Gregor von Rezzori's – also scarcely attested in the critical literature – *Memoirs of an Anti-Semite* of 1979. The humor, the perspective of the first person narrator as reflected and presented in the shape of lived memories of an *alter ego*, and the open and uninhibited display of uncomfortable truths concerning Jews and Germans are what both texts have in common. While von Rezzori's is significantly more radical when it comes to the explicit naming of antisemitic prejudice on the part of the narrator as well as within the historic context, this bluntness is not surprising since his timeframe is that of Weimar Germany right before World War II. The tension between German Holocaust guilt and Jewish identity is, similar to von Rezzori, directly invoked via the detailed descriptions of the German and not Jewish protagonist. Yet, in Flohr's case, he is currently on a one-year visit to Israel. Religious, cultural, and political themes that appear in the Israeli context – as a contrast to the German – are presented as everyday issues in a contemporary narrative style. Frequent topics among the different characters are the multiple and diverse attitudes and opinions vis-à-vis Judaism (the positions represented reach from ultra-Orthodox to Reform to not religious at all).

Yet, what seems important in answer to our questions is the fact that Flohr's narrative is, first and foremost, a love story. On the one hand, it is about love – and this is meant also as a powerful erotic attraction – toward Israel as a place of a different and exotic culture that contains implicit dangers and the experiences of a cultural other. On the other hand, the protagonist himself experiences a love in Israel that highlights the German Jewish conflicts, and that might also be contributing to their very resolution. The love that is described here takes place between the protagonist, the German son of a priest, and Noa, a Sephardic Jew from Jerusalem. Noa is described as an empathetic, lovable, loving, and impulsive young woman, whose political attitudes and idiosyncrasies seem both contemporary and emancipated. This love story, complicated by Noa's family who expect her to marry a – Sephardic – Jew, shows two young people in love, connected in a liberated, unconstrained friendship, and openly discussing their religious and ethnic differences while celebrating what joins them. At the same time, the first person narrator openly and purposefully addresses and then subverts any antisemitic clichés via humor and an especially unexpected straightforwardness: "I have never been clearer about who the Nazis really were, who was responsible for the Holocaust, who had wanted to kill the Jews all over the world, than on this day when I stood in Yad Vashem in between soldiers chewing gum, and I was ashamed to speak my own language."[7] Israel and, more specifically, the location of Yad Vashem, here functions as a catalyst to release the emotions of the German non-Jewish protagonist, and make him aware of the meaning of Holocaust guilt. Through these images, he – and the German reader – becomes aware of the multiply determined meaning of German Holocaust guilt: it is precisely not a *German* memorial site, or the site of a concentration camp in Germany that elicits this kind of revelation of guilt and shame. Instead, the place of Israel as both foreign and strange, bordering on the exotic (including the drama of an attack in Gaza – overall the portrayal of Israel here is less unambiguous than in Gorelik's text), yet also familiar and known due to the protagonist's love for Noa – has, quite unexpectedly, become a site for such identification. Any questions about Zionism, the conflict between Jews and Palestinians, and the role that Jewishness and a Jewish state might play politically seem to be put aside just as are any explicit scenes of war and violence. This might be considered a problem, especially since the politics of Israeli settlement are frequently likened to Nazi occupation. At the same time, however, Israel – and especially the location of Jerusalem – seems to be a place that German readers can relate to through the positively connoted figure of Noa. It is in this nexus where Israel becomes a place in which the German guilt of the past is explicitly thematized.

A depiction that rather avoids direct conflict might be rooted in the fact that it is a "typical German" projection, one where the imagination of a Jewish place – Israel – can be explained with a strong philo-Semitic imagination of coping with German guilt. Because, as opposed to for example in Gorelik's text, this narrative is, due to its non-Jewish narrator, always told from the perspective of the

---

7 "Nie ist mir klarer geworden wer die Nazis waren, wer den Holocaust verbrochen hatte, wer die Juden aus aller Welt umbringen wollte, als an diesem Tag, als ich in Jad Vaschem zwischen den Soldaten mit ihren Kaugummis stand und ich mich schämte meine eigene Sprache zu sprechen." Flohr, *Wo samstags immer Sonntag ist*, 160.

outsider, an outsider who might have a naïve view of Israel, and one that might have been fueled by colonial fantasies and evoked by the wishful projection of a *locus amoenus*. Yet, the specificity of Israel as a location may contradict the very notion of "cosmopolitanism," or in the case of addressing trauma, "cosmopolitan memory." The memory of Holocaust trauma gets subliminally conflated with the trauma of the Israeli-Palestinian conflict, even if that conflict itself appears momentarily eclipsed. The particularity of Israel as a physical and concrete place seems to be what is needed for remembering the past. Trauma as it is related in Flohr and Gorelik becomes palpable to the protagonists, and, thus, to the readers in a precise and specific place.

Important work has been done relating to the different and differing forms of historical narration and its function in contemporary literature especially as memory mediation.[8] More recently, the width and breadth of new forms of fiction, and the problematic role of fiction in Holocaust memory in the German-speaking context has been presented by Hammermeister, Fischer, and Kramer.[9] What this new research shows is already implied in Adorno's dictum. The Holocaust remains, to this day, not equivalent in either scope or magnitude to any other genocide, and is thus also not directly comparable with other historical moments of genocide, discrimination, persecution, racism, or terror – even if individually perceived "other" histories of trauma can loom large in one person's (family) memory trajectory. Comparing the discourses of trauma according to some absolute value therefore seems not fruitful or even ethical. It thus seems important to shift the attention from the relative value of different discourses of trauma to questions of representation, the how of literature, in other words, to questions of the aesthetics of representation and the new conditions of this aesthetic.

If one engages these questions by interrogating, for example, the texts under discussion here according to their aesthetic and thematic qualities, one might arrive at a conclusion that seems, at first glance, less than satisfactory. Yet, it is important to recognize that these are works whose literary quality might vary, but which are usually positively received by the daily press. Furthermore, the attention that they attract in public – and sometimes within academic discourse – makes them important. Thus, even if we don't always see the aesthetic qualities of the works under discussion, we can read them as features characteristic of contemporary discourse. In some cases, they can easily measure up to more stringent

---

[8] Dominick LaCapra, *Writing History, Writing Trauma* (Baltimore: Johns Hopkins University Press, 2001).
[9] Torben Fischer, Philipp Hammermeister, and Sven Kramer, eds., *Der Nationalsozialismus und die Shoah in der deutschsprachigen Gegenwartsliteratur*, Amsterdamer Beiträge zur neueren Germanistik 84 (Amsterdam, New York: Rodopi, 2014).

criteria of aesthetic quality. If we take seriously the questions posed at the outset, and we now primarily look for the *symptoms* of societal change in our evaluation of contemporary discourses on the Shoah, then inquiries into literary and aesthetic value judgment have to take a back seat to the more pressing question of new themes and modes of fiction in contemporary literature. This point of view may help complete our image of the contemporary discourse on Holocaust guilt and responsibility, and where this discourse is rooted.

Benjamin Stein's critical and particularly academic success *Die Leinwand* (2010; *The Canvas* 2012) addresses these issues more comprehensively, clearly, aesthetically, and more earnestly than either Flohr's or Gorelik's narratives. Born in East Berlin in 1970, and converted to Judaism as a young adult, Stein wrote three more novels. Now living in Munich, he is the owner of a small and exclusive literary publishing house. With *Die Leinwand*, his second novel and first critical success, Stein wrote a story that is complex, imposing a high degree of reader participation, and requiring a good deal of contextual knowledge. Two separate first-person narratives can be read from either end of the book, in parallel or in succession. No text is privileged over the other; both coexist and are equal in length. The story of Amnon Zichroni, who grew up as an Orthodox Jew in Israel, and who encourages the Swiss Holocaust survivor Minsky to record his traumatic childhood memories, intersects with that of Jan Wechsler, an East German Jewish journalist seeking to expose Minsky's memories as the lies of a Holocaust remembrance-poseur. The core narrative of course draws on the widely known scandal around Binyamin Wilkomirski's memoir *Fragments: Memories of a Wartime Childhood* (1997). Yet most significantly, it performs, via its intricate narrative structure, the unreliability of memory, identity, and history. The allegorical play that enacts the canvas as the site of projection in the end reveals Zichroni and Wechsler to be one and the same character, further unsettling our perception of what is real, what is imagined, and how memory is mediated. Most striking for our theme, however, is the crucial scene where these questions are enacted: a *mikvah* in Israel, tucked away deep in a forest. The *mikvah* is also the apparent crime scene of the murder of one of the two protagonists. The site and the aestheticizing description of the spiritual place remind us again of a *locus amoenus*, even though it is not love that is the theme here, but rather the characters' search for their (Jewish) identity.

The immersion of Jan Wechsler and Amnon Zichroni into the waters of the spiritual bath, in a hidden and sacred place, is where the revelation of the characters but also the *erasure of memory* takes place. As opposed to, for example, Thomas Bernhard's novel *Auslöschung*, where the unreliability of memory and the increasing insecurity and instability of the subject is a theme in the context of Holocaust remembrance, Stein evokes a specifically anti-intellectual or -cerebral gesture. Touch, here the touch of the water and the sensuality of bathing, are at the core of this narrative. The immersion into the spiritual waters causes both the extinction and the physical recollection of Holocaust memory. At the same time, the immersion into water can be read as a Jewish tradition that has been appropriated as the Christian sacrament of baptism. When the memories of Minsky are revealed as questionable, the identity of the one who does the uncovering, Jan Wechsler, is questioned. Touch, in this case the touch of the water, figures as both a washing-away and a homecoming of Holocaust memory (even though this particular homecoming ends, as noted, with the death of one of the protagonists). Zichroni furthermore has the supernatural ability to feel others' memories when he touches them. Physical touch (of people and of the water) is thus converted to the spiritual work of remembering. Inside the *mikvah*, the immersed body of Jan Wechsler turns into a death by murder, but also into a question, since we don't know for sure who of the protagonists drowned, and who is murdered. "Did this man [Jan Wechsler] really believe that the waters of the mikvah meant a new life for him, a different life from the one he had tried to escape from with his lies? Did he believe he could cleanse himself of the crime of destruction that he had caused and that could never be made good again?"[10] Perpetrator guilt and the guilt of inventing a story to gain personal (psychological) profit is made visible and tangible via the location of the *mikvah*, hidden away in the woods of Israel. To be sure, the novel by Stein invokes the location of Israel, and the *mikvah*, as a place of spiritual renewal, as a catalyst for German and Jewish Holocaust remembrance at a more allegorical, almost mythical level when compared to the lighthearted and immediate style of Flohr and Gorelik. Unlike Flohr's and Gorelik's narratives, his text is not first and foremost a love story (although love and the absence of love play an important role, especially in Zichroni's biography). But, it is significant that in all of these texts addressing German Holocaust guilt and German Jewish relations, Israel is the location where healing and transformation of memory take place. Both Stein's and Flohr's narratives imagine Israel as a home that is familiar and exotic, known and foreign, and where the protagonists' memories are productively aroused.

In order to understand more fully the possibilities that Israel evokes, like we see in Stein's text, it is useful to consider briefly the West German projection of Israel. The immediate postwar period was particularly formative for German-Israeli relations and provided important indices to German perceptions. As Gilad

---

10 "Glaubte dieser Mann [Jan Wechsler] etwa, in den Wassern der Mikwe beginne für ihn ein neues Leben, ein anderes als jenes, aus dem er versucht hatte, sich herauszulügen? Meinte er, sich reinwaschen zu können vom Vergehen der Zerstörung, die er angerichtet hatte und die nicht wieder gutzumachen war?" Stein, *Die Leinwand*, 193.

Margalit reveals, even the strongly philosemitic reports of German journalists of the immediate post-war period and their reports on Israel were not necessarily designed to reduce German prejudice against Jews.[11] On the contrary, the orientalist view of Israel as a progressive farming state with its *kibbutzim* is used more often to substantiate and endorse stereotypes against Jews in the diaspora. This is because, due to their different living circumstances, they can be viewed as "helpless" vis-à-vis the Zionists and thus stereotyped even further. The view of Israeli Jews as "Prussians of the Middle East" and the maintenance of a mythically coded image of Israel make it possible for intellectuals to experience Israelis both as Jewish and as not Jewish at the same time. While there are other aspects to post-war images and imaginations of Israel in Germany too, and more official accounts would provide a different picture, such an exoticization of Israel serves to promote the West German antisemitism that arises from German Holocaust guilt than to reduce it.

Yet, imagining Israel as an exoticized "other" vis-à-vis the West is not a feature of contemporary German literature alone. Jewish American writer Jonathan Safran Foer's latest novel *Here I Am* imagines Israelis as physical, muscular, and dark (in stark opposition to the protagonist Jacob, an American Jew who is cerebral, pale, and weak).[12] Jacob has this conversation with his Israeli cousin Tamir, where Tamir asks: "'And let me also ask you: Is Israel the Jewish homeland?' – 'Israel is the Jewish *state*.' ... 'It depends on what you mean by homeland,' Jacob said. 'If you mean ancestral homeland – 'What do *you* mean?' Tamir asked. 'I mean the place my family comes from.' 'Which is?' 'Galicia.' 'But before that.' 'What, Africa?'"[13] The conversation then degenerates into their grandfather stating that he feels Jewish, and Jacob saying that he feels American, followed by a discussion of Steven Spielberg's – uncircumcised – penis, and similar more or less superficial invocations of stereotypical Jewish obsessions.

The novel eventually careens into an implausible story line in which Israel is destroyed by an earthquake that sets off a cataclysmic war in the Middle East emerging from the humanitarian catastrophe in that region. In other words, it is a force of nature – and not the political conflict – precipitating the catastrophe that is loosely linked with Holocaust trauma. The actual plot of the novel focuses on the disintegration of Jacob's marriage. The destruction of Israel merely serves as a colorful backdrop against which the trauma of the emotional destruction haunting Jacob in his unhappy marriage is acted out physically in Israel while

---

11 Gilad Margalit, "Israel through the Eyes of the West German Press 1947–1967," *Jahrbuch für Antisemitismusforschung* 11 (Berlin: Metropol, 2002), 235–48, here, 248.
12 Jonathan Safran Foer, *Here I Am* (New York: Farrar Straus & Giroux, 2016).
13 Ibid., 232.

circuitously linked with his Jewish and Israeli identity. Throughout the narrative, Tamir seems, in spite of his physical strength, helpless and at the mercy of his insecure Jewish American cousin. "What was Israel to him? What were Israelis?" Jacob muses. "They were his more aggressive, more obnoxious, more crazed, more hairy, more muscular brothers ... *over there*."[14] And even though, in Foer's rendition of an exotic Israel, Jacob acknowledges that Israelis were also *his*, important to his identity, the entire discussion of Jewish identity and Israel as a place remains curiously abstract, removed, and uninvolved with the actual plot of this novel. In contrast to the German texts, where the protagonists spend time in Israel, Jacob's encounters with his Israeli cousin and his adjacent worry about the war take place entirely on American soil. Yet, just as the destruction of Israel – and, by association, of a part of the protagonist's identity – is caused by a random act of nature, so also is the imagination of Israel abstractly removed from the actual emotional trajectory of the story. In this American narrative, the image and imagination of Israel serve a purpose not dissimilar from that of West German journalists' imagined Israel. Israel is described as a scene of trauma more than desire, and it remains oddly abstract. Ultimately, Foer's *Here I Am* is about rescuing the Jewish American self, naming the other as other, and imagining a scenario in which the catastrophe of the exotic other affirms and heals the broken self.

When *Die Leinwand*'s Jan Wechsler decides to travel to Israel and when he meets up with Zichroni there, this is connected to the practical reason of his wanting to verify his own story, the story where the history of his memory and his personal culpability in connection with Zichroni's disappearance is put into question. As Silke Horstkotte shows, the *mikvah* scene in the text instrumentalizes Jewish mysticism in order to evoke "associations of death and rebirth." Still, the liberation from guilt remains unfulfilled for Wechsler, because the pool of the *mikvah* is empty.[15] The kabbalistic meaning of the *mikvah* might be overdetermined, in order to metaphysically frame the question of personal truth and authenticity, and to point to the limitations of the possibilities of objective and subjective truth. As Horstkotte points out, with this explicit way of thematizing fiction within fiction, the possibility of Holocaust memory is newly evaluated and reconfigured. More importantly however, Israel is now for the first time viewed skeptically as a location of reconciliation and positive working-through of Holocaust trauma. Yet, in the Wilkomirski affair itself, Israel is not named as a place

---

14 Ibid., 541
15 Silke Horstkotte, "'Ich bin woran ich mich erinnere.' Benjamin Steins *Die Leinwand* und der Fall Wilkomirski," *Der Nationalsozialismus und die Shoah in der deutschsprachigen Gegenwartsliteratur*, ed. Torben Fischer, Philipp Hammermeister, and Sven Kramer, Amsterdamer Beiträge, 115–32.

or as an explicit theme, making it all the more exposed in Stein's text. *Die Leinwand* can therefore also be read as suggesting the idea that a concrete and explicit working-through of guilt and trauma in the discourse of Holocaust remembrance via Israel as a location is not possible. Personal recollection fails, just as a spiritual healing via a bath in the *mikvah* can't take place. Truth and an authentic Holocaust narrative are no longer immediately possible to recall, just as the idea of Israel as a mythical place for overcoming collective or individual Holocaust guilt is no longer feasible. Such a complex and possibly overdetermined rejection of a just recently established discourse on Israel as a place of overcoming Holocaust guilt presents two separate functions. On the one hand, on the level of content, the question of the individual's possibilities of working through Holocaust trauma is posed anew. To do so, a physical place is referred to metaphysically, and this location becomes more and more the center of attention, with all its possibilities for sensual experiences (including physical touch). Whereas Foer's novel describes Israel as a removed and abstract concept, Stein's text is all about the physicality of the experience. On the other hand, the possibilities of fiction are referred to on a meta-textual level. We will now examine this nexus by considering two more novels.

Olga Grjasnowa's novel *Der Russe ist einer der Birken liebt* (2012; *All Russians Love Birch Trees*; 2014) is probably the most conspicuous recent example for this kind of productive conflation of several different traumas. Yet, the chronological narrative of the author who was born in 1984 and who, like Gorelik, came to Germany at age 11 as a refugee and today lives in Berlin, is simple in style. Grjasnowa is by now a well-established writer, even though she is read more commonly as a writer of "migrant literature," a term she herself rejects.[16] Young, Jewish, Azerbaijani immigrant, first-person narrator Masha lives in Frankfurt, is fluent in five languages, and her best friends are Muslims. Her grandmother was a Holocaust survivor, and when her great love Elias dies tragically as a result of a neglected sports injury, Masha moves to Israel where she finds hope, renewal, and an unexpected confrontation with her family's past trauma that is deeply embedded into her family history. More noticeably than in the other texts by Gorelik and Flohr, Masha permanently lives without a home, seemingly without any identifiable roots. The narrator says about Masha "she could live anywhere. But she doesn't need a home (*Heimat*)." This characterization alongside the experiences of significant post-traumatic memory haunting her suggests that

---

[16] Cf. an interview with the author conducted in Berlin on July 14, 2016, in: *German Jewish Literature After 1990*, Dialogue and Disjunction. Studies in Jewish German Literature, Culture, and Thought (Rochester, NY: Camden House, 2018), 223–28.

concepts like home or identity don't carry meaning for this protagonist. At least they do not in the traditional and expected sense of providing safety or security. When her family's memories haunt her in Israel, memories of being persecuted with her family as a child in Azerbaijan become stark and lasting. Masha's memories of the escape from Azerbaijan are increasingly joined with thoughts of Elias/Elisha, and the different traumas are interwoven in this fiction so as to not be completely clear which narrative strand we are currently dealing with: memories of Azerbaijan, memories of Elias, or the narrative time frame of the experiences in Israel. The reality of the Israeli-Palestinian war that is here – in opposition to the texts by Flohr and Gorelik – clearly delineated, is the cause for the war memories from Masha's childhood. Experiences of flight and persecution, as they shaped Masha as a child since her family was persecuted due to their Jewishness, are associated with Holocaust memory. When Masha arrives in Israel, her aunt forces her to eat: "I asked myself whether this desire to smother the following generation in food was a result more of my grandmother's Caucasian mentality or of her Holocaust legacy. My grandmother and her younger brother had arrived in Baku, half starved to death. They had been the sole survivors of the family."[17] At the same time, we are dealing with trauma that is significantly shaped by conflation. In Israel, Masha calls her parents: "What I longed for were familiar people, but one of them was dead, and the others I couldn't stand any longer. Because they were alive."[18] Israel, here, is no longer a *locus amoenus* as in Gorelik and Flohr, or even the more positive parts of Stein's novel. The novel ends when Masha, after a particularly traumatic war experience in Jerusalem, calls her friend Sami and asks him to rescue her and bring her back from Israel.

One interpretation of the narrative is that Masha ultimately fails in her attempt to work through the trauma of her past – even though Israel provides her with a space for new friendship, new relationships, and a new outlook on life. Yet the Armenian–Azerbaijan war – the actual cause for Masha's personal trauma – is not the source of this failure. Instead, Masha fails in working through her trauma because she recognizes intuitively that the structures that cause trauma – be they in Israel and Palestine, or in the Caucasus – are not changing

---

[17] "Ich fragte mich, ob dieser Drang, die nachfolgende Generation im Essen zu ersticken, mehr mit der kaukasischen Mentalität oder dem Holocaust-Erbe meiner Grossmutter zu tun hatte. Meine Grossmutter war mit ihrem kleinen Bruder halb verhungert in Baku angekommen, sie waren die einzigen Überlebenden in ihrer Familie." Olga Grjasnowa, *Der Russe ist einer der Birken liebt* (Munich: Carl Hanser Verlang, 2012), 174.

[18] "Wonach ich mich sehnte waren vertraute Menschen, nur war der eine tot, und die anderen ertrug ich nicht mehr. Weil sie lebten." Ibid., 203.

and haven't changed. It's the notion of perceiving others as "other" and "foreign" alongside developing social behaviors that reflect this perception that are structurally problematic.

Instead of imagining Israel as a place where memory can be engaged productively to come to terms with a traumatic past, Grjasnowa's novel presents the location of Israel as a catalyst. Yet, at the same time, Israel also appears as a concrete and specific place – of war – in order to shed light on the conflation of different and historically divergent memory discourses and how they are structurally linked. Israel is no longer exoticized, and the more realistic view as a place of war and destruction makes possible the dealing with personal trauma. Similar to the narrative by Stein but carried out very differently, at stake here is the physical experience of Israel as a specific location, where the text, especially as it concerns Masha's sadness about Elias, evokes bodily and sensual memories. The physical-sensual dimension of the narrative – smell and taste are linked both with Elias's body and with the experiences of war – is no longer associated with metaphysical or religious themes as in Stein. As opposed to the happy love stories in Flohr's and Gorelik's novels, Grjasnowa's protagonist's love dies, literally, in the course of the story unfolding, adding to the trauma of her past, but also bringing it to the fore. Home, ethnic, cultural, or religious identity are decidedly no longer defining markers for Masha's generation – decidedly so, since all of these led to the genocide in the first place. Still, it seems not coincidental that the story is set in Israel and that the structural conflation of genocidal trauma is made visible to the protagonist – and to us as readers – via this very particular location. The detailed descriptions of the physical experiences of the protagonist mark Israel a location to be sensually experienced.

Thus far, we have seen examples of two contemporary German texts that imagine Israel as a place for healing German Jewish relations and overcoming Holocaust trauma, as well as two narratives that are less idealistic regarding the location of Israel while still invoking it clearly and with great insistence. It is probably not an accident that the latter two novels have been translated into English, and received considerably more critical and scholarly attention than the ones by Flohr and Gorelik. There are additional examples by Oliver Polak and Adriana Alteras that I can't fully explore here, where Israel functions not as a place that figures in the tangible plot or story line of the narrative itself, but rather as a remote place of imagined (personal) healing and overcoming the past. In Polak and Alteras, Israel is cast as a place of a fantasy for remediating the past in the protagonists' imaginations. Especially because of the different ways in which Israel in fiction is engaged, these texts taken together provide examples of how Holocaust remembrance can be reconceived as part of a new discourse on the Shoah. Israel becomes productive first, as a place for healing and positive working through the German Jewish guilt of the past (Gorelik and Flohr), second, to ask new questions of the possibilities for experiencing and mediating memory (Stein), and third, to indicate the structural conflations between Holocaust trauma and other personal trauma (Grjasnowa). The notion of Israel as a place of "home," spiritual or otherwise, while still preserved more unambiguously in the happy love stories, is deconstructed but still referenced in the narratives by Stein and Grjasnowa. Especially in Grjasnowa's text, Israel instead appears as a place for a collective of multiply displaced others.

Due to these structural conflations of several different traumas in Grjasnowa's text, it might indeed seem as if the Holocaust, and with that, Holocaust remembrance, for today's German Jews have disappeared behind further, other, and more personal differentiated fates. To think more about these conflations, the recently published *Winternähe* will shed light on this nexus. It is by Mirna Funk (2015) who was born in East Berlin in 1981. The German Jewish Funk is known mostly as a fashion and lifestyle journalist, but her debut was widely reviewed and won a debut prize, and she is now working on her second novel. The thread that runs through the story line of this personal narrative, consistently related from a third person perspective, is the protagonist Lola's search for her father Simon. He had been emotionally absent for most of her life. He is the one who is Jewish and who gives Lola her Jewish identity. Additionally, the story is the fictional narrative of a GDR fate, a theme that generally does not receive sufficient attention in addressing the Holocaust past. Lola observes that in contemporary Berlin there is a "Der-Holocaust-ist-so-over-Seite" (the-Holocaust-is-so-over-side) and a "Wir-dürfen-nicht-vergessen-was-geschehen-ist-Seite" (we-must-never-forget-what-happened-side) – two opposing perspectives that are unresolvable in their seeming contradiction.[19] Lola identifies as unmistakably Jewish even though she knows that she can't be recognized by the Orthodox community because of the *halakha*: "I grew up with a Jewish family, I experienced their sorrow, I absorbed their trauma, I have visited Israel every year since I was eleven years old, I can make *aliyah* and become an Israeli citizen, but I can't marry, and my children would be discriminated against and disadvantaged."[20]

Lola's mother Petra is portrayed negatively as a typical German of her generation: superficial, thoughtless, and materialistic. Lola's father had fled

---

[19] Mirna Funk, *Winternähe* (Frankfurt am Main: S. Fischer Verlag, 2015), 21.
[20] "Ich bin bei einer jüdischen Familie groß geworden, ich habe ihr Leid erfahren, ihr Trauma aufgenommen, ich habe Israel seit meinem elften Lebensjahr jedes Jahr besucht, ich darf Alija machen und israelische Staatsbürgerin werden, aber ich darf nicht heiraten, und meine Kinder würden diskriminiert und benachteiligt werden." Ibid., 259.

the GDR in 1987, when Lola was still a child and growing up in East Berlin. Via Simon's parents, and Lola's grandparents, GDR history and memory are productively interwoven with the history and memory of the Shoah. In this text, just as in the one by Grjasnowa, the overarching themes are loss and healing and the recalling and resuscitating of memory. Due to the continuing and visible antisemitism in the midst of German society, which Lola feels acutely in Berlin, making her angry, she acts out in public gestures that are destructive rather than contributing to healing the conflict of her German Jewish identity. The first scene of the story is set in Berlin, where Lola persecutes a couple for depicting her image with a photoshopped Hitler moustache on social media. As opposed to the novel by Grjasnowa, the question of the German-German memory of the Holocaust is thus clearly set front and center of the plot line.

Lola meets her great love Shlomo, an Israeli, via Tinder in Berlin. When her life in Berlin unravels, she decides to visit Shlomo in his hometown Tel Aviv, where also her grandparents had lived and where her grandfather is still living. Upon her arrival in Tel Aviv Lola experiences the war of the summer 2014, occasioned by the kidnapping and then the murder of three Israeli teenagers by Hamas members. Shlomo, too, is traumatized. When he served in the Israeli army, he had accidentally killed a Palestinian boy and as a result became a peace activist. Shlomo never tells Lola about the boy, she finds out from his friend by coincidence. Both traumas – personal in both cases, but in Lola's case evoked by the German Jewish history of antisemitism, and in Shlomo's case by the Israeli-Palestinian conflict – induce a particular kind of intimacy for the lovers. At the same time, due to Lola's inner conflicts, they are also both suspended in a state of uprootedness. In Jerusalem, Lola observes on the occasion of viewing the exhibit of the glass booth in which Eichmann sat during his trial, that the Holocaust is neither explicable nor forgivable: "But what happened has happened. If it was terrible then one doesn't have to forgive. To forgive someone is as misguided as it is to forgive oneself." Instead one is supposed to "Accept. Live with it. Not forget. Remember."[21] However, Lola doesn't immediately live up to this notion. The days with Shlomo that she experiences as conflict laden are defined by the terrifying noise of the war. Instead of a *locus amoenus*, Israel is here turned into a *locus terribilis*. When Lola's grandfather suddenly dies in the midst of the war and Lola learns a secret about the grandmother's past, she travels to Thailand without

---

21 "Aber das geschehene ist geschehen. Wenn es furchtbar war dann muss man es nicht verzeihen. Jemandem zu verzeihen ist genauso bescheuert, wie sich selbst zu verzeihen." And: "Annehmen. Akzeptieren. Damit leben. Nicht vergessen. Sich erinnern." Ibid., 183.

saying good-bye to Shlomo. Thailand is here coded as an exotic other and also as other vis-à-vis Israel. It almost seems as if Lola wants to live in a diaspora, but in a diaspora that frees her from both the German and the German Jewish and Israeli past.

The love between Lola and Shlomo is free and beautiful, but also fragile because it has to withstand so much: both of their traumatic pasts and the conflation of German-Jewish and Israeli-Palestinian conflicts. However, most difficult for Lola is dealing with her contested identity as half-Jewish and half-East German. The memory of the Holocaust past for an East German Jewish woman is entwined with the losses she experiences as a result. Lola understands that Shlomo is a killer. "What does it feel like when a murderer comes – in Lola's mouth? And when he closes the door behind him?" she asks.[22] This recognition of Shlomo's identity as a murderer, as someone with the burden of guilt, brings her own German and non-Jewish identity into sharp focus. When she accompanies Shlomo to the funeral of the Palestinian boy who was killed by Israelis as a result of the Hamas murder of the three young boys, she is keenly aware that it is not this particular boy who is on Shlomo's mind, but the boy who he had accidentally killed earlier. Curiously, the funeral is set in Jerusalem, and Jerusalem is coded as the place where both Shlomo and Lola visit as tourists (they disguise themselves as journalists to gain access to the funeral). It is interesting that Jerusalem functions as a more ambiguous place, whereas Tel Aviv is positively coded as a place of love and family. After the funeral, Lola's love for Shlomo is not diminished by her knowledge of his culpability.

With differently coded markers – in a shift from *locus amoenus* to *locus terribilis* – Israel is in Mirna Funk's text clearly signified as a place of terror and violence. As opposed to the novels by Flohr and Gorelik, the constant fear occasioned by the attacks and loud detonations of the missile defense system is the dominant emotion of Lola's experience in Tel Aviv. Lola associates those emotions with her German Jewish identity, specifically with the German antisemitism that resulted from Holocaust guilt,[23] and finally with Shlomo's trauma concerning his past guilt. What in Gorelik's text is still articulated as humorous and trivial, namely that the Germans are more concerned with the war in Israel than the Israelis themselves, is now, in Funk's novel, the subject of serious consideration.

---

[22] "Wie ist es wenn ein Mörder kommt – in Lolas Mund? Und wie, wenn er die Tür hinter sich zuzieht?" Ibid., 185.
[23] Cf. Agnes C. Mueller, *The Inability to Love: Jews, Gender, and America in Recent German Literature* (Evanston: Northwestern University Press, 2015), for a full consideration of secondary antisemitism in Germany, especially as it pertains to guilt induced antisemitism.

"For Lola everyone was a potential victim and a potential perpetrator. ... Only those who were not conscious of those contradictions viewed themselves exclusively as victims even though they had turned into perpetrators a long time ago. Lola called it *Schuldangst*."[24]

Holocaust memorial culture is thus, still, and similar to the previously discussed texts, moved to a different, non-German, exotically heightened location. Love and desire play an important role in this narrative: Lola's love for Shlomo initially makes her go to Israel where she then reflects on her family history and identity. Lola's personal and individual engagement with what she calls "*Schuldangst*" (guilt anxiety) only starts in Israel, because of the physical experience of the terror of war. Israel as a place of desire as well as terror or trauma thus becomes, in Funk's period novel, a physical space for the experience of working through the past. The resulting terror, anxiety, and insecurity function as catalysts for confronting trauma, a confrontation that seems impossible in Germany. Lola says: "Every time I take a breath in Berlin or Munich or Hamburg, I know that I inhale the ashes of the dead Jews. The only thing I can't understand is why the Germans haven't already suffocated from these ashes."[25] Lola thus names Germany as the place for the physical experience of guilt and mourning, a place where this physical experience turns into an existential threat (through suffocation). To write poetry after Auschwitz is thus perhaps no longer barbaric. But in Germany it may well have become increasingly difficult. As a result of this difficulty it might not, as Adorno revised, "falsch gewesen sein, nach Auschwitz liesse kein Gedicht mehr sich schreiben." Because: "Weil jedoch die Welt den eigenen Untergang überlebt hat, bedarf sie gleichwohl der Kunst als ihrer bewußtlosen Geschichtsschreibung."[26] And while Foer, for the American Jewish context, also designates the location of Israel as a place of terror and trauma, his invocations

---

24 "Für Lola war jeder Mensch ein potentielles Opfer und ein potentieller Täter. ... Nur jene die sich dieser Widersprüche nicht bewusst waren, sahen sich selbst ausschliesslich als Opfer obwohl sie längst zu Tätern geworden waren. Lola nannte das Schuldangst." Funk, *Winternähe*, 85.
25 "Jedes Mal, wenn ich die Luft in Berlin oder in München oder in Hamburg einatme, weiß ich, dass ich die Asche der toten Juden einatme. Das Einzige, was ich nicht verstehe, ist, wieso die Deutschen nicht längst an dieser Asche erstickt sind." Ibid., 312.
26 Theodor W. Adorno, "Jene Zwanziger Jahre [1962]," in *Gesammelte Schriften*, Vol. 10.2 (Frankfurt am Main: Suhrkamp, 1977), 506, The discussion on the (mis)understanding of Adorno's quote is best explained here: https://persistentenlightenment.wordpress.com/2013/05/21/poetry-after-auschwitz-what-adorno-didnt-say/

Also, Samuel Weber's translation of the original quotation firms this up: "Cultural criticism finds itself today faced with the final state of the dialectic of culture and barbarism. To write poetry after Auschwitz is barbaric. And this corrodes even the knowledge of why it has become impossible to write poetry today. Absolute reification, which presupposed intellectual progress

are much less palpable and leave no visible trace, emotional or physical, in the Jewish protagonist. Experiences of guilt and mourning are, in Foer, located in the private and personal space. Israel remains abstract, an outsider to American Jewish identity. The experiences of war, trauma, and terror are in Foer's novel not directly linked with Holocaust guilt, and Jewish identity is here, for the American context, removed from the location of Israel.

The important question as to how art today can remember the Shoah and how this discourse of remembrance – or the "bewusstlose Geschichtsschreibung" – might remain relevant for future generations is therefore not only a question of "how" we engage in dealing with the past and memory. Instead, today we must also ask questions of "where" and "from where." What Rothberg and Snyder touch on in their interpretations of a new and changed minority discourse, but don't directly name, points straight to diachronic as well as synchronic questions of a changed locality. Who is speaking, and from which position? For whom? A view from the outside and a view of that which is seen differently allow for a new point of view. In several German and German Jewish fictional works, we see examples of the projection of love and trauma, via an imagined place that leads to actual and physical experiences of working through trauma. The imagination of the "other" – images of Jews, images of Israel, images of Germans – become, via fiction in literature, a part of the self. The new and changed conditions of the aesthetic in the discourse of Holocaust remembrance, as they are seemingly naively related in Flohr and Gorelik, indicate new markings in both form and content. Already for Flohr, Israel is the place where a German Jewish love can flourish. Additionally, these texts engage in a complex staging of fiction – fiction and aesthetic difference reference itself. While the self-referentiality of fiction is also a theme in Foer's novel, the invocation of Israel as a place to work through trauma is decidedly not, rendering it a specifically German feature. In Stein's novel fiction is furthermore itself set as a player in the text. Conflations of different discourses of trauma and genocide – as in Grjasnowa – also participate in a staging of fiction, although this no longer relies on the archaeological memory work as in the traditional family novel, but rather interweaves different places and times. Such an emphasis on place and position in fiction gains its fullest expression in Funk's novel, because it is precisely *not* possible for the German and Jewish protagonist to name and call out the antisemitism that she finds herself confronted with in Germany. When interpreting this new form of remembrance it is important to not gloss over textual differences where new media and hybrid forms (as they appear

---

as one of its elements, is now preparing to absorb the mind entirely. Critical intelligence cannot be equal to this challenge as long as it confines itself to self-satisfied contemplation."

in many of the recent texts) are seen as synonymous with a new, "post-migrant" or "global" narrative. In the texts under discussion here, it is precisely not true that remembrance is taking place at a random location or in a fictional context, since Israel is clearly presented as the new location for an articulation of trauma.

Especially the latter two texts by Grjasnowa and Funk can be read as the beginning of a new discourse on Holocaust remembrance. They achieve this by imagining Israel as a place of exotic desire, but also as a place of a productive engagement of horror and *personal* trauma. "Multidirectional memory" is here coalescing into specific, personal, local, and empirical markers of remembrance. The conflations that take place in the fictional texts – for example of Holocaust memory with the war in Azerbaijan or with the trauma of having killed a Palestinian boy – precisely do not relativize the horrors of the Shoah. Neither do they suggest that the memory of the Shoah and the adjacent discourse on antisemitism can be easily located in a globalized, post-migrant and multi-cultural society. Rather, the memory and working through of what had not been worked through by previous generations is invoked, and this time without attempting a universalizing, Europeanizing, or orientalizing impulse of the victim–perpetrator discourse. The implications of a "cosmopolitan" memory discourse, a term that on the outset seems naïve and counterproductive due to its conflicting stance toward universal Enlightenment emancipation while glossing over local specificity, seems productive in this context. With Kwame Anthony Appiah, this cosmopolitan memory discourse lies "beneath the facts of globalization."[27] As opposed to the more narrow invocation of Israel as a global place of exotic desire and terrible destruction in Foer's American Jewish identity paradigm, German Jewish Holocaust remembrance utilizes Israel's particularity to advance an emergent discourse that significantly expands on previous notions of empathy. Rather than engaging in a didactic stance – what Adorno tried to refute earlier – these literary texts confront the reader directly with the fictional and raw experiences of a new yet specific location. At stake here is not so much a "post-didactic" memorial culture, as formulated elsewhere, but rather a move to make traumatic memory emotionally and personally accessible. A memorial culture that is changed in this way still includes, as before, the strong German desire for a refutation of guilt of the German Nazi past. Yet, in this moment of an emergent cosmopolitan memory, Holocaust memory is now displaced to an attractive and terrible place, a precise place of trauma and desire, to make individual pain and individual guilt accessible – in Israel.

---

[27] Kwame Anthony Appiah, *Cosmopolitanism. Ethics in a World of Strangers* (New York and London: W. W. Norton, 2006), xx.

Bibliography

Adorno, Theodor W. "Kulturkritik und Gesellschaft." *Gesammelte Schriften*. Vol. 10.1: *Kulturkritik und Gesellschaft I, "Prismen. Ohne Leitbild."* Frankfurt am Main: Suhrkamp, 1977.
Appiah, Kwame Anthony. *Cosmopolitanism. Ethics in a World of Strangers*. New York/ London: W. W. Norton, 2006.
Bernhard, Thomas. *Auslöschung. Ein Zerfall*. Frankfurt am Main: Suhrkamp, 1988.
Flohr, Markus. *Wo samstags immer Sonntag ist*. Munich: Kindler, 2011.
Foer, Jonathan Safran. *Here I Am*. New York: Farrar, Straus & Giroux, 2016.
Funk, Mirna. *Winternähe*. Frankfurt am Main: Fischer, 2015.
Gopnik, Adam. "Blood and Soil. A Historian Returns to the Holocaust." *The New Yorker*, September 21, 2015. http://www.newyorker.com/magazine/2015/09/21/blood-and-soil
Gorelik, Lena. *Hochzeit in Jerusalem*. Munich: SchirmerGraf, 2007.
Grjasnowa, Olga. *Der Russe ist einer der Birken liebt*. Munich: Hanser, 2012.
Hammerstein, Katrin / Julie Trappe. *Aufarbeitung der Diktatur – Diktat der Aufarbeitung? Normierungsprozesse beim Umgang mit diktatorischer Vergangenheit*. Göttingen: Wallstein, 2009.
Horstkotte, Silke. "'Ich bin woran ich mich erinnere.' Benjamin Steins Die Leinwand und der Fall Wilkomirski." In *Der Nationalsozialismus und die Shoah in der deutschsprachigen Gegenwartsliteratur*. Hg. Von Torben Fischer, Philipp Hammermeister, und Sven Kramer, 115–132. Amsterdamer Beiträge zur neueren Germanistik 84. Amsterdam, New York: Rodopi, 2014.
LaCapra, Dominick. *Writing History, Writing Trauma*. Baltimore: Johns Hopkins University Press, 2001.
Levy, Daniel, and Natan Sznaider. *The Holocaust and Memory in a Global Age*. Philadelphia, PA: Temple University Press, 2006.
Margalit, Gilad. "Israel through the Eyes of the West German Press 1947–1967." *Jahrbuch für Antisemitismusforschung* 11(2002): 235–248.
Miron, Dan. *From Continuity to Contiguity. Toward a New Jewish Literary Thinking*. Stanford: Stanford University Press, 2010.
Mueller, Agnes C. *The Inability to Love: Jews, Gender, and America in Recent German Literature*. Evanston, IL: Northwestern University Press, 2015.
Rothberg, Michael. *Multidirectional Memory. Remembering the Holocaust in the Age of Decolonization*. Stanford: Stanford University Press, 2009.
Seyhan, Azade. *Writing Outside the Nation*. Princeton, NJ: Princeton University Press, 2001.
Stein, Benjamin. Die Leinwand. Munich: Beck, 2010.
Taberner, Stuart. "The Possibilities and Pitfalls of a Jewish Cosmopolitanism. Reading Natan Sznaider through Russian-Jewish Writer Olga Grjasnowa's German-language Novel *Der Russe ist einer der Birken liebt (All Russians Love Birch Trees)*." *European Review of History: Revue europeenne d'histoire* 23, nos. 5–6 (2016): 912–930.
Wilkomirski, Binyamin. *Fragments. Memories of a Wartime Childhood*. Translated from German by Carol Brown Janeway. New York: Schocken Books, 1996.

Doerte Bischoff
Paper Existences: Passports and Literary Imagination

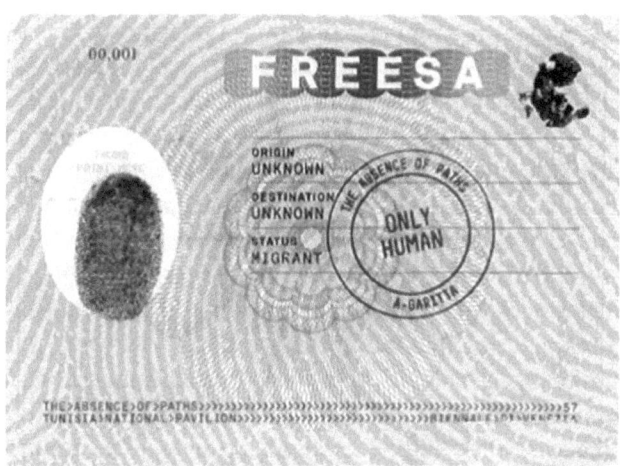

Figure 1: Passports as Art: the Tunisian pavilion at the Biennale Arte in Venice 2017 issued this individualized document to visitors.

Usually, passports are known as documents issued by state authorities to signify a person's citizenship and his or her belonging to a national community. Thus, they appear mainly as an instrument of political governance and not as a means of individual self-expression or creative imagination. It may therefore seem surprising that references to passports and other identity papers in literature and the arts are fairly common and appear to be closely related to their capacity of opening up alternative spaces subverting and transcending actual political boundaries, which often limit or hinder individual mobility. Especially in literature reflecting non-authorized travels or displacement and exile, where political boundaries assume an existential dimension, passports often become central to the narrative plots and experiments. In dealing with identity papers – their appearance, materiality and functions – literary texts explore not only the conditions of individuality and belonging under the conditions of modernity, they also delineate decentered, transnational, and transformed visions of communities that challenge the model of the nation state and the related concept of identity.

This logic can be discerned clearly in some recent art exhibitions or performances that have shown a remarkable interest in passports. Passport collections, passport adaptions, or staging that either integrates passports as material objects or imagines contexts in which they unfold or lose their power, could be seen in many places. In 2017, dance choreographer Helena Waldmann brought out a piece called "Good Passports, Bad Passports," and in the Venice Biennale the same year, the Tunisian pavilion presented itself as a kind of decentered and multiplied booth issuing passport-like documents that could be found at different places in the exhibition area and the city (Figure 1). This in itself was remarkable because it rejected the traditional concept of the Biennale that relies on the idea of an assembly of presentations of nationally framed and, as such, localizable art. A document, called "Freesa," was issued to visitors who then were asked to mark and validate it with an individual thumbprint. The holder of each document was characterized only in the most general way as a migrant and – by means of a stamp – as "only human," while "origin" and "destination" were not specified by geographical or political sites. The "Freesa," which was produced in cooperation with a global company specializing in security documents, also contained information about passports worldwide, for example, the very different range of mobility they allow. Thus, the project titled *The Absence of Paths* raised awareness of the impact passport regimes have on human lives, while at the same time hinting at possible communities beyond the nation.

New books not only thematize questions of identity and belonging in a world of nation states that is increasingly challenged by migrants and exiles, they sometimes also imitate the format and features of passports in their own formal and haptic appearance, as in the case of Janne Teller's novel *War, What If It Were Here* (2004). Even in journalistic commentaries on the outstanding features of recent book publications, passport-like covers are used to illustrate the assumption that contemporary literature engages in politics (again), meaning that with its own artistic devices it reflects on life stories in their connection with identity politics as well as economic and legal issues.

Considering this remarkable evidence of passport-related art and literature at the present time, the question arises if this phenomenon has a historical dimension as well. So before coming back to an example of a contemporary novel about migrants whose lives are centered on the passport issue, some historical constellations will be sketched out which show that passports have spurred the literary imagination not only in our times of mass migration and reinvigorated nationalisms but already in much earlier contexts. As will be shown, these texts do not just share a topic because they happen to refer to similar political situations. They also establish a dense network of textual references by recurring literary motives and narratives in texts of different times and places – which as such, undermines the notion of literature merely representing preceding facts and realities and instead enforces the idea that literature can assert its proper realm with textual strategies and "paper work" of its own.

Representation is a key concept governing not only modern states with their claim to encompass and integrate all their citizens; it is also decisive for the concept of modern identity papers. While before the French Revolution passports were typically issued for specific cases of border crossing and travel requirements, they now developed into a universal means of registering and controlling the population.[1] If at the beginning passports carried by travelers above all included information about the issuing authority, they gradually changed into an identity document containing a *signalement* – for example a description of the person's gender and certain outward characteristics, often also profession and information about his or her date and place of birth – which was closely intertwined with the signs of the issuing nation-state. From World War I on, also passport photographs became obligatory. Since their authenticity is certified by an official stamp, the interleave between signs of the person and the authority becomes most obvious here. The following readings will show how this interleave is weakened, ironized, or even disrupted by texts that foreground the semiotic and textual nature of identification processes.

1 Identification and Reading: Digressive Paths in Sterne's *Sentimental Journey*

In Lawrence Sterne's novel *Sentimental Journey*, which was first published in 1768, signs of the impending changes in the regime of identification can already be discerned. Remarkably, in this paradigmatic travel narrative focusing on the inner sentiments and reflections of the traveler rather than giving precise descriptions of famous sights or historic-political contexts, six chapters are titled "the Passport." The British narrator, having somewhat clandestinely crossed the Channel to come to France, is confronted there with the necessity to present a passport (originally a French word from the Middle Ages meaning a paper permit to pass the gate of a city) as a foreigner. The French-British colonial wars intensified the need to draw clear lines between national affiliations. While the whole undertaking to cross borders and travel to a foreign enemy country already runs counter to

---

[1] John Torpey, *The Invention of the Passport. Surveillance, Citizenship and the State* (Cambridge: Cambridge University Press, 2000); Andreas Fahrmeir, *Citizenship: The Rise and Fall of a Modern Concept* (New Haven, London: Yale University Press, 2007).

the efforts of drawing clear lines and setting boundaries, the narrator also keeps musing about national stereotypes which, to the traveler, soon appear as untenable prejudices. Having been in Paris for a while, he is informed that he should report to the police and present his passport. It is significant for this prerevolutionary setting that the case that somebody does not have a passport is taken as one, if dangerous, possible state for which there can be relief, if the person has influential friends in the country. The narrator, who at first reacts widely unworried to the situation, does not know anybody in France personally. However, after having realized that he is actually threatened with imprisonment he turns to a nobleman in Versailles. When it turns out that at the *Monsieur le Duc de Choiseul* he has to wait several hours, he drives around in Versailles where a conversation with the coachman reminds him that the day before a bookseller had praised another local nobleman, the Count de B****, for his erudition and especially his appreciation of English literature.[2] So by deciding "to tell him his story," he changes his addressee for the passport matter, a choice that also indicates a closer intertwinement of the two kinds of paper he is concerned with: books and identity documents. Remarkably, the new orientation comes about only after a transgressive and aimless movement through foreign places and is the result of accidental encounters and conversations. Thus it evokes random and uncontrollable paths undermining the idea of supervised borders and movement control. While the notion of cultural entanglement is embodied by the French count who is an enthusiast of English literature and the British traveler who converses with him in French, making the text itself bilingual – it is generally associated here with an ongoing process of traveling and self-development through encounters and impressions in a foreign land. Interestingly, this digressive mode of movement is also referred to the act of identification. When the narrator finally faces the Count he is expected to tell his vis-à-vis "who he is," which for him, as he confides to the reader, is always a very "perplexing affair in life."[3] Thus he resorts to the edition of Shakespeare which is lying on the table between them, opens the *Hamlet* volume, and points to the name "Yorik," who as a character in that play is the king's jester who, however, only has his (famous) appearance after death, as a skull. When the narrator thus introduces himself as Yorick just by pointing to the text, adding "*Me voici*" (that's me), this act ironically revives the drama figure conflating "real life" and dramatic imagination, past and present, dead letter

---

[2] In the novel autobiographical experiences resonate. In 1762 Lawrence Sterne had traveled to France and was confronted with the necessity to obtain a passport. He was finally granted one thanks to the intercession of a Comte de Bissie. See Arthur Cash, *Lawrence Sterne. The Later Years* (London, New York: Methuen, 1986), 116–29.

[3] Lawrence Sterne, *A Sentimental Journey* (Oxford, New York: Oxford University Press, 1968), 85.

and living person. The Count responds to this playful introduction quite affirmatively, since he is more than willing to accept that before him miraculously stands Yorick, the king's jester: "*Et Monsieur, est il Yorick?* cried the Count. – *Je le suis*, said I. – *Vous? – Moi – moi qui ai l'honneur de vous parler, Monsieur le Compte – Mon Dieu!* said he, embracing me – *Vous etes* [sic] *Yorick.*"[4] After this act of identification exposing the blending of real and fictional persons, the Count disappears and after a short while comes back with the passport which was "directed to all lieutenant governors, and commandants of cities, generals of armies, judiciaries, and all officers of justice, to let Mr. Yorick, the king's jester, and his baggage, travel quietly along."[5] In a final attempt to correct this erroneous ascription, the narrator insists that he is not a jester and that at the British court jesters no longer have a place anyway: "our manners have been so gradually refining, that our court at present is so full of patriots, who wish for *nothing* but the honours and wealth of their country – and our ladies are all so chaste, so spotless, so good, so devout – there is nothing for a jester to make a jest of."[6] To this the Count only cries out: "*Voila* [sic] *un persiflage!*" implying that the narrator's description of British spotlessness is really an ironic mimicking of a narrow-minded patriotism which denies jest and playfulness and with them also spaces of transgression and encounters which can be opened up by literature.

Thus, at the verge of the development of the European nation states, which engendered a new kind of homogenizing discourse of belonging as a national affair, Sterne's novel not only focuses on a sensitive traveler, his digressive paths, and various border crossings, it also evokes literary modes and spaces of identification that subvert simple and exclusive national categorizations of individuals. Remarkably, the passport, which soon after the publication of the novel gained influence as a means for nations to register people and control their movement, plays an important role here in that it is precisely the perceived necessity and growing pressure to have one that spurs the narrator's imagination and activities. This connection is also reflected in an episode about a bird in a cage which the narrator perceives just after the idea has entered his mind that not having a passport might bring him to the Bastille. The fact that the bird speaks – somebody has taught him the words "I can't get out," which it now repeats over and over again – facilitates identification with it and its state of confinement.[7] The singing bird in the cage – which is a recurring theme in the literature of sensibility (usually it

---

4 Sterne, *Sentimental Journey*, 86.
5 Ibid., 88.
6 Ibid.
7 At the same time, the bird which has been trained to speak like a human being appears as a parody of the notion of the unmediated voice of the creature.

appears in connection with sensitive women who sympathize with the agony of the imprisoned creature and set it free) – is here explicitly intertwined with the passport issue. Sterne's Yorick, too, feels that he has "never had [his] affections more tenderly awakened"[8] than in this identificatory encounter with the captive starling. He also immediately tries to set it free, but when he does not succeed he starts figuring to himself "the miseries of confinement."[9] Before this, he had rather lightheartedly imagined himself living in the Bastille with pen and ink and a lot of time to think and write – everything at the expense of the king of France. Now he dismisses this idea as mere "systematic reasonings," without a real understanding of the mental state of confinement. Interestingly, this self-development indicated by a new sense of compassion with "fellow creatures born to no inheritance but slavery,"[10] then results in his decision to get himself a passport. Thus, two features of the discourse about modern individuality appear closely intertwined: the inward turn toward individual sensitivity, which is supposed to enable him/her to connect to all other feeling (human) beings on the one hand and the turn toward new forms of political organization and social coherence, which rely essentially on the idea of the nation, on the other.[11] Confinement obviously can no longer be regarded as exerted by an external power radically opposed to the individual's freedom of thought and imagination, which can blossom even in prison. Rather,

---

8 Sterne, *Sentimental Journey*, 71.

9 Ibid., 72.

10 Ibid. The hint to slavery may also be read here as a reference to the issue of slavery in the Seven Years' War. In this war, England succeeded in expanding its slave trade by conquering French slave trade stations. Wolfgang Reinhart, *Die Unterwerfung der Welt. Globalgeschichte der europäischen Expansion 1415–2015* (Munich: Beck, 2016), 445. Considering this context, one could suggest that by transgressing the borders of his own country, Sterne's traveler is also affected by the colonial dimension of the national enterprises of the time. While European nations develop a system of separated nation states, which claim to be grounded in ethnic homogeneity and specific cultural characteristics, they conceal that they owe their prosperity and feeling of superiority largely to colonial endeavors and the exploitation of people who are beyond any protection by a nation state. He who crosses his country's borders gets closer to an understanding of this logic by temporarily identifying with the outcasts beyond the national border who at the same time help to define it.

11 In an intriguing reading of the novel, Jesper Gulddal has recently suggested that the topic of borders and travel on a political and geographical level is closely intertwined with the idea of transgression of "intersubjective borders and the associated barriers between genders and classes." The double feature of the passport, to give and to restrict access, is seen as a model for human contact and exchange which need to be regulated by "porous" borders enabling transgression while at the same time guarding the integrity of the self. However, to state that Sterne "does not appear to be interested in the political aspects of the passport," seems to reduce the complexity of the text. Jesper Gulddal, "Porous Borders: The Passport as an Access Metaphor in Laurence Sterne's *A Sentimental Journey*," *Symploke* 25, nos. 1–2 (2017): 53, 56.

confinement must now be conceptualized as ingrained in the modern individual who is granted freedom and protection only as a member of a state, which requires registering and inscribes the individual's name into documents which are based on uniformity and serialization. In Sterne's novel this scenario only announces itself from afar, since the way he finally receives the passport is still quite distant from the normalized bureaucratic operations that later become standard for the praxis of issuing passports. Also, the passport Yorick receives does not seem to contain a lot of information about the bearer of the document. While this reflects the situation in prerevolutionary times, when passports mostly bore the signs of the authorities or noblemen who issued them,[12] the text also attributes the absence of personal traits in the document to the uneasiness the protagonist articulates about having to reveal his name and identity in public, which then results in the digressive scene with the Shakespearean character. Literature here reflects its potential to introduce and follow a person without identifying him or her unequivocally, thus leaving space for association and uncontrollable dynamics. As identity here is presented as connected to a reading process which implies references to other texts and contexts, literature challenges the claim to identification and control typical for state bureaucracies. Unlike state bureaucracies, literature does not rely on the possibility of definite authentication, which it rather exposes as a phantasm as it interferes with identifying operations such as the issuing of passports.

2 Statelessness and Storytelling: B. Traven's Yorikke

Having looked at Sterne's text from this perspective, it seems not altogether surprising that the name Yorick reappears once more in a piece of literature that explicitly deals with passports – or rather the problems that arise when people do not have any. After a somewhat large leap skipping the nineteenth century, which for different reasons was not primarily a century of passports, I will now focus on the interwar period in Europe, which actually is heavily marked by a tightening of passport regulations and the debates about them.

---

12 Valentin Groebner, "Der Schein der Person. Bescheinigung und Evidenz," in *Quel Corps? Eine Frage der Repräsentation*, ed. Hans Belting, Dietmar Kamper, and Martin Schulz (Munich: Fink, 2002), 319.

One of the most impressive literary texts reflecting the changes brought about by the new rule that everybody, not only travelers or other people crossing borders, must possess a passport is B. Traven's novel *The Deathship*, which first came out in German in 1926. As a reminder, B. Traven is not a surname with the abbreviation of a first name, but rather a pseudonym for a writer who has succeeded in carefully masking his real identity by using different names (B. Traven can also be read as "be Traven") – others were Ret Marut, Otto Feige, Traven Torsvan, Hal Croves. This lifelong playing with identities was facilitated by the fact that he had been involved in revolutionary activities as a journalist supporting the council republic in Munich at the end of World War I and was politically persecuted afterwards, changing countries of residence several times. His life, or rather the mysterious aura surrounding it, has fascinated many literary historians who finally seem to have concluded their detective work by finding out that his real name was in fact Otto Feige, the others aliases assuming "fake" identities.[13]

For the purpose of this chapter, it does not matter so much who the author of *The Deathship* and other successful stories of their time really was. Instead, what is of interest here is the subversive character of playing with identities which is very much in accordance with the concerns articulated in the novel. The novel has three parts: in the first we get to know the protagonist, a young sailor who misses his ship after a shore leave in Antwerp. With the ship he has lost not only his workplace but also his sailor's card, which is the only identification paper he ever possessed. At first, he – like Sterne's protagonist – takes it very lightly, as he is confident to be able to find a new ship soon. However, when it turns out that after the war the world has changed dramatically and that without an identity document he cannot get work or a residence permit anywhere, he slowly realizes his fatal situation. Even though he claims to be an American citizen, the American consul refuses to do anything for him because he cannot prove his national identity. No country can rightfully grant him residency, which is why he is constantly deported and repeatedly finds himself in police detention. Everywhere he is exposed to the same interrogation:

> "Where do you have your sailor's card?"
> "I have lost it."
> "Have you got a passport?"
> "No."
> "Citizen paper?"
> "Never had any."[14]

---

[13] Jan-Christoph Hauschild, *B. Traven – Die unbekannten Jahre* (Vienna, New York: Springer, 2012).
[14] (Translation mine, D.B.) B. Traven, *Das Totenschiff* (Hamburg: Rowohlt, 1954), 23.

As a *sans-papier* he is treated everywhere like a criminal and deprived of any possibility to get back into "normal society." In fact, because there is no way back and no possible place for him in the societies of the nation states, his status in a certain sense is worse than that of a criminal for whom there are at least rules and "dwelling" places like prisons. If Hannah Arendt has analyzed the problem of statelessness as a structural outcome of the reinforcement of the model of the nation state in large parts also of Eastern Europe after the war, it is Traven's novel that most acutely portrays the consequences of this development by means of literature.[15]

In the second part of *The Deathship*, the endlessly repeated deportations from one European state to the next, which already conflate movement with stagnation,[16] come to an end as the protagonist enters a new space and the story changes its scene. In many ways, however, the new space is also the old, since on the ship he is finally admitted to are only seamen like him who do not have appropriate papers and have lost all civil rights. Even before he enters this "deathship," the protagonist had felt like a nobody and had described his state as that of a man who is socially dead.[17] Now he joins a community of outlaws who do not belong anywhere, are not protected by any government, and in case of death not missed by anybody, which means that they are totally at the disposal of the capitalist forces for which "deathships" present an ideal opportunity for cheap, slave-like laborers. The name of this ship, however, is "Yorikke," the feminine version of Yorick and, as such, a clear intertextual reference to Sterne and Shakespeare.[18] It is described as a frightfully decrepit vessel which does not operate under any national flag. Although it is definitely not a place chosen voluntarily by any of the seamen, and although they often curse life there as hell, they nevertheless establish close ties with it. By addressing the *Yorikke* as a woman, the narrator makes

---

15 For this connection see Burkhardt Wolf, "Es gibt keine Totenschiffe. B. Traven's Sea Change," in *DVjs* [Deutsche Vierteljahrsschrift für Literaturwissenschaft und Geistesgeschichte] 80, no. 3 (2006): 435–55; Doerte Bischoff, "Kriegszustand: Logiken des Militärischen und die Macht der Pässe in literarischen Reflexionen über Staatsbürgerschaft seit 1918," *Exilforschung* 36 (2018): Ausgeschlossen. Staatsbürgerschaft, Staatenlose und Exil, ed. Doerte Bischoff and Miriam Rürup, 165–83.
16 This aspect is stressed by Jesper Gulddal, "Passport Plats: B. Traven's *Das Totenschiff* and the Chronotope of Movement Control," *German Life and Letters* 66, no. 3 (2013): 292–307.
17 Traven, *Das Totenschiff*, 122.
18 This connection has been frequently noted in research literature, see e.g., Ernst-Ullrich Pinkert, "Travens Mär vom 'einfachen Erzählen.' Zu den intertextuellen Bezügen in dem Roman *Das Totenschiff*," in *B. Travens Erzählwerk in der Konstellation von Sprachen und Kulturen*, ed. Günter Dammann (Würzburg: Königshausen & Neumann, 2005), 23–35. However, possible implications of the intertextual references have rarely been explored.

clear that this ship is the only companion for those who can neither get married nor have a family because they are not "legal."

At the end of the second part, the *Yorikke* is explicitly called a lover whose fate resembles that of the narrator. Thus, although the protagonist of this novel is not directly called "Yorick," he is closely associated with the personified vessel of that name, which also brings out his own status as a disposable thing rather than a living human being. As a deathship, the *Yorikke* is a floating space where those who do not appear in any official register and who in a broader sense cannot be represented by the normative discourses on citizenship and belonging reside. By focusing on them and their stories, the novel in a way revives the dead by making them part of a narrative and thus rewriting them into the cultural knowledge and memory. Here it resembles Sterne's text which, by introducing Shakespeare and the figure of the jester (who is present on stage there as a skull) into the context of a French regime of passports and identification, subverts their impact. Although in Travens's novel the name of the protagonist is mentioned several times at the beginning as "Gerard Gales," other names, origins, and nationalities that he invents for himself play an increasing role in the course of the narrative.[19] This underscores the notion that his "real" name no longer matters, whereas his invented identities can sometimes be convenient if adjusted to a specific situation. In fact, especially in the first part of the book Gales, who registers all the grotesque incidents in police stations and consulates from a seemingly naïve perspective, appears as a kind of jester or picaresque figure.[20] By reproducing the operations of the administrative complex and the effects it has for individuals in his narrative he brings out their absurdities. That his true name gives way to invented identities also corresponds to a self-reflexive episode in the first part of the book where the protagonist is first introduced as a storyteller. When the destitute young man meets an obviously wealthy American couple on the street, he introduces himself telling them a fictive story. This proves to be so interesting and entertaining – for the American the question if it is a true story is not relevant, he praises the narrator for being a "true artist" – that the man rewards him with a considerable tip. The narrator, for whom a little money at this point is also a matter of survival, perceives it as his first earning by storytelling. This little episode reflects the structure of the novel as a whole in that an imaginative narration of supposedly literary quality

---

19 Pinkert suggests that Gales's decision not to reveal his real name on the *Yorikke* should be read as a direct intertextual reference to the passage in Sterne where Yorick confides to the reader that he doesn't like to be identified by his name in public. Pinkert, "Travens Mär," 30.
20 The protagonist has been read as a picaro, the ship as a ship-of-fools, however without reference to Sterne as intertext by Thorsten Czechanowsky, "Die Irrfahrt als Grenzerfahrung. Überlegungen zur Metaphorik der Grenze in B. Travens Roman *Das Totenschiff*," *mauerschau* 1 (2008): 47–58.

appears as a life-saving procedure under the condition of bureaucratic identification, exclusion, and confinement.

This structure is taken up again at the end of the novel when the narrator is the only survivor of an organized shipwrecking involving another deathship in which he and others one day find themselves. The shipwrecking with the calculated deaths of most of the crew is no coincidence but staged by the shipping company for insurance fraud. This is presented as the ultimate consequence of a system that produces people situated outside any law who can then be abused until their deaths. That the story of *The Deathship* – or rather of the phenomenon of deathships in general – can be told at all depends on an unlikely case of survival. The existence of the narration of *The Deathship*, however, is marked as precisely this kind of survivor's story which is framed by the address of a person as "Sir" without further identifying him. It could be a reference to the American in the story who positively reacts to the invented life-story of the paperless sailor. But it could also be a reference to one of the American consuls in different European countries who usually do not listen to individual stories but reduce every person to a paper document and set of normalized and registered information. Thus, the precarious state of the narration that aims at raising attention to the excluded and at questioning prevailing identification practices is underscored. However, by entangling the narrative with famous intertexts such as Sterne's *Sentimental Journey* or Dante's *Inferno*, the literary treatment of paper existences here again evokes at least two possible readings. While the notion of a "man cut of cardboard,"[21] that is, a person reduced to paperwork, demonstrates the mortifying effects of exclusive national passport regulations, interweavings with texts from different times and languages also open up alternative spaces of imagination and thinking concerning identity formation.

3 Transference and Adaption: Passports in Remarque's Exile Novels

In the literature of exile during and after the Nazi era the topic of passports and visa stamps as existential prerequisites to cross borders and reach safe countries of refuge becomes – not surprisingly – again very prominent. The experience that the life of a person depends on a mere piece of paper, which in decisive moments must bear the correct seals, is expressed in numerous different ways in these

---

21 Traven, *Das Totenschiff*, 25, 47.

texts. Typically, as in the case of Erich Maria Remarque, the literary treatment of passports and citizenship in times of their being a means of social control and exclusion by a totalitarian regime relies on biographical experiences. Remarque, who as a critic of national socialism and author of the famous anti-war novel *All Quiet on the Western Front* (1929) had attracted the rage of the fascists already before their coming to power, had moved to Switzerland in 1931 and, after his expatriation by the Nazis in 1938, went to the United States in 1939 where eight years later he was granted citizenship. In his first novel written in European and American exile, *Flotsam*,[22] which was first published in sequences in an American journal (*Collier's Weekly*, 1939) and later appeared in German under the title *Liebe deinen Nächsten* with the exiled publishing company Bermann Fischer in Stockholm in 1941, the fate of refugees resembles in many ways that of the *sans-papiers* depicted in Traven's novel. Unlike Gales, the protagonists here once had valid passports for the country of their birth, but after having been expatriated as Jews or political dissidents by the Nazis, they are now stateless and likewise without identity papers. Their stalemate situation resulting from their being pushed off from one country to another is depicted as a paradoxical life on borders which constitute the only home ("*Heimat*") left to them.[23] The fatal situation arises from the fact that for stateless refugees it is extremely difficult to enter and stay in another country since every national state normally grants rights of residence only to its citizens. The following passage, in which the student Ludwig Kern who is seized in Switzerland without a passport after having crossed the border illegally, shows the consequences:

> "Why didn't you report to the police after illegally crossing the border?" [the judge] asked. "Then I'd had been put straight out of the country again," Kern answered wearily. ... The judge shrugged. "I cannot help you. It is my duty to sentence you. ...That is the law. We have it to protect our country from being flooded with refugees." "I know." ... "All I can do is to make a recommendation on your behalf to the Superior Court that you be given detention and not a prison sentence. ... it is of great importance for full civil rights. If you are simply placed in detention you will have no prison records." ... Kern looked for a while at the good-natured, unsuspecting man. "Full civil rights..." he said then. "Full civil rights. What would I do with them? ... I am a shadow, a ghost, a dead man in the eyes of society. ...We no longer exist as far as Germany is concerned. And for the rest of the world we exist only as prey for the police."[24]

---

22 As a book it was published under the same title in 1941 in the United States by Little, Brown and Company. In the same year a screen adaption directed by John Cromwell came out with the title *So Ends Our Night*.
23 Erich Maria Remarque, *Liebe Deinen Nächsten* (Frankfurt am Main., Berlin, Vienna: Ullstein, 1974), 180.
24 (Translation mine, D.B.) Remarque, *Liebe Deinen Nächsten*, 254.

Although the Swiss judge suddenly becomes aware of the enormity of the problem that far exceeds the individual case in front of him, he cannot do anything as long as there are no supranational passport regulations, such as by the League of Nations.

However, another narrative thread around the figure of the political exile Josef Steiner, whom Kern meets at the beginning as a fellow *sans-papier* in Austrian police detention, develops in a different direction. Instead of lamenting his fate and trying to get on without papers, Steiner successfully attempts to get a false passport. A Russian acquaintance in a somewhat macabre business-like manner advises him to buy a foreign passport: "I'd like to recommend the dead Austrian. There are Rumanians, too, and they are cheaper. But who knows how to speak Rumanian?"[25] After Steiner has purchased the passport, which is issued to a worker called Johann Huber from Graz and has his own photograph inserted, he is full of satisfaction. Looking at the passport with his new identity, he addresses its former holder: "You are dead ... but your passport lives and is valid for the administration. I, Josef Steiner, am alive; but without a passport I am dead for the officials. He laughed. Let's switch, Johann Huber! Give me your paper life and take my paperless death! If the living do not help us, the dead will have to do it."[26] This implies the idea that in such times a piece of paper cannot only function as a "social weapon by which one may kill men without any bloodshed,"[27] as Hannah Arendt once put it, but that it can in fact also be used to give new life to an otherwise practically dead person. Both possibilities underscore the tight relationship between human existence and paper document. There only seems to be one way to regain agency: circumventing the all-encompassing power of state-controlled identification papers by appropriating and imitating them for one's own purposes.[28]

In *The Night in Lisbon*, a later novel by Remarque, published in 1962, the motif of surviving in exile with the passport of a stranger is taken up. There the protagonist explicitly admits that the new identity paper is much more than a mere instrument to achieve certain aims: it actually changes the ways he conceives of himself and the world. In fact, the new name has already inscribed itself

---

25 Ibid., 88.
26 Ibid., 93.
27 Hannah Arendt, "We Refugees," in *Altogether Elsewhere. Writers on Exile*, ed. Marc Robinson (Boston, London: Faber & Faber, 1994), 118.
28 For the connection of passport forgery and art see Burcu Dogramaci, "Die Kunst der Passfälschung: Exil, Flucht und Strategien der Grenzüberschreitung," *Exilforschung* 36 (2018): Ausgeschlossen. Staatsbürgerschaft, Staatenlösigkeit und Exil, ed. Doerte Bischoff and Miriam Rürup, 184–209.

into his kind of movement across borders: passing borders as (Josef) Schwarz (black) in German means to cross them illegally. It also connects him to other people with different origins and national affiliations who have been in the possession of the passport before and will be after him (he passes the passport on to a young refugee on his way to Mexico at the end), thus again subverting the idea of clear national distinctions and unambiguous identification.[29] Unlike *Flotsam*, the novel *The Night in Lisbon* is presented by a narrating I, however, neither of the two novels foreground self-reflexive moments which would connect the passport stories to the respective narratives themselves and, with that, to the possibilities of literature as such.

4 Mortification and Writing On: The Powers of Paper in Seghers's *Transit*

This is altogether different in Anna Seghers's seminal novel *Transit* – written while Seghers herself was fleeing from the Nazis through France and finally concluded in Mexican exile – in which some of the constellations described resonate in a complex narrative setting. At the beginning, the protagonist is introduced as an emigrant sitting in a pizzeria in Marseille with another refugee with whom he shares his story – which apparently is also the story we read. Remarkably throughout the novel we do not get to know his original name.[30] This corresponds with the fact that we hardly learn anything about his life before the time of the Nazis. If he himself feels a loss, he can no longer identify (with) what exactly has been lost.[31] The experiences that have most strongly shaped his life since then are connected to his time as a detainee in different camps and on his flight. His youth has all gone wrong, as he once says.[32] He has a feeling of emptiness, without relations with his past or commitments for the future, thus he really embodies the

---

[29] This aspect is highlighted by Charlton Payne, "Der Pass zwischen Dingwanderung und Identitätsübertragung in Remarques' *Die Nacht von Lissabon*," *Exilforschung* 31 (2013): Dinge des Exils, ed. Doerte Bischoff and Joachim Schlör, 343–54. Payne concludes here that the people who find themselves forcefully displaced have to invent alternative networks of circulation in order to survive. Remarque's novel, it is further suggested, foregrounds a non-genealogical passing on of an identity document which thus brings about cosmopolitical connections.
[30] Anna Seghers, *Transit* (Berlin: Aufbau, 2001), 32. "My own name never entered the picture." English translation cited after Anna Seghers, *Transit* (New York: New York Review of Books, 2013), 27.
[31] Seghers, *Transit*, 41.
[32] Ibid., 88.

flotsam giving the title to Remarque's book in English. When names play a role in connection with his story, they are alien names that he assumes more or less accidentally in the course of the events. One name – we don't even get to know which one it is – he invents when checking into a hotel in Paris, another one, Seidler, he receives after an acquainted French family has managed to get him a refugee certificate somebody else had just returned, obviously after having received "a better set of documents."[33] "Seidler was the name of the man whose second-best certificate ended up being a better one for me. ... We looked up Seidler's village in a school atlas and concluded from its location that, fortunately for me, the village along with the registry of its inhabitants, had probably been burned to the ground."[34] Here a pattern can be discerned governing the narration: identification documents, which ensure getting on and surviving in a situation of persecution, are structurally connected to catastrophic events implying loss and destruction. Although Seidler's certificate is not directly connected with the burning of his village, its subversive transmission to another person seems to function better the less the paper refers to any existing place and person, developing a life of its own instead.

Later in the book, a file described as full of the best and useful documents appears to be the file of a dead person.[35] This obviously has two opposing implications: first, it indicates that the state bureaucracy has established a highly self-referential and self-fulfilling system in which human beings are substituted by serialized card files and the related documents. Second, it also implies that the means to intervene must also rely on paper – and its potential to be reproduced, circulated or "creatively" appropriated. As long as – as in Traven's dystopian narration – there is a clear-cut distinction between those who have passports and those who do not, the mortifying effects of passports – as Hannah Arendt and Remarque note – do not really become visible because those without are socially dead and therefore, like the crew of the *Yorikke*, invisible for "normal people." As soon as this line between passport holders and *sans-papiers* however is blurred, the deathly nature of exclusionary effects of a certain kind of passport regime comes to the fore.

In Seghers's novel this becomes clear when yet another name is introduced with which the narrator in the course of the events becomes associated. Like in Remarque's novels it is the name of a dead person – whereby his death is explicitly connected with the events of the Nazi persecution. The writer Weidel – like the

---

33 Seghers, *Transit*, 33 (English version).
34 Ibid.
35 Seghers, *Transit*, 103.

historical Ernst Weiß – had killed himself in a hotel in Paris when the Germans entered the city and he lost any hope (a similar story is, of course, that of Walter Benjamin who committed suicide as a refugee close to the French-Spanish border when he heard of new visa regulations in Fascist Spain). Although the narrator who is given the suitcase of the deceased does not pretend to be Weidel, he is mistakenly identified with him when he appears at the Mexican consulate in Marseille. He goes there because in Weidel's suitcase he found letters indicating that he has a visa to Mexico and that his separated wife to whom he could hand over Weidel's belongings, might also come there. While all other refugees in the cafés and consulates in Marseille are anxiously waiting for paper documents to get out of Europe as soon as possible, the narrator himself seems uninterested and even bored by the monotony of the visa "ceremonies" and the stories of fellow emigrants who seem to circle around the same issues all the time and thus have lost any individual character. It is this attitude which puts him in a position, however, to observe and register what is happening from a distance seemingly without being existentially involved.

> I suddenly felt a tiny degree of superiority over the official. Had Weidel still been alive, the official would have had the advantage over him; he would have looked right through him, maybe even would have been amused by him. But now watching the official carefully study the file with a rather excessive attention, I was the one who was amused. A specter among the visa applicants, a shadow who readily relinquished all his rights. I decided that instead of immediately explaining things to him, I would leave him for a moment to his useless activity.[36]

As a detached observer, the narrator watches and describes for the reader the absurdity and self-referred logic of the visa bureaucracy whose executives do not even realize that they are not dealing with living human beings any more. The administrative acts of identification have assumed the character of a religious ceremony, implying that death is no longer conceived as being in the hands of God but is produced and administered by the bureaucratic complex itself. This becomes especially explicit as the text cites a liturgic formula, part of Christian funeral ceremonies, and transposes it into the very worldly context of visa administration: "I stared at the papers on the desk, which were the last remains of the dead man. Visa to visa, paper to paper, file to file. In perfect and confident hope."[37]

---

[36] Seghers, *Transit*, 48 (English version).
[37] Translation mine (in the published English edition this aspect is neutralized in the translation as "file by file"). For the German version see Seghers, *Transit*, 56: "Ich starrte auf die Papiere

By implicitly analyzing this logic, the narrator – and with him the narrative – does not succumb to it but opens up a more distanced perspective. In fact, as the narrator does not vehemently contradict the official's assumption that he is Weidel, a name the official supposes to be the *nom de plume* for Seidler, he does finally get involved in the Weidel case. However, as he is not just eager to use (or misuse) this name for himself, he becomes affected by the name and life of the dead man in very different ways. It is not only that he develops a relationship with Marie, Weidel's former wife who still hopes to find him in Marseille, the perhaps most important impulse for him to cling to Weidel's suitcase, his belongings, his papers and in fact his life-story, is an experience he has when first opening his suitcase in the hotel in Paris. It contains, as he notices with surprise, "little more than paper."[38] When, out of curiosity, he starts reading it, he is drawn into a story told with such vividness that he gets completely absorbed by it following the actions and delusions of the characters involved including one in which he recognizes himself. Reading, which for the narrator who admits to never have read a book to the end before, is an altogether new and exciting experience. It obviously implies an act of identification and, at the same time, a distanced, analytical perspective which enables the reader to recognize himself and the conditions of the world around him from a new angle. However, the manuscript of the dead writer abruptly ends, and the protagonist is left alone with an unfinished story cut off at the point when the Germans enter Paris. Together with two letters he also finds in the suitcase, this experience – which is also explicitly marked as an encounter with the rich and moving quality of his mother-tongue quite different from what Nazi propaganda had made of it – induces him to turn to the consulate and pursue the "Weidel case" on his own terms.

Thus the novel very artfully interweaves two kinds of papers: identification documents controlled by national administrations on the one hand, and a literary manuscript reflecting on the impact of exclusive categorization and totalitarian control on the individual, on the other. By somehow inheriting Weidel's papers (in both senses of the word), the narrator is confronted with a responsibility: as the only witness to the death of the writer and the only reader of his unfinished manuscript, he now appears as the only one left to tell his story and to remember the conditions of his death. Thus the narrative of *Transit*, as such, appears as the redemption of this responsibility to take up the threat of narration in times of catastrophic destruction, persecution, and death. That the narrator

---

auf dem Schreibtisch, die von dem Toten übrig waren! Visa zu Visa, Papier zu Papier, Dossier zu Dossier. In vollkommener und gewisser Hoffnung."
38 Seghers, *Transit* (English version), 20.

remains without clear identity and just assumes the name of a dead person accentuates the fact that his story is marked by deep caesurae and breaks. These also are reflected as breaks with tradition – or even civilization – as they imply the absorption and destruction of religious and cultural identification practices by the totalizing momentum of modern bureaucracy. In a certain way, Seghers' narrator is alive and dead at the same time. Like Traven's narrator, he appears as a survivor who bears witness to the lives of those who have been excluded from the social sphere and from human life altogether. By reading the narrator's account of reading Weidel, however, and by taking part in his getting involved in the deathly mechanisms of identification practices as well as his attempts "to tell the whole story. ... 'From the beginning',"[39] the readers themselves are also implicated in the story. Because it is marked by caesurae and breaks and cannot be told by those who experienced it and died, it is our story with which we are invited to identify as well.

5 Asylum Laws and the Invention of Life Stories: Abbas Khider's *A Slap in the Face*

If one keeps in mind that the passport is originally a travel document and a means of border control, it is evident that its function is challenged especially by mass migration and exile, which might have been provoked by restrictive passport regimes in the first place. If this is documented in German exile literature of the Nazi-period, as has been shown above with respect to Remarque and Seghers – and one could add other authors such as Joseph Roth, Franz Werfel, Bertolt Brecht, Hans Natonek, Bruno Frank, Theodor Balk or Hans Sahl – it is also a central theme in contemporary German literature reflecting exile in, and migration into, Germany. That this is not an entirely new phenomenon in the history of literature in German but appears in many ways entangled with historical exile literature is reflected in the reappearance of motifs, narrative constellations, and explicit references within the contemporary texts themselves. It is also reflected in the literary field where awards in memory of famous writers of exile are increasingly given to writers of a non-German background. In 2013, Abbas Khider, who was born in Iraq in 1973 and has been living in Germany since the year 2000, was awarded the Hilde Domin Prize for "Literature in Exile." In his acceptance speech he explicitly underscored the potential of literature to cross national borders: "In

---

39 Seghers, *Transit* (English version), 5.

literature you don't need a visa, a residence permit or a citizenship to arrive."⁴⁰ From this it cannot be inferred, however, that identity documents are not an issue in his novels. Quite the contrary: already in his first novel *Der falsche Inder* (The False Indian), which depicts the flight and odyssey of a young Iraqi through different countries around the Mediterranean Sea, passport controls seem to accompany the refugee's routes all along. As in many of the historical exile texts, the question of their authenticity or forgery has completely given way to the question if they are useful in a certain situation or not. Thus, to move on as a refugee means to adjust to the respective rules of different countries and try to avail oneself of the "correct" papers. That "friends," smugglers, and forgers are involved, is the first lesson a refugee has to learn. This is presented as standard knowledge among exiles in Germany also in Khider's recent (fourth) novel *Ohrfeige* ("box on the ear," also meaning: slap in the face, in a metaphorical sense). "In exile many peculiar problems and mysteries arise which normal people could never imagine. Difficulties of all kinds befall you like natural catastrophes. We are completely exposed to them. To survive and not to become totally insane, we need the mediators, the Mafiosi, the greedy, the smugglers, the corrupt policemen and officials, we need all the bloodsuckers who want to profit from our situation. We need them much more than all the people working for AMNESTY INTERNATIONAL together."⁴¹ Thus, in the midst of the "normal world" of those with correct citizenship and papers live the exiles (widely unnoticed by the former), with a completely different conception of reality: with the permanent threat of police controls and detention, a city like Munich appears like a huge prison. Obviously, freedom and freedom of movement is not granted to everyone, but even in times of intensified global movement of goods and information, the free movement of people, to a large extent, still depends on where somebody happens to be born.

If the German asylum legislation is partly a heritage of this country's history of violent persecution and expulsion in the twentieth century, the bureaucratic ways to categorize and register people haven't changed much. This at least is suggested by the text which presents Germany as a country virtually buried under paragraphs and rules and administered by bureaucrats who usually are not interested in human beings but only in the mindless execution of paragraphs. One of these clerks is "Frau Schulz" who is responsible for Karim, the protagonist, in the foreigners' registration office. In his narrative, he describes her as one of those who decide the way in which he may exist. Entrenched behind her

---

40 https://www.heidelberg.de/hd,Lde/HD/service/18_09_2013+Hilde_Domin_Preis+2013 +fuer+Abbas+Khider_.html.
41 (Translation mine, D.B.) Abbas Khider, *Ohrfeige* (Munich: Hanser, 2016), 28.

computer screen and protected by mountains of files she fidgets about in the air with her sharp pen as if she wanted to stab flies."[42] This description recalls a very similar passage in Traven's *Deathship* where the protagonist observes that the officials in the consulates constantly play with their pencils, for instance by tapping them on the desk "as if they wanted to nail down a word with every tap."[43] Against this attitude of fixing creatures and language to only one controllable meaning – which practically amounts to killing them – the text develops a different relation between language and identity. After Karim has been involuntarily stranded in Germany, he is given a Green identity card and sent to a home for asylum seekers where he meets several other refugees who give him important advice: "if you want to be stuck here for the rest of your life, then tell them the truth. ... I tell you something: you have to invent a completely new life story for yourself."[44] One of them, Salim, recalls having once made up a highly adventurous story in court, so that, "After my trial I seriously considered becoming a writer."[45] The connection between the confining situation of the refugee vis-à-vis the asylum laws and the impulse for literary imagination is also taken up in the frame of the novel itself. In the opening scene Karim has just tied Frau Schulz to her office chair and gagged and given her the box on the ear which lends the book its title. Thus she is silenced, which finally gives him the opportunity to speak and tell his story. Ironically, before he starts his narration, he lights himself a special cigarette: "I sit opposite her on the visitor's chair, take a piece of paper from her desk, mix some hash into my tobacco and draw myself a cigarette. I light it and inhale deeply. With relish. ... I enjoy the lightly burning pain in my chest. I feel as alive as I haven't felt for a long time."[46]

Here the abusive use of bureaucratic paperwork opens up new ways of perceiving reality – and of transforming it imaginatively. In fact, at the end of the story, the motif of Karim smoking a joint is taken up again. Salim wakes Karim, who has been sleeping in his apartment, from a hash dream, and tells him to get ready for the smuggler who will get him out of Germany. There is no Frau Schulz anywhere, the whole story turns out to be imagination. Considering this framing of the whole "real life story," Karim appears as a prototypical unreliable narrator. This, however, does not mean that we are to dismiss everything he narrates as not true. Instead, we are confronted with the fact that realities and life stories are constructs following certain rules and possibilities of what can and cannot be

---

42 Khider, *Ohrfeige*, 11.
43 Traven, *Totenschiff*, 23, 45.
44 Khider, *Ohrfeige*, 69.
45 Ibid., 73.
46 Ibid., 9.

expressed. These constructs are highly dependent on political, economic and legal discourses and constellations and pertain to only specific people and perspectives. Life itself cannot be captured by any narrative – especially in contexts of violence, persecution, and exile.

This is reflected in two of the stories told within Karim's story. One is about a fellow student who at school in Baghdad had dared to make fun of Saddam Hussein. He was then arrested and never heard from again. Karim presents the story of the defiant boy as his own in face of the German asylum officials – only with a happy end that he escaped seizure. Thus the story he tells about himself is not a false story, it did happen, but the one who experienced it cannot tell it anymore. To understand why Karim fled his country, to understand the whole situation of thousands of asylum seekers, combined, enriched, and transposed stories like this one have to be told. In the literary context they assume a higher reality than the mere reconstruction of single life stories could have. That the latter is always prone to be told and received according to certain prevailing narrative concepts and expectations is reflected in the second internal story. It tells about Hayat, a beautiful, deaf-mute girl who had been Karim's childhood friend in his home town. One day when she had grown into a teenager she is lured into a car by three men who, after raping and killing her, abandon her corpse like a piece of garbage. Karim admits that it is not easy for him to tell this story, for he is deeply traumatized by it. He even relates his own constant uneasiness, his lack of belonging, to this incident at the threshold of his own transition to adulthood. His story thus cannot be any other coming-of-age story, instead he tells about a monstrosity that characterizes his adult body and makes it impossible to perceive him according to the usual categories. Thus he confides to the reader (and to Frau Schulz who definitely would not have a category for him) that he has grown breasts indicating his intense identification with the murdered girl whom he cannot forget. This is certainly a different kind of identification: it transcends borders – here borders of gender – and keeps the killed ones alive in one's compassionate imagination. This kind of identification is also explicitly associated with literature in the text: for her thirteenth birthday, Karim had given Hayat a book she cannot read because she is not allowed to go to school. But she identifies with the girl on the cover who seems to open new spaces and realities – *Alice in Wonderland*. Hayat is not any name, it is the Arabic word for "life" which, as the narrator reflects, has also been adopted by the Turkish language. As a word it had the capacity to cross borders while the reality of "Hayat," life "itself" continues to be defiled in so many places of the world.

The story of Hayat, the deaf-mute girl, does not necessarily have to be true, nor is the narrator's secret about his monstrous body of which he is ashamed, necessarily the "true story" for him to tell when he can finally raise his voice in the asylum office. However, they show that literature can give a face and a story to those who have been murdered and silenced – not only by real dictators, but also by the power of categorizing who is in and who is out and by the same discourses in which we all construct our truths and stories. It also shows that the attempt to grant asylum according to certain categories of life-stories necessarily misses the pluralities, contradictions, and dynamic qualities of life and that it cannot, of course, account for the traumatic voids and breaks which define the life stories of so many refugees.

6 Conclusion

Literary texts centering on passports reveal the effects of identification practices which, in modernity, tie the individual to a political regime and its economies of control and belonging. By focusing on those who are excluded from certain or all kinds of citizenship – illegal travelers, outlaws, exiles, and asylum seekers – they shed light on the semiological and bureaucratic operations which ensure the self-preservation of the nation state.[47] The remarkable preoccupation with passports and identity papers that can be discerned in literature from the eighteenth century until the present shows that questions of alternative identifications in and by literature are not necessarily developed in sharp contrast to the functioning of state regulated identity regimes. Instead, it is the playful convergence of identity paper and literary manuscript or book, the performance of their shared features, which typically becomes the focal point for narrative explorations of identity. By revealing processes of reading and transformative adaptation as being involved in identifying operations the texts also bring out associations and intertextual networks which go beyond specific historical or biographical instances, thereby subverting national identification. That the protagonists' name and identity are often disseminated by a plurality of names and by the blurring of fact and fiction does not imply a general arbitrariness but appears as a means to subvert the determining power of identification. Instead, a different mode of literary identification as an ongoing process without definite reference or closure is enacted which does not aspire to represent and control life but aims at imaginatively recollecting and reviving what has been excluded by normative denotations.

---

[47] This perspective, observing the "[g]atherings of exiles, and émigrés and refugees" at the frontiers, is also the one Bhabha describes as the starting point of his analyses of the nation from its margins. Homi K. Bhabha, *The Location of Culture* (London, New York: Routledge, 1994), 139.

Bibliography

Arendt, Hannah. "We Refugees." In *Altogether Elsewhere. Writers on Exile*. Edited by Marc Robinson, 110–119. Boston, London: Faber & Faber, 1994.
Bhabha, Homi K. *The Location of Culture*. London, New York: Routledge, 1994.
Bischoff, Doerte. "Kriegszustand: Logiken des Militärischen und die Macht der Pässe in literarischen Reflexionen über Staatsbürgerschaft seit 1918." *Exilforschung* 36 (2018): 165–183. Ausgeschlossen. Staatsbürgerschaft, Staatenlose und Exil. Edited by Doerte Bischoff and Miriam Rürup,
Cash, Arthur. *Lawrence Sterne. The Later Years*. London, New York: Methuen, 1986.
Czechanowsky, Thorsten. "Die Irrfahrt als Grenzerfahrung. Überlegungen zur Metaphorik der Grenze in B. Travens Roman *Das Totenschiff*." *mauerschau* 1 (2008): 47–58.
Dogramaci, Burcu. "Die Kunst der Passfälschung: Exil, Flucht und Strategien der Grenzüberschreitung." *Exilforschung* 36 (2018): 184–209. Ausgeschlossen. Staatsbürgerschaft, Staatenlosigkeit und Exil. Edited by Doerte Bischoff and Miriam Rürup.
Fahrmeir, Andreas. *Citizenship: The Rise and Fall of a Modern Concept*. New Haven, London: Yale University Press, 2007.
Groebner, Valentin. "Der Schein der Person. Bescheinigung und Evidenz." In *Quel Corps? Eine Frage der Repräsentation*. Edited by Hans Belting, Dietmar Kamper, and Martin Schulz, 309–323. Munich: Fink, 2002.
Gulddal, Jesper. "Passport Plats: B. Traven's *Das Totenschiff* and the Chronotope of Movement Control." *German Life and Letters* 66, no. 3 (2013): 292–307.
Gulddal, Jesper. "Porous Borders: The Passport as an Access Metaphor in Laurence Sterne's *A Sentimental Journey*." *Symploke* 25, nos. 1–2 (2017): 43–59.
Hauschild, Jan-Christoph. *B. Traven – Die unbekannten Jahre*. Vienna, New York: Springer, 2012.
Hilde Domin Preis 2013 für Abbas Khider, https://www.heidelberg.de/hd,Lde/HD/service/18_09_2013+Hilde_Domin_Preis+2013+fuer+Abbas+Khider_.html
Khider, Abbas. *Ohrfeige*. Munich: Hanser, 2016.
Payne, Charlton. "Der Pass zwischen Dingwanderung und Identitätsübertragung in Remarques *Die Nacht von Lissabon*." *Exilforschung* 31 (2013): 343–354. Dinge des Exils. Edited by Doerte Bischoff and Joachim Schlör.
Pinkert, Ernst-Ullrich. "Travens Mär vom 'einfachen Erzählen.' Zu den intertextuellen Bezügen in dem Roman *Das Totenschiff*." In *B. Travens Erzählwerk in der Konstellation von Sprachen und Kulturen*. Edited by Günter Dammann, 23–35. Würzburg: Königshausen & Neumann, 2005.
Reinhart, Wolfgang. *Die Unterwerfung der Welt. Globalgeschichte der europäischen Expansion 1415–2015*. Munich: Beck, 2016.
Remarque, Erich Maria. *Liebe Deinen Nächsten*. Frankfurt a. M., Berlin, Vienna: Ullstein, 1974.
Seghers, Anna. *Transit*. Berlin: Aufbau, 2001. English translation: *Transit*. New York: New York Review of Books, 2013.
Sterne, Lawrence. *A Sentimental Journey*. Oxford, New York: Oxford University Press, 1968.
Torpey, John. *The Invention of the Passport. Surveillance, Citizenship and the State*. Cambridge: Cambridge University Press, 2000.
Traven, B. *Das Totenschiff*. Hamburg: Rowohlt, 1954.
Wolf, Burkhardt. "'Es gibt keine Totenschiffe.' B. Traven's Sea Change." *DVjs* 80, no. 3 (2006): 435–455.

Judith Müller
Neither *Heimat* nor Exile: The Perception of Paris as a Historical Blind Spot in Three Israeli Novels

1 In Parallel

For the last three centuries, Paris has attracted writers as a city to live and write in. Among the French literary greats are Honoré de Balzac, Charles Baudelaire, Victor Hugo, Marcel Proust, Jean-Paul Sartre, and Simone de Beauvoir. Among the long list of foreign writers who came to the French metropolis by choice or as exiles are Heinrich Heine, Rainer Maria Rilke, F. Scott Fitzgerald, Gertrude Stein, Ernest Hemingway, as well as the émigré group of Russian poets called the *Paris Note*, which included writers like Georgii Adamovich, Anatolii Shteiger, and Lydiia Chervinskaia.[1] Apart from providing a physical home, the French metropolis has also long served as the object of literary fascination, and though Paris never regained the crucial role it played during *les années folles*, its image and appeal remain vibrant for many whereby the reflections of Parisian natives on the city are rather ambiguous compared to numerous outside perspectives.[2] Yet, for all of Paris's popularity in various literary circles, the city played a smaller role in the history of Modern Hebrew fiction and poetry before World War II, overshadowed by the great centers of Modern Hebrew literature such as Odessa, Warsaw, and Berlin. Nonetheless, in the 1920s, as the city's role and importance in the modernist and avant-garde art scene reached its apogee, Hebrew poets like Rachel Bluwstein, Zalman Shneur, David Vogel, Nathan Alterman, Avraham Shlonsky, and Yocheved Bat-Miriam, arriving from Eastern or Central Europe,

---

[1] Johannes Willms explains that the influence and importance of Paris has not been diminished over the centuries. Whereas cities like Florence, Prague, or Rome lost their influence over time that of Paris grew even stronger. The crucial factors for this development were the increasing centralization of France and the power of the monarchy, hence its peak in the nineteenth century when it became the informal capital of Europe. See Johannes Willms, *Paris. Hauptstadt Europas 1800–1914* (Munich: C.H. Beck, 2000), 8. For a deeper analysis of the conception of home and exile by Russian émigrés, see Maria Rubins, "The Diasporic Canon of Russian Poetry: The Case of the Paris Note," in *Twentieth-Century Russian Poetry. Reinventing the Canon*, ed. Katharine Hodgson, Joanne Shelton, and Alexandra Smith (Cambridge: Open Book Publishers, 2017).
[2] A point noted by several essays in the *Yale French Studies* special issue on *Paris in Literature*, edited by Joseph H. McMahon (New Haven: Yale University Press, 1964).

or from *Eretz Israel*, did write in and about the city on the banks of the Seine.³ Importantly, throughout the second half of the twentieth century, Israeli writers like Yehoshua Kenaz, Yaakov Shabtai, Moshe Ben-Shaul, Haim Gouri, and David Shahar have traveled to Paris to live, write, and find inspiration there. Although they did not always write specifically about Paris, their works are often filled with allusions to French culture, quotes from French poems, *chansons*, or characters who dream of studying in the City of Light.

In this chapter, I would like to explore how the longing for and imagination of Paris functions in three Israeli novels, A.B. Yehoshua's *Five Seasons* (מולכו, 1987), Judith Katzir's *Matisse Has the Sun in His Belly* (למאטיס יש את השמש בבטן, 1995), and Lizzie Doron's *On the Brink of Something Beautiful* (התחלה של משהו יפה, 2007), thus taking into consideration not only canonical authors of the generation mentioned above, but the next generation as well. These novels are, moreover, very diverse in their literary ambition, language and style as well as their narrative content, yet they all include short but pivotal episodes featuring a couple's journey to Paris. It is my intention here to explore how Paris serves as a space for desire and longing in the novels. As it will become clear, Yehoshua, Katzir, and Doron, through various means, describe Paris as the metropolis of European high culture embodying traditional French lifestyle and the ideal of the European "capital of the nineteenth century." In this depiction, Paris appears as if untouched by the historical events of the twentieth century. The characters in these three novels do not only travel to Paris to experience personal happiness – the sometimes kitschy motif of the City of Love is reflected in various ways in all three texts – but also to find a place in Europe that is seemingly devoid of the traumatic experience of the Holocaust, unlike Austria, Germany, or Poland. While all of the narrators mention other European places, and some characters even continue their voyage eastward (into the darkness of the past), Paris is still imagined as the ideal, Western European city. Given the breach of civilization, the extermination of European Jewry, and the Israeli perspective of the three novels, such a presentation of Paris tells a curious story. It is thus my intention here to elaborate on the city's depiction in relation to other European realms in the context of the characters' relation to Holocaust memory. In other words, it is my aim to discuss how Paris is imagined by the narrators and in so doing to point to how Paris, in these works, emerges as an ahistorical blind spot.

---

3 For further elaboration on this topic see Yuval Ben-Atiya, "תמונות פריזאיות.' דיוקן פריס בשירה העברית בין שתי מלחמות העולם" ("'Parisian Pictures.' The Image of Paris in Hebrew Poetry between the Two World Wars"), M.A. thesis, Tel Aviv University, 2002.

According to the textbook on ophthalmology by Fritz Hollwich, the blind spot is "an area of complete blindness in the visual field."[4] In a similar way, the narrators and characters in the chosen novels do not visualize European Jewish history, and especially the Holocaust, when directing their gaze to Paris. This is surprising since Paris is the very opposite of an ahistorical place. Only typing "Paris" and "Memory" into a search engine reveals pages of Holocaust-related memorials and ceremonies in and around the French capital. Even when leaving the Nazi occupation and the deportation of Parisian and French Jews aside, Paris abounds with *lieux de mémoire* of French history, such as the Arc de Triomphe and the Bastille, to name but two. Moreover, the city itself is listed in the collection of Pierre Nora as a *lieu de mémoire* under the category "identifications," meaning that Paris shapes French identity and memory of the society and nation.[5] Furthermore, memory also plays a crucial role when looking at Paris from a non-French perspective. The volume *Paris, From the Image to Memory* (*Paris, de l'Image à la Mémoire*)[6] focuses on the perception of the city through the eyes of foreigners – mostly from neighboring European countries. In the introduction, Marie-Christine Kok Escalle writes that our image of Paris is formed by the memory we inherit: "This heritage is loaded with emotions that provoke admiration or love, anxiety or hostility; it is a 'memory' that links the place with a history and a symbolic meaning; it is a set of mental and emotional representations developed from images which are occasional or involve a longer period."[7] However, as it will become clear in the following pages, Paris is not only a place formed by memory, but it can turn into a realm where the latter is avoided and ignored. Phrased differently, the perception of Paris as outside the natural flow of time, leads to the depiction of an urban realm deprived of a tragic chapter in history. Unlike Rome and Jerusalem, Paris's reputation is less "eternal"; more saliently, the City of Light is neither an ancient city nor loaded with religious meaning. Furthermore, perceiving Paris as the European capital of the nineteenth century, an image that seems to persist one way or another, first and foremost focuses on

---

4 Fritz Hollwich, *Ophthalmology: A Short Textbook*, trans. Frederick C. Blodi, 2nd ed. (Stuttgart/ New York: Georg Thieme Verlag/Thieme Stratton, 1985), 7.
5 Pierre Nora, *Les lieux de mémoire* (Paris: Gallimard, 1997).
6 Marie-Christine Kok Escalle, ed., *Paris, de l'Image à la Mémoire: Représentations Artistiques, Littéraires, Socio-Politiques* (Amsterdam/Atlanta: Rodopi, 1997).
7 "Cet héritage est chargé d'émotions, que celles-ci provoquent l'admiration ou l'amour, l'angoisse ou l'hostilité, il est 'une mémoire' qui associe à un lieu une histoire et une signification symbolique; c'est une ensemble de représentations mentales et affectives élaboré à partir d'images, que celles-ci soient ponctuelles ou qu'elles concernent une durée plus longue." Marie-Christine Kok Escalle, Introduction to Escalle, *Paris: De l'Image à la Mémoire: Représentations Artistiques, Littéraires, Socio-Politiques*, 1.

Paris's cultural impact and the development of modernist art and literature and not political power – which France was already losing.

In undermining the status of Paris as a *lieu de mémoire*, or put another way, in perceiving an idealized urban realm that is a product of the lasting picture of a life-celebrating Parisian culture that emerged in the nineteenth-century capital of Europe and the modern avant-garde scene of the 1920s, the novels discussed here thus reveal a historical blind spot. The fact that all three were published from the 1980s onward, a time by which the Holocaust had become increasingly present in the Israeli public discourse, makes this blind spot all the more noticeable, and unlike places in Austria, Germany, and Poland, Paris serves as neither *Heimat* nor exile, but rather as an artificial vanishing point from reality. Marcy E. Schwartz describes a similar phenomenon in Latin American literature, where, when it comes to Europe, Spain and Portugal are mostly excluded from a positive depiction since they provoke memories of the dark time of colonialism. Paris, on the other hand, becomes, according to Schwartz, the European model of urbanness that influences the conceptualization of urban identity especially in, but also beyond literature.[8]

As I have mentioned above, Paris as such is obviously not ahistorical, nor is the perception I propose in this context necessarily modernistic. Nevertheless, first, a modern understanding of history is necessary to identify the lack of discussion on one particular chapter of history that is emotionally very close to the protagonists; and second, a specific modern concept plays a great role in exploring the city: strolling around. Thus, Paris's importance for modern literature lies not only in its ability to inspire or in the setting it offers; indeed, the very experience of observing and wandering its many streets and passages turns into a literary figure itself. One of the best-known representations of this activity is the concept as developed by Walter Benjamin, a thinker who also promoted the idea of Paris as the European capital of the nineteenth century. Interestingly, he explored this figure through Baudelaire, one of the key poets of the modernist Parisian literary scene. However, the *flâneur* was conceptualized over time from different perspectives and it could be argued that the fictional characters from the novels I am going to address are not *flâneurs* simply because they are visitors and tourists.[9] And still, strolling is important for how they perceive Parisian space.

---

[8] Marcy E. Schwartz, *Writing Paris: Urban Topographies of Desire in Contemporary Latin American Fiction* (Albany: State University of New York Press, 1999), 2–4.

[9] See Victoria E. Thompson, "Telling 'Spatial Stories': Urban Space and Bourgeois Identity in Early Nineteenth-Century Paris," *The Journal of Modern History* 75, no. 3 (2003): 523–56.

Although Michel de Certeau states that "to walk is to lack of place,"[10] the characters make the cityscape their own through walking, as will become clear later. But, although it seems as if they belong there for a certain amount of time in one way or another, the spiritual homeland, the imagined Paris, that is neither *Heimat* nor exile, evokes a vague longing and yearning, oftentimes for that which is not. De Certeau moreover elaborates on what he calls the *Wandersmänner* and their subjective use of the cityspace: "These practitioners make use of spaces that cannot be seen; their knowledge of them is as blind as that of lover's in each other's arms."[11] The blind spot that has been described above is caused by willingly not seeing or willingly not referring to a certain aspect that is part of the place's history, but by doing so, the place itself turns into a blind spot; it is characterized by the presence of an absence to put it in de Certeau's terms one more time.[12] He moreover emphasizes that the depiction depends on what unfolds before us: "Places are fragmentary and inward-turning histories, pasts that others are not allowed to read, accumulated times that can be unfolded but like stories held in reserve, remaining in an enigmatic state, symbolizations encysted in the pain or pleasure of the body."[13] This individual perception of space is what also constitutes a spiritual homeland that is neither a historicized *Heimat*, nor an ahistoric exile. Rather, the fact that it is spiritual gives way, in my understanding, to a personally transformed space that is perceived subjectively according to the needs of the perceiving individual. How this is dealt with in the three fictional narratives will be the subject of the following discussion.

2 Paris in White and Grey: A Winter Voyage

The novel *Five Seasons*, published in 1987, is among a number of transitional texts that point to important changes in A. B. Yehoshua's writing, moving as he did from symbolism to realism, and approaching new topics in the process.[14] The plot of *Five Seasons* revolves around the protagonist, Molkho, in the first year

---

10 Michel de Certeau, *The Practice of Everyday Life*, trans. Steven Rendall (Berkeley/Los Angeles/London: University of California Press, 1984), 103.
11 Ibid., 93.
12 Ibid., 108.
13 Ibid.
14 Gilead Morahg gives a short summary of the discussion among critics on A. B. Yehoshua's stylistic transition before elaborating upon the deficits of this thesis and explaining why his style is to be seen not as realism but rather as realistic symbolism. Gilead Morahg, "Reality and Symbol in the Fiction of A. B. Yehoshua," *Prooftexts* 2, no. 2 (1982): 179–96.

after his wife's death from a long and terminal illness. With her passing, Molkho needs to find his own, and certainly a new, place in the world.[15] During the year of mourning he travels twice to Europe. The episodes set in Paris are rather short but essential to Molkho's stages of grieving and his return to a life by himself without sickness and death; moreover, they shed light on the relationship he had with his late wife.

Molkho comes to Paris, the city he had visited with his wife already three times. Therefore, the city is no stranger to him. Yehoshua, who himself lived in Paris from 1963 to 1967,[16] about two decades before he wrote the short episode on Molkho's voyage to the city, does not project idealized visions of Paris onto his protagonist. Moreover, Molkho does not just come to Paris to escape his reality back home or for a restorative vacation. He returns in January, four months after his wife passed away, to see once more the place they both loved: "Three times he and his wife visited Paris, and each time they reassured themselves again of their common love for this city."[17] Yehoshua appeals thusly to the trope of Paris as the City of Love, but suggests that it was their common love for the city itself rather than their love for each other that draws Molkho back. The memories of their trips make Paris unique for Molkho, and the narrator emphasizes that he now travels alone on this his fourth visit.[18] The trip to Paris thus marks the beginning of Molkho's new life. Unlike his time in Vienna and Berlin, his stay in Paris is not filled with dark, non-personal memories, but rather with pleasant memories connected to his wife and their former visits to the French capital.

The plans for Molkho's journey to remember are disrupted from the very beginning. First, he had planned to stay at the same hotel in which he had stayed with his wife on their last visit, but her cousin insists on hosting him at her home. Molkho cannot help but feel that their motivations are emotionally complicated: "As if they decided to compensate him with an overload of warmth, out of guilt

---

15 A. B. Yehoshua's thoughts about this novel were influenced by the death of a good friend of his wife who passed away while he was writing. The couple was in the United States, and when they came back, Yehoshua's wife went to see her friend's husband. What she told Yehoshua afterwards had an impact on how he wrote and described the scenes around the death of Molkho's wife. Bernard Horn, *Facing the Fires. Conversations with A. B. Yehoshua*, (Syracuse: Syracuse University Press, 1997), 67–68.

16 Nitza Ben-Dov, "על א"ב יהושע ויצירתו" (On A. B. Yehoshua in His Work), in *מבטים מצטלבים: עיונים ביצירת א"ב יהושע* (Intersecting Glances. Studies of the Work of A. B. Yehoshua), ed. by Amir Banbaji, Nitza Ben-Dov, and Zavi Shamir (Tel Aviv: Hakibbutz Hameuhad, 2010), 9.

17 "שלוש פעמים ביקרו הוא ואשתו בפאריז, ובכל פעם אישרו לעצמם מחדש את אהבתם המיוחדת לעיר הזאת." Abraham B. Yehoshua, מולכו (Tel Aviv: Hakibbutz Hameuhad, 1987), 79.

18 Ibid.

that they did not come to the funeral and sent only a telegram."[19] The guilt not only disturbs the purity of Molkho's commemoration, but also turns the journey to remember her life into a journey to remember that she died: when she was alive, they had always stayed at hotels. Molkho's relationship to his wife's cousin is ambiguous. Although he feels distant at first and a bit disturbed in his plans, he enjoys the busy mornings, the loud French-speaking family, and the chaos in the house – a stark contrast to the silence he had experienced at home with his dying wife in the months before.[20] Although Molkho had never lived in Paris, he nevertheless represents the "anti-tourist": he speaks the language, even if his French is not good enough to discuss with the Parisian relatives all the medical details around his wife's death.[21] Moreover, he chooses to visit only one historical site, Versailles, a site that is neither directly connected to the Holocaust nor to his or his wife's personal history. Furthermore, this *lieu de mémoire* is situated outside of the city itself. In other words, the little historical memory Molkho encounters during his visit is placed at the outskirts of Paris and in the periphery of his perception.

The cold weather symbolizes once more his position as a non-tourist; for example, the beautiful gardens of Versailles are covered in snow and the palace appears inhospitable. But the meteorological circumstances reflect more than just the regular continental European weather one must expect in January: "The next morning the wind became stronger and the temperatures fell and the announcers of the weather forecast on the radio had an alarming tone … The people at the tables around him talked with enormous excitement about the weather."[22] The cold weather has a rather positive effect on Molkho. Not only does he feel hungry after his frosty tour of Versailles,[23] but also the news and the constant conversations about the snowstorm are a nice alternative to the news in Israel. As Risa Domb has observed, "the renewed encounter with Europe triggers admiration and attraction as well as hostility and repulsion. Some protagonists escape to Europe and others from Europe, but in both cases Europe never serves as just a tourist's sightseeing spot abroad but as a world which stands in total contrast

---

19 Ibid. "כמו מתוך אשמה על שלא באו להלוויה ורק שלחו מיברק החליטו לפצות אותו עכשיו בחמימות יתרה."
20 Ibid.
21 Ibid.
22 [...] "למחרת בבוקר גברה הרוח והטמפרטורה ירדה מאוד, ולנגישי חדשות מזג-האוויר ברדיו היה טון מאיים. האנשים ליד השולחנות שסביבו דיברו על מזג-האוויר בהתעוררות רבה."
Yehoshua, *מולכו*, 80.
23 Ibid.

to Israel."[24] Moreover, the snow blankets the scene in a peaceful atmosphere: "Around midnight when they left the opera, they were surprised by a clear sky and the whole city rested under a white and thick layer of glowing snow."[25]

As already mentioned, Molkho does not visit Paris for sightseeing. The first morning and reencounter with the city is therefore described against the background of his hosts' daily routine: "They dropped him off to stray under the grey sky in the Latin quarter, on the boulevards, at places he loved, known to him from previous travels, and when the huge stores opened he went from one floor to another to check the prices and to collect initial ideas for the presents he needed to bring to his children."[26] The department stores as well as shopping for presents are rather opposed to the Benjaminian arcades and the practice of strolling. It is Molkho's first day in Paris and he seems a bit lost. Unlike regular tourists, he does not have a plan for which site to visit first and which should follow it; and although shopping for gifts, especially souvenirs, can be rather touristic, most people would explore the city first, something Molkho does not feel the need to do because he already knows his way around. Moreover, rather soon he gets back to wandering around and because Molkho does not have a special spot that he wants to visit first, his walks seem aimless. Even a few days later: "[He] walked around in the city, between heaps of snow despicable as long as the sky shone in a callous blue, he delved into the small streets behind the opera house..."[27]

Five Seasons is the first transitional text in Yehoshua's oeuvre that suggests his growing interest in *Mizrahim* in Israel and *mizrahi* identity.[28] In Molkho's case,

---

24 Risa Domb, "Home and Abroad: Israel and Europe in Hebrew Fiction of the 1980s," *Israel Affairs* 1, no. 2 (1994): 326.

25 "לקראת חצות, כשיצאו מן האופרה, הופתעו למצוא שמיים נהירים והעיר כולה נחה תחת מעטה לבן ועבה של שלג זורח."
Yehoshua, *מולכו*, 81.

26 "הורידו גם אותו לשטט תחת שמיים אפורים ברובע הלטיני, בבולבארים המפולשים, במקומות שהיו מוכרים ואהובים מהמסעות הקודמים, וכאשר נפתחו חנויות הענק החל עולה מקומה לקומה לבדוק מחירים ולאסוף רעיונות ראשונים למתנות שיצטרך להביא לילדיו."
Ibid., 79–80.

27 "[הוא] הסתובב בעיר, בין ערימות השלג שנעשה מסואב מכל שהשמיים הבהיקו בכחול בוטה. הוא העמיק ברחובות קטנים מאחורי בניין האופרה..."
Ibid., 83.

28 At this point, I would like to clarify that I do not use the term *Mizrahi* in this context as referring to Jews who immigrated to Israel from the Arab countries and North Africa in the 1950s. This is neither the background of Molkho the fictional character nor of Yehoshua the author. The fact that this explanation is needed already hints at the difficulties that come with these terminologies. For obvious reasons, the term Oriental is problematic as well as is Sephardic, which does not only refer to the Jews whose ancestors fled from the Iberian Peninsula, but describes also a religious tradition.

his deep connection to his Levantine roots influences his Israeliness, which is defined, inter alia, by the land and its geographical location in the Levant and decidedly not in Europe. I suggest that we can thus read Yehoshua's Paris episode within the context of the discussion about a Levantine identity.

Bernard Horn and A. B. Yehoshua discuss this issue in the conversations Horn published and come to the conclusion that Molkho's identity is stable and that neither the fact that his wife was of European origin, nor the fact that he travels to Europe and is even familiar with Paris as a European city lets him merge with the Parisian society or make him question where he comes from and belongs to: "In *Five Seasons*, though the story is told in the third person, the point of view is rigorously Molkho's, and never is there any question of the borders of identity. Rather, as the novel moves from Israel into France, Austria, and Germany, we stand well within the human borders of 'Molkho, Israeli,' and, as he struggles with his private identity as an adult male and a lover, he has the sort of stability and particularity of the characters of nineteenth-century Russian literature."[29] As opposed to his Berlin-born wife, Molkho identifies solely with the realm of the Levant and feels a deep connection to the land and its tradition. He struggles as a man and husband, but feels rooted in the land his Sephardic forefathers already lived in. Whereas he just travels to Europe in order to assure that he has a home, many others like his wife and mother-in-law have been uprooted from the old continent. The fact that they found a place in Israel after their flight from Germany does not lead automatically to the same feeling Molkho has about his Levantine homeland. They are still connected to European history and culture and see it as part of their own identity that takes up time and space in their daily life. Moreover, it is his wife's cousin whom they visit in Paris, whereas Molkho does not have any family ties in Europe. Nevertheless, the fact that Paris enables another encounter for him and his wife that does not take place either in her former homeland or in the land they lived in and wherein Molkho sees his roots, makes this city a spiritual homeland to Molkho that does not claim to be his *Heimat*.

France and Paris can be seen as a cultural space of transition from Europe to the Levant and therefore as a connecting factor between Molkho and his wife. In her writings, Jacqueline Kahanoff emphasizes the influence of French culture on Levantine identity. She describes France as "a Latin nation, which by means of the church had inherited the essence of cultured Levantinism as it was embodied in Byzantium."[30] Israel is seen by Kahanoff as the "ambivalent Levantine,"[31]

---

29 Horn, *Facing the Fires*, 85.
30 Deborah A. Starr, Sasson Somekh, eds., *Mongrels or Marvels. The Levantine Writings of Jacqueline Shohet Kahanoff* (Stanford: Stanford University Press, 2011), 182.
31 Ibid., 193.

since it is geographically located within the Levantine realm, but is, through Zionism, strongly based on European thinking and conceptualization. This characterization can be also applied to Paris, which is geographically located in Europe but has a strong – although partly negative, due to its colonial history – lingual and cultural connection to the Levant. Like Paris, the Levant is a realm of boundaries, a realm where one meets the other. France is, moreover, situated on the Mediterranean, but Paris is perceived as a, or even *the*, European city; or in other words, it is the Europe of the Levantines. Thus, Molkho is not looking for a new *Heimat* in Paris, but he does not feel as distant and as non-European in the capital of this Mediterranean country as he does in Berlin and Vienna. This might not be as strongly connected to the Holocaust as we think, but again to the fact that Molkho speaks the language of Paris, which is also widely spoken in the Levant.

The fact that Molkho has no personal or family history in Europe allows him to have a fairly "neutral" attitude about the old continent and its past. This is reflected in the author's own claim that his approach toward the Holocaust was rather intellectual and less emotional since he is an Oriental Jew and his family was not directly affected.[32] Horn does recall in their conversations his own family history and Yehoshua consequently elaborates on how personal and family history effect the perception of specific places and cities in Europe:

> Yes, when Jews deal with their past in Europe now – imagine, for example, a Jew who goes back to Russia: he isn't concerned with his village as a geographical place; he is concerned with the community that was, let's say, in Lvov or in Lida or your father's Sambor.
>
> When he goes back, he deals with families and with the structure of human relationships, but he does not see Vilna, for example, first of all as a place, in a geography, near a river, near all those things that make Vilna's smells and colors whatever they are.[33]

Molkho's own experience is juxtaposed to what Yehoshua describes in these lines as a characteristic encounter of Jews who had family members that fled from Europe during World War II or perished in the Holocaust. The encounter he has is not one with the historical past, but rather with his and his wife's personal history. Even in Berlin where he looks for the house his wife was born in, there remains a distance between Molkho and the place. Nevertheless, as Risa Domb emphasizes, the encounter with Europe is for most literary characters not a "new" one – not even for Molkho as I would like to add.[34]

---

32 Horn, *Facing the Fires*, 129.
33 Ibid. 106.
34 Domb, "Home and Abroad," 326.

For Molkho, Paris is indeed a contrast to Israel – also on a personal level, as are the other European cities he visits. But, it is first and foremost in the French capital that he reencounters family life while staying with his wife's cousin, her husband, and their two little children, a family life that seems to differ enormously from the one he led with his dying wife. The French family's lively and chaotic daily routine contrasts with his and his wife's months-long wait for death. The children do not only stand at the beginning of their own journey, they symbolize Molkho's new journey, his new beginning.

Although the young family brings him back to life, Molkho visits Paris primarily to stay in the past. He chooses Paris to say his final goodbyes and only in leaving Paris behind can he move on; Paris is Molkho's closure. Molkho learns how to be by himself again, he walks alone in the rather grey and cold winter streets, but he can still come home to a warm and welcoming environment. For all its dreary weather, Paris reminds him of the love he shared with his wife. It is not associated with an idealized picture of Europe as the elderly home where his mother-in-law lives and in which Amir Banbaji identifies the "Weimar idyll."[35] Nevertheless, Molkho is not confronted with the historical past either and remains in the comfort zone of his personal memories.

3 Paris of Art, Literature, and Music

Personal memories are what the young protagonist in Judith Katzir's *Matisse Has the Sun in His Belly* who was, like Molkho, in Paris before, still creates, and she does so on the visit discussed in the following. In contrast to Molkho and his wife, on her prior visit, art student Rivi saw only the Eiffel Tour and the Louvre while on an organized tour of Europe.[36] The second visit that is recalled in detail in the novel is again integrated into a longer tour, but nevertheless she and her lover Yigal manage to see more than she did the last time.

Judith Katzir was born in 1963 in Haifa and started publishing novellas and novels in the late 1980s during the "female revolution," when she gained critical attention together with other women writers including Zeruya Shalev and Michal Govrin. "[A]lthough entirely different from each other in tone, style, and literary sensibilities, these authors undermined the 'oedipal masterplot' through

---

35 "האידיליה הוויימרית."
Amir Banbaji, "הכישלונות של מולכו: ראליזם, מודרניזם, מזרחיות," in *ביצירת א״ב יהושע: עיונים מעטלבים*, ed. by Amir Banbaji, Nitza Ben-Dov, Zavi Shamir (Tel Aviv: Hakibbutz Hameuhad, 2010), 173–194.
36 Judith Katzir, למאטיס יש את השמש בבטן, (Tel Aviv: Hakibbutz Hameuhad, 1995), 50.

a 'poetics of the body' and often focused on mother-daughter duos," writes Nili Gold, who identifies these poetics of the body in Katzir's descriptions of Haifa that appear in almost all her texts: "Haifa surrenders itself to the feminine voice of her native. The city of curvy bays, mountains, rounded treetops, and lush nature recalls in its contours the feminine body."[37]

In *Matisse Has the Sun in His Belly*, Rivi goes through the ups and downs of an affair with a married man with a child – Yigal. Throughout their relationship, they travel to Italy, France, Spain, and Egypt. Each country represents a different stage in their liaison, which continues until Rivi realizes that she will always come in second after Yigal's family. They split and thereafter only meet one more time after Rivi's mother dies from cancer. The novel is narrated precisely, even overloadingly, and there are few details of their personal and sexual relationship that remain vague.

Early in their relationship, Rivi and Yigal travel together to Europe. First, they spend some time in Italy before they finish their trip with a few days in Paris, where they live the romantic cliché. The city for lovers turns into a heterotopian space where they exist as an almost regular couple. In Italy, on the other hand, they had not yet entered into a clear routine, and in Spain their connection to each other suffers from its first ruptures. It is self-evident that their daily routine is even more complicated in Israel. Rivi's statement in a room full of Matisse paintings is therefore not surprising: "And I would like for the moment not to end, that we would stand together in front of all that red in the heart of Paris forever."[38] However, not to move and to stay in the moment is contradictory to Rivi's regular behavior. She and Yigal do not calmly stroll and explore, but are driven by Rivi's excitement and restlessness:

> [T]hey went by foot from their hotel in Saint Germain to the Centre Pompidou, and she rejoiced next to him like a foal, she stopped in front of every café and every shopping window, sticking her nose into every bakery and perfume and tobacco shop … she was thrilled, wandered around among the paintings, not in order but according to what caught her eye, like she read books from time to time, from the middle, and from the beginning and from the end without patience.[39]

---

37 Nili Gold, "The Topography of the City and the Body: Yehudit Katzir's Haifa," *Hebrew Studies* 47 (2004): 282–83. For more on Katzir's biography see Shay Rodin, "קציר, יהודית" in לקסיקון הקשרים לסופרים ישראלים ed. Zissi Stavi, Yigal Schwartz (Or Yehuda: Kinneret, 2014), 813–14.
38 "ורציתי שהרגע הזה לא ייגמר, שתמיד נעמוד יחד בלב פאריס מול כל האדום הזה." Katzir, *Matisse*, 51.
39 "הלכו ברגל מן המלון שלהם בסן-ז'רמן למרכז פומפידו, והיא צהלה לצידו כסייחה, מתעכבת ליד כל בית-קפה וליד כל חלון ראווה, תוחבת את חוטמה בפתחי המאפיות וחנויות הבשמים והטבק, [...] שוטטה נפעמת בין הציורים, לא לפי הסדר, אלא לפי מה שצד את עינה, כמו האופן שבו קראה ספרים לפעמים, מן האמצע ומן ההתחלה ומן הסוף

The frequent use of the conjunction "and" further increases the feeling of unrest. Rivi's excitement dominates the way their trip to Paris is narrated, from the beginning when she opens the window of their hotel room on the first morning. It is oddly described as a big "French window."[40] The brightness that might come through that window is a link to Paris as the City of Light, but the scenery outside is neither flooded with light nor is it anything more than ordinary everyday life: "And she looked at the grey sky and at the roofs as dark as basalt, and then at the narrow and long street that twisted five floors under her, only two sanitation workers in orange jumpsuits were seen at six in the morning, and the lines of toy cars along the sidewalk, and a few men who entered and left a bistro on the corner."[41] Nevertheless, the simple fact that Rivi is in Paris and that she watches this scene through a "French window" together with her almost child-like attitude to explore adds this scene to her particular perspective on Paris while remaining in the sanctuary of the hotel room and not participating in daily life.

Another sanctuary realm that is even more detached from daily Parisian life is the art scene they partly re-imagine for themselves. From an art historian's point of view, Rivi and Yigal stroll mostly in the post-World War II era. However, it is intertwined with the colorful 1920s represented by, for example, Brecht and Weill's *Three Penny Opera* they go to see together. Throughout the novel, it is mostly their beloved bookseller Golden who connects first Rivi but also Yigal to a bygone European world and culture. The text is full of nods to Stefan Zweig in general and his autobiography in particular.[42] In *The World of Yesterday*, Zweig describes the Paris before the destruction by Nazi Germany as characterized by "the divine colourful, the blessed cheerful, the melodiousness and the unwittable blossom of this harmonic entity."[43]

"באיזה חוסר סבלנות...‟

Ibid., 51.

40 Ibid., 50.

41 „...והביטה בשמיים האפורים ובגגות הכהים כבזלת, ואחר ברחוב הצר והארוך שהתפתל חמש קומות מתחתיה, רק שני פועלי ניקיון בסרבלים כתומים מצוחצחים נראו בשעה ו, ושורת המכוניות צעצועיות לאורך המדרכה, וכמה גברים שנכנסו ויצאו מביסטרו בפינה.‟

Ibid., 50.

42 For further elaborations on Golden the book trader and the references to Zweig's *The World of Yesterday* in *Matisse Has the Sun in His Belly*, see Judith Müller, "Auf der Suche nach dem letzten Europäer in Judith Katzirs *Matisse hat die Sonne im Bauch* – Eine israelische Nebenfigur aus einer *Welt von Gestern*," *Germanica Revues. Regards croisés sur l'Europe et les voisins européens* 56 (2015): 15–26.

43 "[D]as göttlich Farbige, das selig Heitere, den Schmelz und die unverwelkbare Blüte dieses harmonischen Gebildes." Stefan Zweig, *Die Welt von Gestern. Erinnerungen eines Europäers*

In *Matisse Has the Sun in His Belly*, the rupture in the city's cultural life after Paris was occupied by the National Socialists is not mentioned. It rather seems as if the cultural life continued to flourish throughout the most catastrophic decades of modern European history. Rivi and Yigal go to the Picasso museum to see paintings of the Spanish-born artist from the early twentieth century through the decades after World War II. The couple sits in the Closserie de Lilas at the tables of people who shaped the culture in those decades like Ernest Hemingway, Jean-Paul Sartre, André Gide, and Gertrude Stein. Moreover, they visit the postmodern building of the Centre Pompidou that has "red and blue tubes gaping out its head as a periscope"[44] and was built only in the 1970s. The unsorted mix of styles, epochs, names of artists and works causes a rather blurry picture of what Paris might be, but the colorfulness and diversity help again to omit the memory of dark times.

However, Rivi recalls memories. First of all, she recalls her own, and she does so in Paris when she tells Yigal the story about her now-divorced parents and how they first met. Moreover, she "manages to extract memories" from Yigal. Leon I. Yudkin argues that, "Rivi looks both backward and forward; her memorialization is both recollection of the past and protection against the vicissitudes of the future."[45] However, these are all personal and not historical memories connected to Paris. In fact, the French capital provides stability rather than a stormy and insecure history: "She walked through the narrow streets, dwelling near the windows of the galleries and the antique shops. I would be happy to live in one of these houses, she thought. Indifferent, great, with the assurance of centuries they rest on, and everything, stores and restaurants and people, moves with a by-the-way refinement, without any effort, and the light is comforting in its greyness, not demanding, moderate."[46] In sum, although Rivi and Yigal seem to live the cliché of the City of Love, they do not imagine the idealized nineteenth-century capital of Europe. Nevertheless, the long chain of places they go to, the paintings they see, and the names of French cultural personalities they talk about are a path to a blind spot. Although the same could be said about Italy, Spain, and Egypt, Paris

---

(Frankfurt am Main: Fischer Taschenbuch Verlag, 2012), 151.
44 "שציונרות אדומים וכחולים פעורים מראשו כפריסקופים".
Katzir, *Matisse*, 51.
45 Leon I. Yudkin, "Memorialization in New Fiction," *World Literature Today* 72, no. 3 (1998): 489.
46 "היא פסעה בסימטאות הצרות, מתעכבת ליד חלונות הגלריות וחנויות העתיקות. הייתי שמחה לגור באחד הבתים האלה, היררה, אדישים, גאיונים, רובצים להם בביטחון של מאות שנים, והכל, חנויות ומיסעדות ואנשים מתנהל כאן באיזה עידון שבדרך-אגב, כאילו בלי שום מאמץ, והאור מרגיע באפרוריות, לא תובעני, מתון".
Katzir, *Matisse*, 56.

remains unique since they reach a personal not only a historical blind spot in the French capital: they do not only seem to live the cliché; it is in Paris that historical time appears to stop – the old houses in their assurance of centuries and the red of Matisse paintings that invites Rivi to stay represent this notion.

4 Paris of Love, Light, and Life

For Amalia in Lizzie Doron's *On the Brink of Something Beautiful*, the past and especially the Holocaust is always present. Like the two other protagonists of the novel who grew up in the same neighborhood, she is the daughter of Holocaust survivors, as is the author herself. Lizzie Doron was born in 1953 in Tel Aviv. In the past years she has written about the Middle East conflict starting with *Who the Fuck is Kafka* (German, 2015), a novel which has not been published in Hebrew due to its content. This book in particular is highly critical of how Israeli society deals with the other and how it accepts or rather does not accept Jewish-Arabic encounters, friendships, and love. However, in the 1990s, Doron began her career as a writer of fiction about the second generation, thus joining other "second generation" writers like Nava Semel and Savyon Liebrecht. In that decade, the narrative of Israeli literature became more pluralistic – or in other words, the Zionist narrative was not the only one anymore, but rather one among many. It is therefore not a coincidence that female writers such as Judith Katzir and authors of the second generation like Lizzie Doron appeared during and after that change. Neither is it surprising that A. B. Yehoshua's narrative took into account the non-Ashkenazic point of view.

On the Brink of Something Beautiful is divided into three parts, each one dedicated to one of three children, Amalia, Hezi, and Gadi. The reader follows their problems as they live with their survivor parents and later follows their lives as adults, which are still influenced by what they and their parents experienced.[47] For the purposes of our study, we will focus on Amalia and Hezi and a short episode in which they think about living together in Paris. They are both in their fifties; Amalia works at an Israeli broadcasting station and Hezi is a historian teaching at the Sorbonne. When Hezi comes home for his father's funeral, he hears Amalia on the radio and they agree to meet. A short time later, she travels to Paris to be with him: "Two weeks ago I landed at the Charles de Gaulle airport.

---

[47] For an analysis and description of the trauma of the second generation and its impact on their behavior and daily life see Dina Wardi, *Memorial Candles. Children of the Holocaust*, trans. by Naomi Goldblum (London/New York: Routledge, 1992).

Paris fits me, I thought."[48] This simple thought shows the naiveté in Amalia's behavior. She does not really know if Paris fits her because she has never been there for any substantial amount of time. And, she does not know Hezi either. She remembers Hezi the child who lived next door to her, but she has never spent enough time with him to know him as a grown man. She is nevertheless convinced that he is committed to her and their future in the City of Love where she plans to marry him. However, Amalia never truly arrives in Paris although she lands at the Charles de Gaulle airport on the outskirts of the city. Hezi picks her up and instead of leaving the airport, he surprises her with tickets to Poland where they fly immediately in order to rebuild the former *Heimat* of their parents.

Traveling to Europe is a crucial issue in second-generation literature. In her study *Past Present: Biography, Identity and Memory in Second Generation Literature*, Iris Milner elaborates:

> Works of second-generation literature can be considered as travel literature in two different ways that often coexist in one single work. In a concrete form, as when the works describe a real voyage to specific geographical destinations which were not the places of killing and remembrance in Europe, or in a symbolic way – such as when the works focus on the mental, imaginary journey that is psychoanalytical in character, towards the bottoms of the archaeological piles that cover up a silenced past, and a repressed identity.[49]

For Amalia traveling to the geographical places in Poland triggers memories of a silenced past whereas her imaginary journey to Paris promises a new beginning. Connected by alliteration, Paris and Poland are presented as opposed poles. Although Hezi tries to convince Amalia that Kraków can be their new Paris, she cannot stop noticing the differences. After all, there is no Arc de Triomphe in Kraków, neither is there the Champs Elysée.[50] Moreover, Kraków is dark at night in contrast to the City of Light, and the memories connected to Poland are even darker. Already before she arrives, the sheer thought of being in Poland makes Amalia sick: "For three hours I threw up into a bag and imagined my death under the sky of Poland."[51] Her dramatic experience came partly from shock, since Hezi

---

48 "לפני שבועיים, אולי קצת יותר, נחתי בשדה התעופה שארל דה גול. מתאים לי פריס, אמרתי לעצמי". Lizzie Doron, *התחלה של משהו יפה* (Jerusalem: Keter, 2007), 44.

49 "יצירות הסיפורת של הדור השני הן בבחינת ספרות מסעות בשני מובנים שונים, אשר לעתים קרובות מתקיימים זה לצד זה באותה יצירה עצמה: במובן הקונקרטי, כלומר בהיותן יצירות המתארות מסע ממשי אל יעדים גיאוגרפיים מסוימים, הלא הם אתרי הרצח והזיכרון באירופה, ובמובן הסמלי – בהיותן יצירות הממוקדות במסע מנטאלי, דמיוני פסיכואנליטי באופיו, אל תחתיתם של תלים ארכיאולוגיים המסתירים עבר מושתק וזהות מודחקת".
Iris Milner, *קרעי עבר. ביוגרפיה, זהות וזיכרון בסיפורת הדור השני* (Tel Aviv: Am Oved, 2003), 95–96.

50 Doron, *Something Beautiful*, 46.

51 "שלוש שעות הקאתי לתוך שקית, ודמיינתי את מותי בשמי פולין". Ibid., 44.

undermined her imagined but seemingly tangible future, but she surrenders to her childhood trauma as a second-generation child in particular. Poland is full of Holocaust memories and is therefore a place of death for Amalia. It is at the least not where she believes they could live happily ever after. Amalia prefers a house in Paris, but Hezi says that they already have one there and that it is time to build a new one in the former homeland of their parents.[52]

Hezi is obsessed with the Holocaust. His Parisian ex-girlfriend even calls him "the Holocauster." For him, too, his dream is fulfilled when he moves to the French capital for his studies. He had been learning French for several years with his parents' friend Wolf Katzenelnbogen, and when he finally arrives, he is full of excitement. However, the perspective of the historian and his professor with whom he has a good relationship provide him with deeper insights, and he starts to ask questions about the past. He was brought up with the narrative of the *résistance* and when he arrives in France, he accepts this perspective on history as a reality for a long time. However, with his growing obsession, he discovers more and more details until he finally bursts out: "'You are another people,' I told her [Solange, Hezi's Parisian girlfriend], 'you are a people wrapped in crème brûlée and spread in butter and chocolate, a people that covers up its sins with make-up and powder.'"[53]

The idealized perception Hezi has of France in general, and of Paris in particular, is the result of the stories Wolf Katzenelnbogen tells him. The first French word he teaches the young boy is *"amour"* and the French teacher emphasizes that the military support for Israel comes from *"le peuple français."*[54] However, when Hezi finally lives in Paris and studies and teaches there on a daily basis, the spectacle ceases to be idealized. Moreover, as opposed to Amalia and the characters from the two novels discussed above, he does not flee to Paris in order to avoid the everyday reality of his Israeli life. Hence, the city neither plays a redemptive role for him, nor does it function as a blind spot in Hezi's personal narrative. He confronts the French people with their responsibility and makes clear that they participated in persecuting the Jews under the Nazi occupation. Nevertheless, the places of horror remain, even in Hezi's account, *outside* of Paris: Drancy on the one hand and Eastern Europe on the other.

Although Amalia and Hezi never live together in Paris, and Amalia's description of the city consists therefore only of fantasies, her perception of Paris as an

---

52 Ibid., 46.
53 "'את עם אחר,' אמרתי לה, 'את עם עטוף בקרם ברולה ומרוח בחמאה ושוקולד, עם שמכסה את חטאיו במייק-אפ ופודרה.'"
Ibid., 141.
54 Ibid., 118.

ahistorical place is the most explicit among the three novels. Amalia's dreams are "kitschy," even more than Rivi's, but this is relativized by her sarcasm and Doron's ironic style of writing. In a certain way, the enormous discrepancy between Paris and Poland in Amalia's imagination contributes even more to the irony as does the fact that for Hezi, who has lived in Paris for many years already, the dark history beyond the façade comes to the surface. To Amalia, Paris means light not darkness, happiness not death, whereas Poland represents mass killing and is a country where every stone could be from a Jewish grave or the house their parents and grandparents were taken from.

5 Conclusion

All three protagonists, Molkho, Rivi, and Amalia, go to Paris in couples, though it does not seem so at first glance. Molkho travels alone, but does so in memory of his late wife. Therefore, she is in a sense "with him." Rivi and Yigal go there to be a regular couple at least for a few days, and Amalia and Hezi travel together and she envisions their life there, even if they do not stay in Paris. Outside of Paris, Amalia and Hezi are haunted by their parents' trauma, and their happiness fails even before Amalia leaves Poland to go back to Israel. Moreover, in all the three novels the voyage to Paris is only a short episode of the plot. However, it becomes clear that the voyage to Paris resembles an escape from the character's daily life as well as a blind spot. The latter is realized by portraying the city mostly in contrast to other places in Europe – Vienna and Berlin in *Five Seasons*, Poland in *On the Brink of Something Beautiful*, and Italy and Spain in *Matisse Has the Sun in His Belly*. The fact that the southern European countries are generally not the first associated with European-Jewish Holocaust memory and trauma does not necessarily diminish the meaning of Paris, but rather widens the space of an imaginary, positive, ahistorical Europe; although, in Katzir's novel, these places are of course portrayed as all but ahistorical from a cultural and artistic point of view. The places Rivi and Yigal see in Italy and Spain are, thus, left out of the traumatic Jewish experience as well and serve as romantic sites and historical blind spots. The fact that they never went to Poland together, where Yigal came from, speaks for itself. Central and Eastern Europe as well as Germany are those realms where most characters in Hebrew literature and Jewish Israelis and non-Israelis with a European background in general go to when they want to explore their family history and their ancestors' lives. Many of those places disappeared; they represent the erasing of history and come often with traumatic memories, although it is a sense of belonging that brings people there. The fear of disappearance is something rather characteristic for Central Europe and is deeply inscribed into the historical conscience of its small nations. This feeling has led to a distrust in history, as Milan Kundera argues in his essay, "The Tragedy of Central Europe."[55] This Central European notion of uncertainty and constant menace is, as he continues, a factor that constitutes European Jewish history even more. As opposed to this, we read in Katzir's novel of the notion that the buildings of Paris remain, however, indifferent and great with the assurance of centuries behind them. Thus, Paris attracts them through a longing for stability or even only an idealized image.

Europe is in general a place with a long past and an enormously complex history. A. B. Yehoshua talks to Bernard Horn about his love for the visible and touchable history: "When I think about the place itself, we don't have the past like the Europeans, like a Parisian, for example, who can go out into the street and touch a church that was built in the eighteenth century or the seventeenth century. Europeans can visit a library that holds old manuscripts and a whole physical environment. But we don't have the past in the present physically."[56] This is the past Molkho sees in Versailles or the history for which Rivi loves the old houses. It is not the past of traumatic memories.

Some of the protagonists do have memories of Paris, but they are personal and mostly happy memories – as is the case with Molkho. Moreover, these memories are not embedded in a historical time. In general, it can be said that Paris is a place where time stands still for the characters: Rivi and Yigal pause for a few days in the development of their relationship that first ignites in Italy and then gets its first scratches in Spain. Molkho breathes for the first time after his wife died; he realizes that he will travel alone from now on and he needs this time to remember her. For Amalia, it is the thought of going to Paris that lets her imagine that time can stop, because for her time is the endless circle of Holocaust trauma and remembrance. The impression of a timeless Paris in Hebrew literature leads to the conclusion that it is a stable point in the chaotic European landscape of memory and therefore a historical blind spot, an area with no image detection.[57] This is what happens to Molkho, Rivi, and Amalia in Paris. They are unable and often do not want to detect the image of history unlike at other European places and the fact, that all three novels are written in a rather realistic tone, does contribute to this effect since leaving out a specific chapter of Parisian

---

[55] Milan Kundera, "The Tragedy of Central Europe," in *The New York Review of Books*, April 26, 1986.
[56] Horn, *Facing the Fires*, 106.
[57] David M. Gamm, Daniel M. Albert, "Blind Spot," in *Encyclopaedia Britannica*, accessed September 1, 2015. https://www.britannica.com/science/blind-spot.

history becomes even more unique. The described perspective leads on the one hand to the characters' utopian ideas, and the impression that Paris seems to be a museum, exhibiting its own myths. Rivi and Yigal, for example, sit at the Closserie de Lilas at the tables of Henry Miller, Gertrude Stein, and Jean-Paul Sartre. And on the other hand, the alleged absence of history brings a feeling of security and stability.

Regarding the perception of the cityscape, Molkho explores Paris often from within buildings and houses, but the narrator mentions the typical boulevards. Except for that, the protagonist dwells in unremarkable streets "behind (!) the opera house" or visits the department stores. In *Matisse Has the Sun in His Belly*, Paris is described in much more picturesque terms, referring to specific Parisian characteristics like the typical houses with their black roof or a bistro situated on a street corner, as well as narrow streets between small shops and houses in the Latin Quarter. Amalia on the other hand never arrives in the city and she thinks first and foremost of the Eiffel Tower and the Arc de Triomphe when she imagines Paris. In other words, in her narrative there is neither urbanity nor a landscape. Moreover, she thinks of Paris as a city full of light as opposed to the darkness of Poland, whereas the weather throughout Molkho's voyage is everything but bright, and even Rivi sees a grey sky when looking out of the window the first morning. Thus, although the cityscape in Katzir's novel is much more romanticized than in that of Yehoshua, the narrator does not overly idealize his description. However, as opposed to the urban landscape at the center of his writing on Paris, for the characters of Yehoshua, Katzir, and Doron the emotional landscape is of much greater importance.

This emotional landscape emerges from the creation of a timeless space by the narrator; this timelessness is not necessarily a result of the absence of historical time as such, but refers mostly to the lack of commemoration of historical events connected to World War II and especially the Holocaust. This becomes even clearer when comparing the imagination of Paris to fictional writing on Berlin, Vienna, and Poland as I suggested above. Thus, the imagination of Paris is characterised by a historical blind spot the characters are longing for: it is clear that the French capital is neither their *Heimat* nor are they permanently in exile, but the imagined realm provides them with a temporal spiritual homeland free of a traumatic past and its memories.

Bibliography

Banbaji, Amir. "הכישלונות של מולכו: ראליזם, מודרניזם, מזרחיות." In *מבטים מצטלבים: עיונים ביצירת א"ב יהושע*. Edited by Amir Banbaji, Nitza Ben-Dov, and Zavi Shamir, 173–194. Tel Aviv: Hakibbutz Hameuchad, 2010.

Ben-Atiya, Yuval. "תמונות פריזאיות'. דיוקן פריס בשירה העברית בין שתי מלחמות העולם." M.A. thesis, Tel Aviv University, 2002.

Ben-Dov, Nitza. "על א"ב יהושע ויצירתו." In *מבטים מצטלבים: עיונים ביצירת א"ב יהושע*. Edited by Amir Banbaji, Nitza Ben-Dov, and Zavi Shamir, 9–13. Tel Aviv: Hakibbutz Hameuchad, 2010.

Benjamin, Walter. *Charles Baudelaire: A Lyric Poet in the Era of High Capitalism*. Translated by Harry Zohn. London/New York: Verso, 1997.

Benjamin, Walter. "Paris: Capital of the XIX. Century." *Perspecta* 12 (1969): 163–172.

Benjamin, Walter. "Paris die Hauptstadt des XIX. Jahrhunderts." In *Walter Benjamin. Gesammelte Schriften*. Edited by Rolf Tiedemann, V: 45–59. Frankfurt a. M.: Suhrkamp, 1991.

Benjamin, Walter. "Pariser Passagen II." In *Walter Benjamin. Gesammelte Schriften*. Edited by Rolf Tiedemann, V: 1044–1059. Frankfurt a. M.: Suhrkamp, 1991.

Certeau, Michel de. *The Practice of Everyday Life*. Translated by Steven Rendall. Berkeley/Los Angeles/London: University of California Press, 1984.

Domb, Risa. "Home and Abroad: Israel and Europe in Hebrew Fiction of the 1980s." *Israel Affairs* 1, no. 2 (1994): 323–333.

Doron, Lizzie. *התחלה של משהו יפה*. Jerusalem: Keter, 2007.

Gamm, David M., and Daniel M. Albert. "Blind Spot." *Encyclopaedia Britannica*. https://www.britannica.com/science/blind-spot. Accessed September 1, 2015.

Gold, Nili. "The Topography of the City and the Body: Yehudit Katzir's Haifa." *Hebrew Studies* 47 (2004): 281–294.

Hollwich, Fritz. *Ophthalmology: A Short Textbook*. Translated by Frederick C. Blodi. 2nd ed. Stuttgart/New York: Georg Thieme Verlag/Thieme Stratton, 1985.

Horn, Bernard. *Facing the Fires. Conversations with A.B. Yehoshua*. Syracuse: Syracuse University Press, 1997.

Katzir, Judith. *למאטיס יש את השמש בבטן*. Tel Aviv: Hakibbutz Hameuchad, 1995.

Kok Escalle, Marie-Christine. Introduction to *Paris: De l'Image à la Mémoire. Représentations Artistiques, Littéraires, Socio-Politiques*. Edited by Marie-Christine Kok Escalle, 1–7. Faux Titre: Etudes de Langue et Littérature Françaises Publiées 122. Amsterdam/Atlanta: Rodopi, 1997.

Kok Escalle, Marie-Christine, ed. *Paris, de l'Image à la Mémoire: Représentations Artistiques, Littéraires, Socio-Politiques*. Amsterdam/Atlanta: Rodopi, 1997.

Kundera, Milan. "The Tragedy of Central Europe." *The New York Review of Books*, April 26, 1986.

Lauster, Martina. "Walter Benjamin's Myth of the 'Flâneur'." *The Modern Language Review* 102, no. 1 (2007): 139–156.

McMahon, Joseph H. *Paris in Literature*. New Haven: Yale University Press, 1964.

Milner, Iris. *קרעי עבר. ביוגרפיה, זהות וזיכרון בסיפורת הדור השני*. Tel Aviv: Am Oved, 2003.

Morahg, Gilead. "Reality and Symbol in the Fiction of A. B. Yehoshua." *Prooftexts* 2, no. 2 (1982): 179–196.

Müller, Judith. "Auf der Suche nach dem letzten Europäer in Judith Katzirs *Matisse hat die Sonne im Bauch* – Eine israelische Nebenfigur aus einer *Welt von Gestern*." *Germanica Revues. Regards croisés sur l'Europe et les voisins européens* 56 (2015): 15–26.

Netanel, Lilach. *המולדת הישנה*. Jerusalem: Keter, 2014.
Nora, Pierre. *Les lieux de mémoire*. Paris: Gallimard, 1997.
Ofrat, Gideon. *פאריז-תל אביב. הקשר הצרפתי של האמנות הישראלית. מאמרים ורשימות*. Tel Aviv: Ofer Levi Foundation for Israeli Art, 2015.
Rubins, Maria. "The Diasporic Canon of Russian Poetry: The Case of the Paris Note." In *Twentieth-Century Russian Poetry. Reinventing the Canon*. Edited by Katharine Hodgson, Joanne Shelton, and Alexandra Smith, 289–328. Cambridge: Open Book Publishers, 2017.
Schwartz, Marcy E. *Writing Paris: Urban Topographies of Desire in Contemporary Latin American Fiction*. Albany: State University of New York Press, 1999.
Starr, Deborah A., and Sasson Somekh, eds. *Mongrels or Marvels. The Levantine Writings of Jacqueline Shohet Kahanoff*. Stanford: Stanford University Press, 2011.
Thompson, Victoria E. "Telling 'Spatial Stories': Urban Space and Bourgeois Identity in Early Nineteenth Century Paris." *The Journal of Modern History* 75, no. 3 (2003): 523–556.
Wakeman, Rosemary. *The Heroic City: Paris 1945–1958*. Chicago: University of Chicago Press, 2009.
Wardi, Dina. *Memorial Candles. Children of the Holocaust*. Translated by Goldblum Naomi. London/New York: Routledge, 1992.
Westerwelle, Karin. "Paris: Urbanität, Entgrenzung, Flüchtigkeit." In *Handbuch Literatur & Raum*. Edited by Jörg Dünne and Andreas Mahler, 431–441. Berlin a.o: De Gruyter, 2015.
Willms, Johannes. *Paris. Hauptstadt Europas 1800–1914*. Munich: C.H. Beck, 2000.
Yehoshua, Abraham B. *מולכו*. Tel Aviv: Hakibbutz Hameuchad, 1987.
Yudkin, Leon I. "Memorialization in New Fiction." *World Literature Today* 72, no. 3 (1998): 485–492.
Zweig, Stefan. *Die Welt von Gestern. Erinnerungen eines Europäers*. Frankfurt am Main: Fischer Taschenbuch Verlag, 2012.

Notes on Contributors

Esra Almas is an assistant professor of Translation Studies and English literature at Istanbul Sehir University, Turkey. She was a research fellow at the Katz Center of Advanced Judaic Studies at University of Pennsylvania. Her research focuses on the intersections of memory studies and urban imaginary. She has published on Istanbul's modernist literary cityscape and autobiographical narratives.

Asher D. Biemann is a professor of religious studies at the University of Virginia, where he teaches modern Jewish thought and intellectual history. He is the author of a critical edition of Martin Buber's *Sprachphilosophische Schriften* (2003), *The Martin Buber Reader* (2001), as well as of *Inventing New Beginnings: On the Idea of Renaissance in Modern Judaism* (2009) and *Dreaming of Michelangelo: Jewish Variations on a Modern Theme* (2012; German translation *Michelangelo und die jüdische Moderne*, 2016), both of which appeared with Stanford University Press. He is currently completing a book of essays titled *Enduring Modernity: Judaism Eternal & Ephemeral*.

Pierre Birnbaum is an emeritus professor of political sociology at the University of Panthéon-Sorbonne. His books include *Paths of Emancipation. Jews, States, and Citizenship* (co-edited with Ira Katznelson, 1995), *The Jews of the Republic* (1996), *Geography of Hope: Exile, the Enlightenment, Disassimilation* (2008) and more recently, *Léon Blum. Prime Minister, Socialist, Zionist* (2015).

Doerte Bischoff is a professor of modern German literature and chair of the Walter A. Berendsohn Research Center for Exile Studies in German Literature at Hamburg University. Her publications include *Ausgesetzte Schöpfung. Figuren der Souveränität und Ethik der Differenz in der Prosa Else Lasker-Schülers* (2002), *Poetischer Fetischismus. Der Kult der Dinge im 19. Jahrhundert* (2013). She has co-edited several volumes on exile literature, is co-editor of the yearbook *Exilforschung. Ein internationales Jahrbuch* and edits the Center's newsletter *Exilograph*.

Richard I. Cohen is the academic director of the Israel Center of Research Excellence (I-Core) for the Study of Cultures of Place in the Modern Jewish World (Daat Hamakom) and emeritus professor of Jewish history at the Hebrew University of Jerusalem. His publications include *The Burden of Conscience. French-Jewish Leadership during the Holocaust* (1987); *Jewish Icons. Art and Society in Modern Europe* (1998); co-editor and co-curator *From Court Jews to the Rothschilds: Art, Patronage, and Power, 1600–1800* (1996); *Le Juif Errant: Un témoin de temps* (2001).

Nina Fischer runs the research hub Religious Positioning: Modalities and Constellations in Jewish, Christian, and Muslim Contexts at the Goethe University of Frankfurt, Germany. She is a literary and cultural studies scholar whose research interests include Jewish studies, Holocaust and genocide studies as well as Israel, Palestine, and the Middle East conflict. She is the author of *Memory Work: The Second Generation* (2015), a study of the writings of children of Holocaust survivors in Anglophone literatures.

https://doi.org/10.1515/9783110637564-014

Jeffrey A. Grossman is an associate professor and chair of the German department at the University of Virginia. His publications include *The Discourse on Yiddish in Germany from the Enlightenment to the Second Empire* (2000) and a special issue (co-editor) of the journal *Quest: The Great War: Reflections, Experiences and Memories of German and Habsburg Jews* (1914– 1918) (2016). He is currently writing a book titled *Jewish Self-Fashioning and Translating Yiddish: The Case of Germany and Austria, 1890–1939*.

Stefani Hoffman is the former director of the Mayrock Center for Russian, Eurasian, and East European Research at the Hebrew University of Jerusalem. She is currently a freelance researcher, academic editor, and Russian to English translator. Her particular area of interest is Russian and Jewish intellectual history in the Soviet and post-Soviet period.

Judith Lang Hilgartner is a visiting assistant professor in Hispanic Jewish studies at Davidson College in North Carolina. Her forthcoming monograph is entitled *Belonging to Exile: The Elusive Homelands of the Sephardic Jews*. Her research includes the Sephardic community after World War II and Latin American Ashkenazic identities in film and literature.

Agnes C. Mueller is the College of Arts & Sciences Distinguished Professor of the Humanities and a professor of German and comparative literature at the University of South Carolina. Her most recent book publications are *The Inability to Love: Jews, Gender and America in Recent German Literature* (2015) and *German Jewish Literature Since 1990* (coedited, 2018)

Judith Müller is a research associate for Jewish literature at the Centre for Jewish Studies in Basel as well as a Ph.D. candidate in Jewish literature at the Centre for Jewish Studies at the University of Basel and the Ben Gurion University of the Negev (Cotutelle de Thèse). Her research focuses on modern Hebrew literature in its European context. Her latest article "'Glorious, accursed Europe.' A fictional historian, transcultural Holocaust memory and the quest for a European identity" has been published in *History and Belonging. Representations of the Past in Contemporary European Politics*, edited by Stefan Berger and Caner Tekin (2018).

Anna M. Parkinson is an associate professor in the Department of German at Northwestern University. Her research interests include modern German literature and film, critical theory and Holocaust and Memory Studies. Her first book, *An Emotional State: The Politics of Emotion in Postwar West German Culture* was published by the University of Michigan Press in 2015. She is the recipient of a Mellon New Direction Fellowship for 2019–2020, as well as co-convener of the project "Trauma, Politics, and the Uses of Memory" as part of the "Critical Theory in the Global South" Mellon Project at Northwestern University.

Regina Range is an assistant professor and Language Program director of German at the University of Alabama. Her research pertains to the German-speaking émigré writers, autobiographical writing, exile literature, film, and scriptwriting. Her current book project: *The Forgotten Ones: Reinserting the German-Speaking Female Exile Experience in Hollywood History (1930s –1950s)*, is a literary, cultural, and historical examination of Gina Kaus, Vicki Baum, and Salka Viertel, whose work in the Hollywood film industry has long been understudied.

Diego Rotman is a senior lecturer at the Department of Theatre Studies at the Hebrew University of Jerusalem. His current research explores narratives of the reconstruction and deconstruction of the Jewish house in Eastern Europe as reflected in post-Holocaust Yiddish theater and Israeli contemporary art. He is also an interdisciplinary artist, curator, and member of the Sala-manca artists group in Jerusalem. He is the author of the book *The Stage as a Temporary Home: On Dzigan and Shumacher Theater (1921–1980)* (2017), co-editor of *The Ethnography Department of the Museum of the Contemporary*, with Lea Mauas (2017) and *Heara – Independent Art in Jerusalem at the Beginning of the 21st Century*, with Ronen Eidelman and Lea Mauas (2014).

Sarah E. Wobick-Segev is an affiliated research fellow at the Richard Koebner Minerva Center for German History at the Hebrew University of Jerusalem. She is the author of *Homes away from Home: Jewish Belonging in Twentieth-Century Paris, Berlin, and St. Petersburg* (2018) and, together with Dr. Gideon Reuveni, co-editor of *The Economy in Jewish History: New Perspectives on the Interrelationship between Ethnicity and Economic Life* (2011).

Index

Abdulla, Danah 53
Abulhawa, Susan 35, 45, 46, 48
Abu-Lughod, Lila 35, 49, 50
Adamovich, Georgii 277
Adler, Alfred 59, 63
Adorno, Theodor 154, 164, 168, 173, 179, 205–207, 209, 227, 238, 249, 251
Agamben, Sergio 169
Agasfer, the wandering Jew 120, 121, 123
Aksenov, Vasilii 109, 112–115, 125
Ali, Zarefa 37
Alienation 68, 101, 102, 104, 111, 116, 118, 163, 178, 200, 206
Alsace 17
Alteras, Adriana 245
Alterman, Nathan 277
America 11, 18, 19, 26, 27, 33, 35, 36, 41, 43–49, 63, 66–68, 71, 72, 74, 75, 79, 82, 91, 95, 119, 131, 210, 241, 242, 249, 250, 251, 260, 262–264
– Latin America 129, 132, 138, 139–142, 280
Amsterdam 12, 14, 208, 209, 227
Antisemitism 4, 105, 116, 119, 122, 139, 188, 207, 211, 223, 224, 241, 247, 248, 250, 251
Antwerp 260
Appadurai, Arjun 2
Appiah, Kwame Anthony 251
Ararat (Artistisher revolutsionerer teater) 81–85
Arendt, Hannah 261, 265, 267
Argentina 129–149
Armenia 81, 86, 244
Ashkenaz 129, 131, 133, 137–139, 141, 291
Ashrawi, Hanan 35
Asylum 217, 219, 270–274
Auerbach, Erich 2, 184, 195, 197–200
Auschwitz 121–122, 208, 227, 249
Austria 3, 26, 59–61, 64–67, 69, 71, 73, 74, 75, 159, 160, 167, 173, 183, 185, 186, 191, 193, 265, 278, 280, 285
– Austro-Hungarian Empire 17, 183, 184, 185
Avraham Goldfaden Theater 93

Azerbaijan 86, 183, 188, 244, 251
Babylon 12, 18, 25
Baer, Yitzhak 11
Baghdad 273
Balk, Theodor 270
Balzac, Honoré de 277
Banbaji, Amir 287
Baron, Hans 4
Barzilay, Isaac 12, 13
Bat-Miriam, Yocheved 277
Baudelaire, Charles 167, 169, 174, 177–179, 277, 280
Bayonne 17
Beauvoir, Simone de 277
Belonging 3, 5, 6–8, 18, 26, 32, 34–36, 39, 41, 42, 46, 48, 53, 60, 61, 67, 77, 78, 95, 109, 129–149, 207, 212, 214, 216, 224, 226, 227, 253, 254, 257, 262, 273, 274, 294
Ben Israel, Menasseh 12–15
Benjamin, Walter 5, 111, 117, 153–180, 184, 187, 198, 199, 268, 280, 284
– *Berliner Kindheit um 1900* (A Berlin Childhood around 1900) 169, 171, 174, 177
– *Das Passagenwerk* (The Arcades Project) 174
– "Der Begriff der Geschichte" (On the Concept of History) 163–166, 171, 175, 176
– "Paris, Hauptstadt des XIX. Jahrhunderts" (Paris, Capital of the Nineteenth Century) 174
Ben-Shaul, Moshe 278
Berlin 8, 59, 60–65, 67, 69, 183–201, 208, 239, 243, 246–247, 249, 277, 282, 285, 286, 294, 296
Bernstein, Michael André 154, 164, 178
Besht (Baal Shem Tov) 106, 107
Der bialistoker melukhisher yiddisher miniatur-teater 86
Bhabha, Homi 2, 274
Blanqui, Louis-Auguste 166
Blei, Franz 59

https://doi.org/10.1515/9783110637564-015

Bluwstein, Rachel 277
Bordeaux 17, 25
Border 31, 43, 76, 101, 110, 122, 136, 160, 183, 185, 200, 220, 237, 255–258, 260, 263, 264, 266, 268, 270, 273, 285
Borges, Jorge Luis 129, 137, 139–142, 210
Börne, Ludwig 154, 157, 158, 161
Bosnia 131, 190, 191, 194
Bosphorus 189, 193, 197, 198
Boundary, boundaries 1, 14, 24, 60, 61, 70, 77, 78, 115, 133, 189, 200, 201, 218, 221, 226, 253, 256, 286
Brecht, Bertolt 62, 154, 166, 179, 270, 289
Broch, Hermann 59
Broderzon, Moyshe 81–85
Brodsky, Adriana 132
Buber, Martin 117, 187
Buenos Aires 136, 139, 141
Bureaucracy 259, 267, 268, 270
Burke, Peter 6

Cairo 14, 43
Camurri, Renato 67
Carens, Joseph 3, 4
Carlebach, Azriel 93
Cassirer, Ernst 4
Catholic, Catholicism 16, 18, 19, 21, 121, 158
Cemenzamanlı, Yusuf Vezir 189
Censor 63, 73, 86, 92, 93, 103, 115, 157, 159, 160, 162, 208
Certeau, Michel de 281
Chervinskaia, Lydiia 277
Citizenship 3, 11, 12, 16, 24, 25, 34, 112, 129, 186, 212, 226, 227, 253, 262, 264, 271, 274
Commerce 12, 14–16, 18, 19, 21, 23, 177
Community 5, 8, 11, 15, 33, 34, 36, 38, 42, 46, 50, 51, 53, 70, 87, 129, 131, 133, 136, 138, 141, 159, 160, 185, 186, 206, 215, 224, 225, 227, 246, 253, 261, 286
Constantinople. See Istanbul
Conversion 18, 19, 21, 23, 24, 26, 183, 185, 186, 239
Cosmopolitan 2–5, 61, 101, 104, 123, 137, 140, 187, 233, 236, 238, 251
Cosmopolitanism 2–5, 139, 191, 205–228, 233, 238
Crémieux, Adolphe 159, 160, 162

Dabbagh, Selma 35, 50
Damascus Blood Libel 158, 159, 160, 162, 166
Dark Humour 211, 220, 224
Darraj, Susan Muaddi 46
Deir Yassin massacre 39
Deleuze, Gilles 84, 125, 225
Derrida, Jacques 4, 218
Detering, Heinrich 225, 226
Deterritorialization of language 125
Dialectical Images 174, 175
Diaspora 7, 8, 12, 31–53, 83, 91, 92, 95, 96, 101, 102, 105, 110, 117, 118, 120, 123–124, 138, 235, 241, 248
– post-Soviet diaspora 110
Dickens, Charles 179
Diderot, Denis 23
Dohm, Christian Wilhelm 12, 15, 16, 17, 24
Domb, Risa 283, 286
Dome of the Rock 39, 46, 47
Doron, Lizzie 278, 291, 294, 296
Dostoevsky, Fyodor 104, 108
Doumani, Beshara 45
Dreyfus, Alfred 26
Dzigan, Shimen 81–96

Eagleton, Terry 175
Effendi, Abdulkerim 194
Egypt 123, 288, 290
Ehrenfels, Rolf von 186, 189
Eiland, Howard 166
Einstein, Albert 187
Eis, Egon 66
Eis, Otto 66
Elkin, Judith Laikin 139
Elmusa, Sharif S. 43, 44, 46, 48
Emancipation 11, 12, 14–17, 19, 21, 27, 153, 155–158, 162, 251
Émigré, Émigrée 59–61, 67–70, 76, 119, 185, 206, 274, 277
Endelman, Todd 15
Enlightenment 23–25, 153, 155, 156–158, 166, 180, 206, 213, 251
Entanglement 256
Erasmus of Rotterdam 3, 4

Escalle, Marie-Christine Kok 279
Europe 4, 16, 45, 48, 66–68, 81, 85, 88, 91, 95, 103–106, 108, 138, 158, 159, 164, 183–187, 190–192, 194, 198, 199–200, 214, 225, 251, 257–259, 261, 263, 264, 268, 277–280, 282–295
Exile 1–7, 11–27, 32, 37, 38, 40–47, 51, 53, 59, 60, 65–79, 81, 92, 96, 101–126, 129–131, 134–139, 143–149, 153, 155, 156, 162–164, 166, 169–173, 180, 183–201, 205–228, 253, 254, 263–266, 270–274, 277–296
– internal 102–105
– negation of 96
– Parisian 170
Ezrahi, Sidra 31, 53

Feige, Otto (B. Traven) 260
Feuchtwanger, Lion 62, 70
Film 59–61, 63–78, 178
Fischer, Torben 238
Fitzgerald, F. Scott 277
Flohr, Markus 236–240, 243–246, 248, 250
Fodor, Ladislaus 67
Foer, Jonathan Safran 241–243, 249–251
Forster, Georg 169, 170
Foucault, Michel 6
France 12, 17, 19, 21–27, 60, 61, 65–69, 110, 112, 129, 153–180, 255–258, 266, 277, 280, 285, 286, 288, 293
Frank, Bruno 270
Frank, Leonhard 70
Franz Joseph, Habsburg Emperor 167
Freud, Sigmund 175, 191
Friedrich I (Barbarossa) 160
Frischauer, Erich 65
Funk, Mirna 246, 248, 249, 250, 251

Gatrell, Peter 3
Gaza 31, 34, 40, 45, 50, 51, 237
Gelman, Juan 129–149
Gender 6, 7, 61, 63, 64, 70–73, 77, 255, 258, 273
Gerchunoff, Alberto 129, 137–139, 142
German Jews 5, 39, 70, 153–180, 197, 233–251, 246

Germany 20, 59–60, 64, 66, 68, 103, 105, 109–111, 118–120, 124–126, 156–158, 160–164, 171, 172, 180, 183–188, 197, 200, 205, 207, 208, 210–211, 234–237, 241, 243, 249, 250, 264, 270–272, 278, 280, 285, 289, 294
– GDR 246, 247
– Nazi Germany 164, 180, 184, 197, 200, 289
– Weimar Germany 4, 63–64, 73, 78, 166, 183, 185, 186, 188, 208, 236
Gide, André 290
Glatshteyn, Yankev 91
Gold, Nili 288
Gorelik, Lena 234, 237, 238, 239, 240, 243–246, 248, 250
Gouri, Haim 278
Govrin, Michal 287
Graetz, Heinrich 17
Grégoire, Abbé 17–23, 26
Grjasnowa, Olga 243, 245, 246, 247, 250, 251
Guattari, Félix 84, 125, 225

Habermas, Jürgen 213
Habsburg Empire. *See* Austria
Halbwachs, Maurice 34
Hamburg 158, 160, 236, 249
Hammermeister, Philipp 238
Hansen, Rolf 66
Hausmann, George-Eugène 176, 177
Heftman, Yosef 93
Heidegger, Martin 6, 105
Heimat 42, 60, 67, 75, 76, 156, 163, 164, 167–171, 173, 178, 180, 243, 264, 277–296
Heimatfilm 74, 75
Heine, Heinrich 117, 153–180, 277
– "Letters from Helgoland" 157
– "Ludwig Markus" 162, 164
Hemingway, Ernest 277, 290
Herzen, Alexander 104
Hesse, Hermann 187
Hiller, Mischa 44, 50, 51
Hilsenrath, Edgar 211
Hirsch, Marianne 48–50
Hirschman, Albert 11
Historiography 1, 3, 6, 11, 33–35, 38, 42–45, 50–52, 87, 105, 119, 123, 131, 132, 137,

153, 165–167, 170, 173, 174, 176, 177, 179, 194, 198, 205–207, 212, 213, 217, 223–225, 233–239, 242–245, 247, 249, 254, 255, 260, 268, 270, 271, 274, 277–296
Hitler, Adolf 78, 167, 209, 210, 211, 247
Holland 12, 17, 19, 23, 226
Hollywood 60, 65, 66–72, 78, 187, 191, 195
Hollywood (film) industry 65, 68, 70, 78
Hollywood studios 65, 68
Holocaust 4, 33, 38, 45, 48, 81–96, 120–124, 209, 211, 216, 217, 227, 233–251, 278, 279, 280, 283, 286, 291, 293, 294–296
– Holocaust literature [also under literature] 211
– Holocaust memory 233, 234, 235, 238, 240, 242, 244, 249, 251, 278, 293, 294
Homeland, Home 1–8, 16, 18–21, 25, 31–53, 59–96, 101–126, 131, 133–137, 139, 143, 146–149, 153, 156, 160, 162, 163, 167, 168, 170, 190, 191, 192, 195–197, 207, 209, 214, 225–227, 241, 272, 273, 277, 281–287, 291, 293, 296
Honig, Bonnie 213
Horkheimer, Max 178, 205, 209
Horn, Bernard 285, 286, 295
Hourwitz, Zalkind 17, 24, 25
Hugo, Victor 277
Hussar, James A. 138
Hussein, Saddam 273

Identity 2, 6–8, 12, 15, 21, 26, 31–37, 42, 45, 46, 51, 53, 60, 61, 65, 67, 75, 78, 82, 83, 86, 87, 92, 95, 96, 102, 109, 111, 114, 116, 125, 129–132, 137–140, 142, 146, 156, 161, 183–188, 190–194, 196, 197, 200, 208, 211, 215, 224, 234–236, 239, 240, 242, 244–251, 253, 254–256, 259, 260, 262–266, 270–272, 274, 279, 280, 284, 285, 292
Identity Papers. *See also* passports
Imagination 2, 8, 23, 32, 45, 46, 50, 52, 125, 148, 195, 200, 201, 221, 233, 237, 241, 242, 245, 250, 253–274, 278, 294, 296

Irgun 38, 39
Islam 48, 183, 185, 186, 187, 189, 190, 194, 198, 201
Israel 7, 8, 11–12, 15–16, 19, 25, 26, 31, 35, 39–41, 43, 45–53, 82, 87, 88, 92, 93, 95, 96, 101–103, 110, 118, 119, 124, 136, 211, 233–251, 278, 283–285, 287, 288, 293, 294
Istanbul 8, 14, 184–186, 188–191, 193, 197–199
Italy 8, 20, 23, 129, 183, 288, 290, 294, 295

Jacobs, Keith 32
Jaffa 43, 49, 50
Jarrar, Randa 36
Jeremiah 12, 18, 25
Jerusalem 8, 15, 21, 23, 24, 31, 34, 38–42, 44–47, 49, 52, 53, 136, 143, 234, 236, 237, 244, 247, 248, 279
Jesenská, Milena 59, 78
Jews, Jewish. *See* Judaism
Johnson, Penny 32
Joseph II (Habsburg Emperor) 12
Judaism 15, 26, 47, 141, 183, 185, 188, 201, 236, 239
– Orthodox 15, 234, 236, 239, 246
– Reform 236

Kabbalah 117, 139, 148
Kafka, Franz 78, 125, 178
Kahanoff, Jacqueline 285
Kant, Immanuel 4, 212, 213, 224
Kantorowicz, Ernst 4
Karmi, Ghada 38–40
Karp, Jonathan 14, 16
Katzir, Judith 278, 287, 291, 294–296
Kazakhstan 87
Kedourie, Elie 95
Keilson, Hans 205–228
Kenaz, Yehoshua 278
Khalidi, Rashid 33–34
Kharitonov, Mark 115
Khazanov, Boris 101–126
Khider, Abbas 270–271

Kirshenblatt-Gimblett, Barbara 2
Klee, Paul 165
Korsch, Karl 154
Kracauer, Siegfried 5
Kraków 292
Kramer, Sven 238
Kranz, Joseph 62, 77
Kraus, Karl 154
Kristeller, Paul 4
Kundera, Milan 295

Lacis, Asja 154
Ladino 129–131, 133–135, 143, 144, 146
Language 33, 83–86, 90–95, 106–110, 115–117, 119, 124–126, 129–131, 133–134, 137–138, 143, 145
– Hebrew language 92–95, 106, 117, 124, 130, 291
League of Nations 265
Leneman, Leon 88
Levant, Levantinism 285, 286
Levy, Daniel 233
Liberles, Robert 15
Libya 193–196
Liebrecht, Savyon 291
Literature 31–53, 59, 60, 65, 69, 84, 103, 108, 115–116, 124–126, 139, 141, 154, 156, 177, 184, 199, 200, 211, 216, 225, 227, 233–251, 253–259, 261, 263, 266, 270, 271, 273, 274, 277, 280, 285, 287–292, 294
– Exile 31–57, 59–80, 101–128, 129–150, 153–182, 183–203, 205–232
– German Jewish 153–180, 233–251
– Holocaust 211
– Israeli 277–296
– Minor literature 84, 125
– Palestinian 31–53
Livorno 12
Łódź 81–85, 88, 90, 91, 92, 95
Loewendahl, Erika 188
London 14, 19, 50, 51, 179
Longfellow, Henry Wadsworth 131
Longing. See nostalgia
Lorraine 17
Los Angeles 66
Loti, Pierre see Viaud, Julien

Louis XVI 15, 17
Lukács, Georg 45, 154, 175, 227
Luther, Martin 3
Luzzatto, Simone 12–16

Makine, Andreï 110, 111
Malesherbes, Guillaume-Chrétien de Lamoignon de 15, 17
Mann, Heinrich 62
Mann, Thomas 70, 187
Marcus, Hugo 186, 187
Markus, Ludwig 153, 162, 164
Marseille 266, 268, 269
Marton, George 65, 66
Marx, Karl 160, 161, 175
Mason, Victoria 36
Memory 12, 31, 32–53, 65, 92, 106, 111, 114, 115, 122, 124, 125, 138, 139, 155, 161, 168, 170, 189, 191, 193, 233, 236, 238–240, 242–251, 262, 270, 278, 279, 283, 290, 292, 294, 295
Mendelssohn, Moses 160
Mendes, Lothar 63
Merz, Konrad 227
Messiah, Messianism 11, 13, 16, 19, 20–25, 107, 122, 155, 163, 165, 171, 173, 174, 179
(Mass) Migration 3, 7, 33, 36, 43, 46, 47, 52, 85, 101, 103, 105, 107, 108–110, 117, 139, 205–207, 254, 270
Metz 11–27
Mexico 129, 131, 146, 147, 149, 266, 268
Michaelis, Johann David 16, 18, 20
Midrash 117, 122, 123
Miller, Henry 296
Miłosz, Czesław 91
Mirabeau, Count of (Honoré Gabriel Riqueti) 24–26
Miron, Dan 84
Mobility 64, 78, 79, 253, 254
Morgenroth, Ernest Gustave 170
Morocco 138
Moscow 102, 103, 106–115, 119, 126
Motherland 68, 105, 108, 109, 137, 190
Movement 115, 195–197, 200, 256, 257, 261, 266, 271

Munich 67, 103, 109, 185, 234, 239, 249, 260, 271
Musil, Robert 59
Muslim, Muslims 3, 22, 31, 38, 42, 195–188, 194, 197, 243

Nabokov, Vladimir 210
Naficy, Hamid 71
Nahor, Asher 95
Nakba 33, 34, 35, 37–50
Nantes 17
Napoleon Bonaparte 25, 26, 156, 166
Nation 13–26, 33, 34, 60, 61, 65, 72, 91, 92, 95, 126, 130, 138, 192, 206, 212, 216, 220, 225–227, 253–258, 261, 274, 279, 285
Nationalism 3, 5, 34, 50, 51, 69, 76, 78, 91, 102, 105, 108, 118, 124, 132, 162, 163, 188, 193, 197, 198, 216, 219, 254
Natonek, Hans 270
Netherlands 12, 15, 66, 207, 208, 209, 214, 215, 226
– Nazi occupation of 209, 214, 215
Network 5, 6, 254, 266, 274
Neumann, Alfred 70
New York 48, 66, 82, 172, 191, 194–197
Nikoïdsky, Clarisse 129–131, 133
Nirenberg, David 24
Noah, Mordecai Manuel 82
Nora, Pierre 279
Nostalgia 1, 41, 74, 75, 131, 137, 141, 189, 190, 197
Nussinbaum, Lev 183–201

Oppenheim, Max von 186
Orientalism 137, 185–187, 189, 194, 201
O'Ryan, Mariana 140
Ottomans. *See* Turkey

Palestine 16, 18, 20–22, 24–27, 31–53, 104, 119, 244
Paris 8, 63, 65, 66, 133, 154, 155, 157, 159, 164, 166, 167, 169–180, 256, 267–269, 277–296
Passport 45, 49, 85, 116, 253–274
Patriotism 34, 141, 142, 216, 257
Pensky, Max 174

Phantasmagoria 171–180
Polak, Oliver 245
Poland 81, 82, 85–90, 93, 96, 160, 278, 280, 292–294, 296
Pomerants, Grigorii 105, 109, 117
Portugal 18, 19, 280
Prague 125, 277
Pressburger, Arnold 63, 65, 66
Prilutsky, Noah 83
Prose, Francine 211
Proust, Marcel 178, 277
Prussia 12, 15–18, 26, 156, 159, 160, 185, 187

Ramallah 40, 41, 47–49
Ravid, Benjamin 13
Read, Peter 34
Refugee 1, 3, 4, 5, 32, 36, 37, 39, 40, 43–46, 50–52, 68, 93, 173, 184, 185, 188, 206, 217, 220, 234, 243, 264–268, 271–272, 274
Refugee camp 36, 43–46, 50–52
Regeneration 21–22, 24, 26
Reinach, Joseph 26
Reiss, Tom 183, 189, 200
Remarque, Erich Maria 264–267, 270
Representation 45, 64, 90, 91, 141, 176, 188, 189, 198, 199, 238, 255, 279, 280
Rezzori, Gregor von 236
Right of return 36, 40, 51, 52
Rilke, Rainer Maria 277
Roederer, Pierre Louis 17
Rome 108, 277, 279
Rootedness 2, 5, 53, 78, 79, 117, 247
Rose, Alison 61
Roth, Joseph 5, 167, 168, 270
Rothberg, Michael 233, 250
Rozenblit, Marsha 60, 61, 65
Rushdie, Salman 197
Russian culture 110, 118
Russian emigration/ emigrant 108–110
Russian intelligentsia 102–104, 126
Russian Jews 102, 110, 119, 125, 138, 233
Russian language 103, 106, 108, 110, 115, 116, 119, 125
Russian *narod*, worship of 102, 104, 105
Russian nationalism 105, 108, 118, 124
Russian soul 108

Sa'di, Ahmad 35, 37, 49
Sahl, Hans 270
Said, Edward 5, 35, 40, 41, 45, 49, 52, 68, 71, 78, 199, 200, 213, 214
Said, Jean Makdisi 37, 41, 42
Said, Najla 48, 53
Saint-Simon, Henri de 157
Samizdat 103, 105, 118–120
Sammons, Jeffrey 156–158, 160, 161
Sans-Papier 261, 264, 265, 267
Sartre, Jean-Paul 277, 290, 296
Sayigh, Rosemary 34
Schechter, Ronald 24, 25
Schiller, Friedrich 76
Scholem, Gershom 148, 154, 164, 167
Schönberg, Arnold 70
Schutz, Alfred 7
Schwartz, Marcy E. 280
Scriptwriter 59, 60, 66–70, 72, 76, 82
Scriptwriting 70, 71, 74
Segalovitsh, Zusman 84
Seghers, Anna 266–270
Semel, Nava 291
Sepharad 131, 132, 138, 141, 144. *See also* Judaism
– self-sephardization 132, 137
Sepinwald, Alyssa 17
Seyhan, Azade 192
Shabtai, Yaakov 278
Shahar, David 278
Shakespeare, William 256, 259, 261, 262
Shalev, Zeruya 287
Shandler, Jeffrey 91
Shlonsky, Avraham 277
Shneur, Zalman 277
Shoah. *See* Holocaust
Sholem Aleichem 81, 84, 85, 96
Shteiger, Anatolii 277
Shteyngart, Gary 110
Shumacher, Isroel 81–96
Simmel, Georg 196
Skrandies, Timo 176
Solzhenitsyn, Aleksander 104–106, 109
Sosnowski, Saúl 140, 142
Soviet Jewish writers 101, 117
Soviet Union 86, 87, 95, 101–105, 107–110, 112–116, 118, 119, 124, 167

– collapse of 101, 109, 112, 125
Spain 3, 129, 131, 138, 139, 143, 144, 164, 268, 280, 288, 290, 294, 295
Spielberg, Steven 241
Spire, André 26
Stalin, Joseph 102, 113, 114, 188
State 3, 5, 11, 12, 15–17, 19–22, 26, 27, 31, 39, 43, 50, 51, 60, 61, 73, 82, 87, 91–93, 95, 96, 101, 102, 109, 118, 136, 162, 188, 194, 198, 206, 212, 216, 218, 225–227, 237, 241, 253, 254, 255, 258, 259, 261, 264–267, 274
Stateless 214–216, 220, 224, 259, 261, 264
Stavans, Ilan 129, 138, 139, 141
Stein, Benjamin 239, 240, 245, 246
Stein, Gertrude 277, 290, 296
Steiner, George 91
Sterne, Lawrence 256–258, 261, 262
Sternheim, Carl 59
Storywriter 67
Strauss, Johann 75
Strawinsky, Igor 70
Switzerland 65, 187, 264
Sznaider, Nathan 233
Szurmuk, Mónica 139

Talmud 21, 24
Tel Aviv 92, 95, 96, 247, 248, 291
Teller, Janne 254
Theater 7, 76, 85, 211
– Yiddish Theater [also under Yiddish] 81–96
Thiery, Claude-Antoine 17, 22–25
Tihanov, Galin 213, 224, 225
Tokyo 194
Toland, John 12–14, 16, 20
Toller, Ernst 5
Tonnerre, Clermont 25
Torberg, Friedrich 70
Transgression 257, 258
Transnational 2, 37, 38, 41, 48, 52, 59, 67, 71, 74, 110, 115, 192, 253
Trauma 33, 35, 47, 75, 129, 132, 135, 141, 144, 145, 148, 206, 207, 209, 220, 222, 226, 227, 233, 235, 238, 239, 241–251, 273, 274, 278, 291, 293–296

Travel 1, 18, 41, 47, 60, 81, 103, 108, 122, 145, 146, 171, 194, 195, 208, 214, 221, 242, 247, 253, 255, 255–258, 270, 278, 282, 284, 285, 288, 291, 292, 294, 295
Traveler 81, 123, 255–258, 260, 274
Turkey 81, 183, 185, 186, 189, 190, 193, 194, 196–199
– Ottoman Empire 184–186, 189–194, 197, 198

Ukraine 135
Ullstein publishing house 62, 64, 65, 77
Ulmer, Edgar 63, 66
United States 47, 60, 63, 66–73, 88, 110, 129, 184, 188, 191, 201, 205, 264, 282. *See also* America
Uris, Leon 33

Valentino, Rudolfo 187
Venice 12–15, 253, 254
Viaud, Julien (Pierre Loti) 193, 194
Videla, Jorge Rafael 145
Vienna 59–62, 65, 67, 69, 75, 78, 156, 185, 186, 189–191, 193, 194, 195, 196, 282, 286, 296
Vogel, David 277

Wahlheimat 59, 60, 67, 153, 155, 162–164, 166, 171, 173, 175, 179, 180, 207, 211, 215, 226, 227
Waldmann, Helena 254

Wanner, Adrian 110, 111
Warsaw 83–85, 87, 91, 92, 95, 96, 277
Wassermann, Jakob 227
Weil, Simone 53
Weill, Kurt 289
Weiss, Leopold (Muhammad Assad) 186
Werfel, Alma Mahler 59
Werfel, Franz 59, 70, 270
West Bank 31, 34, 40, 43, 45, 50, 51
Wieviorka, Annette 38
Wilhelm II 185, 186

Yehoshua, A. B. 11, 278, 281–286, 295, 296
Yiddish 21, 24, 81–96, 130, 131, 135, 144
– Post-vernacular 81–96
– Volhynia dialect 83
– Yiddish Language 24, 83, 86, 92
– Yiddish Theater 81–96
Di yiddishe bande 85
el-Youssef, Samir 51, 52
Yudkin, Leon I. 290
Yuval-Davis, Nira 35, 56

Zaidan, Ismat 37
Zambrano, María 136, 139
Zhitlowski, Haym 91
Zionism 13, 15, 26, 27, 31, 52, 119, 237, 286
Zirner, Josef 61
Zweig, Stefan 3–5, 227, 289

www.ingramcontent.com/pod-product-compliance
Lightning Source LLC
Chambersburg PA
CBHW031758220426
43662CB00007B/448